RENT-A-GIRLFRIEND

VOLUME 8

REIJI MIYAJIMA

CONTENTS

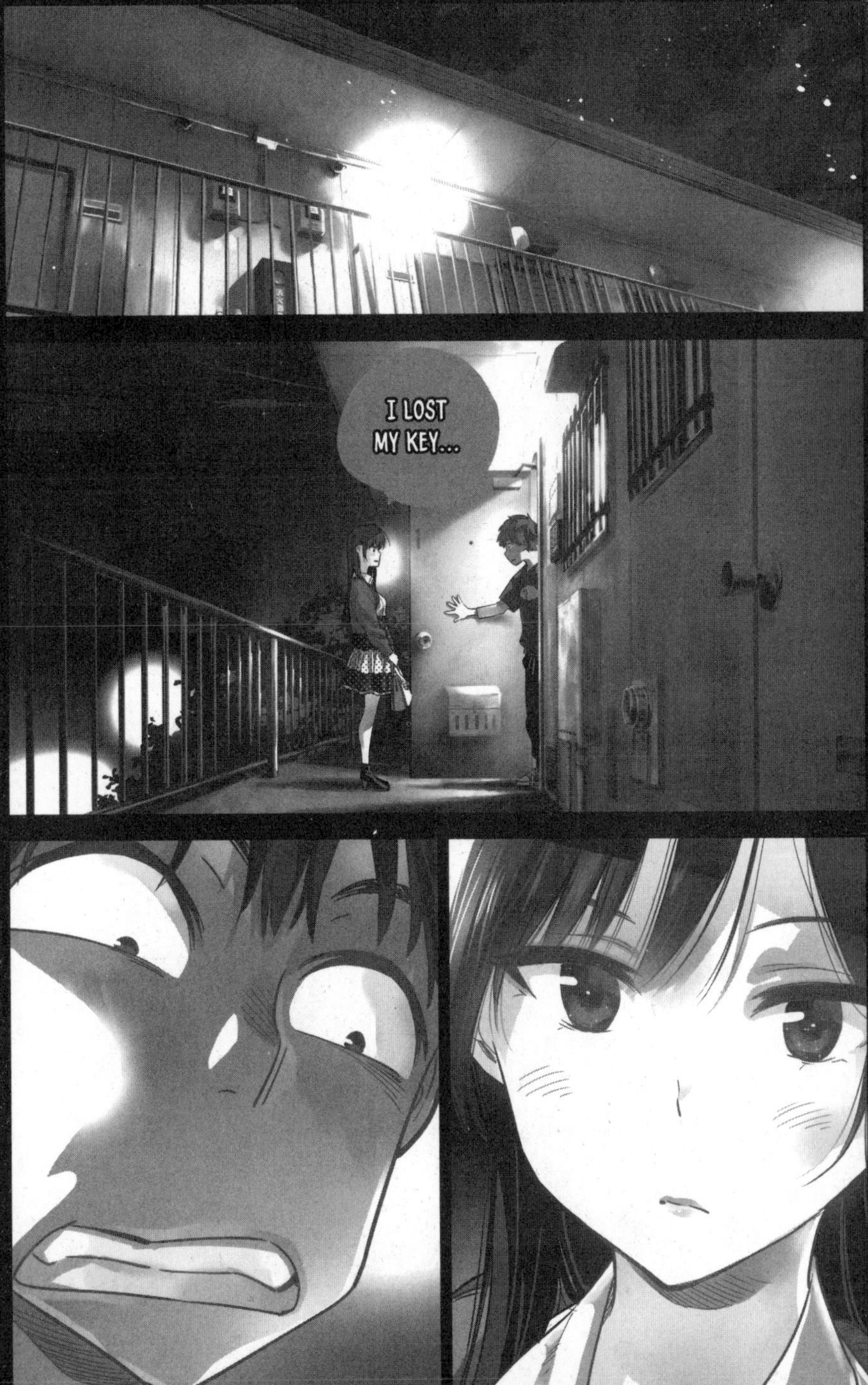
I LOST MY KEY...

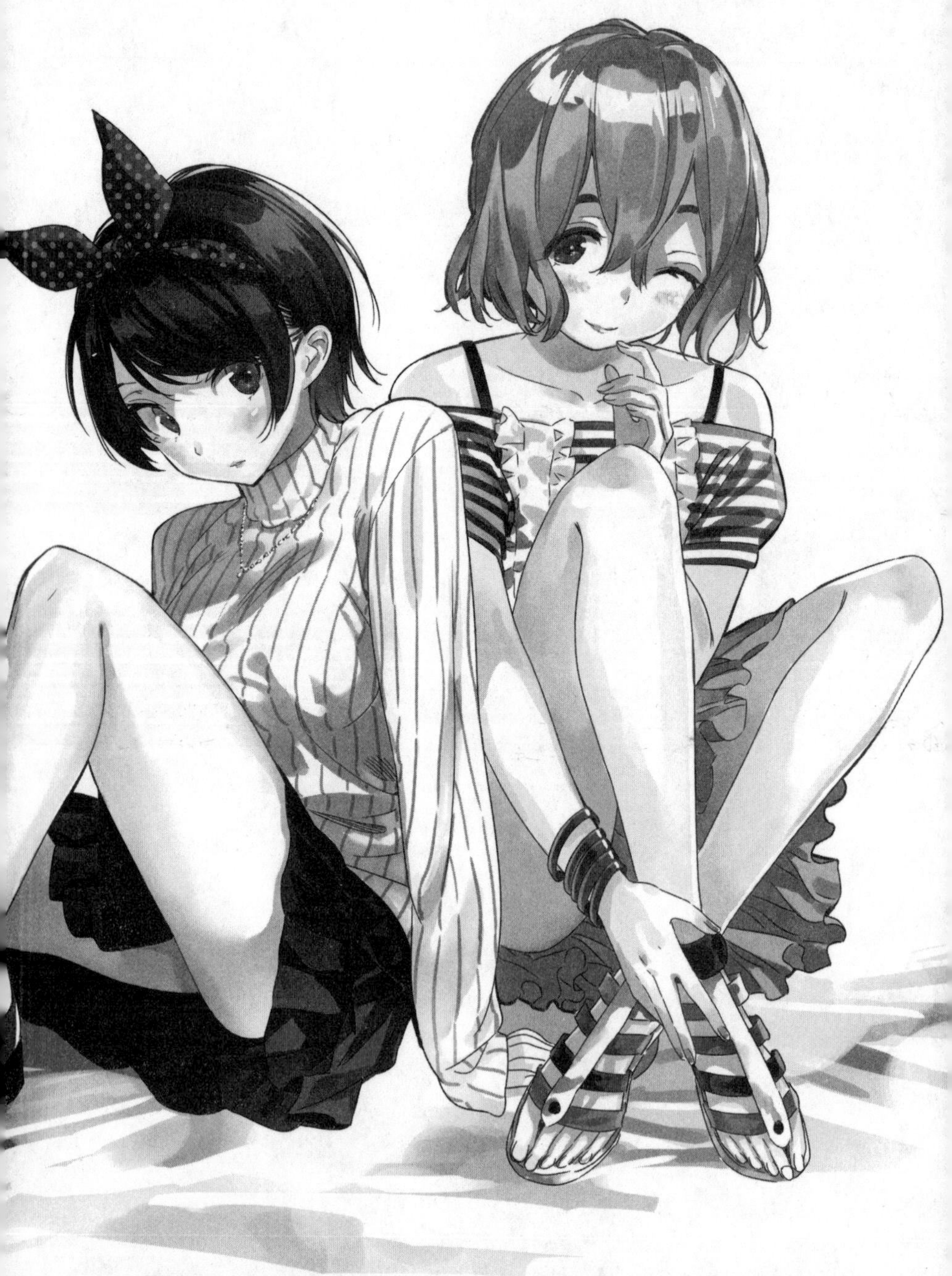

RATING 59 MY "GIRLFRIEND," CHIZURU ICHINOSE 4

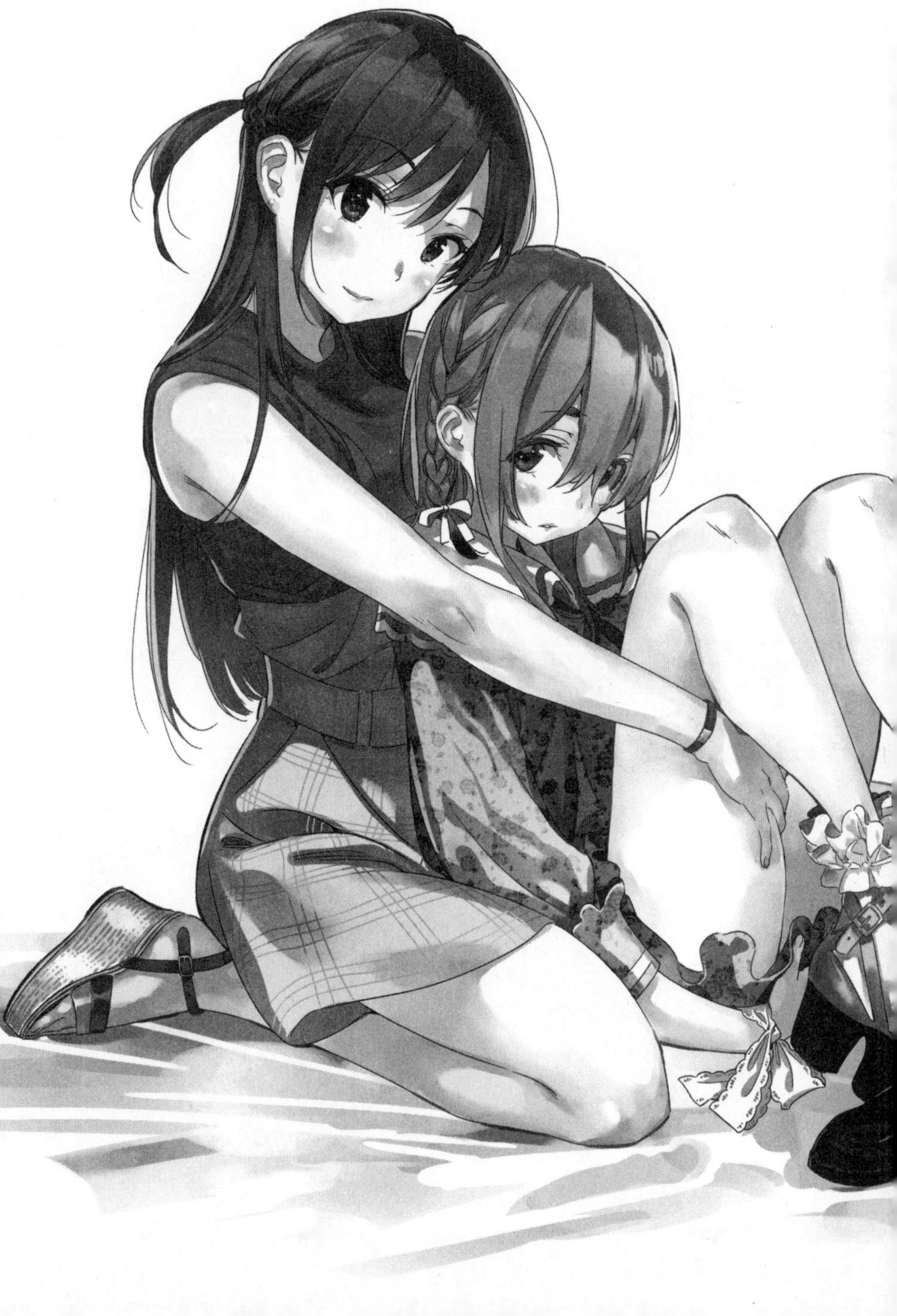

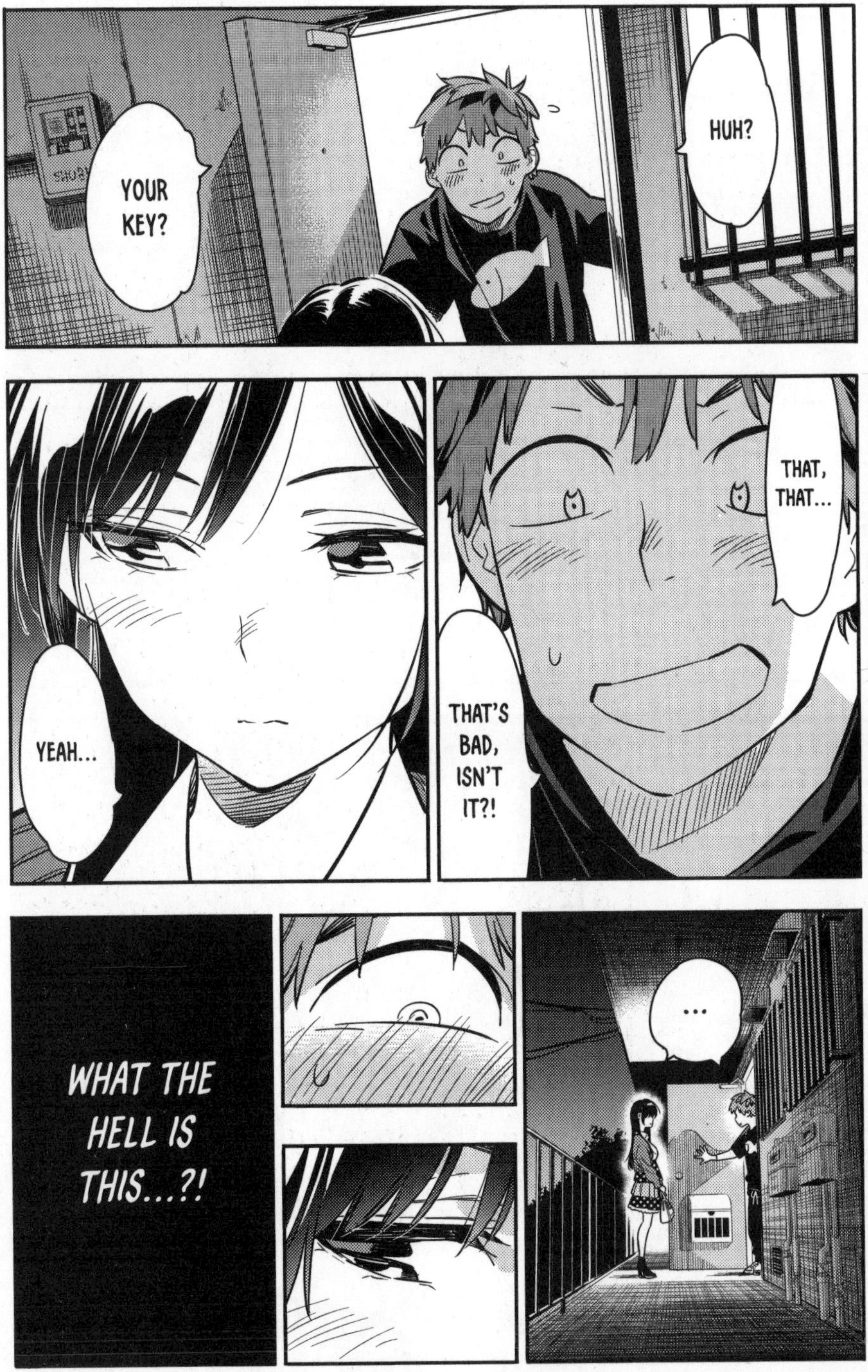
HUH?
YOUR KEY?
THAT, THAT...
THAT'S BAD, ISN'T IT?!
YEAH...
...
WHAT THE HELL IS THIS...?!

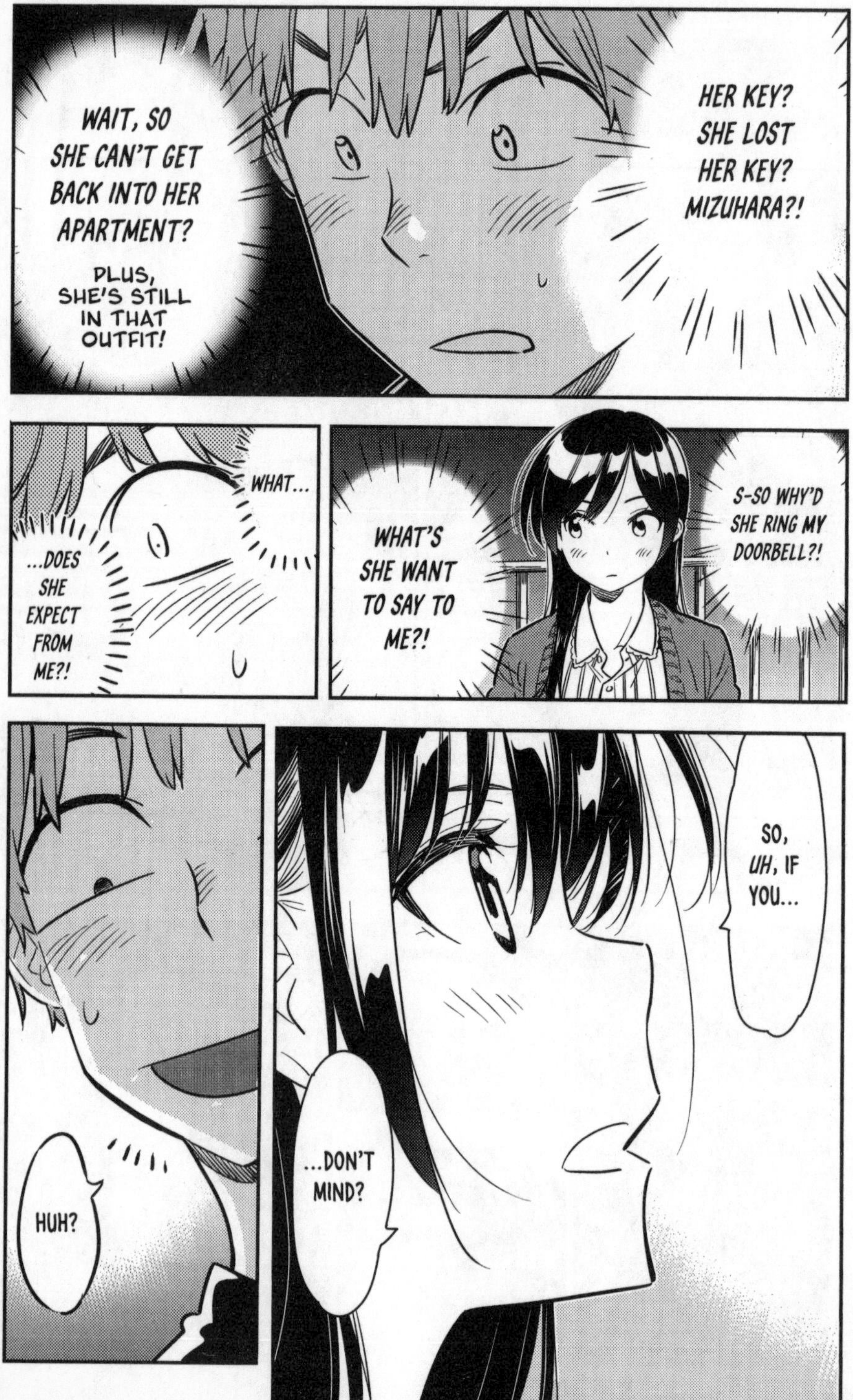
HER KEY? SHE LOST HER KEY? MIZUHARA?!
WAIT, SO SHE CAN'T GET BACK INTO HER APARTMENT?
PLUS, SHE'S STILL IN THAT OUTFIT!
S-SO WHY'D SHE RING MY DOORBELL?!
WHAT'S SHE WANT TO SAY TO ME?!
WHAT...
...DOES SHE EXPECT FROM ME?!
SO, UH, IF YOU...
...DON'T MIND?
HUH?

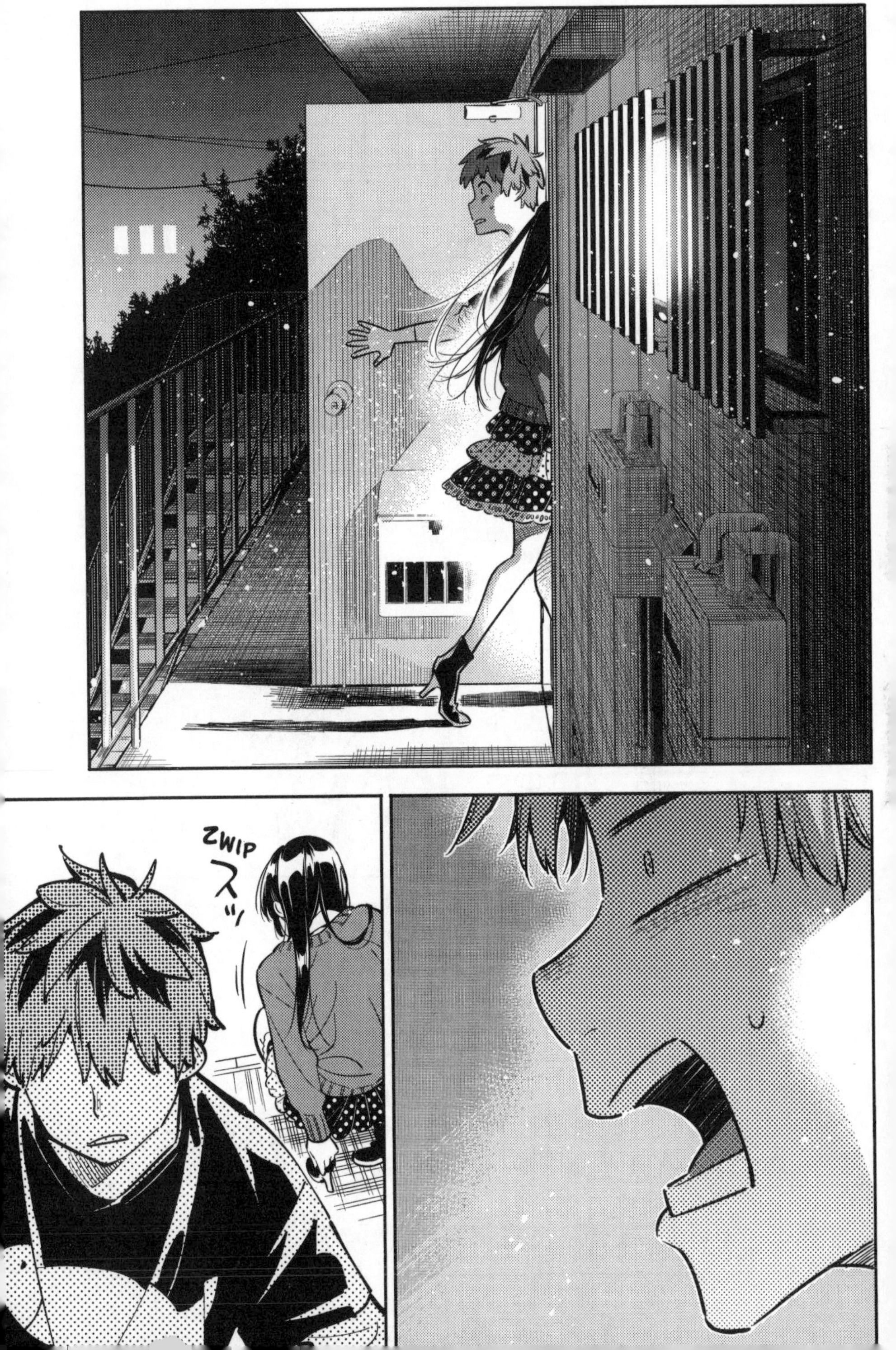
ZWIP
スッ

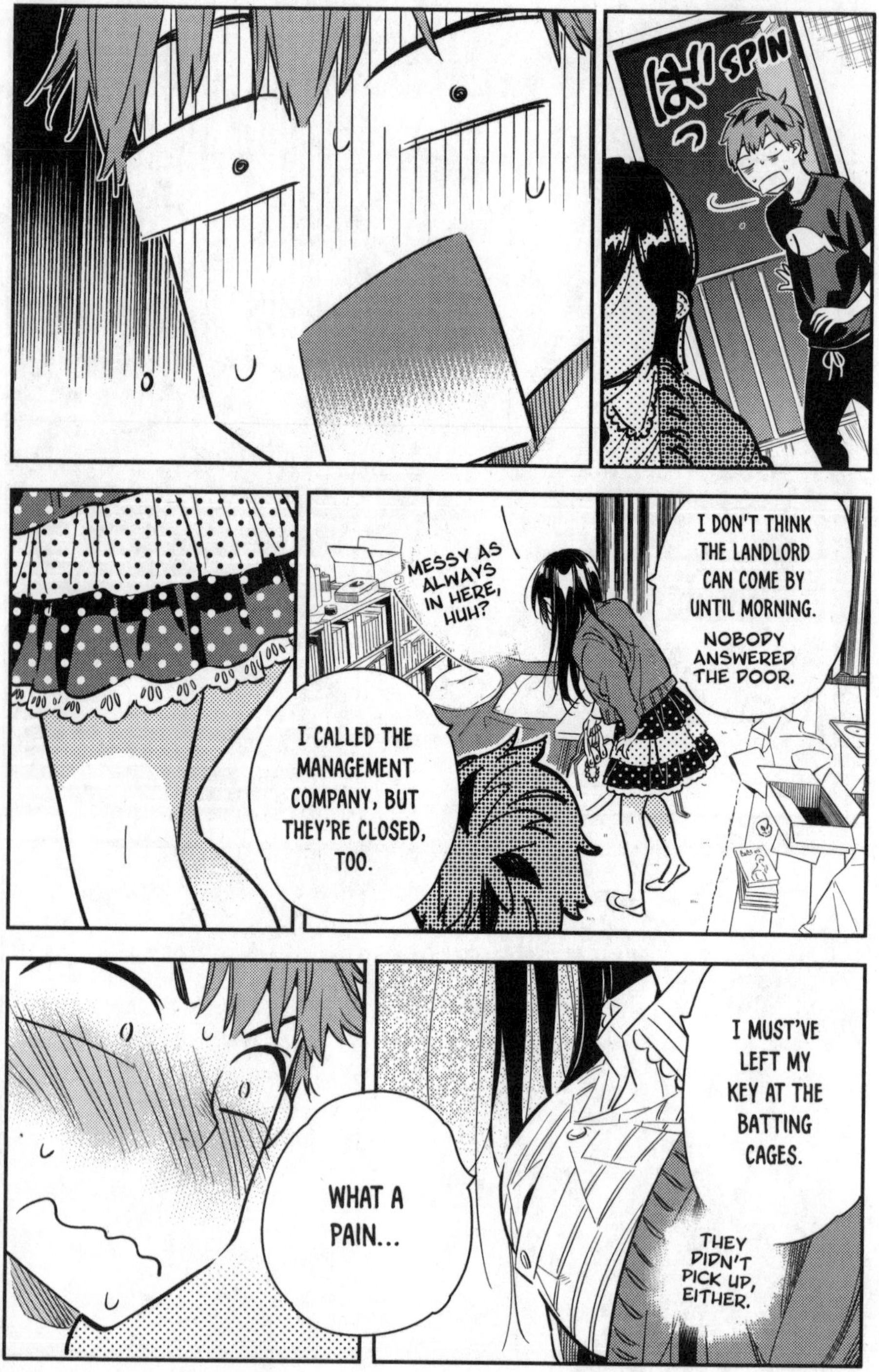
ぱっ
SPIN
I DON'T THINK THE LANDLORD CAN COME BY UNTIL MORNING.
NOBODY ANSWERED THE DOOR.
MESSY AS ALWAYS IN HERE, HUH?
I CALLED THE MANAGEMENT COMPANY, BUT THEY'RE CLOSED, TOO.
I MUST'VE LEFT MY KEY AT THE BATTING CAGES.
THEY DIDN'T PICK UP, EITHER.
WHAT A PAIN...

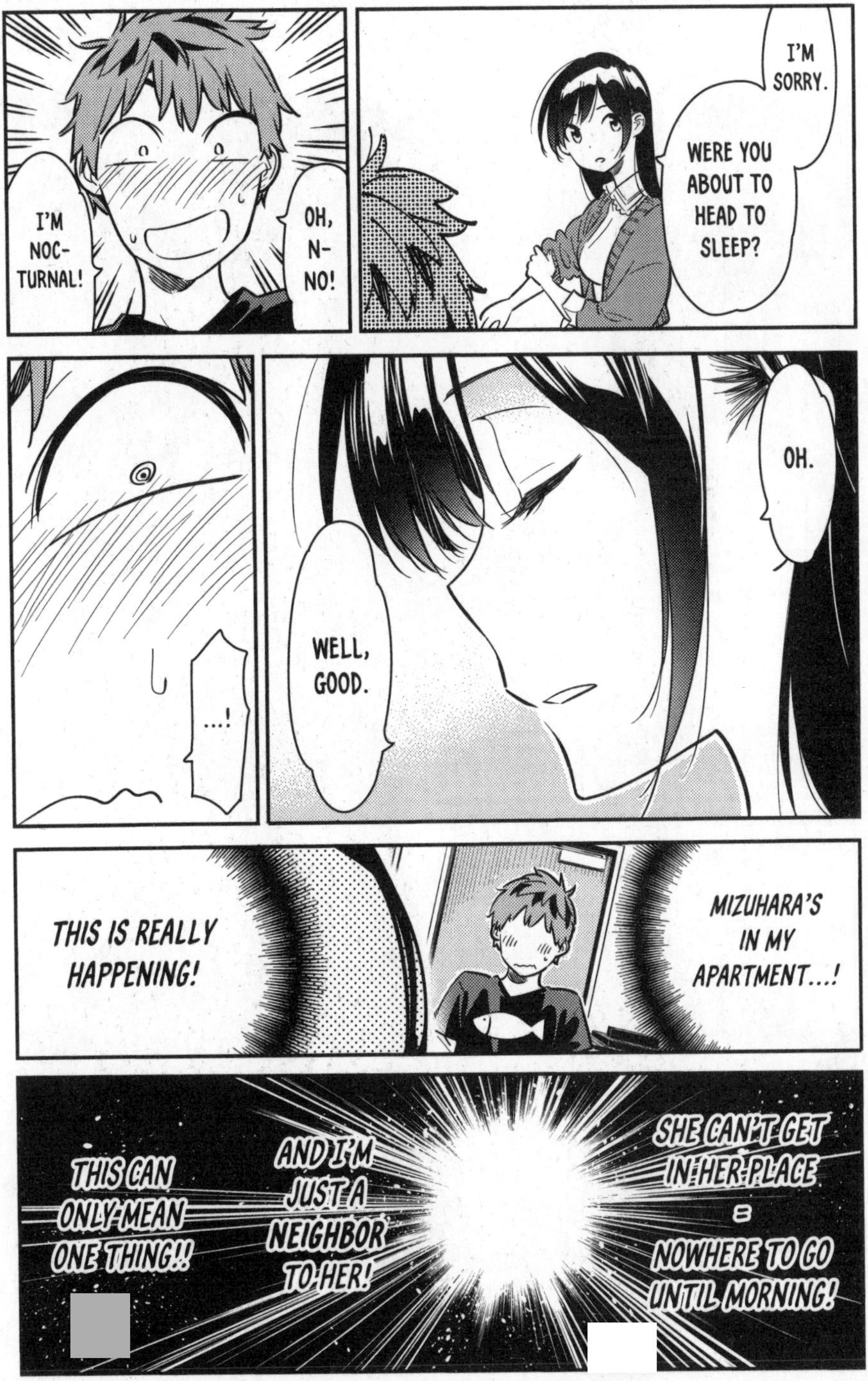
I'M SORRY.
WERE YOU ABOUT TO HEAD TO SLEEP?
OH, N-NO!
I'M NOC-TURNAL!
OH.
WELL, GOOD.
...!
MIZUHARA'S IN MY APARTMENT...!
THIS IS REALLY HAPPENING!
SHE CAN'T GET IN HER PLACE = NOWHERE TO GO UNTIL MORNING!
AND I'M JUST A NEIGHBOR TO HER!
THIS CAN ONLY MEAN ONE THING!!

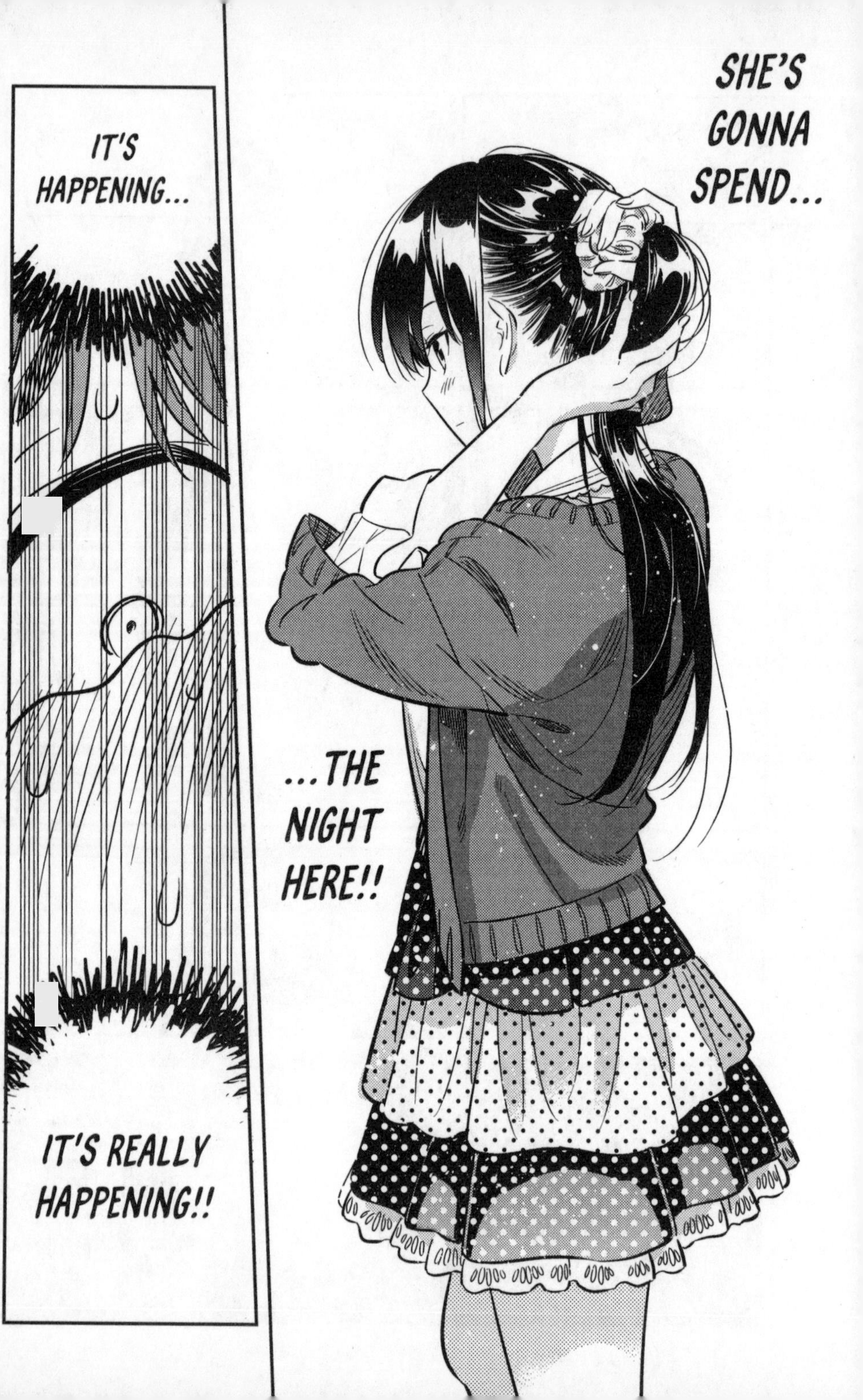
SHE'S GONNA SPEND...
...THE NIGHT HERE!!
IT'S HAPPENING...
IT'S REALLY HAPPENING!!

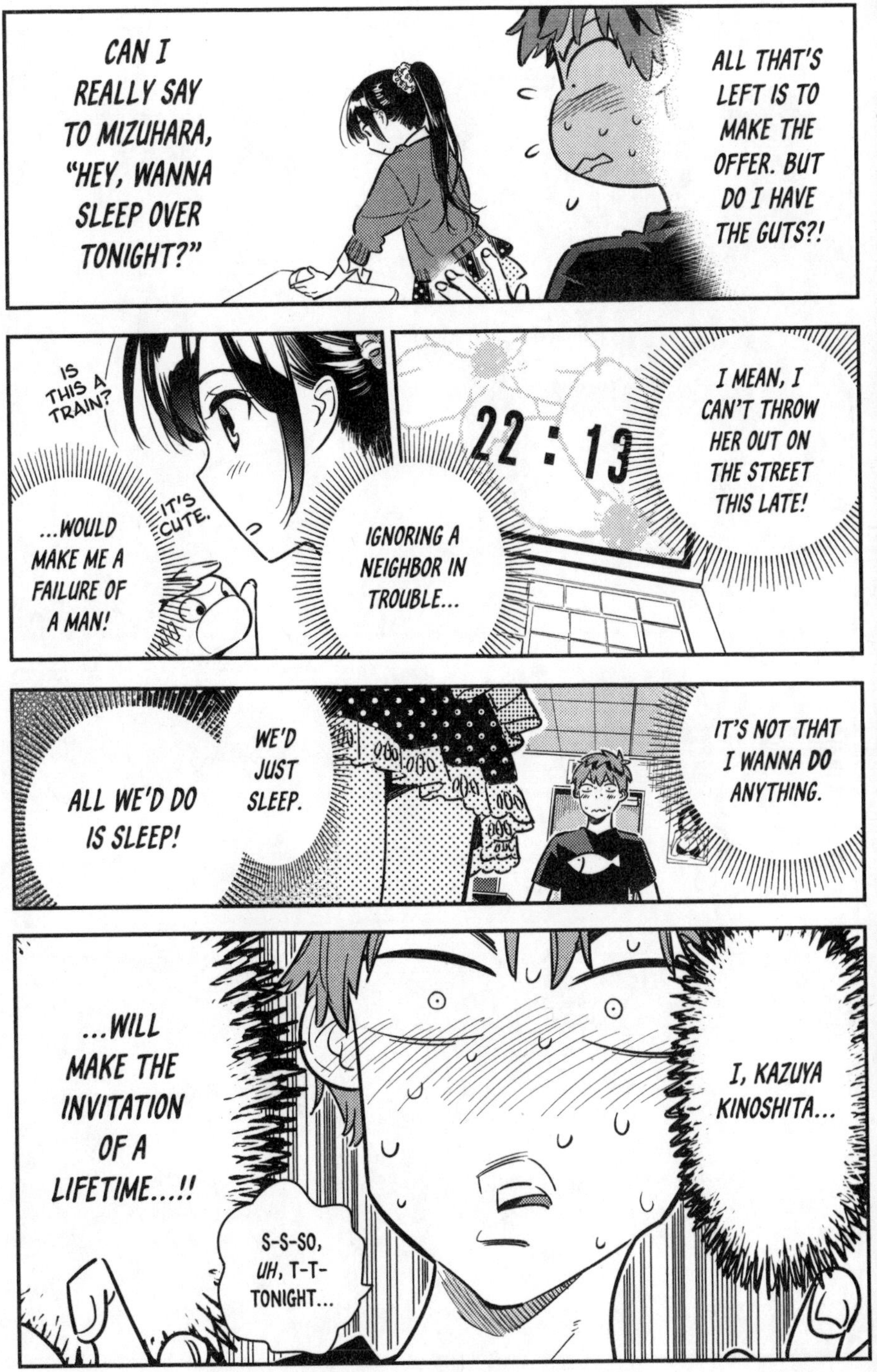
ALL THAT'S LEFT IS TO MAKE THE OFFER. BUT DO I HAVE THE GUTS?!
CAN I REALLY SAY TO MIZUHARA, "HEY, WANNA SLEEP OVER TONIGHT?"
I MEAN, I CAN'T THROW HER OUT ON THE STREET THIS LATE!
22 : 13
IGNORING A NEIGHBOR IN TROUBLE...
IS THIS A TRAIN?
IT'S CUTE.
...WOULD MAKE ME A FAILURE OF A MAN!
IT'S NOT THAT I WANNA DO ANYTHING.
WE'D JUST SLEEP.
ALL WE'D DO IS SLEEP!
I, KAZUYA KINOSHITA...
...WILL MAKE THE INVITATION OF A LIFETIME...!!
S-S-SO, UH, T-T-TONIGHT...

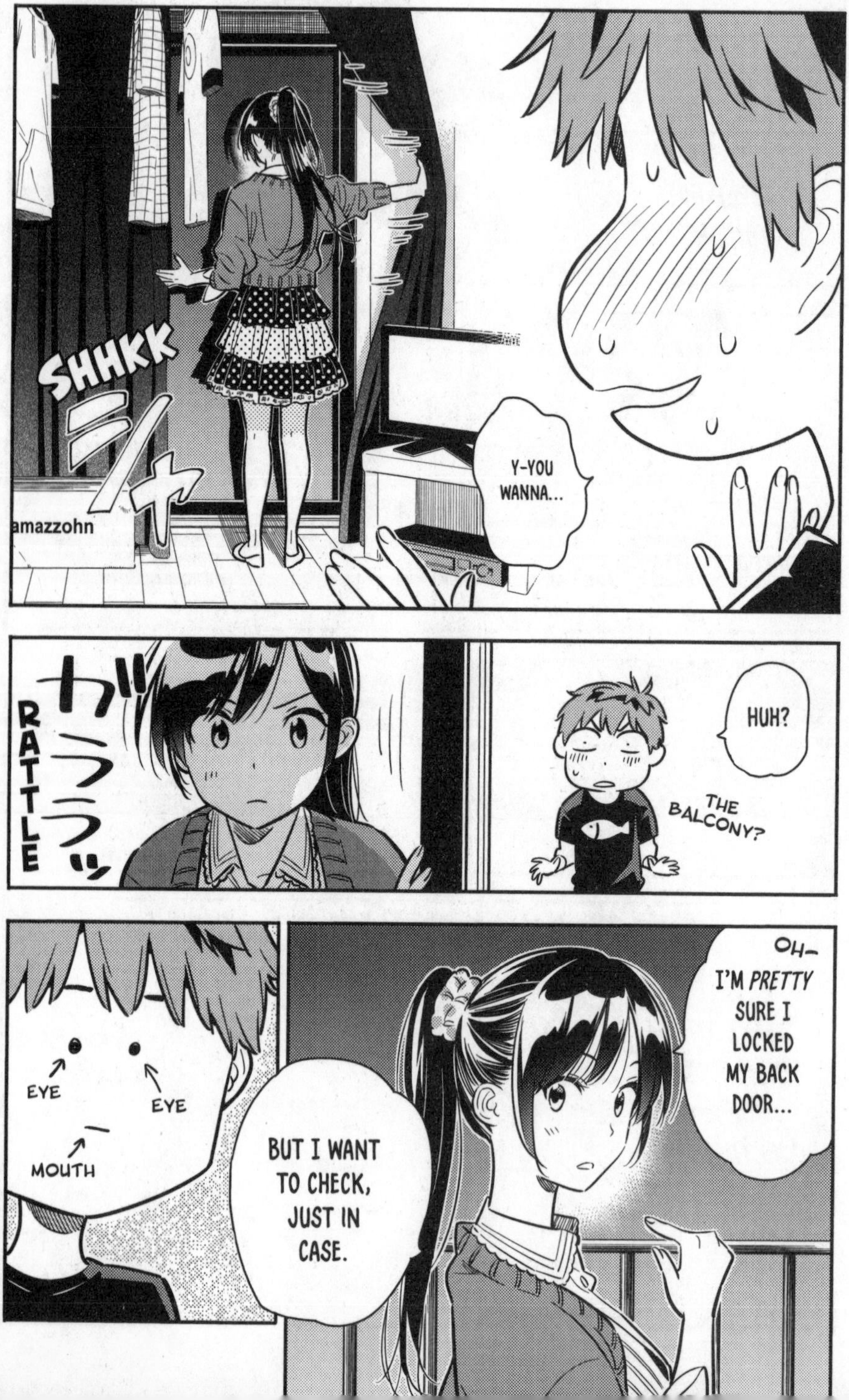
Y-YOU WANNA...
SHHKK
amazzohn
HUH?
THE BALCONY?
RATTLE
OH— I'M *PRETTY* SURE I LOCKED MY BACK DOOR...
BUT I WANT TO CHECK, JUST IN CASE.
EYE
EYE
MOUTH

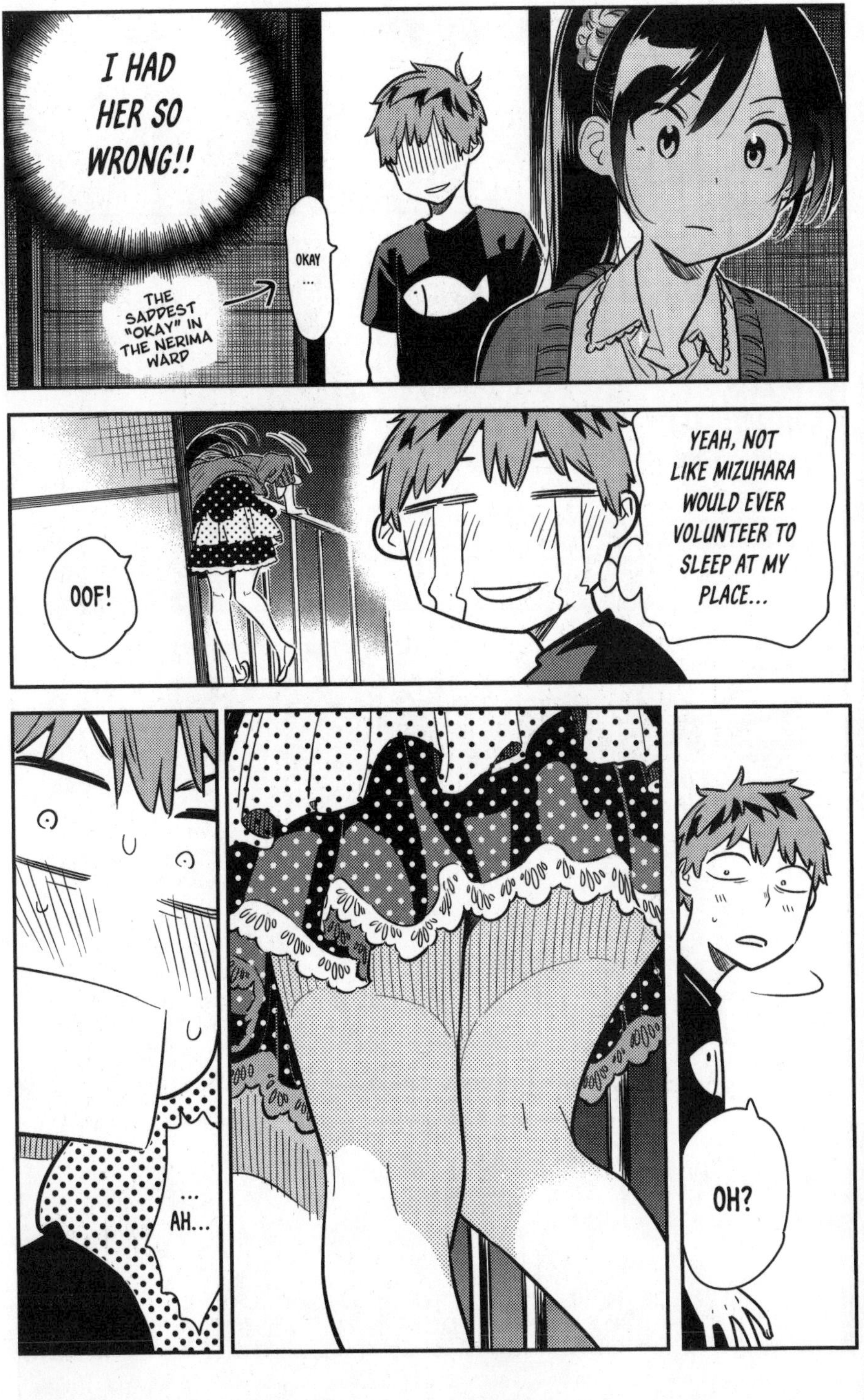
OKAY ...
THE SADDEST "OKAY" IN THE NERIMA WARD
I HAD HER SO WRONG!!
YEAH, NOT LIKE MIZUHARA WOULD EVER VOLUNTEER TO SLEEP AT MY PLACE...
OOF!
OH?
... AH...

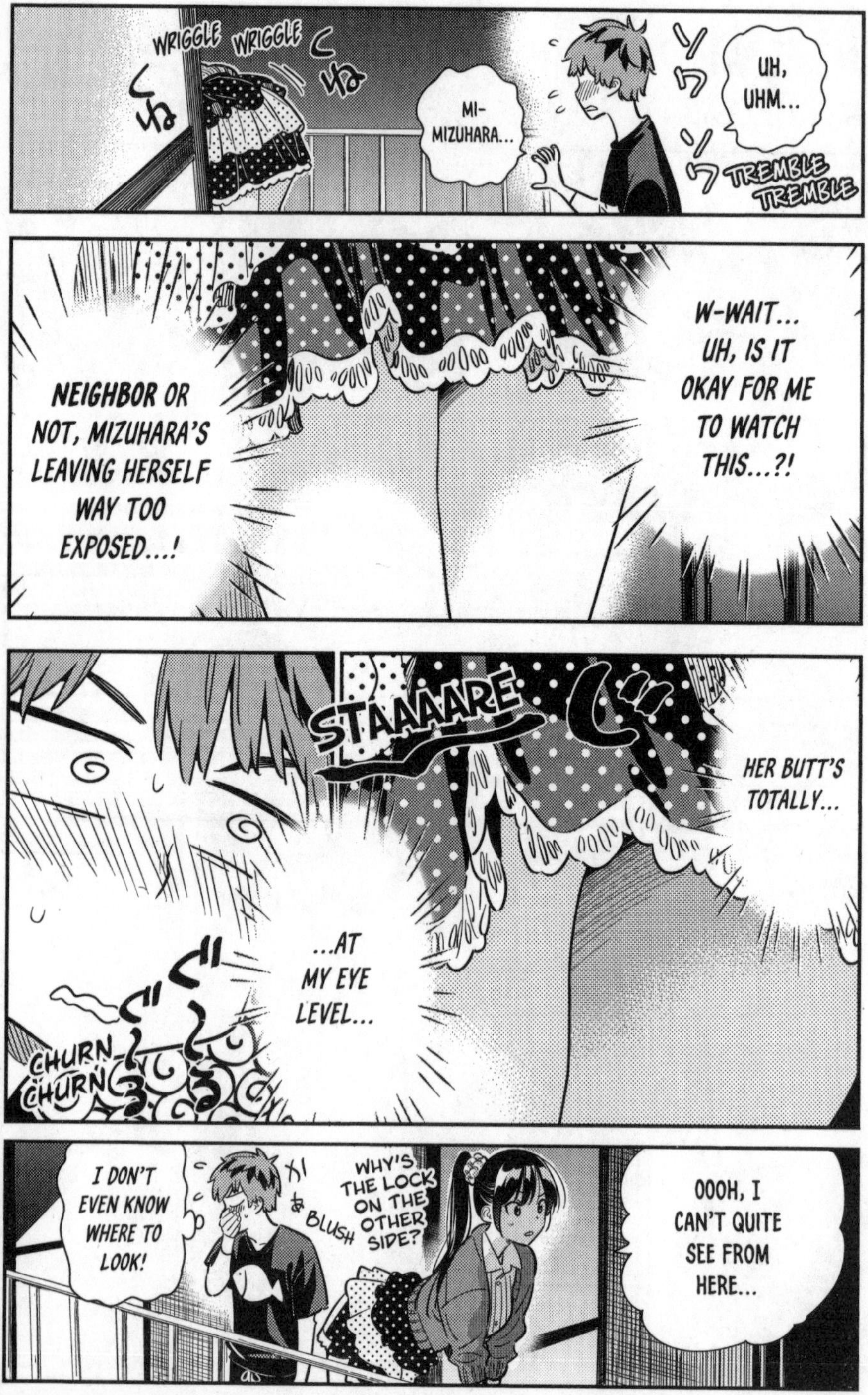
UH, UHM...
TREMBLE TREMBLE
MI- MIZUHARA...
WRIGGLE WRIGGLE
W-WAIT... UH, IS IT OKAY FOR ME TO WATCH THIS...?!
NEIGHBOR OR NOT, MIZUHARA'S LEAVING HERSELF WAY TOO EXPOSED...!
STAAAARE
HER BUTT'S TOTALLY...
...AT MY EYE LEVEL...
CHURN CHURN
OOOH, I CAN'T QUITE SEE FROM HERE...
WHY'S THE LOCK ON THE OTHER SIDE?
BLUSH
I DON'T EVEN KNOW WHERE TO LOOK!

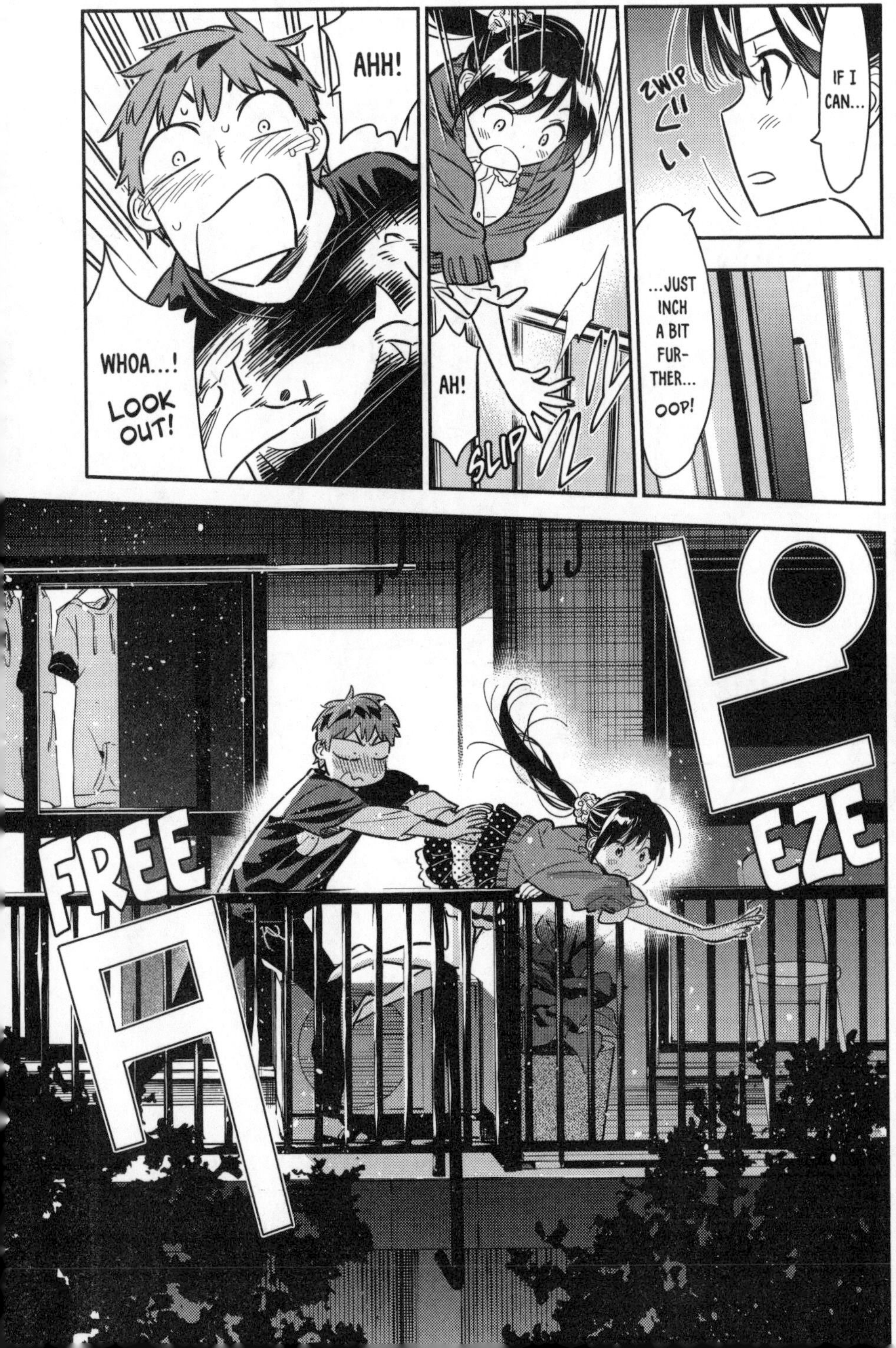
ZWIP
IF I CAN...
...JUST INCH A BIT FURTHER... OOP!
AH!
SLIP
AHH!
WHOA...!
LOOK OUT!
FREEZE

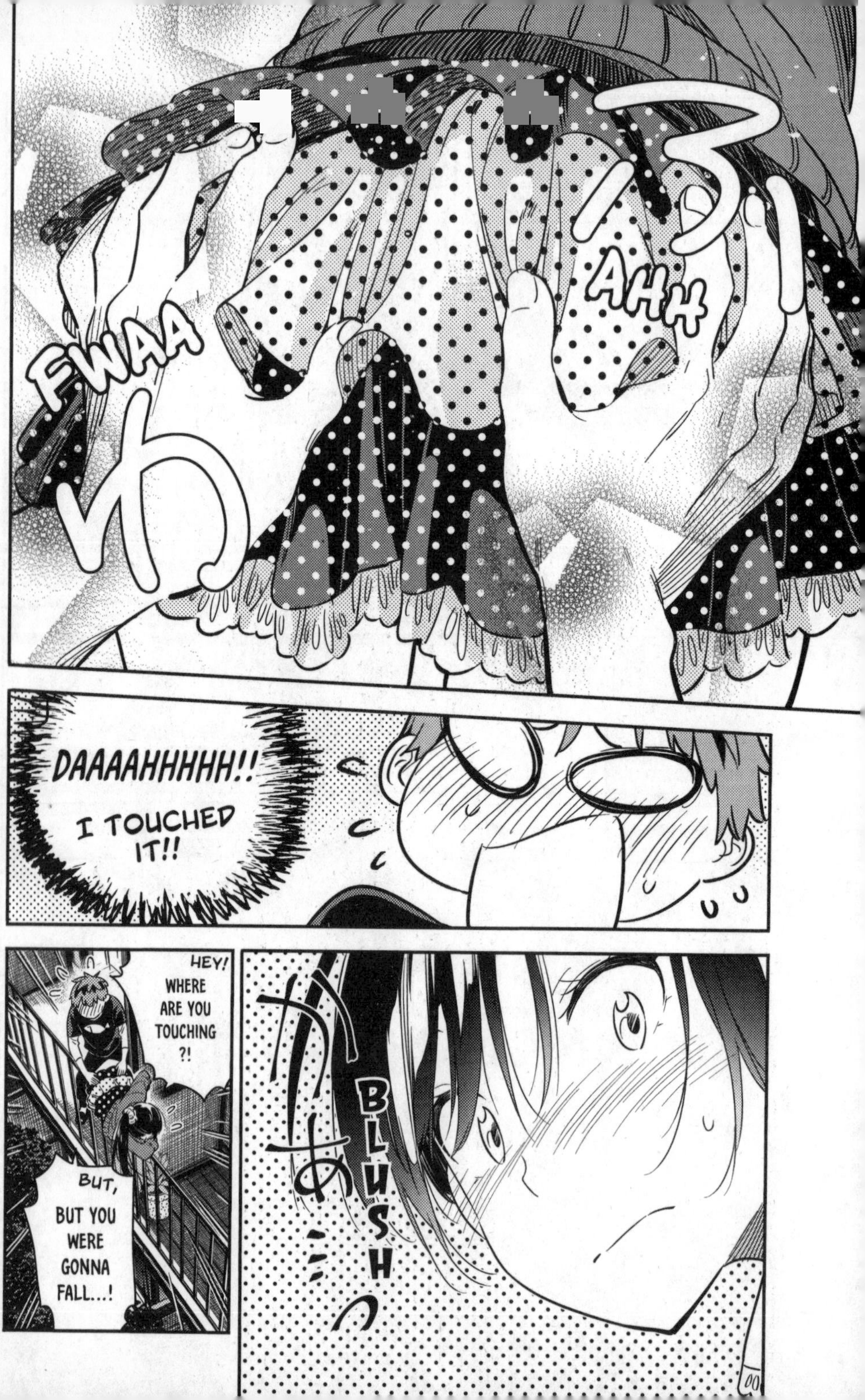
AHH
FWAA
DAAAAHHHHH!!
I TOUCHED IT!!
BLUSH
HEY! WHERE ARE YOU TOUCHING ?!
BUT, BUT YOU WERE GONNA FALL...!

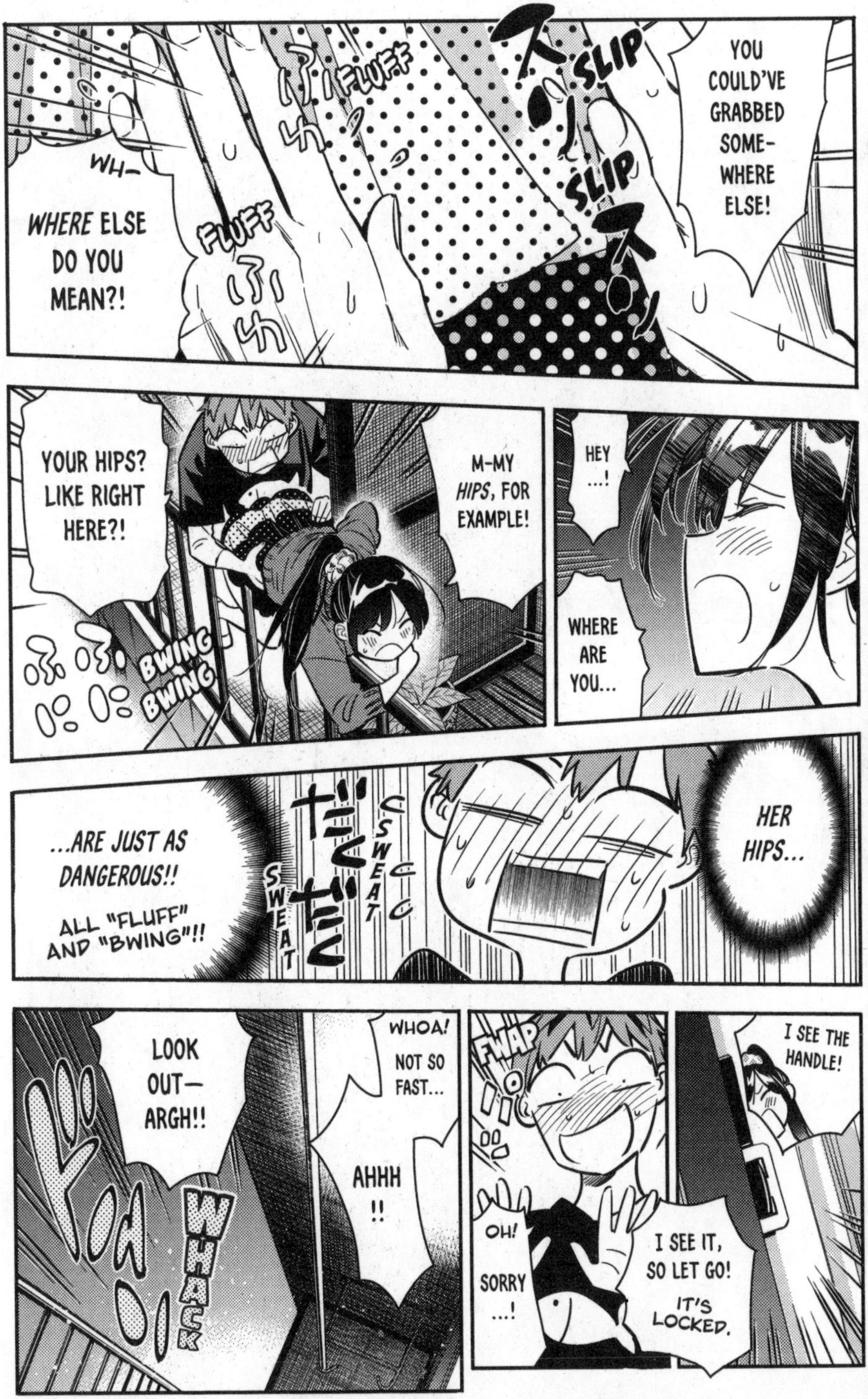
YOU COULD'VE GRABBED SOME-WHERE ELSE!
SLIP
SLIP
FLUFF
FLUFF
WH- WHERE ELSE DO YOU MEAN?!
HEY ...!
WHERE ARE YOU...
M-MY HIPS, FOR EXAMPLE!
YOUR HIPS? LIKE RIGHT HERE?!
BWING BWING
HER HIPS...
SWEAT SWEAT
...ARE JUST AS DANGEROUS!!
ALL "FLUFF" AND "BWING"!!
I SEE THE HANDLE!
FWAP
I SEE IT, SO LET GO!
IT'S LOCKED.
OH!
SORRY ...!
WHOA!
NOT SO FAST...
AHHH !!
LOOK OUT— ARGH!!
WHACK

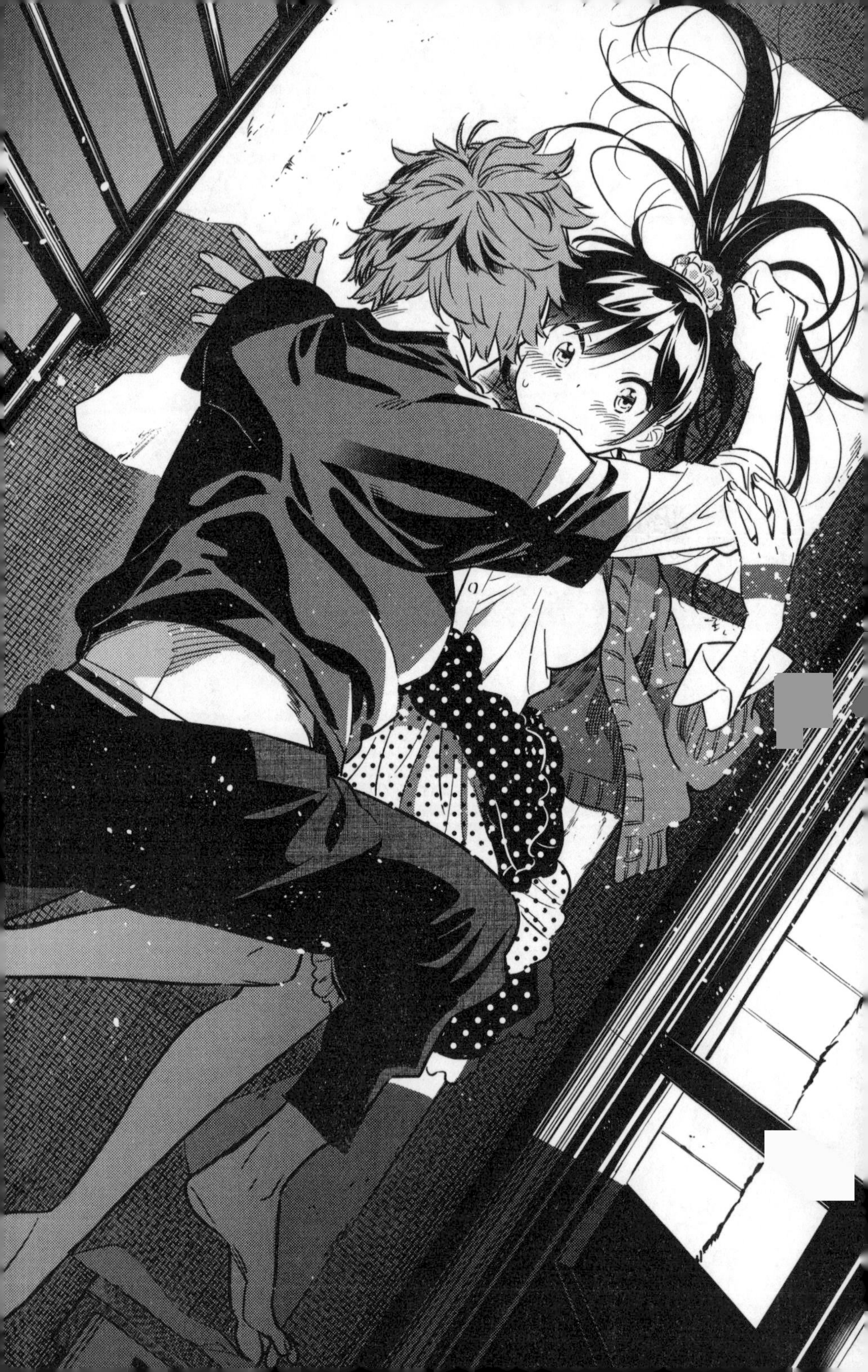

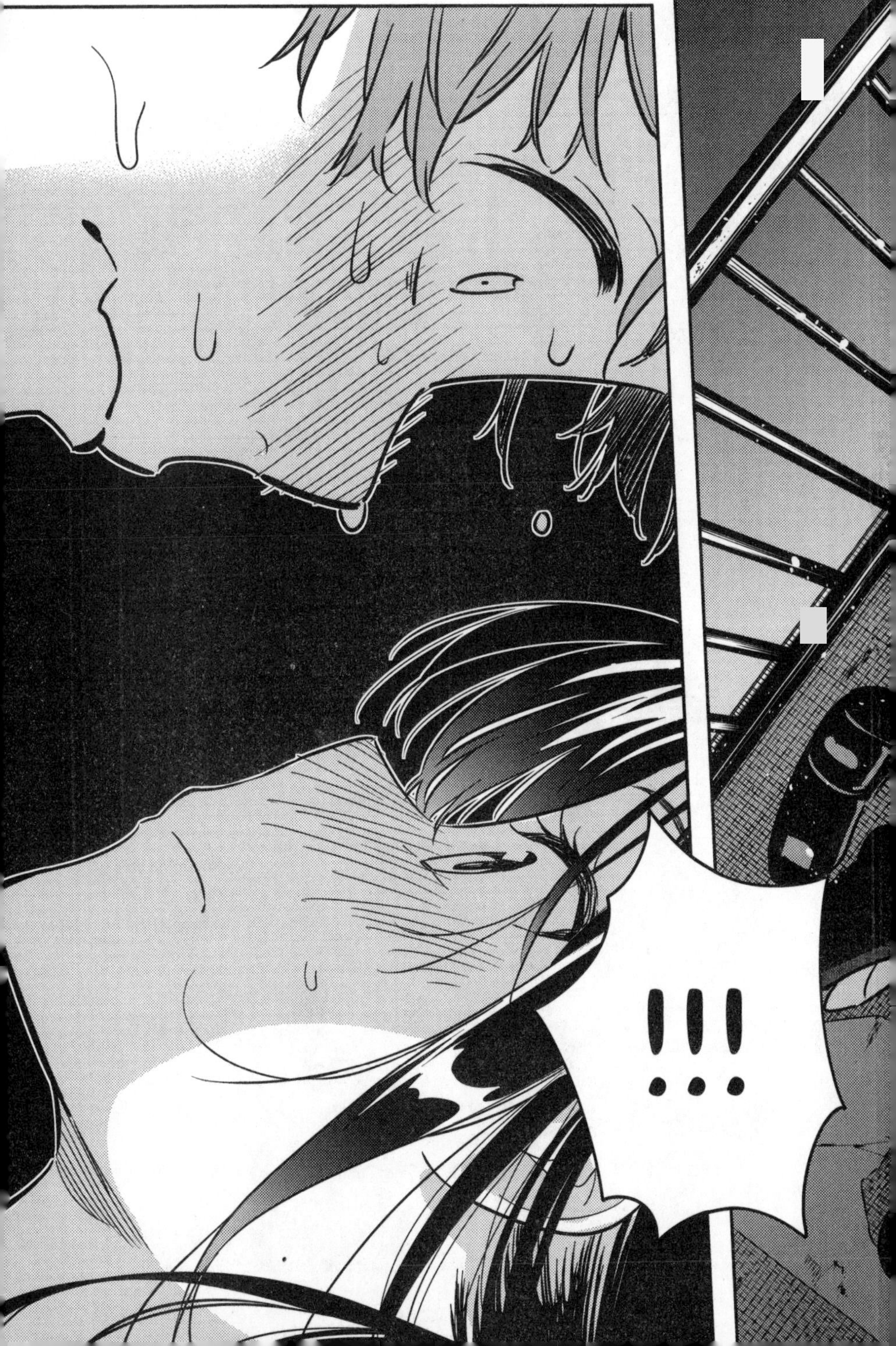
!!!

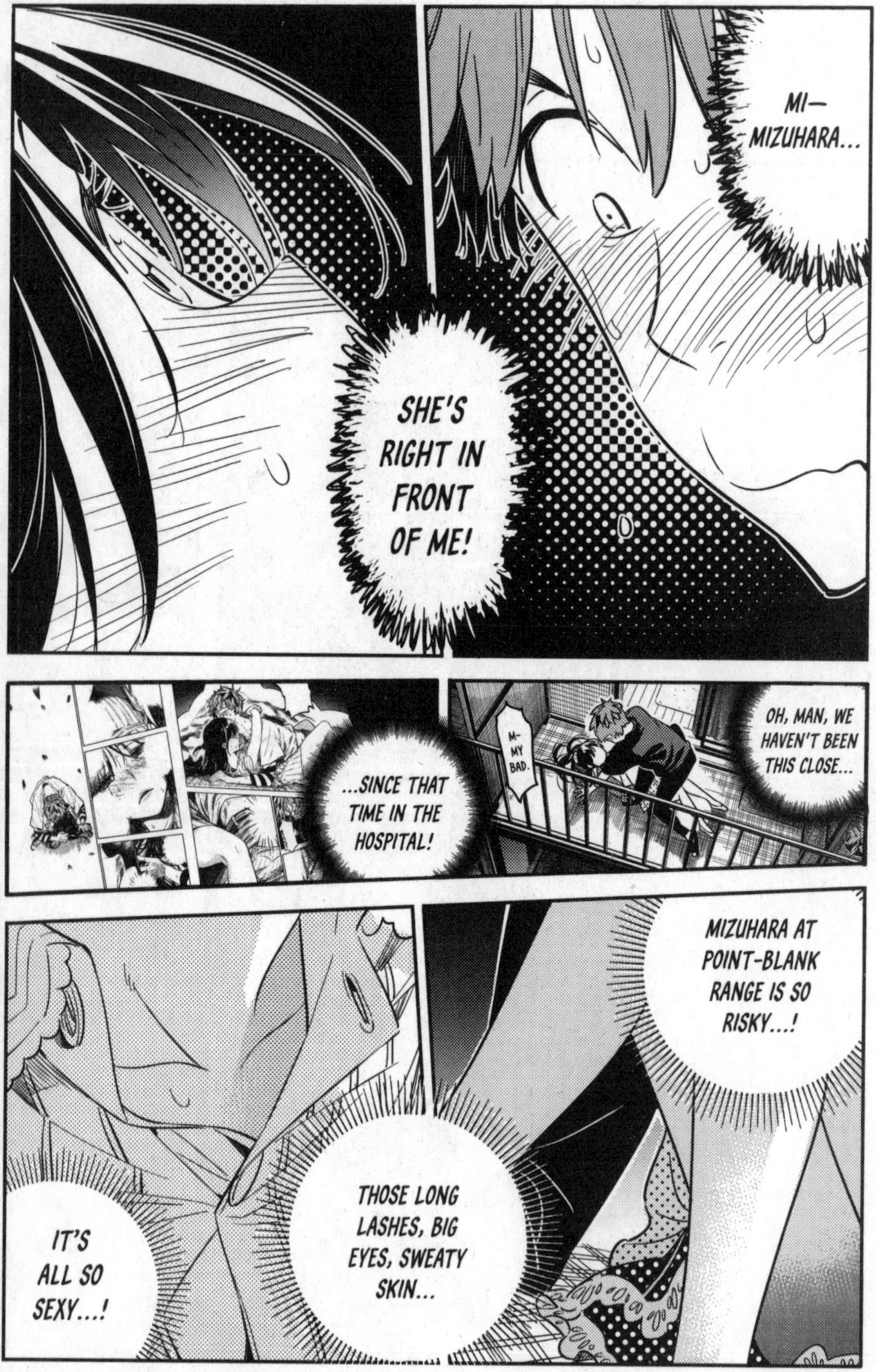
MI—
MIZUHARA...
SHE'S RIGHT IN FRONT OF ME!
OH, MAN, WE HAVEN'T BEEN THIS CLOSE...
M-MY BAD.
...SINCE THAT TIME IN THE HOSPITAL!
MIZUHARA AT POINT-BLANK RANGE IS SO RISKY...!
THOSE LONG LASHES, BIG EYES, SWEATY SKIN...
IT'S ALL SO SEXY...!

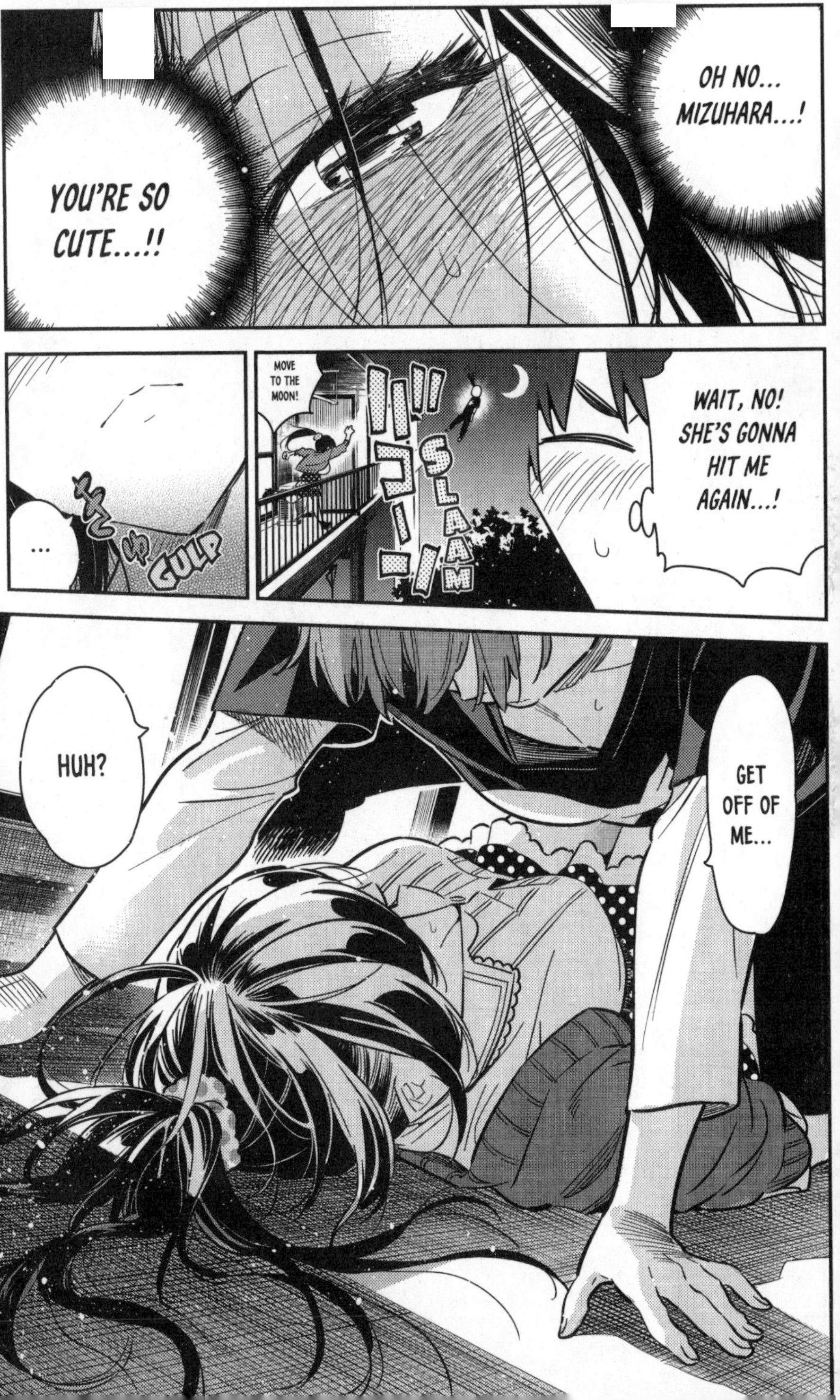
OH NO... MIZUHARA...!
YOU'RE SO CUTE...!!
WAIT, NO! SHE'S GONNA HIT ME AGAIN...!
MOVE TO THE MOON!
SLAAM
...
GULP
GET OFF OF ME...
HUH?

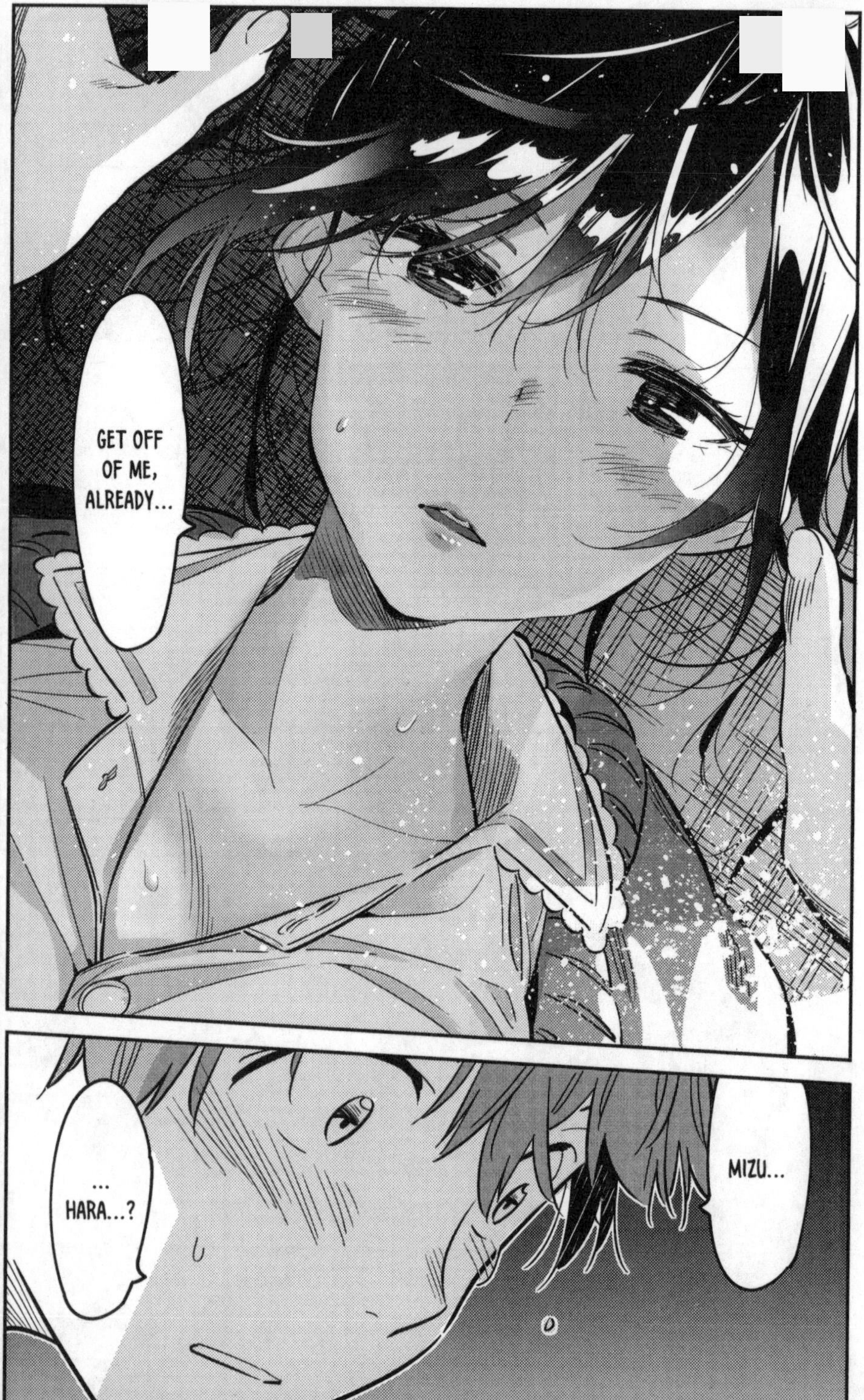
GET OFF OF ME, ALREADY...
MIZU...
... HARA...?

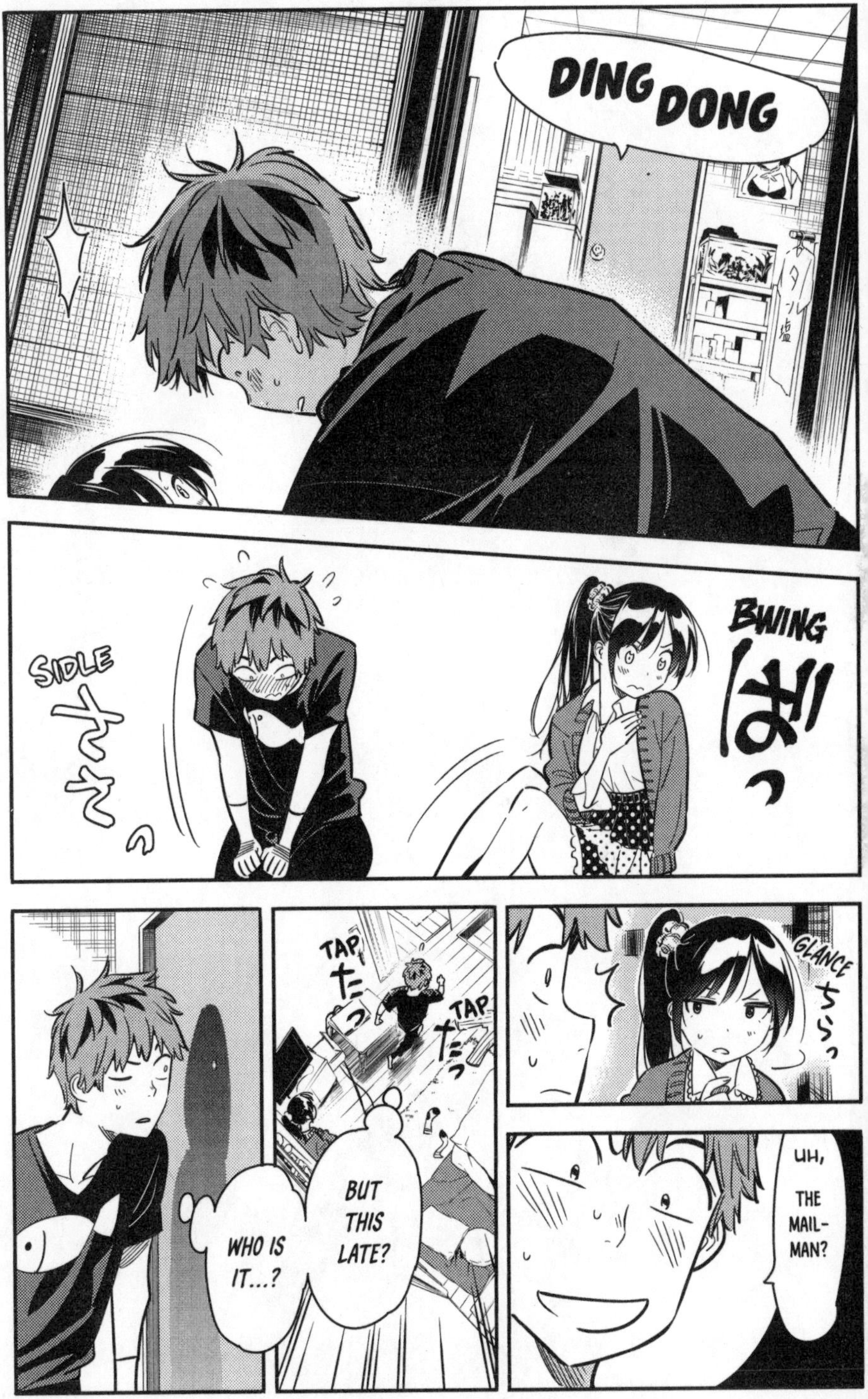
DING DONG
BWING
ぱっ
SIDLE
ささっ
GLANCE
ちらっ
UH, THE MAIL-MAN?
TAP
たっ
TAP
たっ
BUT THIS LATE?
WHO IS IT...?

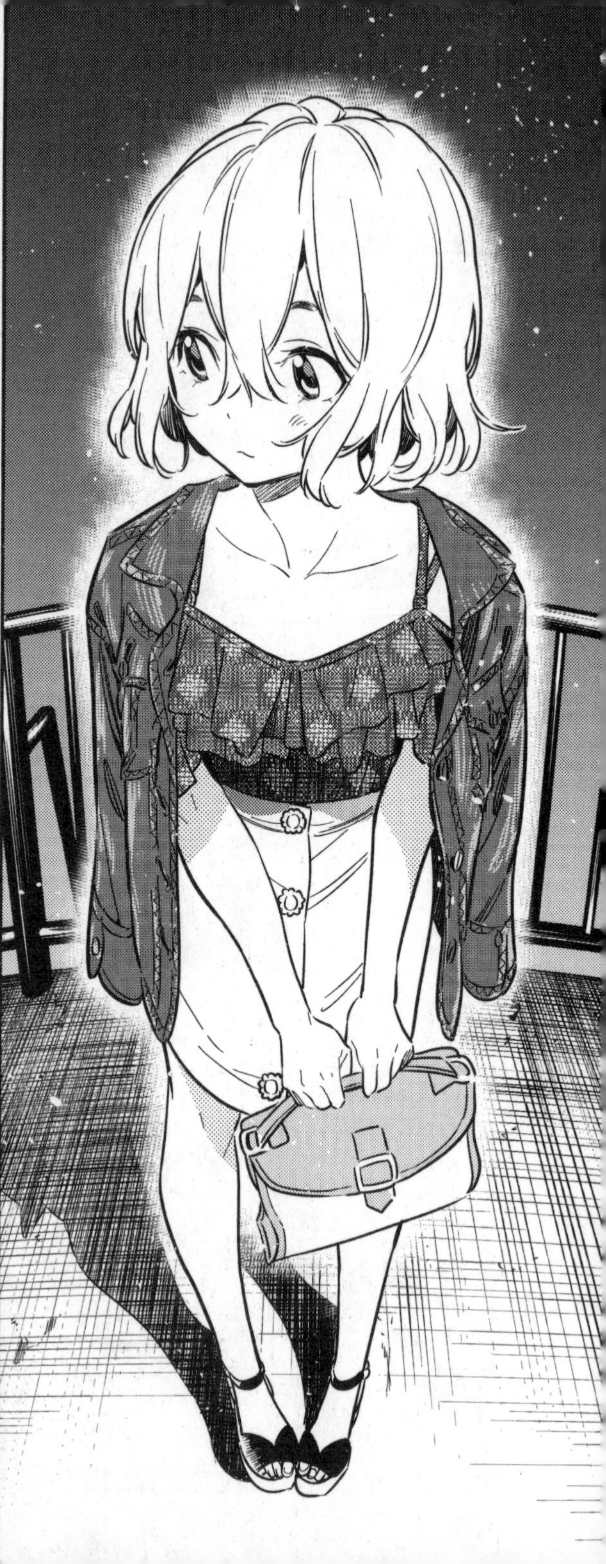
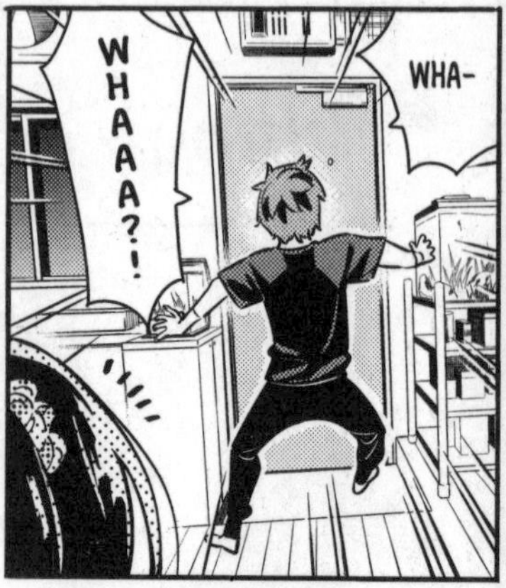
WHA-
WHAAAA?!
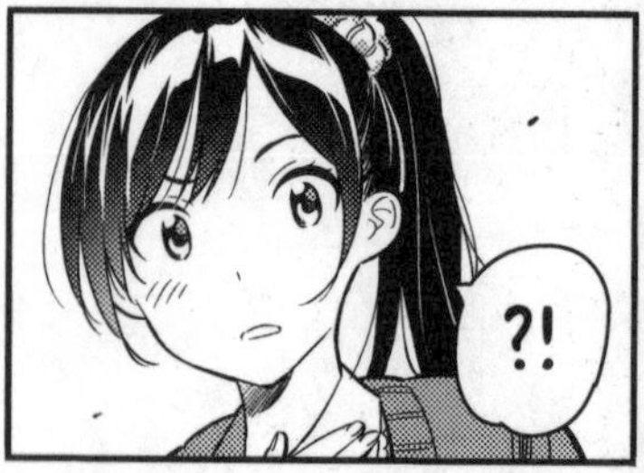
?!
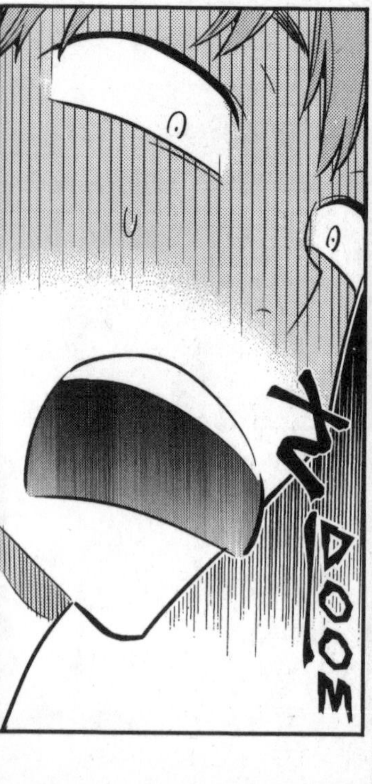
DOOM

RATING 60 MY "GIRLFRIEND," CHIZURU ICHINOSE 5

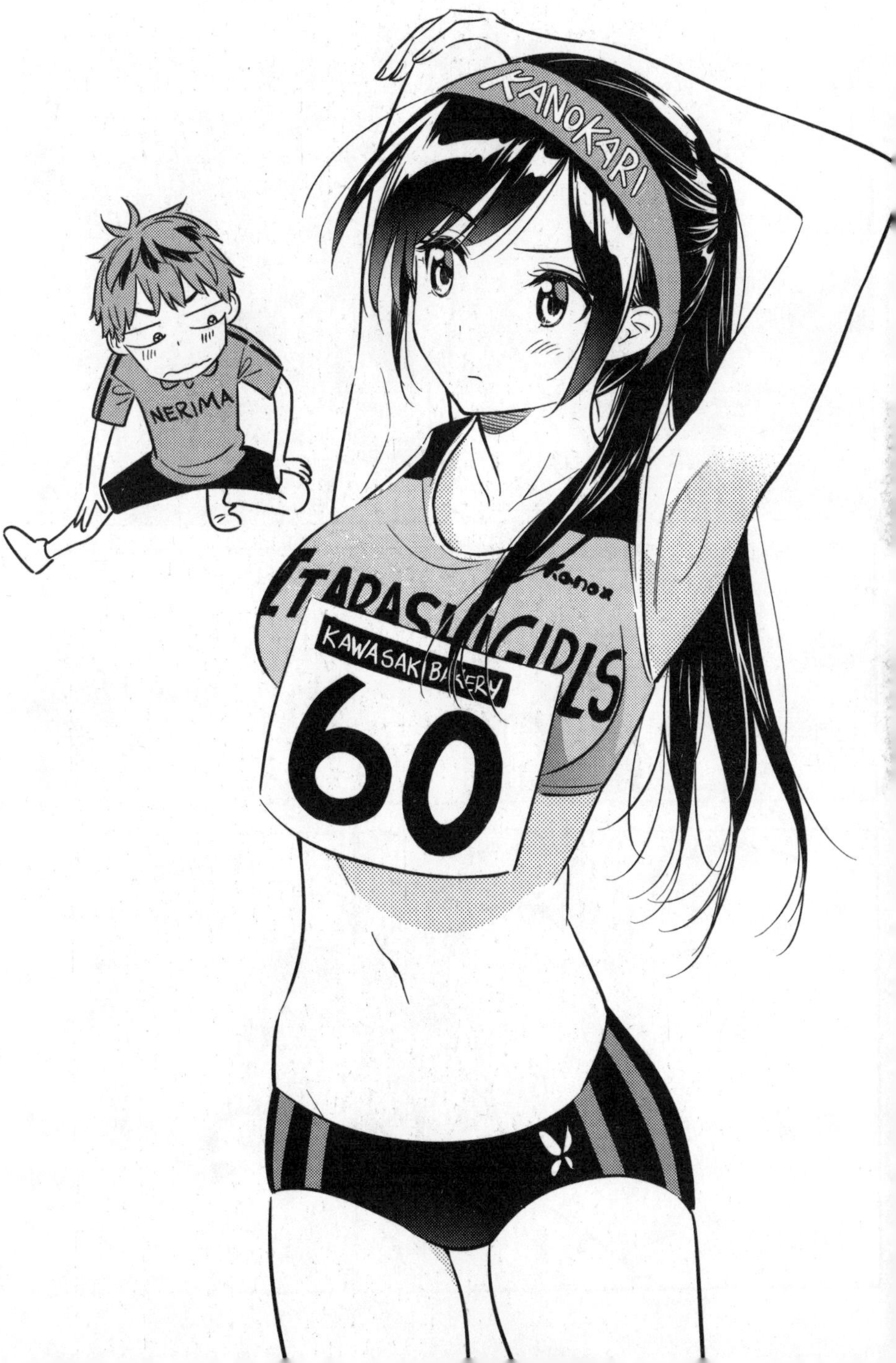
KANOKARI
NERIMA
60

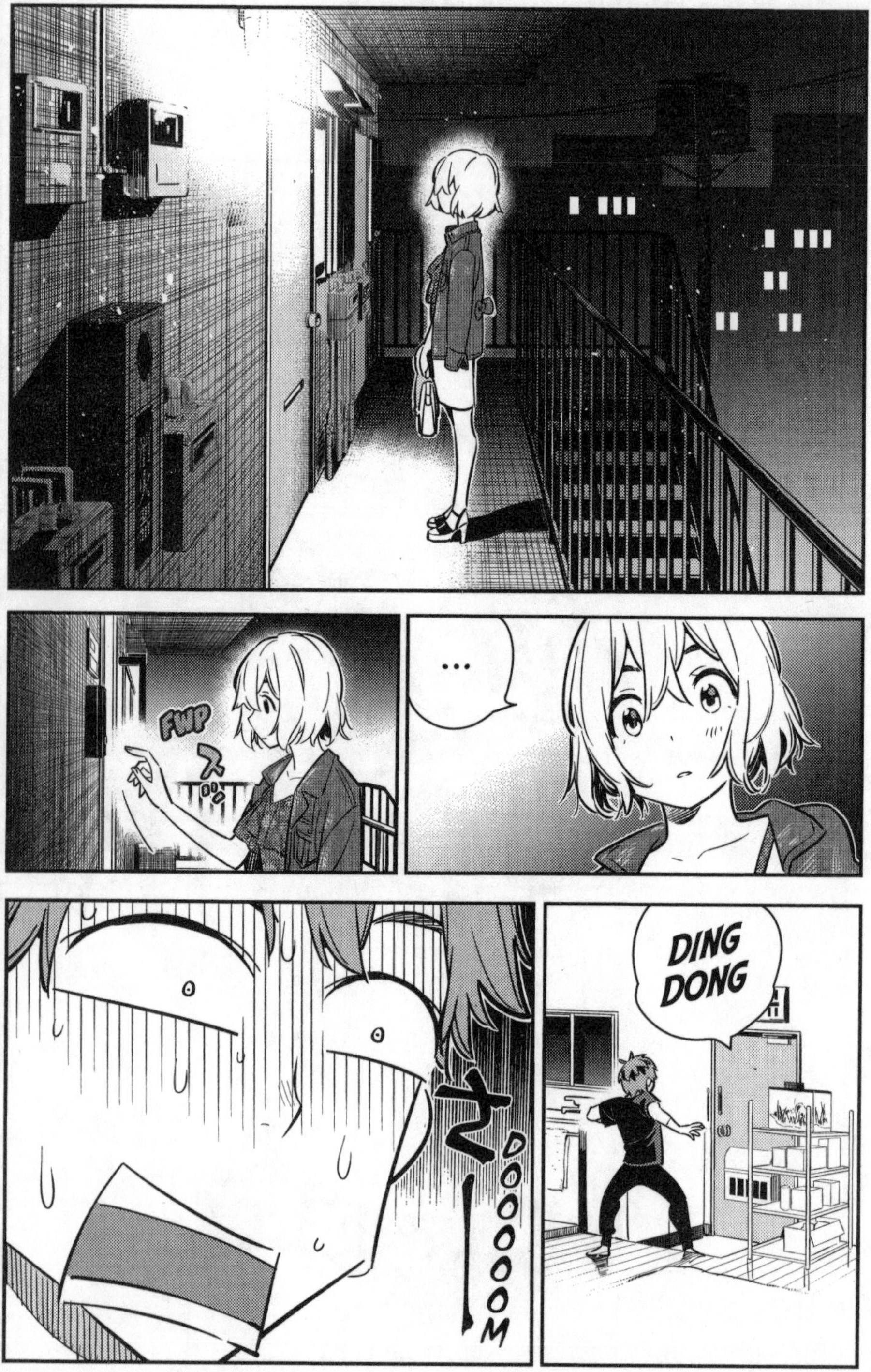
...
FWP
DING DONG
DOOOOOM

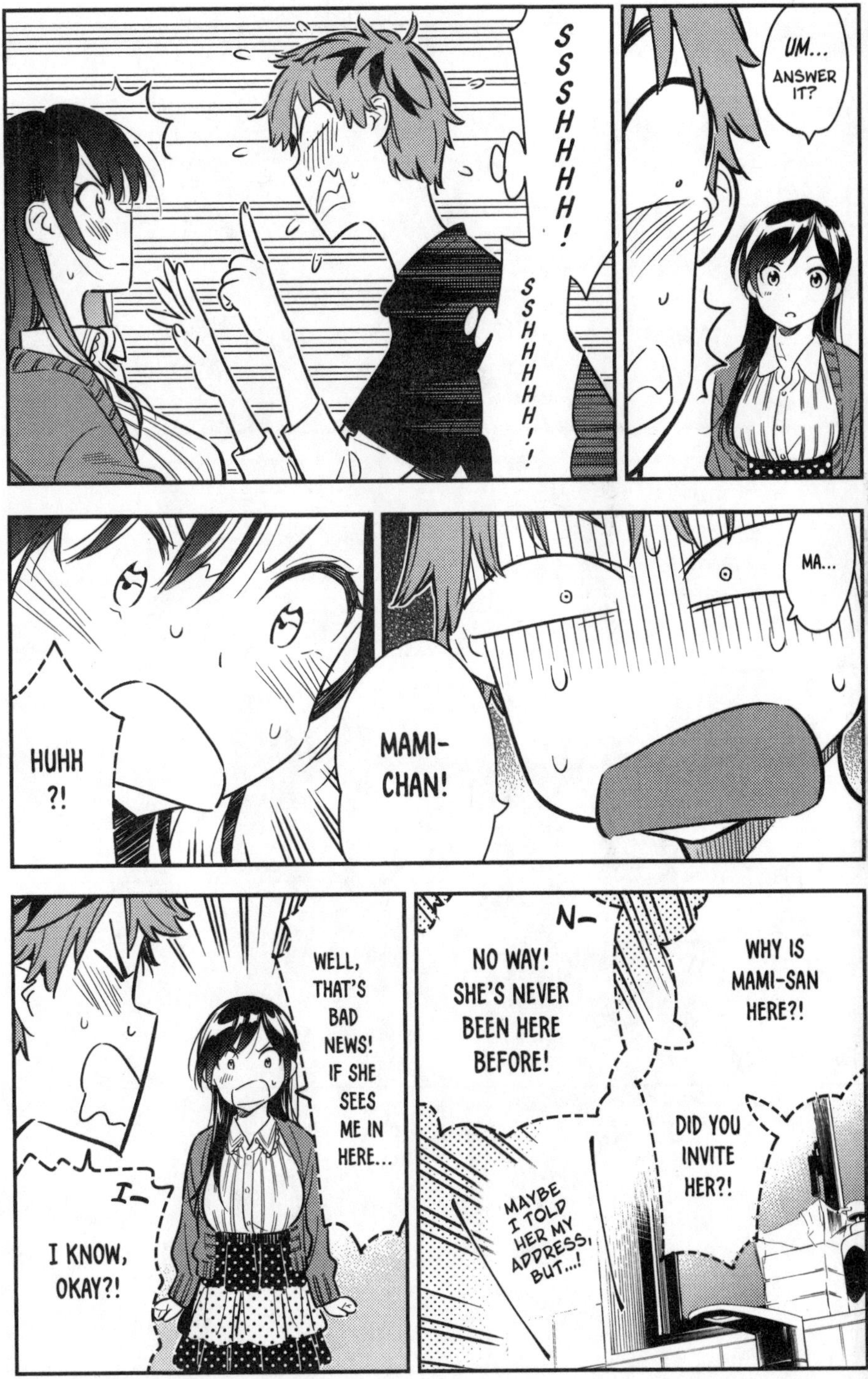
UM... ANSWER IT?
SSSHHHHH!
SSHHHHHH!!
MA...
MAMI-CHAN!
HUHH ?!
WHY IS MAMI-SAN HERE?!
N—
NO WAY! SHE'S NEVER BEEN HERE BEFORE!
DID YOU INVITE HER?!
MAYBE I TOLD HER MY ADDRESS, BUT...!
WELL, THAT'S BAD NEWS! IF SHE SEES ME IN HERE...
I—
I KNOW, OKAY?!

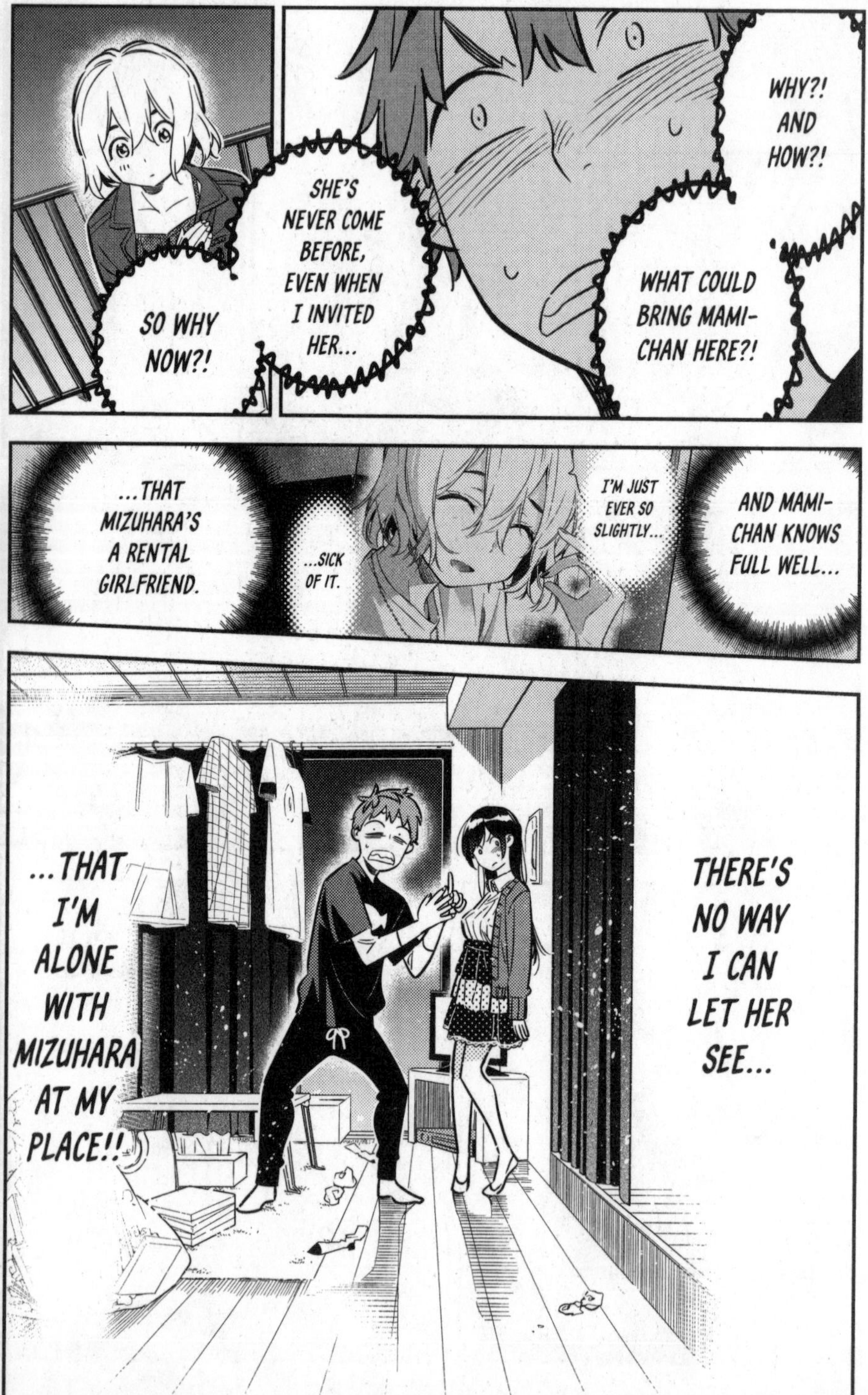
WHY?! AND HOW?!
WHAT COULD BRING MAMI-CHAN HERE?!
SHE'S NEVER COME BEFORE, EVEN WHEN I INVITED HER...
SO WHY NOW?!
AND MAMI-CHAN KNOWS FULL WELL...
I'M JUST EVER SO SLIGHTLY...
...SICK OF IT.
...THAT MIZUHARA'S A RENTAL GIRLFRIEND.
THERE'S NO WAY I CAN LET HER SEE...
...THAT I'M ALONE WITH MIZUHARA AT MY PLACE!!

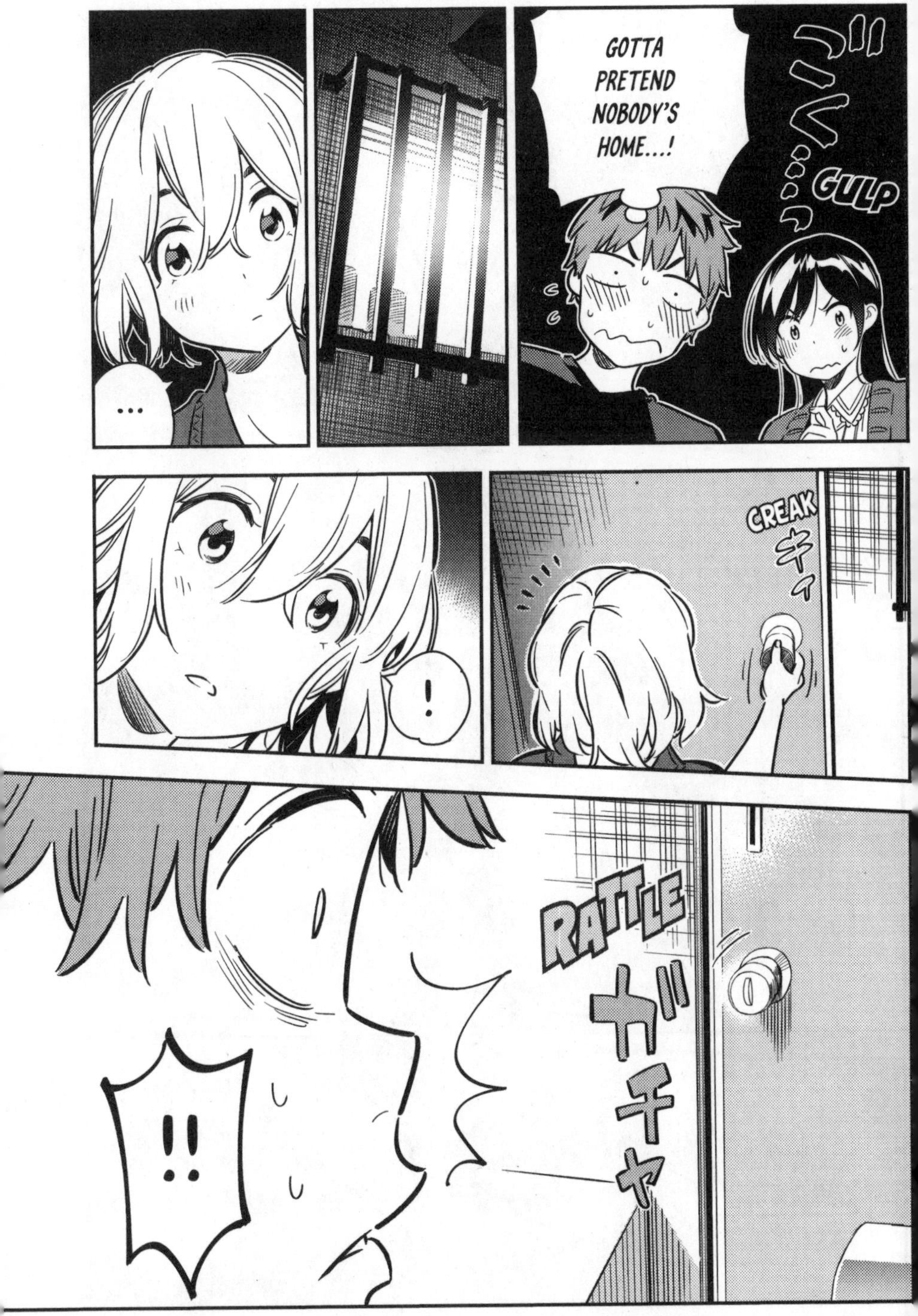
GOTTA PRETEND NOBODY'S HOME...!
GULP
...
CREAK
キィ
!
RATTLE
ガチャ
!!

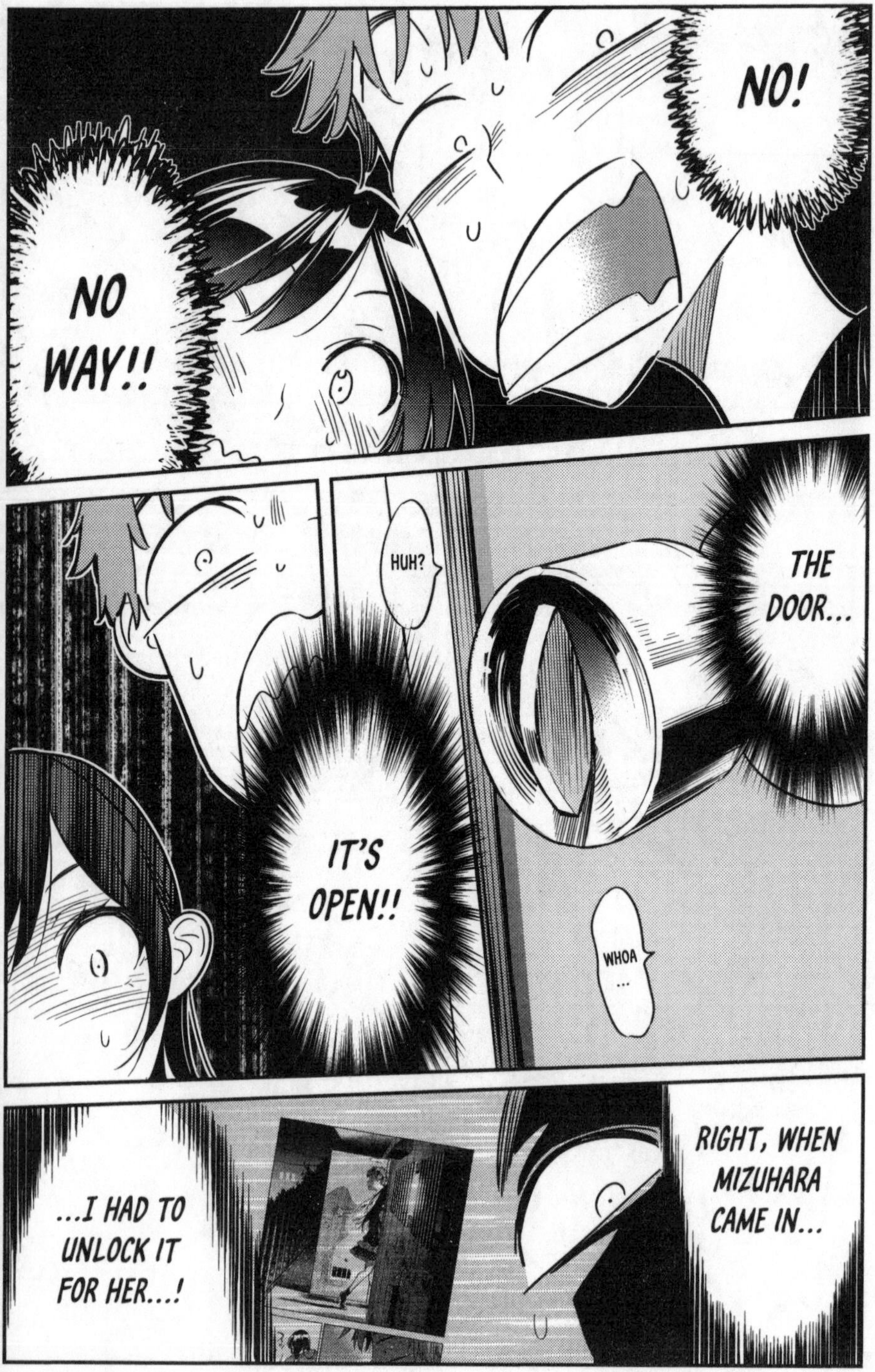
NO!
NO WAY!!
THE DOOR...
HUH?
IT'S OPEN!!
WHOA ...
RIGHT, WHEN MIZUHARA CAME IN...
...I HAD TO UNLOCK IT FOR HER...!

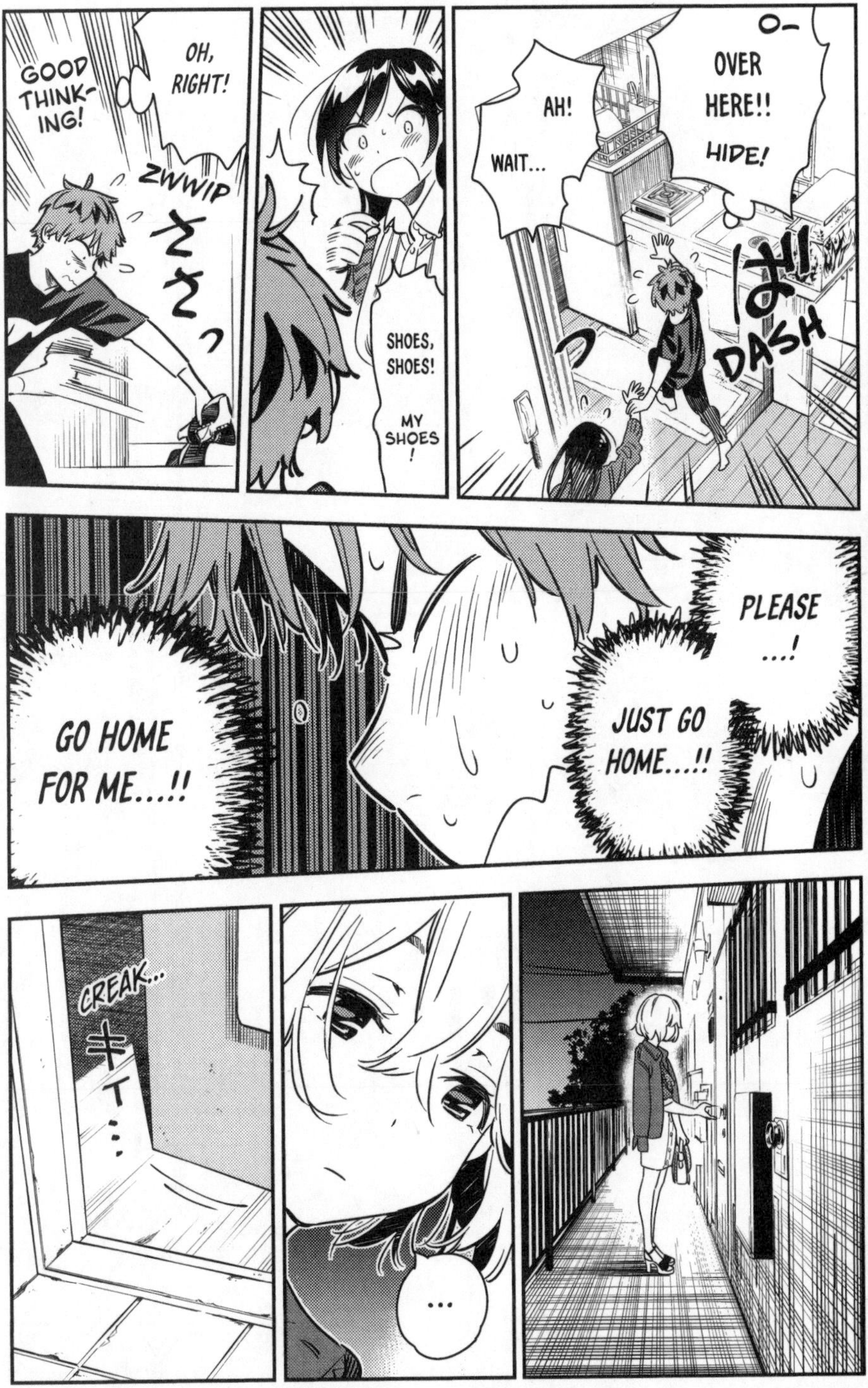
O-
OVER HERE!!
HIDE!
AH!
WAIT...
ぱっ
DASH
つ
SHOES, SHOES!
MY SHOES!
OH, RIGHT!
GOOD THINKING!
ZWWIP
ささっ
PLEASE ...!
JUST GO HOME...!!
GO HOME FOR ME...!!
...
CREAK...
キィ…

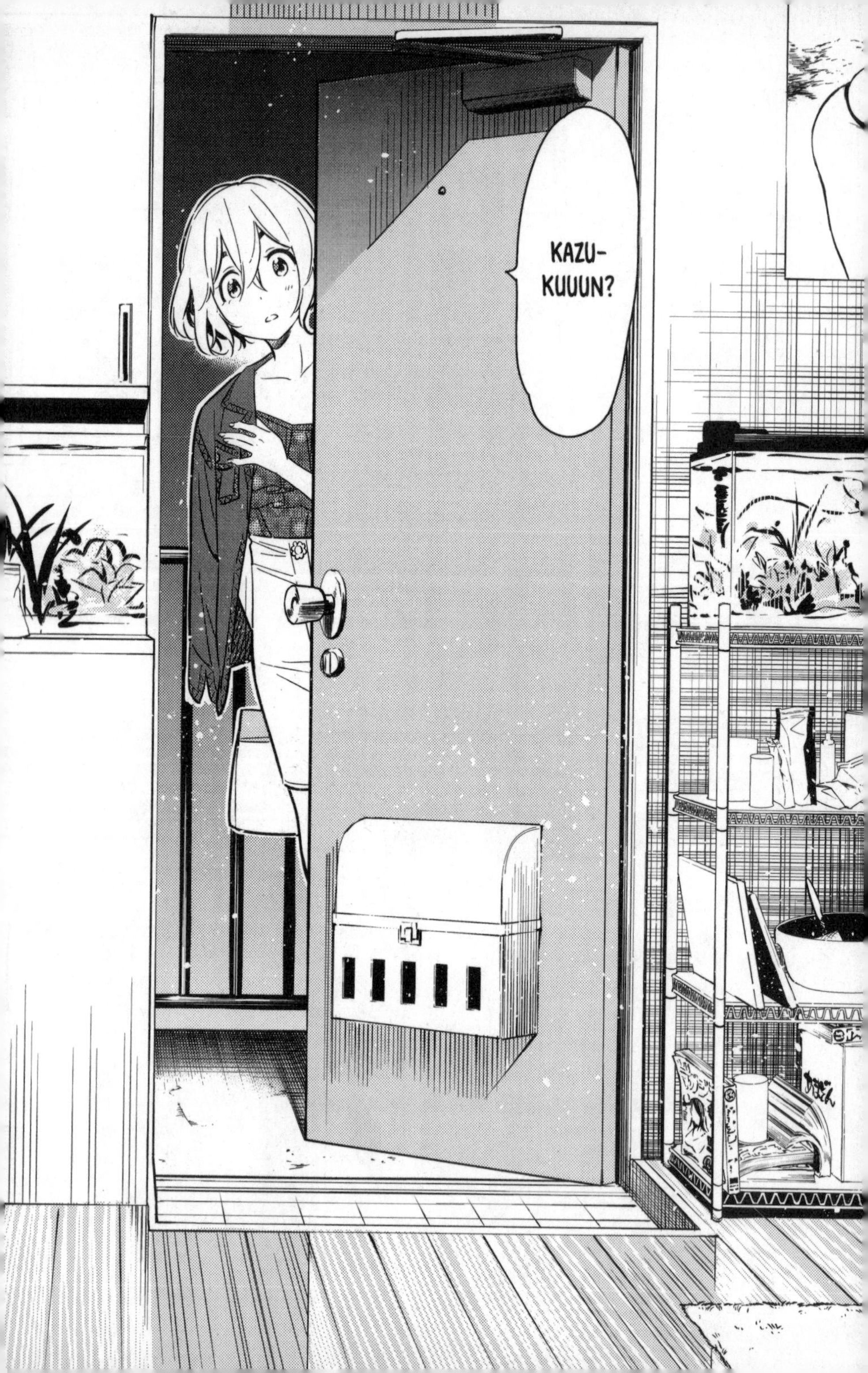
KAZU-
KUUUN?

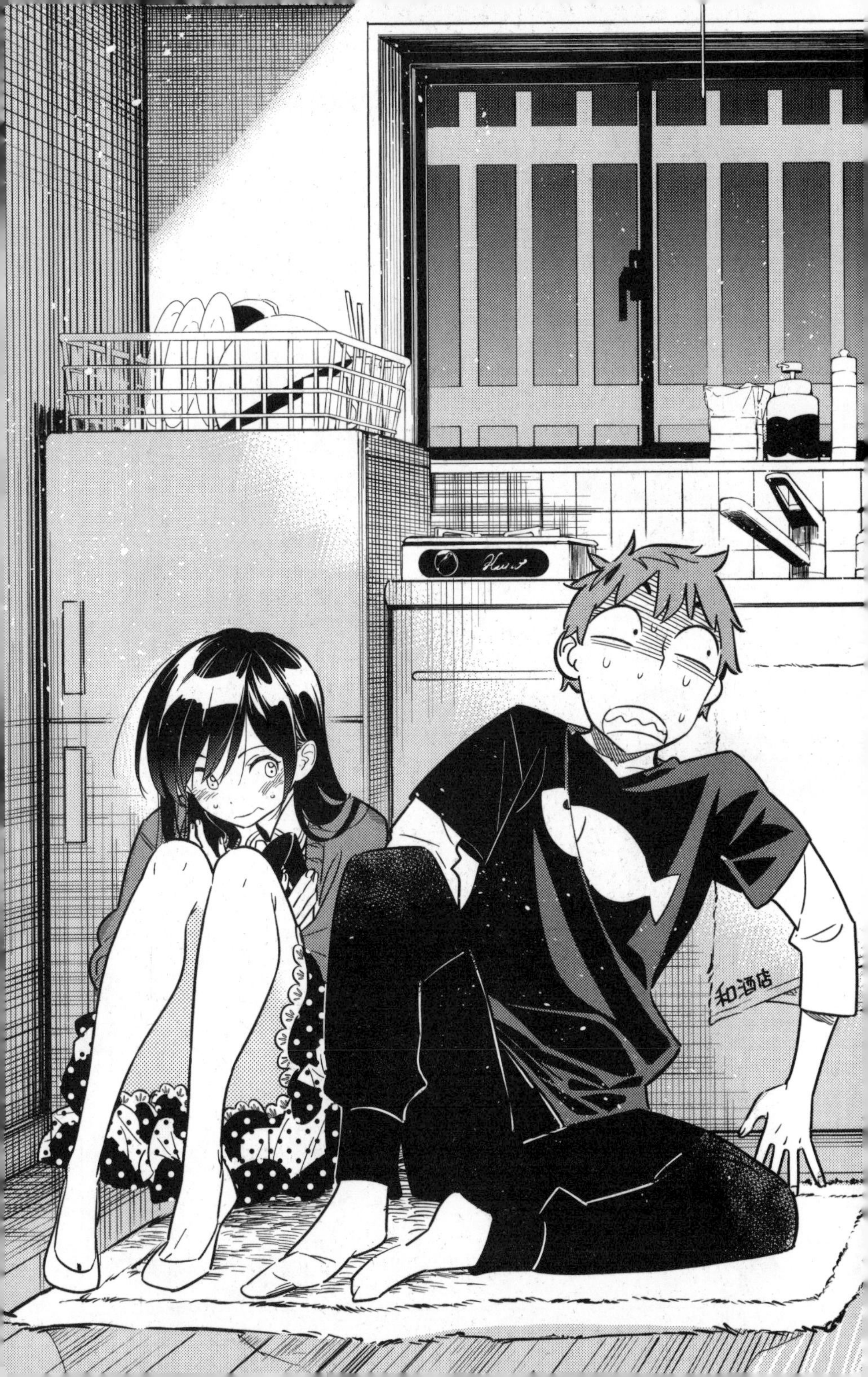
和酒店

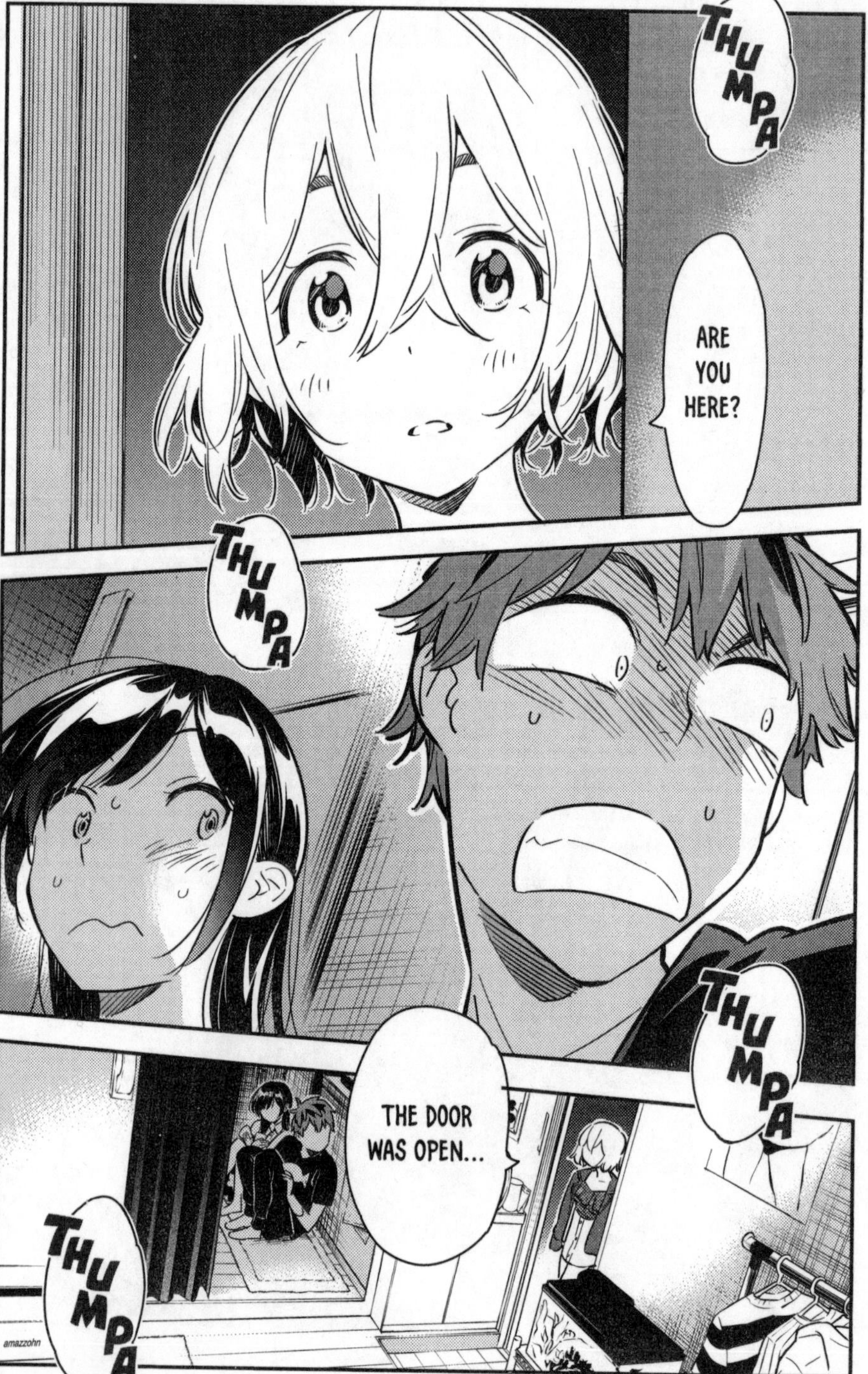
THUMPA
ARE YOU HERE?
THUMPA
THUMPA
THE DOOR WAS OPEN...
THUMPA

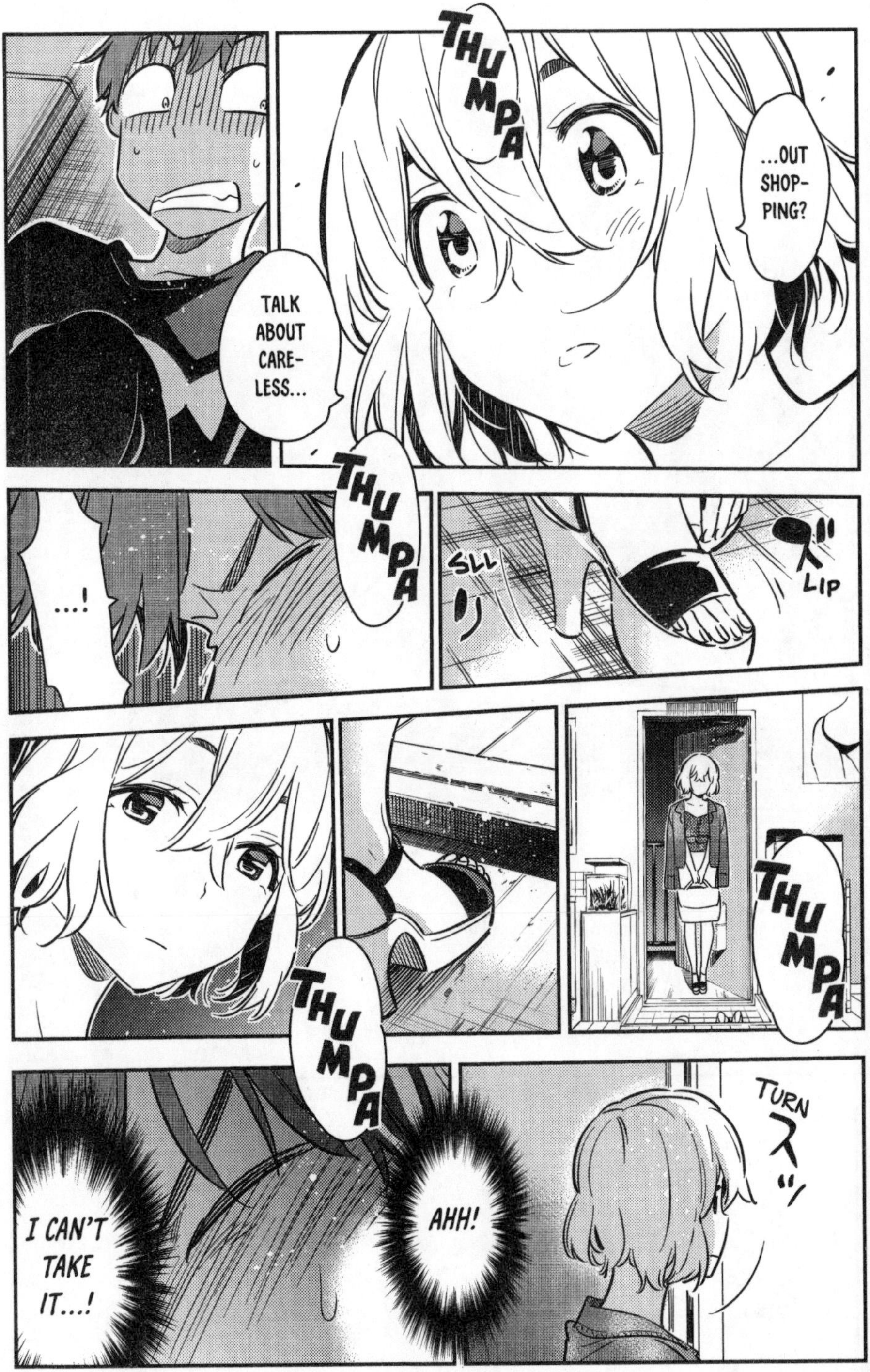
THUMPA
...OUT SHOPPING?
TALK ABOUT CARELESS...
LIP
SLL
THUMPA
...!
THUMPA
THUMPA
TURN
AHH!
I CAN'T TAKE IT...!

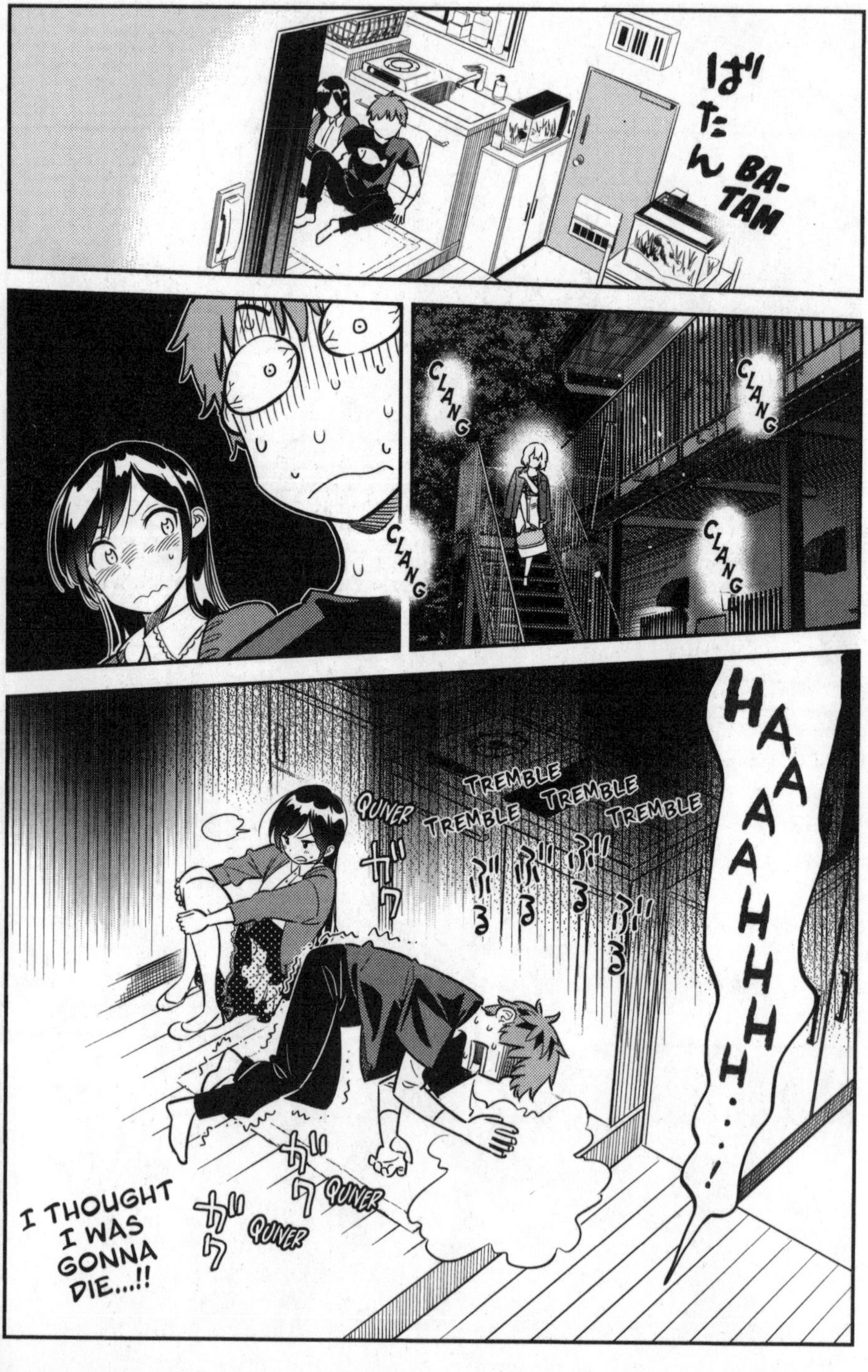
ばたん
BA-TAM
CLANG
CLANG
CLANG
CLANG
CLANG
HAAAAHHHH...!
TREMBLE TREMBLE TREMBLE TREMBLE
ぶるぶるぶるぶる
QUIVER
ガク
ガク
QUIVER
ガク
QUIVER
I THOUGHT I WAS GONNA DIE...!!

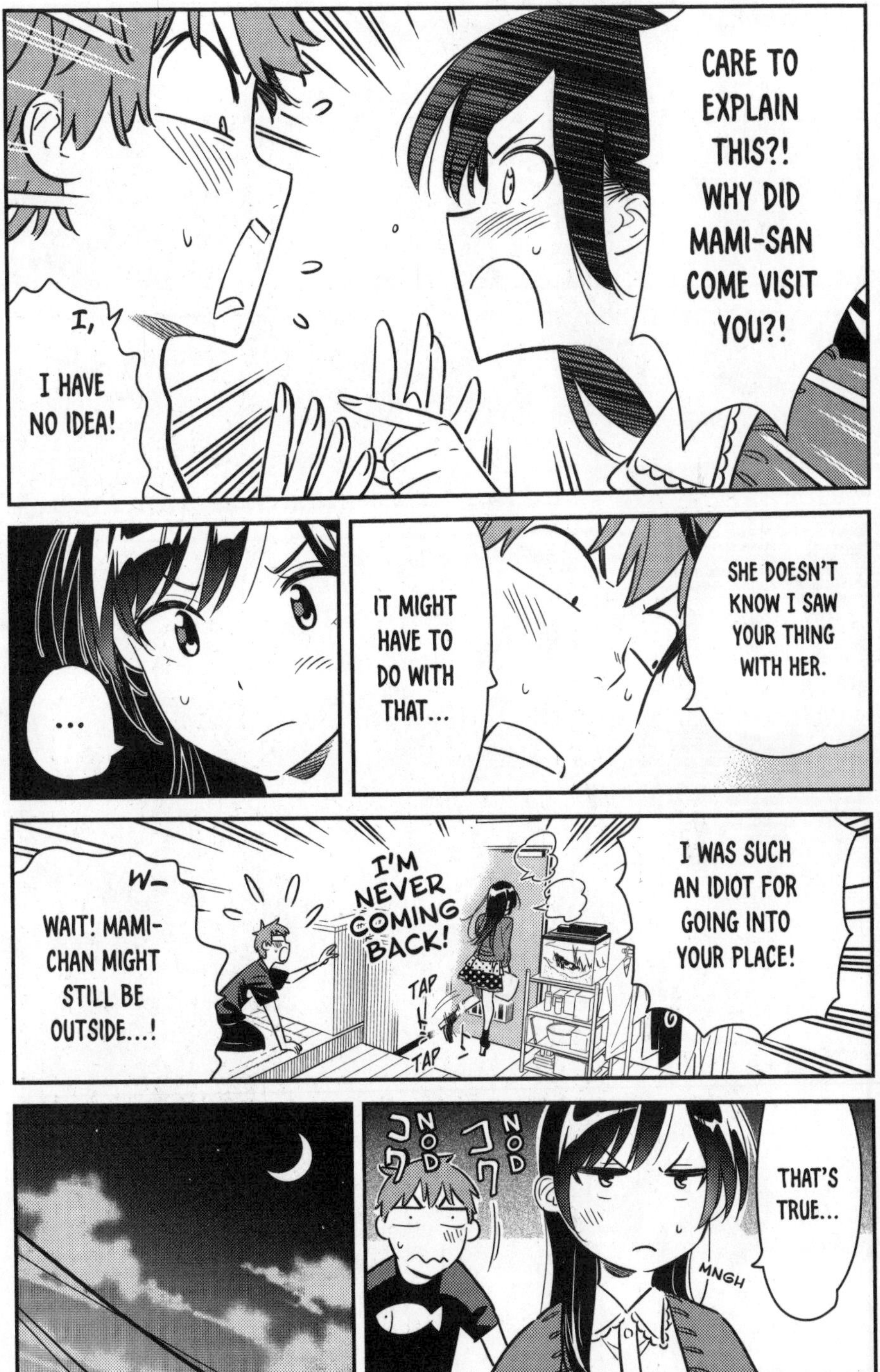
CARE TO EXPLAIN THIS?! WHY DID MAMI-SAN COME VISIT YOU?!
I,
I HAVE NO IDEA!
SHE DOESN'T KNOW I SAW YOUR THING WITH HER.
IT MIGHT HAVE TO DO WITH THAT...
...
I WAS SUCH AN IDIOT FOR GOING INTO YOUR PLACE!
I'M NEVER COMING BACK!
TAP
TAP
W—
WAIT! MAMI-CHAN MIGHT STILL BE OUTSIDE...!
THAT'S TRUE...
MNGH
NOD
コク
NOD
コク

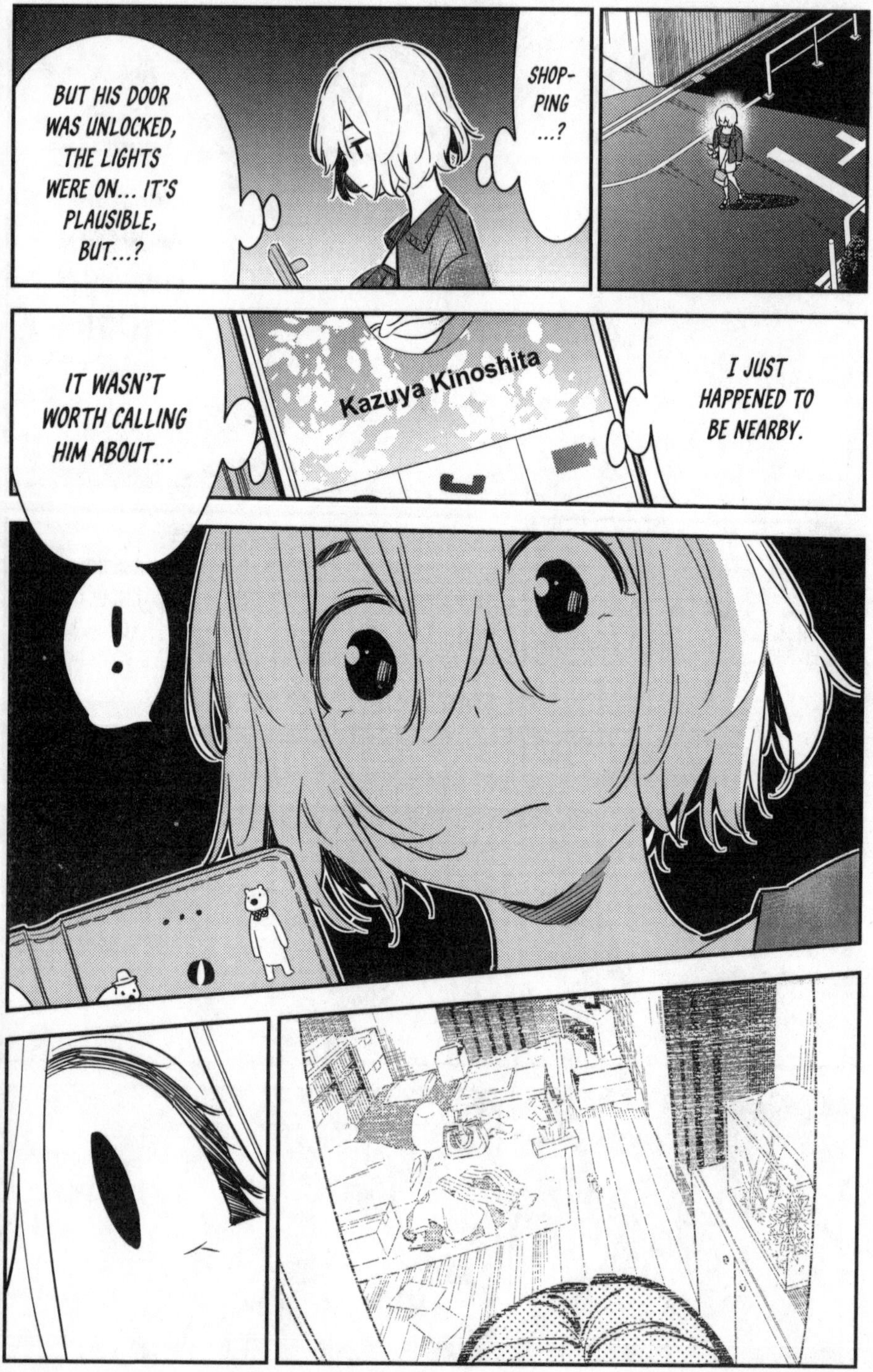
SHOP-PING ...?
BUT HIS DOOR WAS UNLOCKED, THE LIGHTS WERE ON... IT'S PLAUSIBLE, BUT...?
I JUST HAPPENED TO BE NEARBY.
Kazuya Kinoshita
IT WASN'T WORTH CALLING HIM ABOUT...
!
...

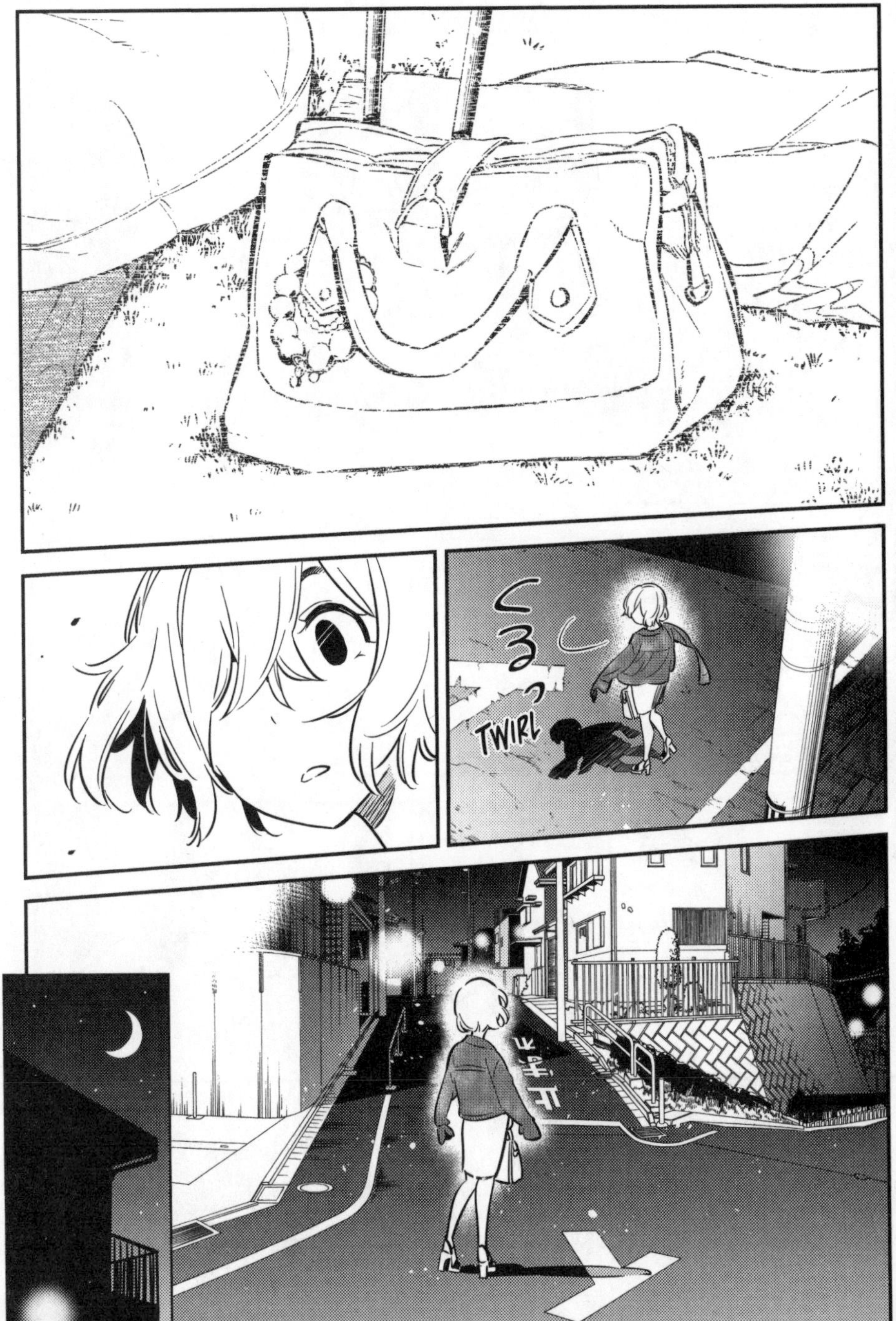
くるっ
TWIRL

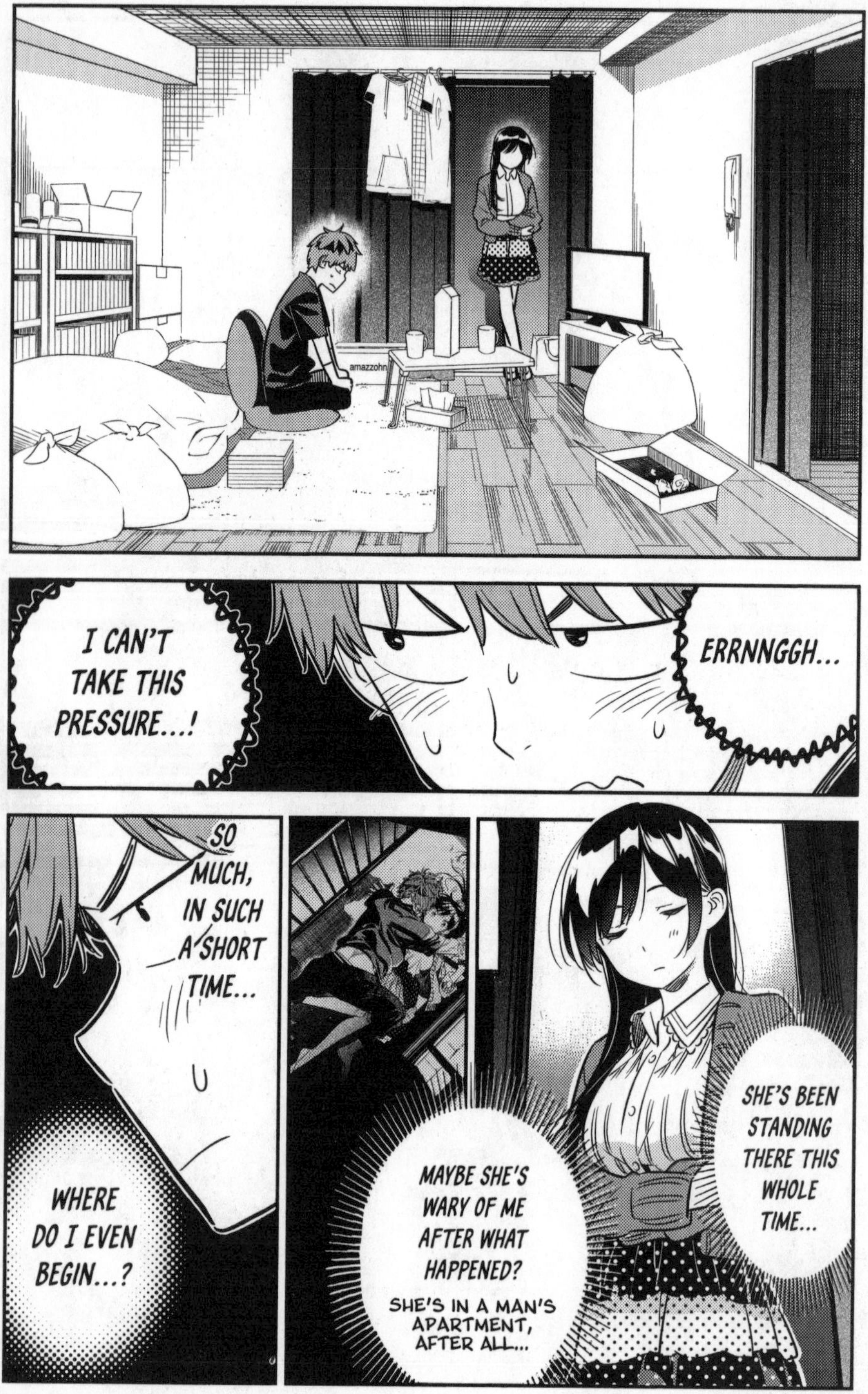
ERRNNGGH...
I CAN'T TAKE THIS PRESSURE...!
SHE'S BEEN STANDING THERE THIS WHOLE TIME...
MAYBE SHE'S WARY OF ME AFTER WHAT HAPPENED?
SHE'S IN A MAN'S APARTMENT, AFTER ALL...
SO MUCH, IN SUCH A SHORT TIME...
WHERE DO I EVEN BEGIN...?

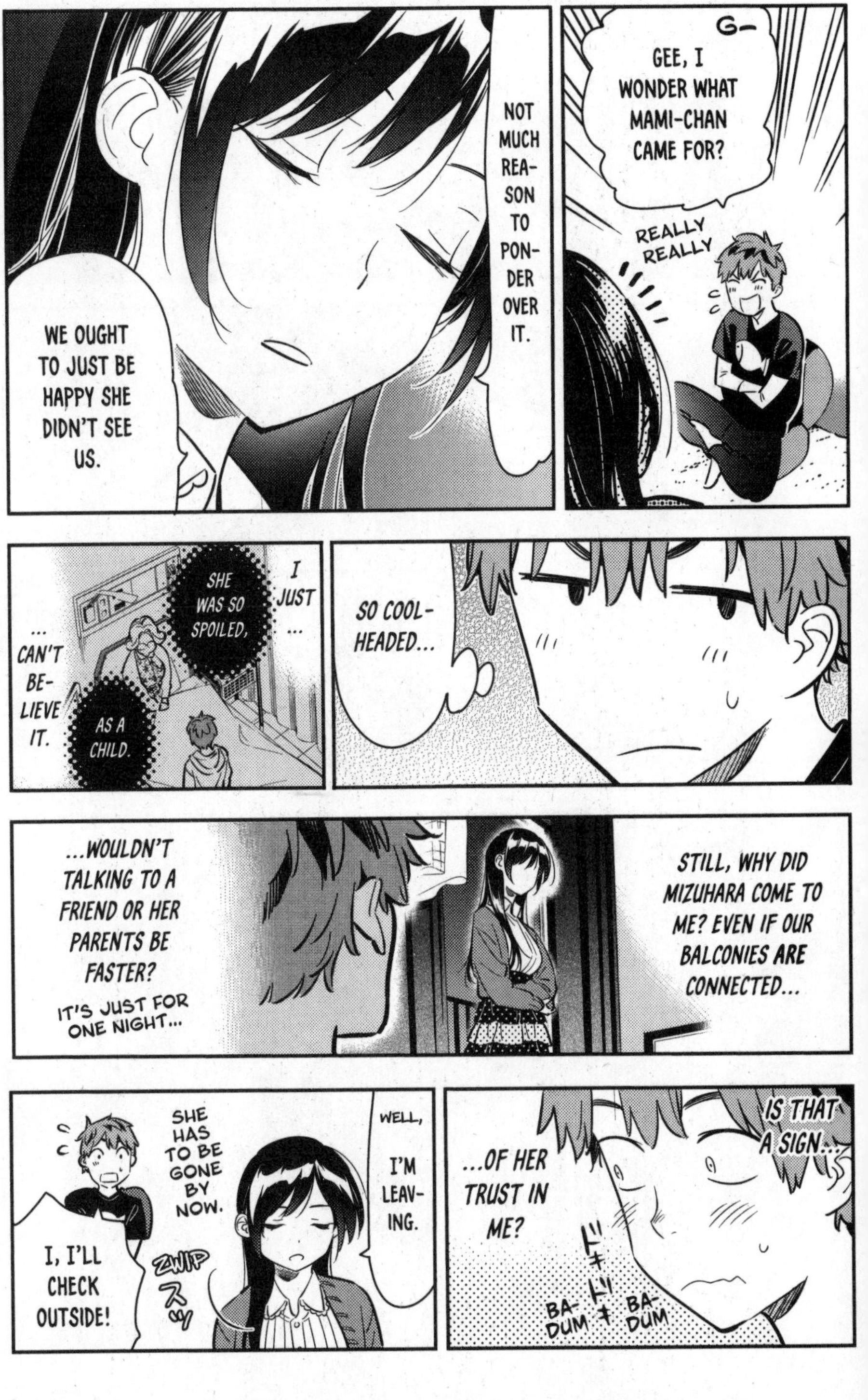
G—
GEE, I WONDER WHAT MAMI-CHAN CAME FOR?
REALLY REALLY
NOT MUCH REA-SON TO PON-DER OVER IT.
WE OUGHT TO JUST BE HAPPY SHE DIDN'T SEE US.
SO COOL-HEADED...
I JUST ...
SHE WAS SO SPOILED,
AS A CHILD.
... CAN'T BE-LIEVE IT.
STILL, WHY DID MIZUHARA COME TO ME? EVEN IF OUR BALCONIES ARE CONNECTED...
...WOULDN'T TALKING TO A FRIEND OR HER PARENTS BE FASTER?
IT'S JUST FOR ONE NIGHT...
IS THAT A SIGN...
...OF HER TRUST IN ME?
ドキドキ
BA-DUM BA-DUM
WELL,
I'M LEAV-ING.
SHE HAS TO BE GONE BY NOW.
ZWIP
スッ
I, I'LL CHECK OUTSIDE!

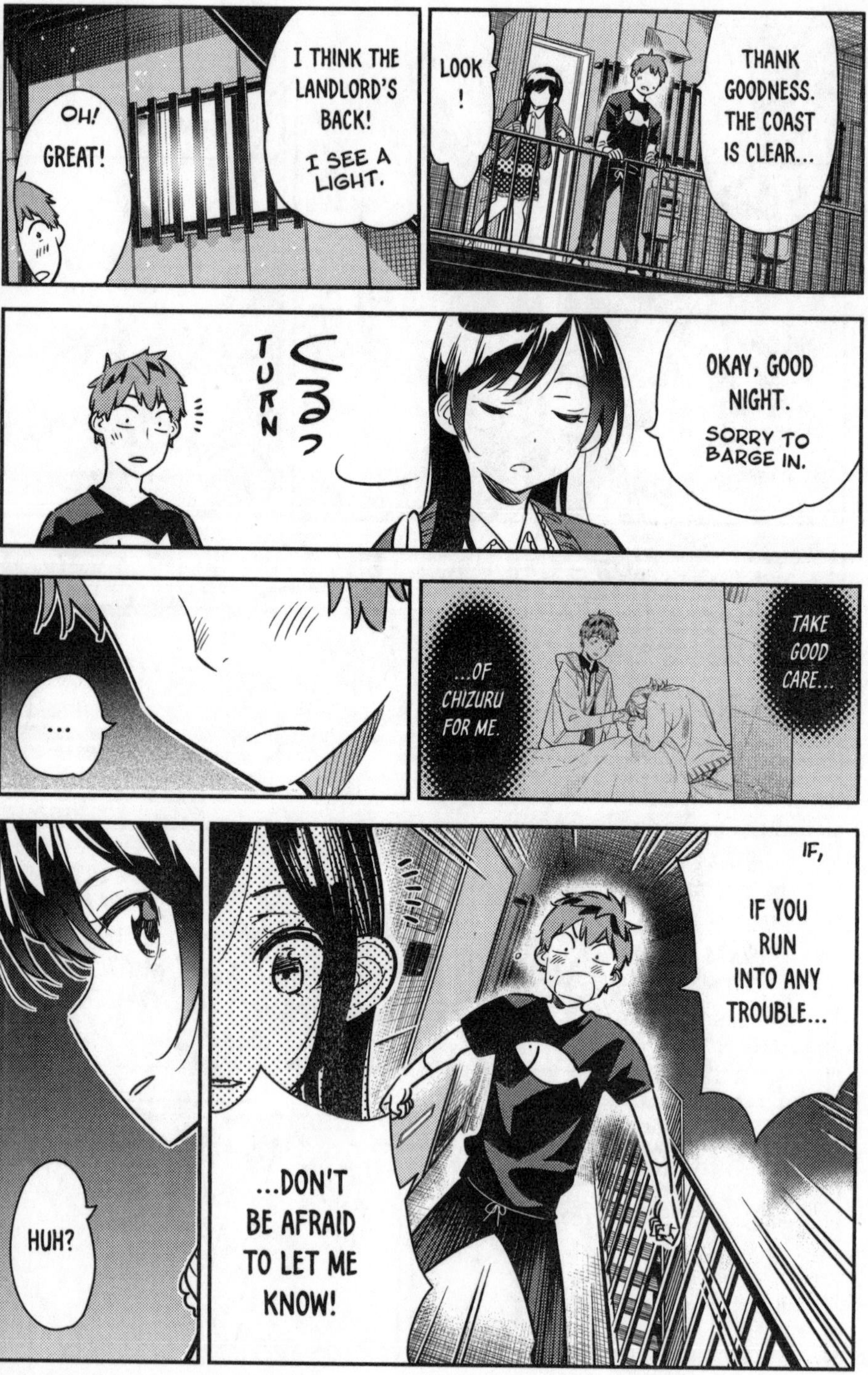
THANK GOODNESS. THE COAST IS CLEAR...
LOOK!
I THINK THE LANDLORD'S BACK!
I SEE A LIGHT.
OH! GREAT!
OKAY, GOOD NIGHT.
SORRY TO BARGE IN.
TURN
TAKE GOOD CARE...
...OF CHIZURU FOR ME.
...
IF,
IF YOU RUN INTO ANY TROUBLE...
...DON'T BE AFRAID TO LET ME KNOW!
HUH?

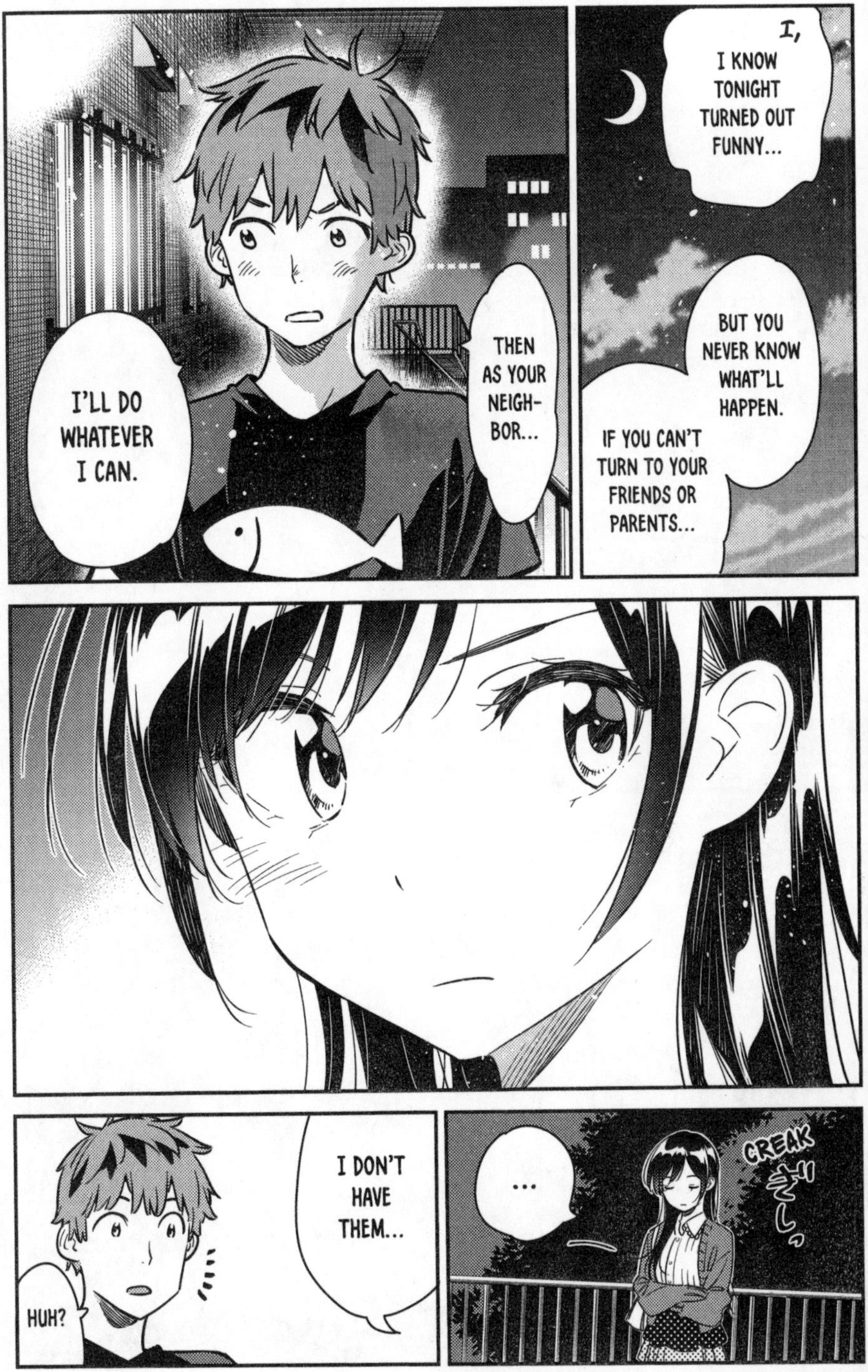
I, I KNOW TONIGHT TURNED OUT FUNNY...
BUT YOU NEVER KNOW WHAT'LL HAPPEN.
IF YOU CAN'T TURN TO YOUR FRIENDS OR PARENTS...
THEN AS YOUR NEIGH-BOR...
I'LL DO WHATEVER I CAN.
...
CREAK
ぎしっ
I DON'T HAVE THEM...
HUH?

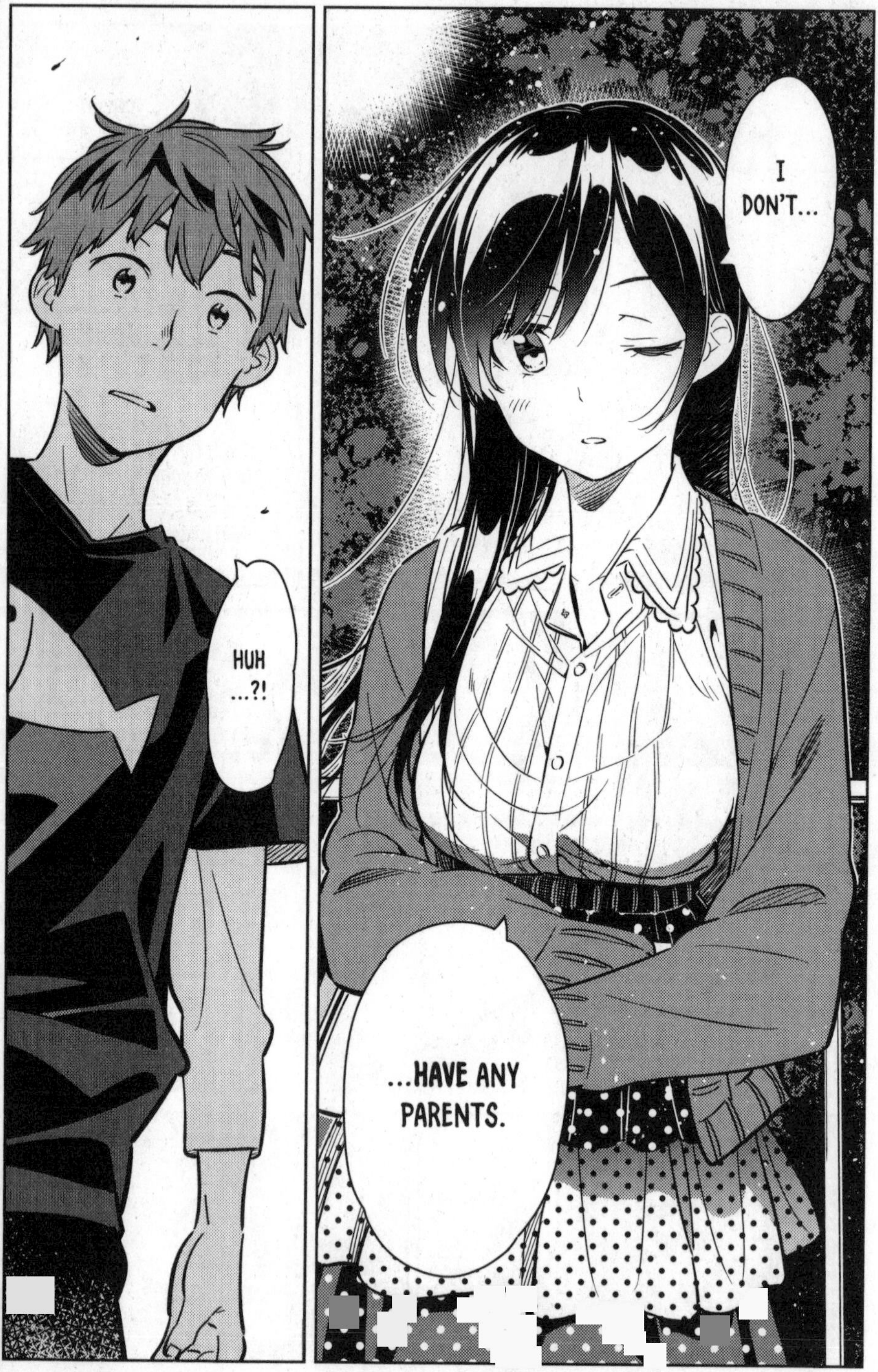
I DON'T...
...HAVE ANY PARENTS.
HUH ...?!

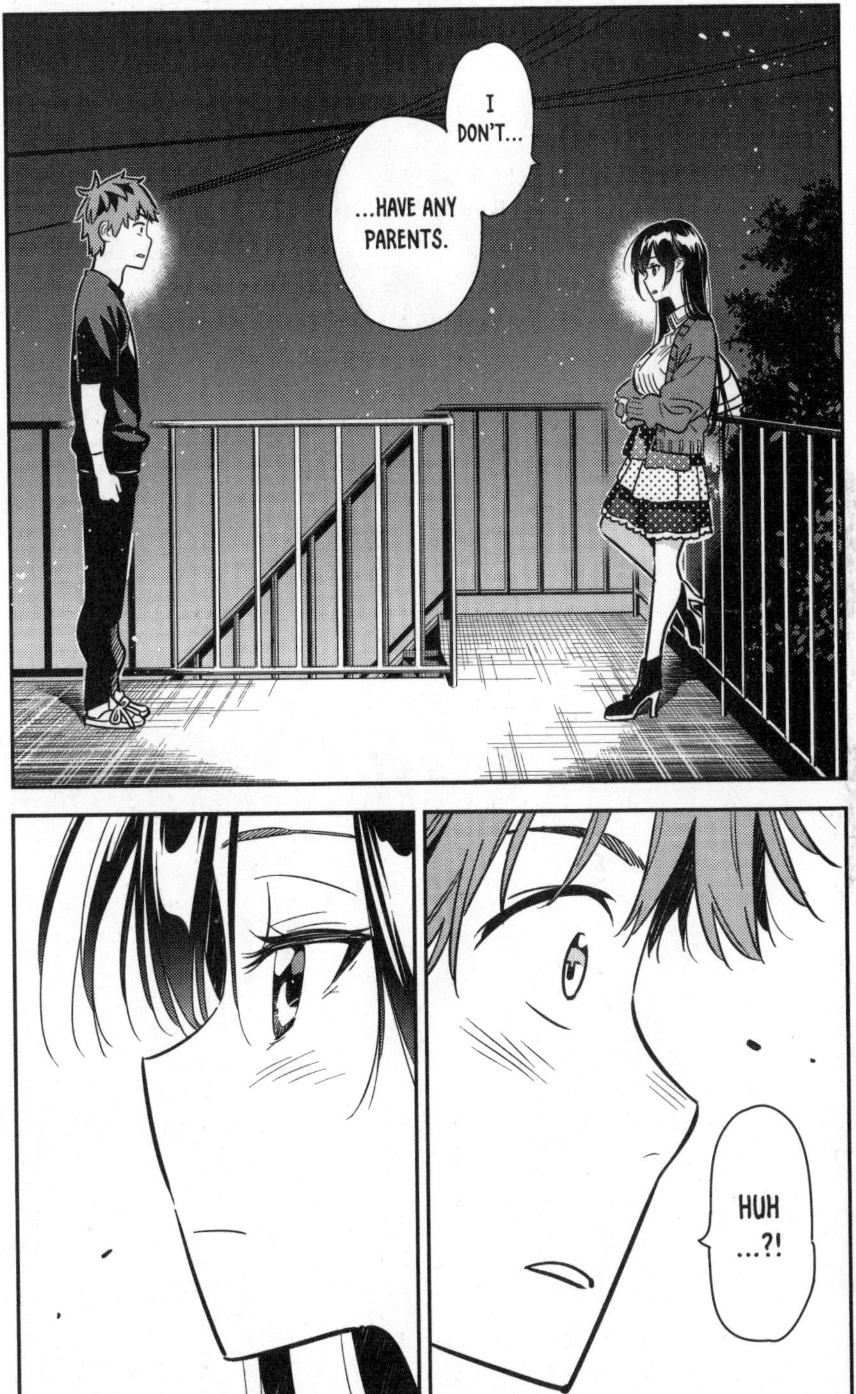
I DON'T...
...HAVE ANY PARENTS.
HUH ...?!

RATING 61 MY "GIRLFRIEND," CHIZURU ICHINOSE 6

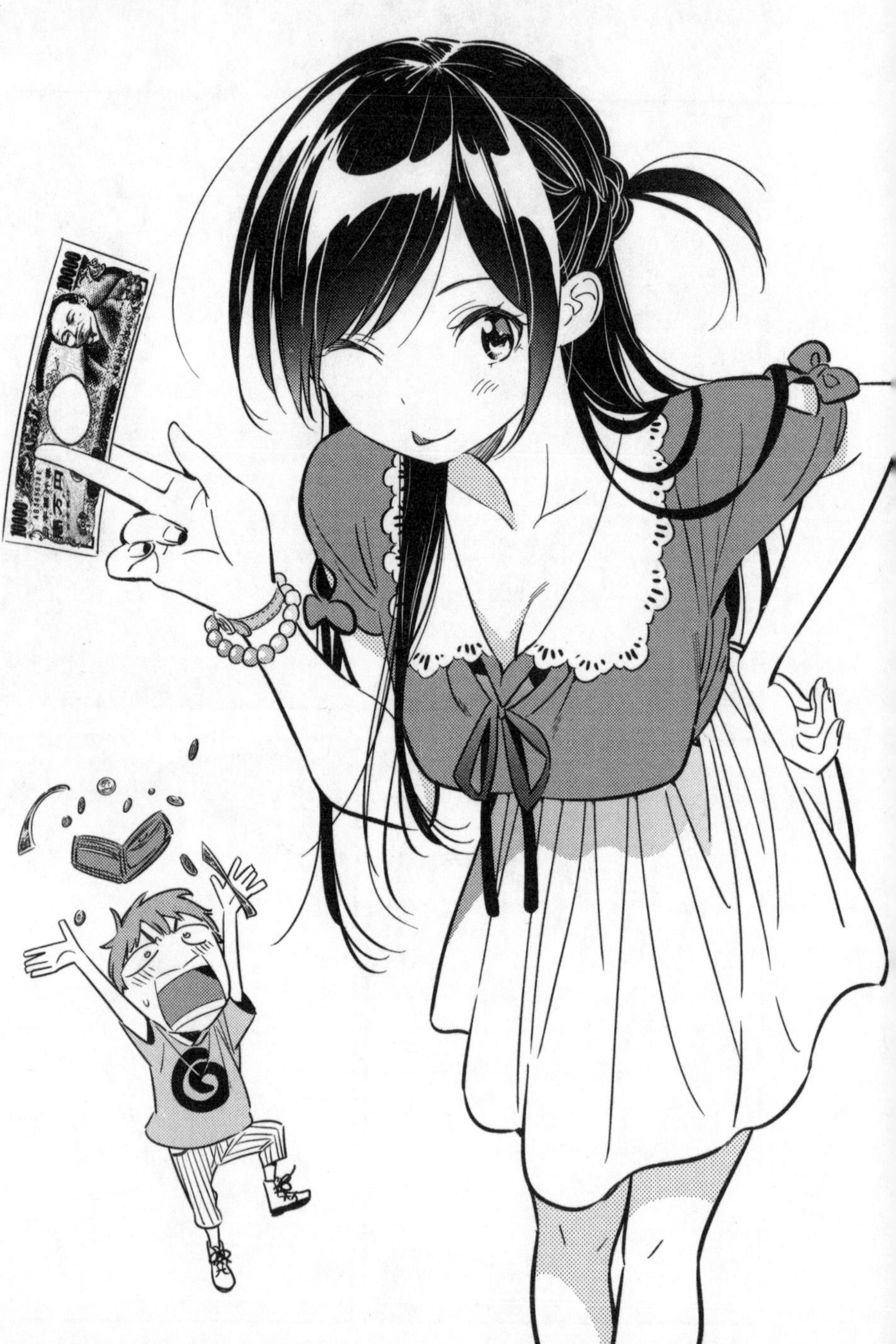

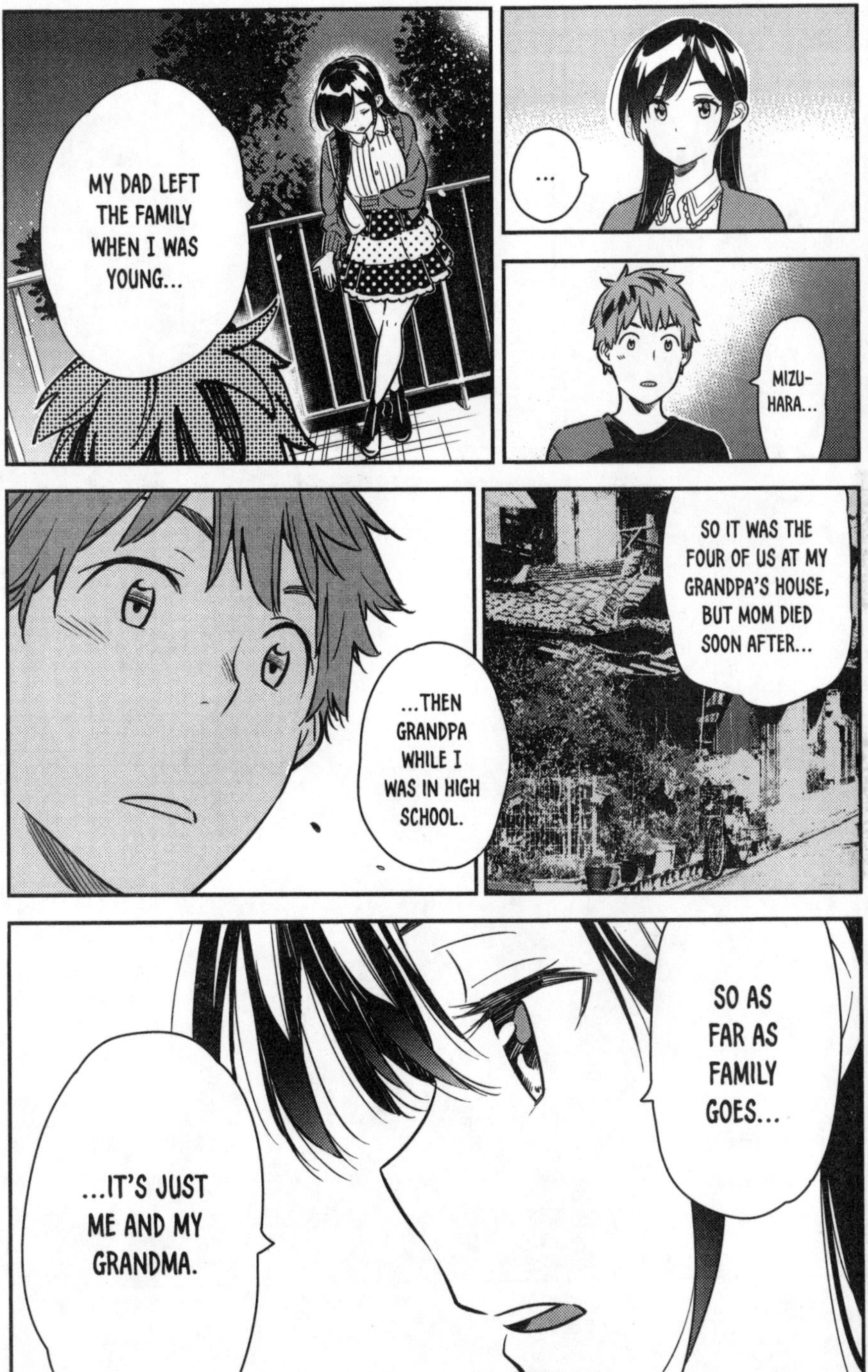
...
MIZU-HARA...
MY DAD LEFT THE FAMILY WHEN I WAS YOUNG...
SO IT WAS THE FOUR OF US AT MY GRANDPA'S HOUSE, BUT MOM DIED SOON AFTER...
...THEN GRANDPA WHILE I WAS IN HIGH SCHOOL.
SO AS FAR AS FAMILY GOES...
...IT'S JUST ME AND MY GRANDMA.

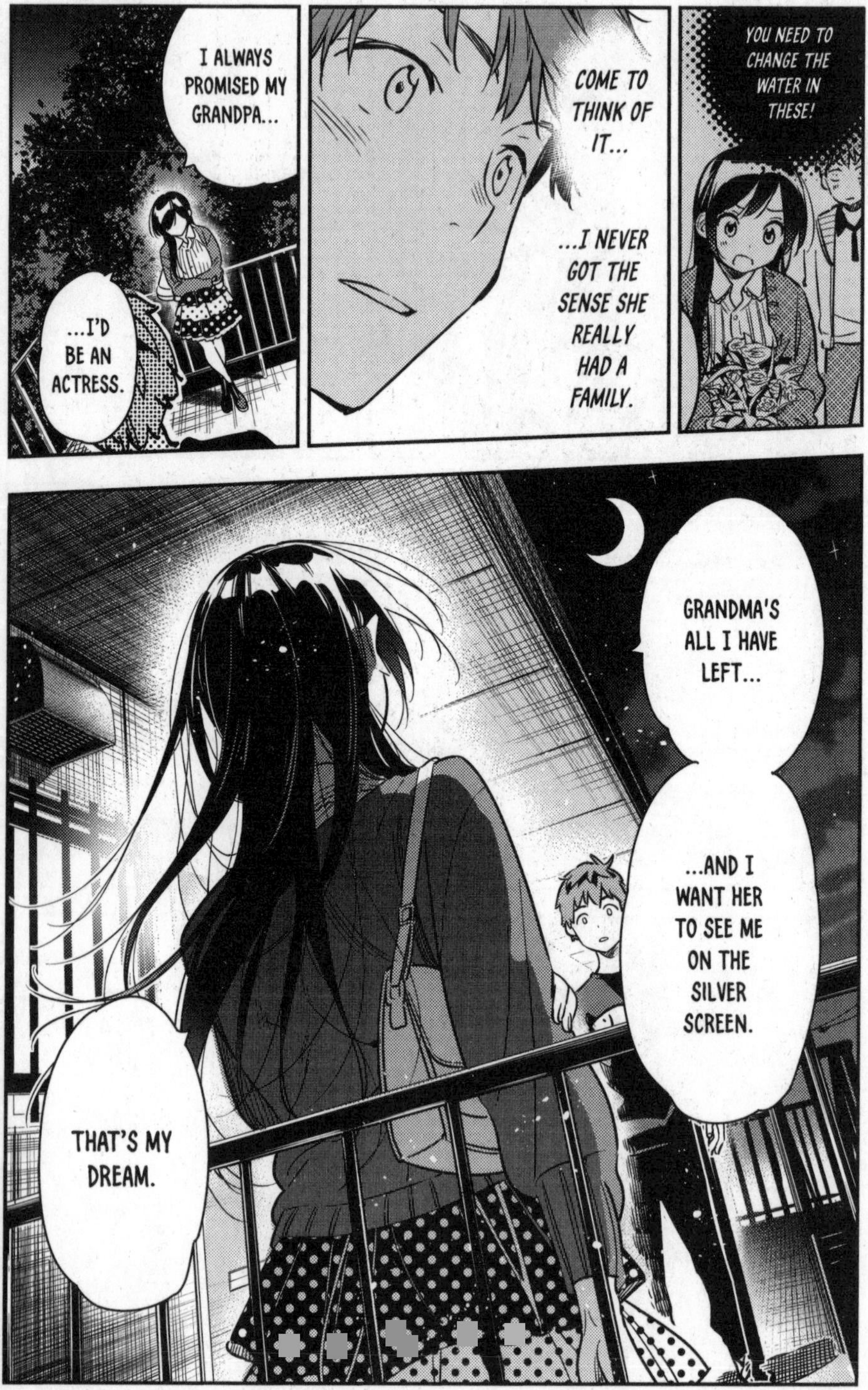
YOU NEED TO CHANGE THE WATER IN THESE!
COME TO THINK OF IT...
...I NEVER GOT THE SENSE SHE REALLY HAD A FAMILY.
I ALWAYS PROMISED MY GRANDPA...
...I'D BE AN ACTRESS.
GRANDMA'S ALL I HAVE LEFT...
...AND I WANT HER TO SEE ME ON THE SILVER SCREEN.
THAT'S MY DREAM.

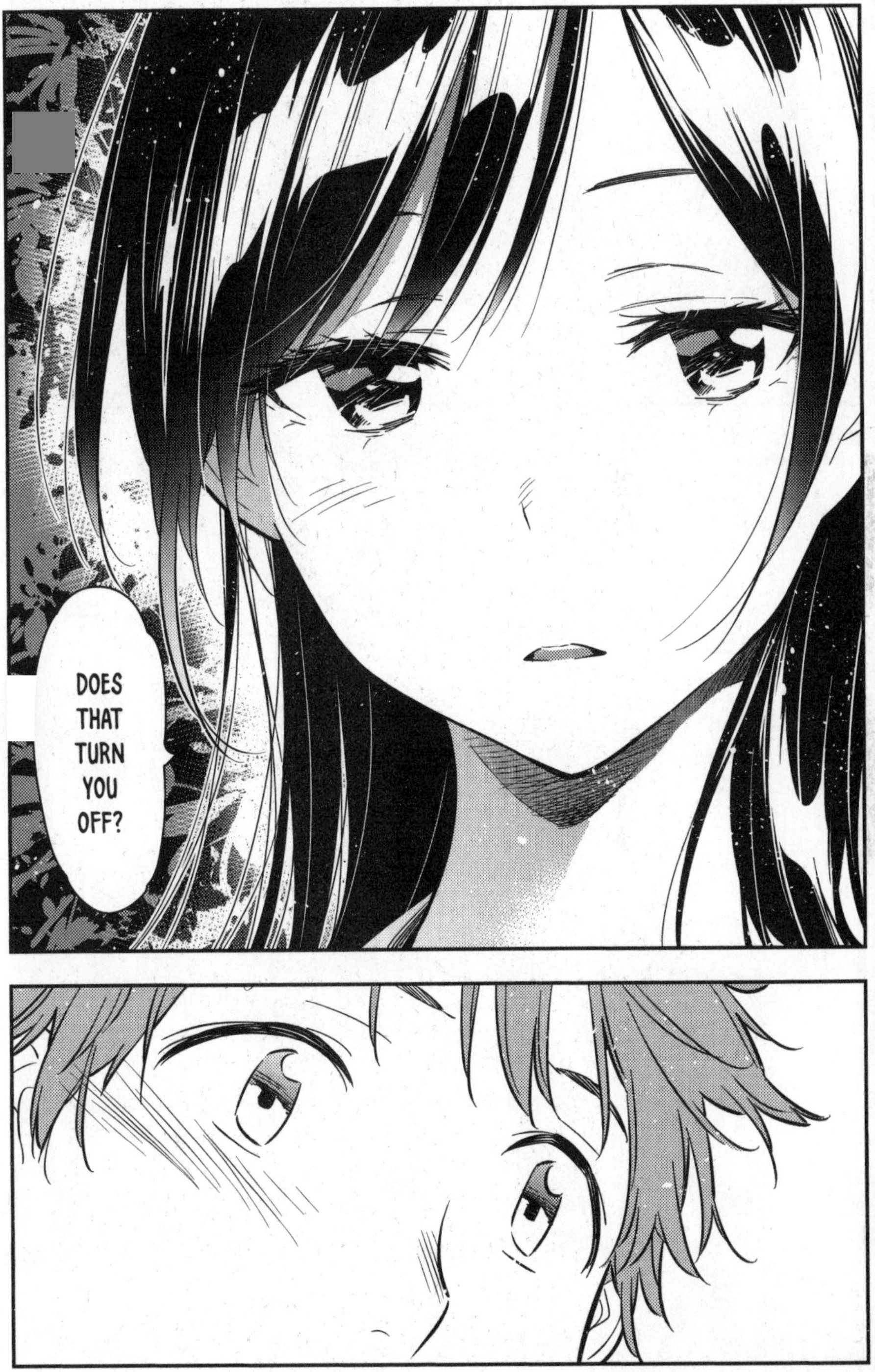
DOES THAT TURN YOU OFF?

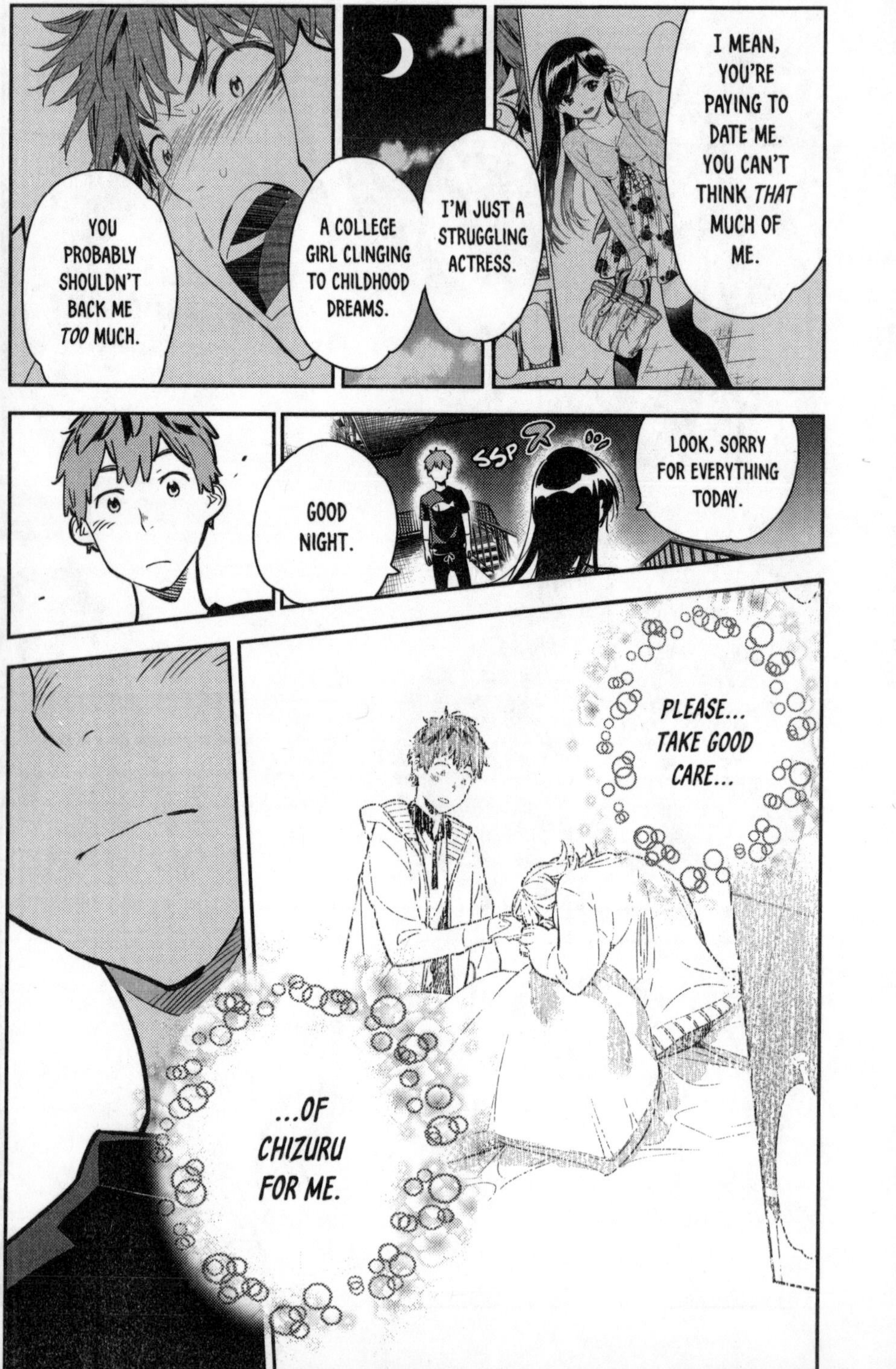
I MEAN, YOU'RE PAYING TO DATE ME. YOU CAN'T THINK *THAT* MUCH OF ME.
I'M JUST A STRUGGLING ACTRESS.
A COLLEGE GIRL CLINGING TO CHILDHOOD DREAMS.
YOU PROBABLY SHOULDN'T BACK ME *TOO* MUCH.
LOOK, SORRY FOR EVERYTHING TODAY.
SSP
GOOD NIGHT.
PLEASE... TAKE GOOD CARE...
...OF CHIZURU FOR ME.

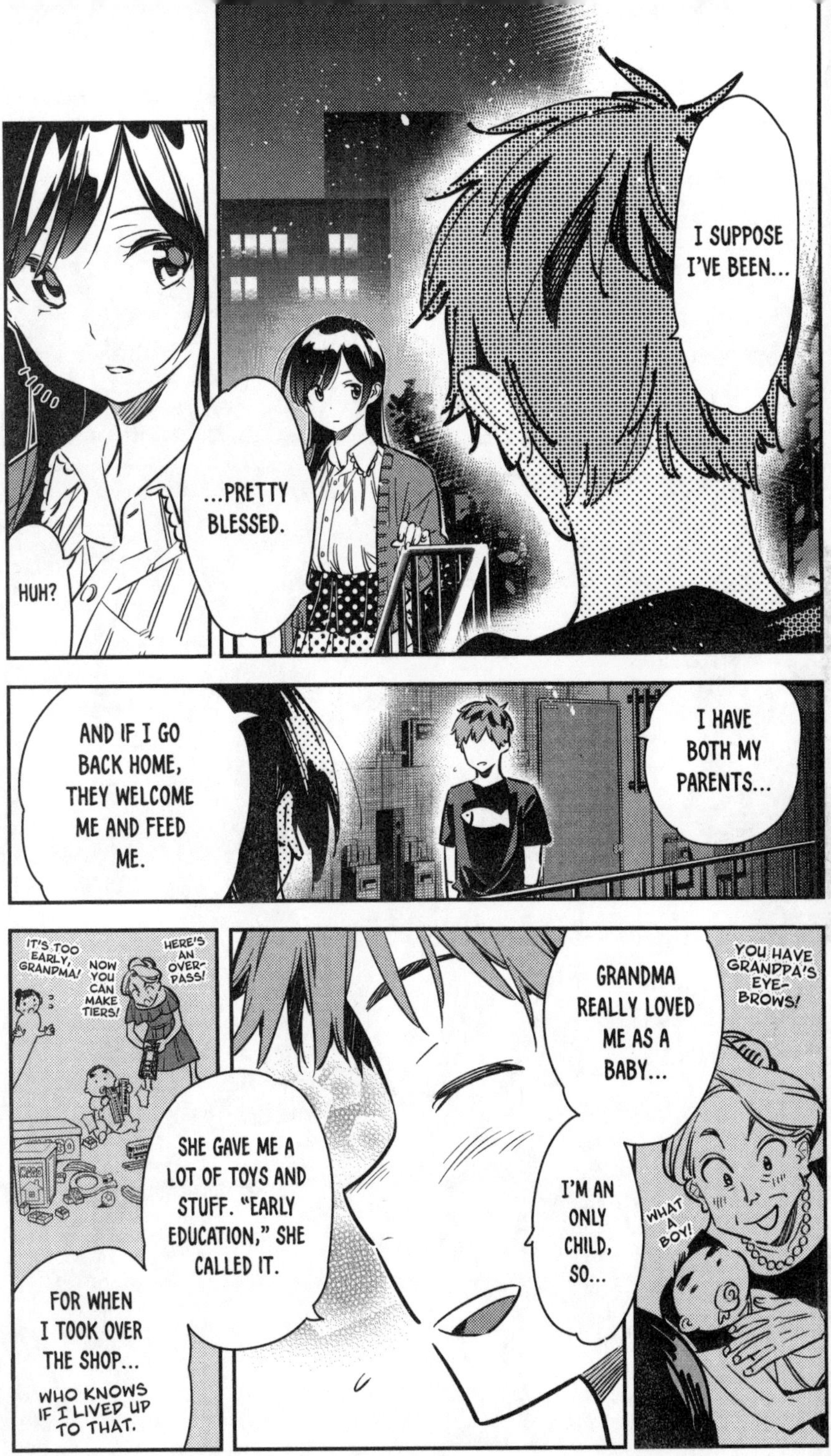
I SUPPOSE I'VE BEEN...
...PRETTY BLESSED.
HUH?
I HAVE BOTH MY PARENTS...
AND IF I GO BACK HOME, THEY WELCOME ME AND FEED ME.
YOU HAVE GRANDPA'S EYE-BROWS!
WHAT A BOY!
GRANDMA REALLY LOVED ME AS A BABY...
I'M AN ONLY CHILD, SO...
SHE GAVE ME A LOT OF TOYS AND STUFF. "EARLY EDUCATION," SHE CALLED IT.
FOR WHEN I TOOK OVER THE SHOP...
WHO KNOWS IF I LIVED UP TO THAT.
HERE'S AN OVER-PASS!
NOW YOU CAN MAKE TIERS!
IT'S TOO EARLY, GRANDMA!

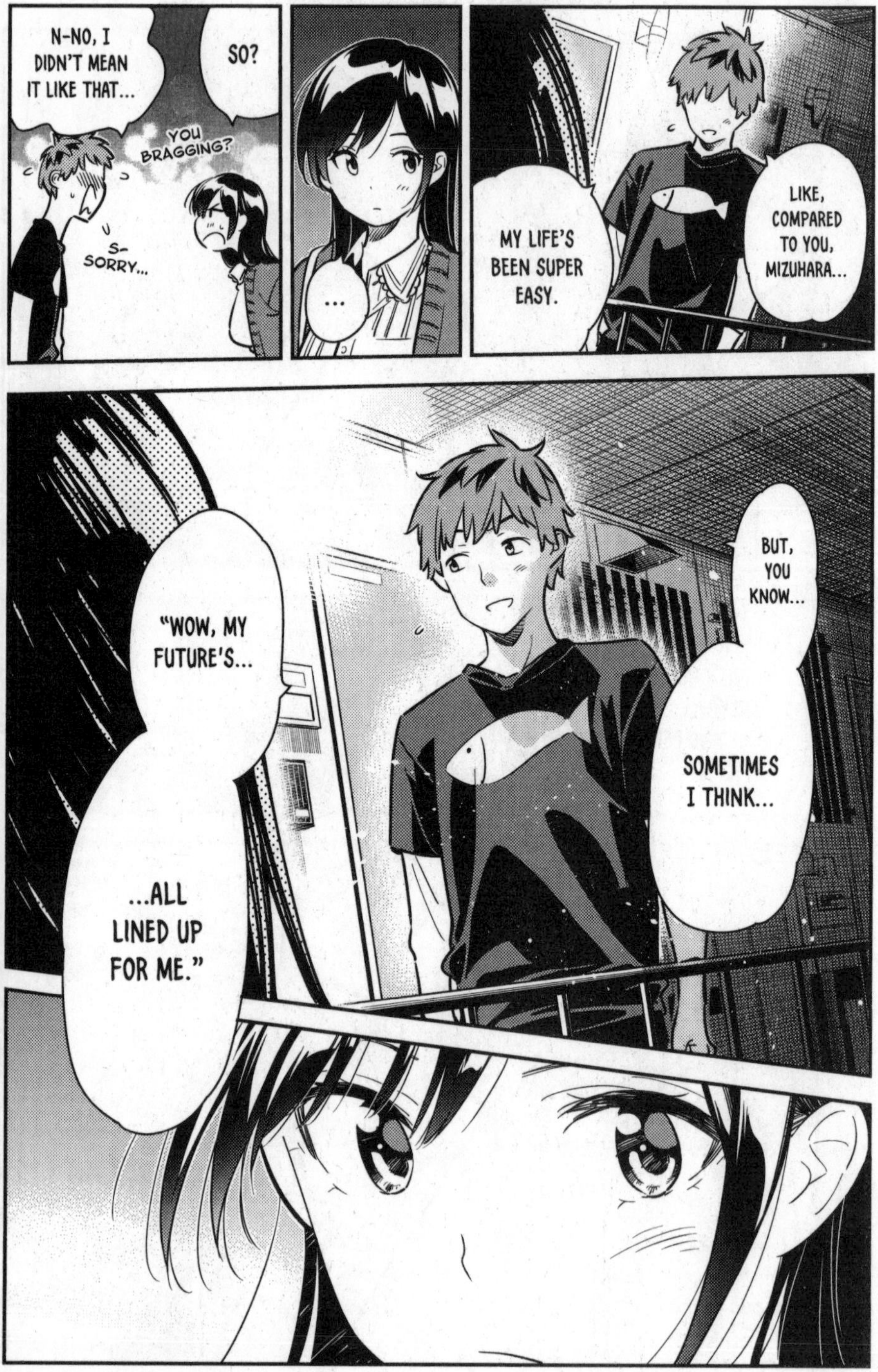
LIKE, COMPARED TO YOU, MIZUHARA...
MY LIFE'S BEEN SUPER EASY.
...
SO?
N-NO, I DIDN'T MEAN IT LIKE THAT...
YOU BRAGGING?
S-SORRY...
BUT, YOU KNOW...
SOMETIMES I THINK...
“WOW, MY FUTURE'S...
...ALL LINED UP FOR ME.”

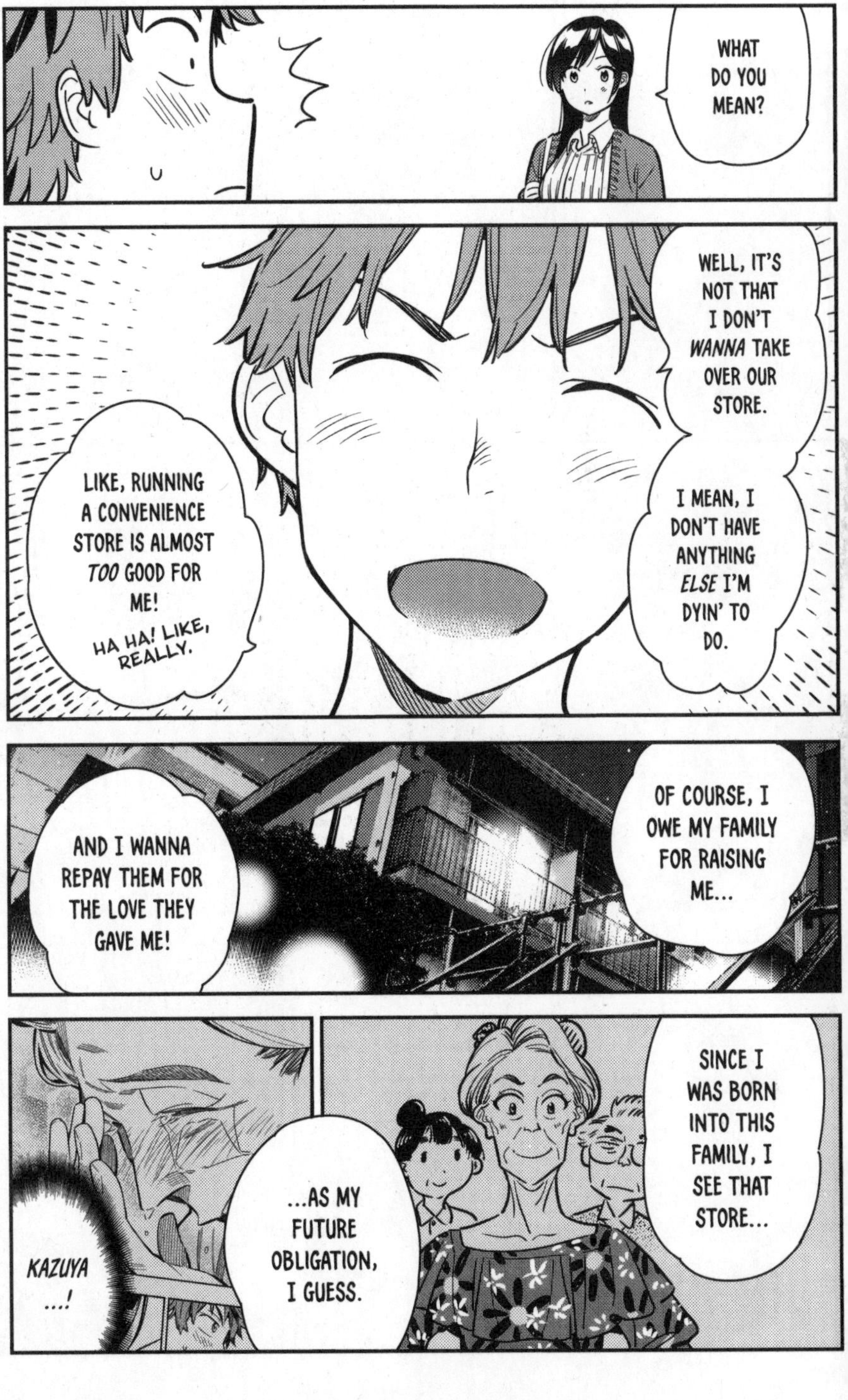
WHAT DO YOU MEAN?
WELL, IT'S NOT THAT I DON'T *WANNA* TAKE OVER OUR STORE.
I MEAN, I DON'T HAVE ANYTHING *ELSE* I'M DYIN' TO DO.
LIKE, RUNNING A CONVENIENCE STORE IS ALMOST *TOO* GOOD FOR ME!
HA HA! LIKE, REALLY.
OF COURSE, I OWE MY FAMILY FOR RAISING ME...
AND I WANNA REPAY THEM FOR THE LOVE THEY GAVE ME!
SINCE I WAS BORN INTO THIS FAMILY, I SEE THAT STORE...
...AS MY FUTURE OBLIGATION, I GUESS.
KAZUYA ...!

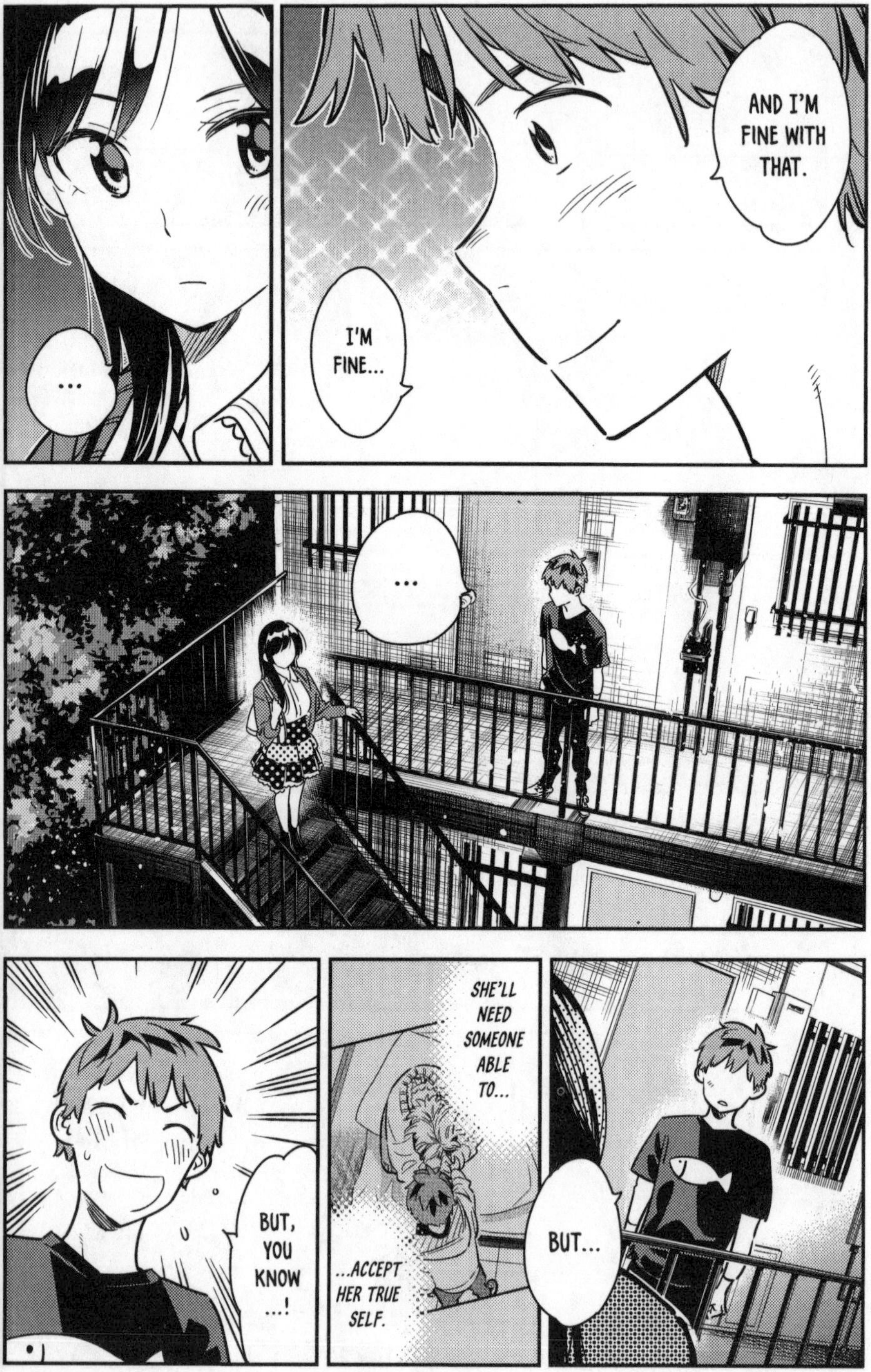
AND I'M FINE WITH THAT.
I'M FINE...
...
...
BUT...
SHE'LL NEED SOMEONE ABLE TO...
...ACCEPT HER TRUE SELF.
BUT, YOU KNOW ...!

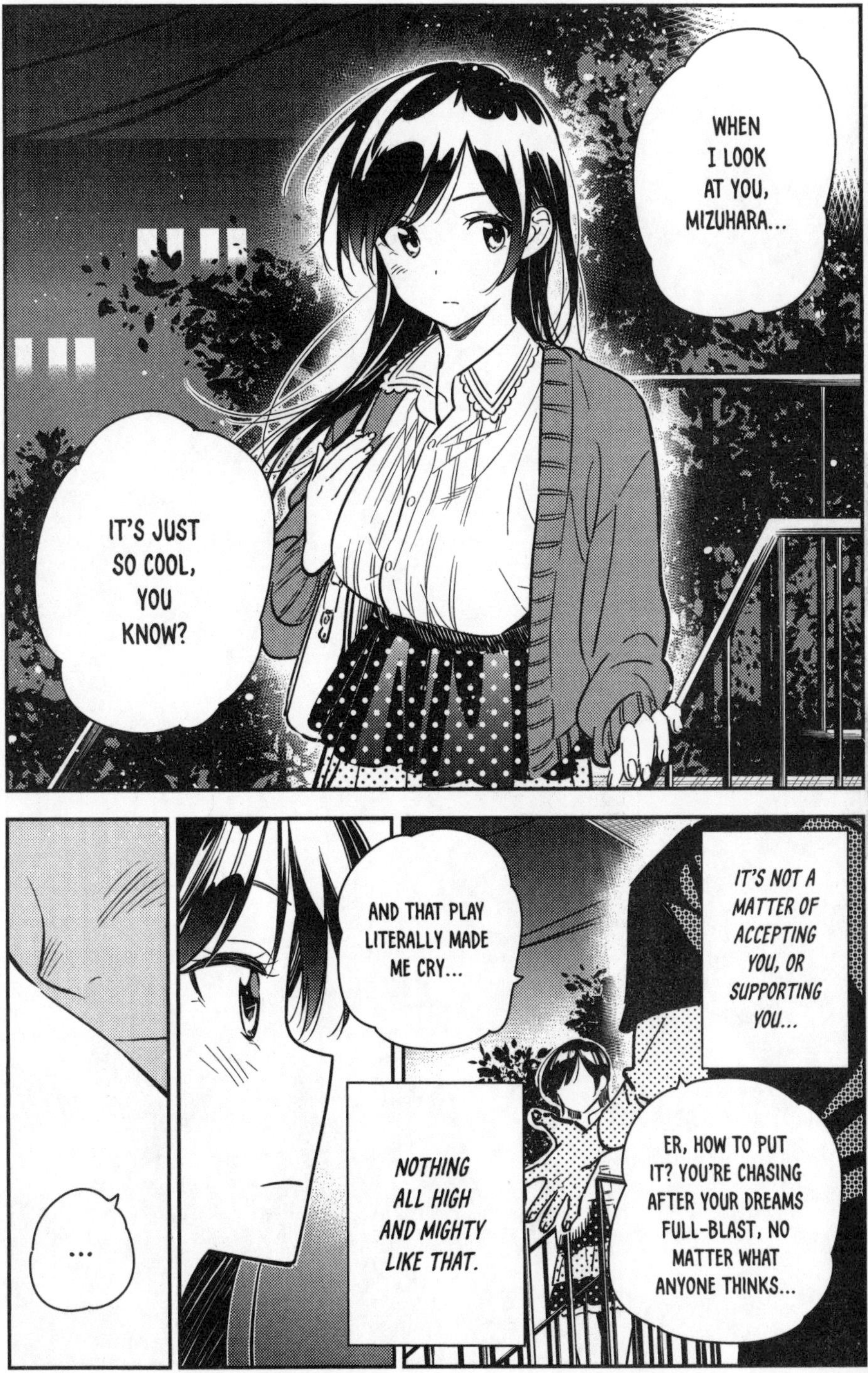
WHEN I LOOK AT YOU, MIZUHARA...
IT'S JUST SO COOL, YOU KNOW?
AND THAT PLAY LITERALLY MADE ME CRY...
ER, HOW TO PUT IT? YOU'RE CHASING AFTER YOUR DREAMS FULL-BLAST, NO MATTER WHAT ANYONE THINKS...
IT'S NOT A MATTER OF ACCEPTING YOU, OR SUPPORTING YOU...
NOTHING ALL HIGH AND MIGHTY LIKE THAT.
...

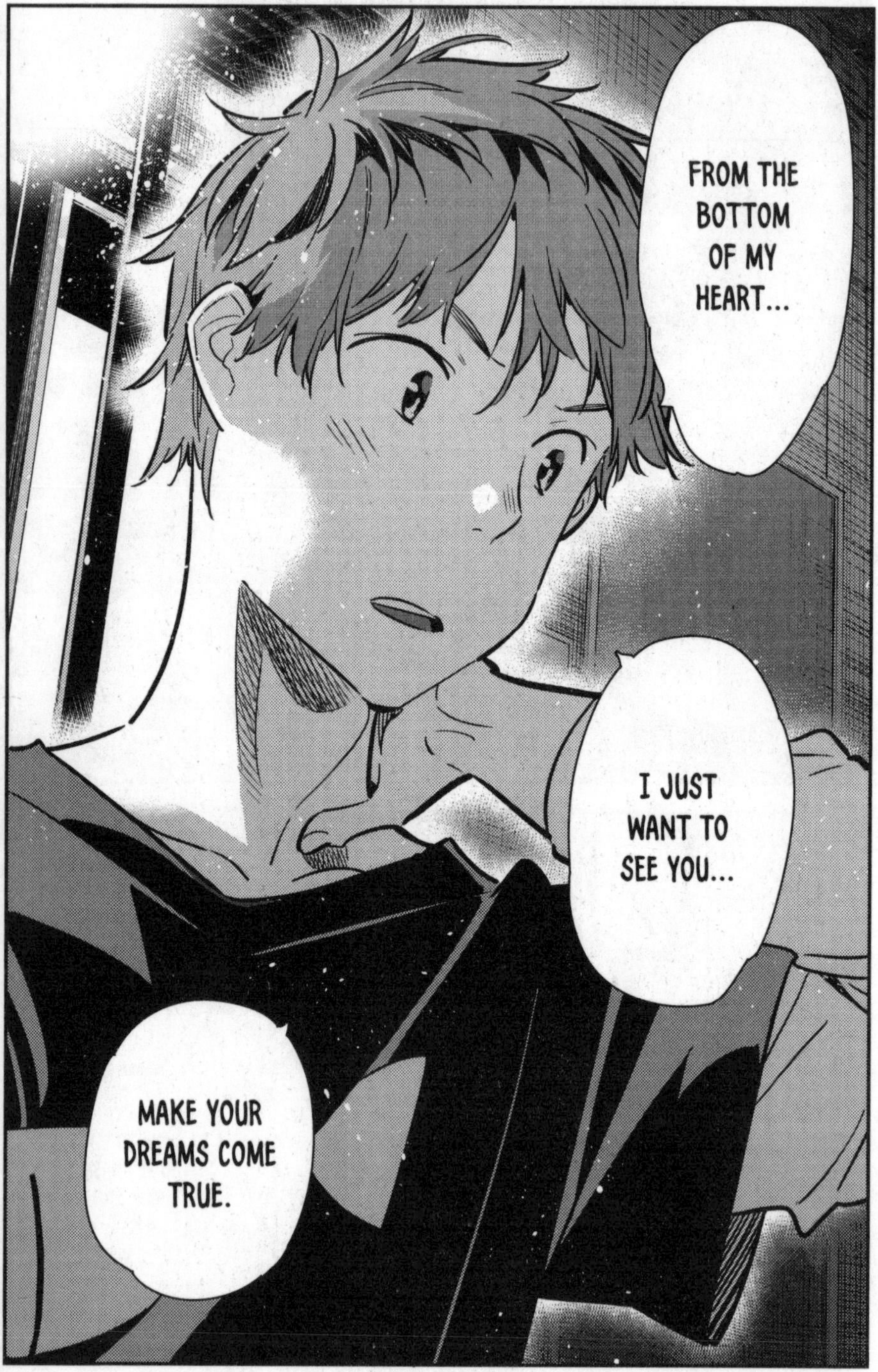
FROM THE BOTTOM OF MY HEART...
I JUST WANT TO SEE YOU...
MAKE YOUR DREAMS COME TRUE.

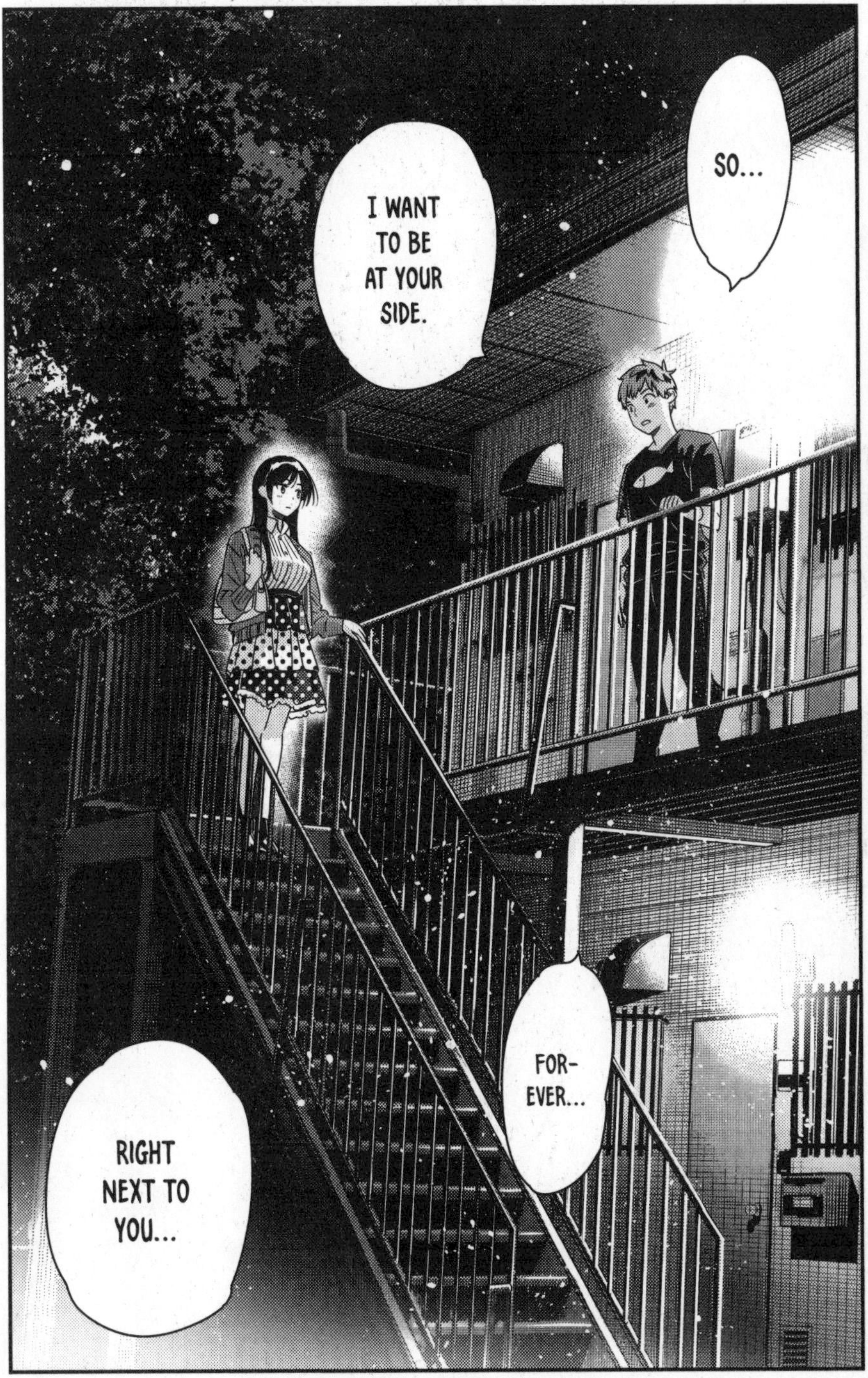
SO...
I WANT TO BE AT YOUR SIDE.
FOR-EVER...
RIGHT NEXT TO YOU...

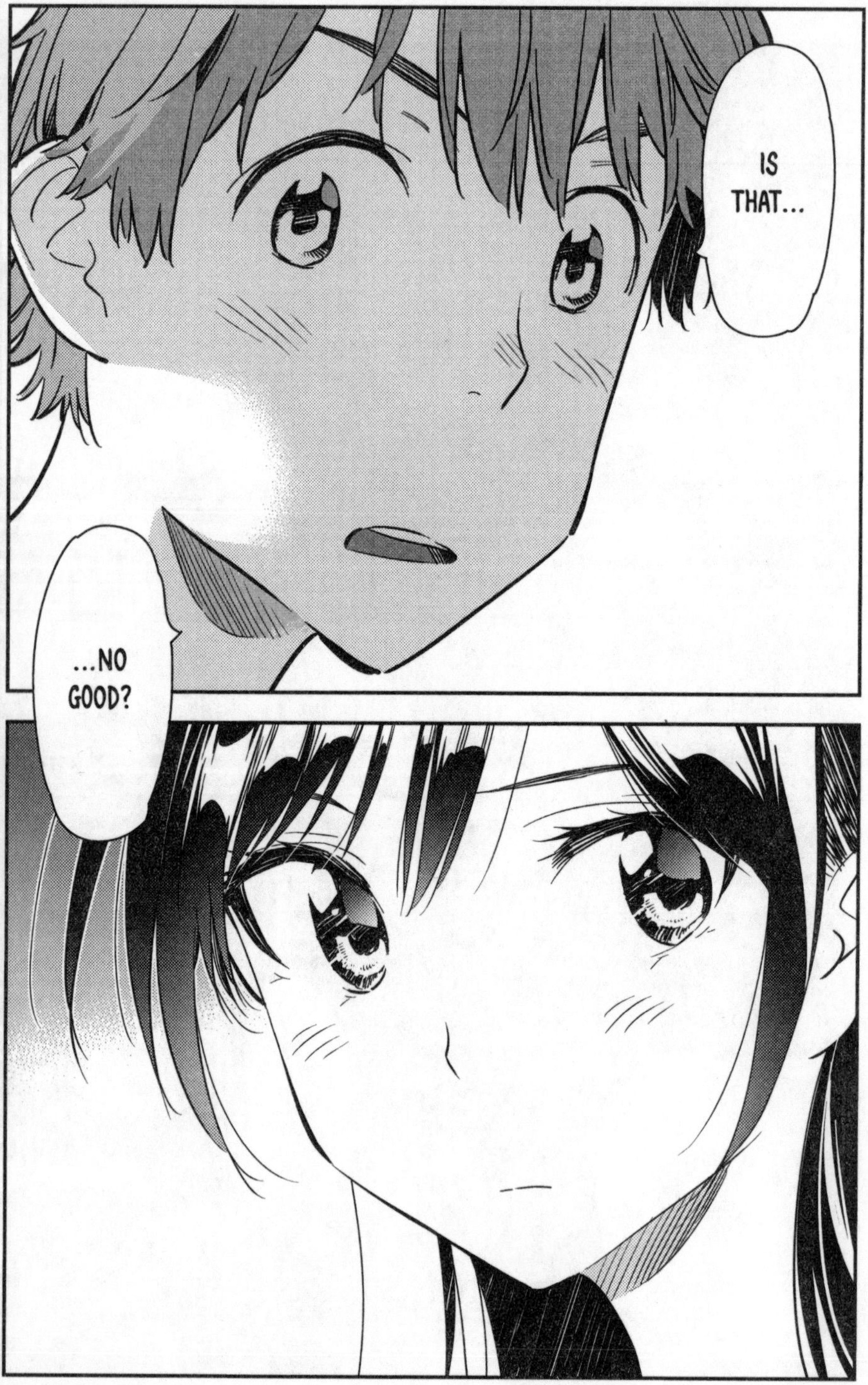
IS THAT...
...NO GOOD?

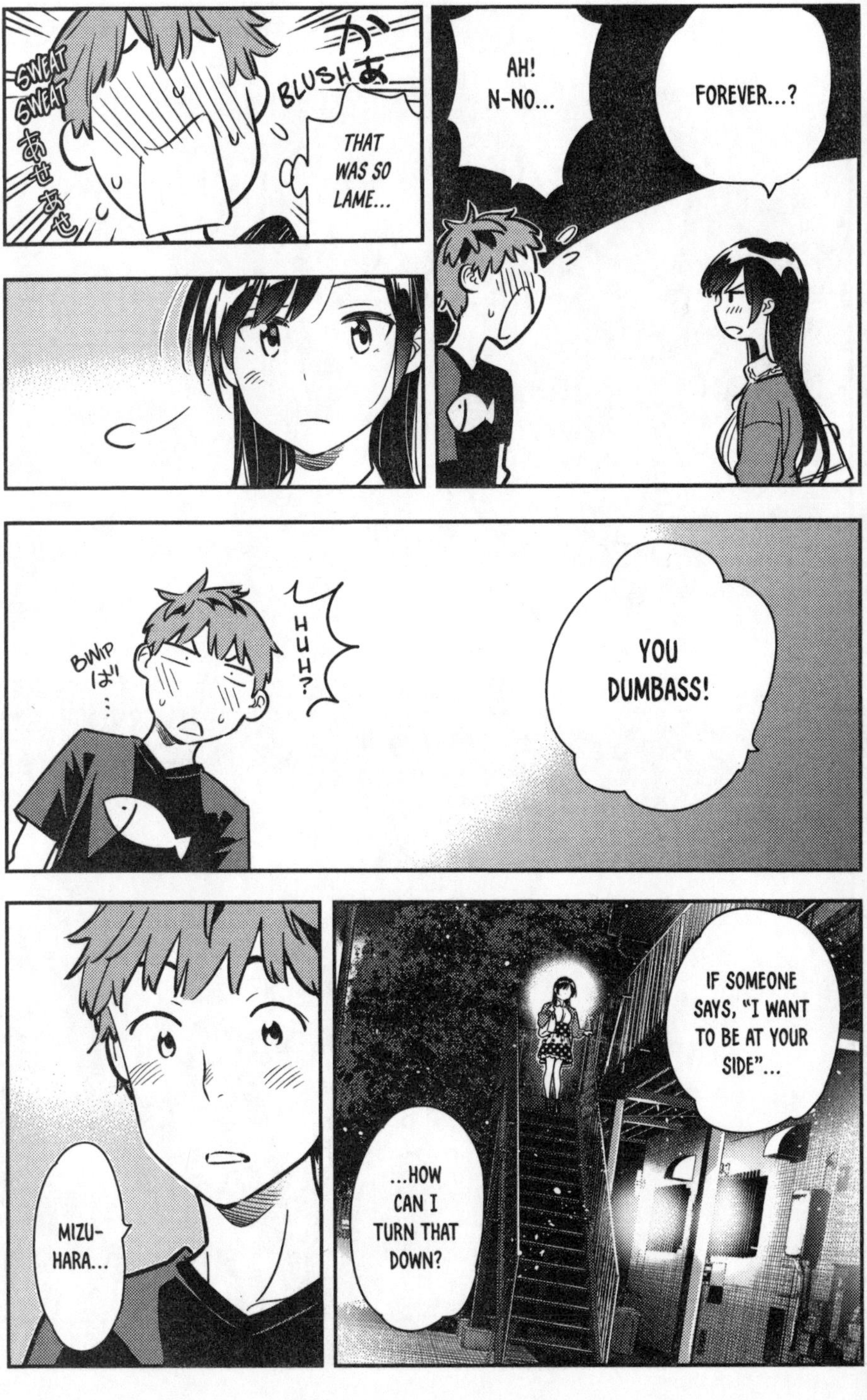
FOREVER...?
AH! N-NO...
BLUSH かあ
THAT WAS SO LAME...
SWEAT SWEAT あせあせ
YOU DUMBASS!
HUH?
BWIP ぱ
IF SOMEONE SAYS, "I WANT TO BE AT YOUR SIDE"...
...HOW CAN I TURN THAT DOWN?
MIZU-HARA...

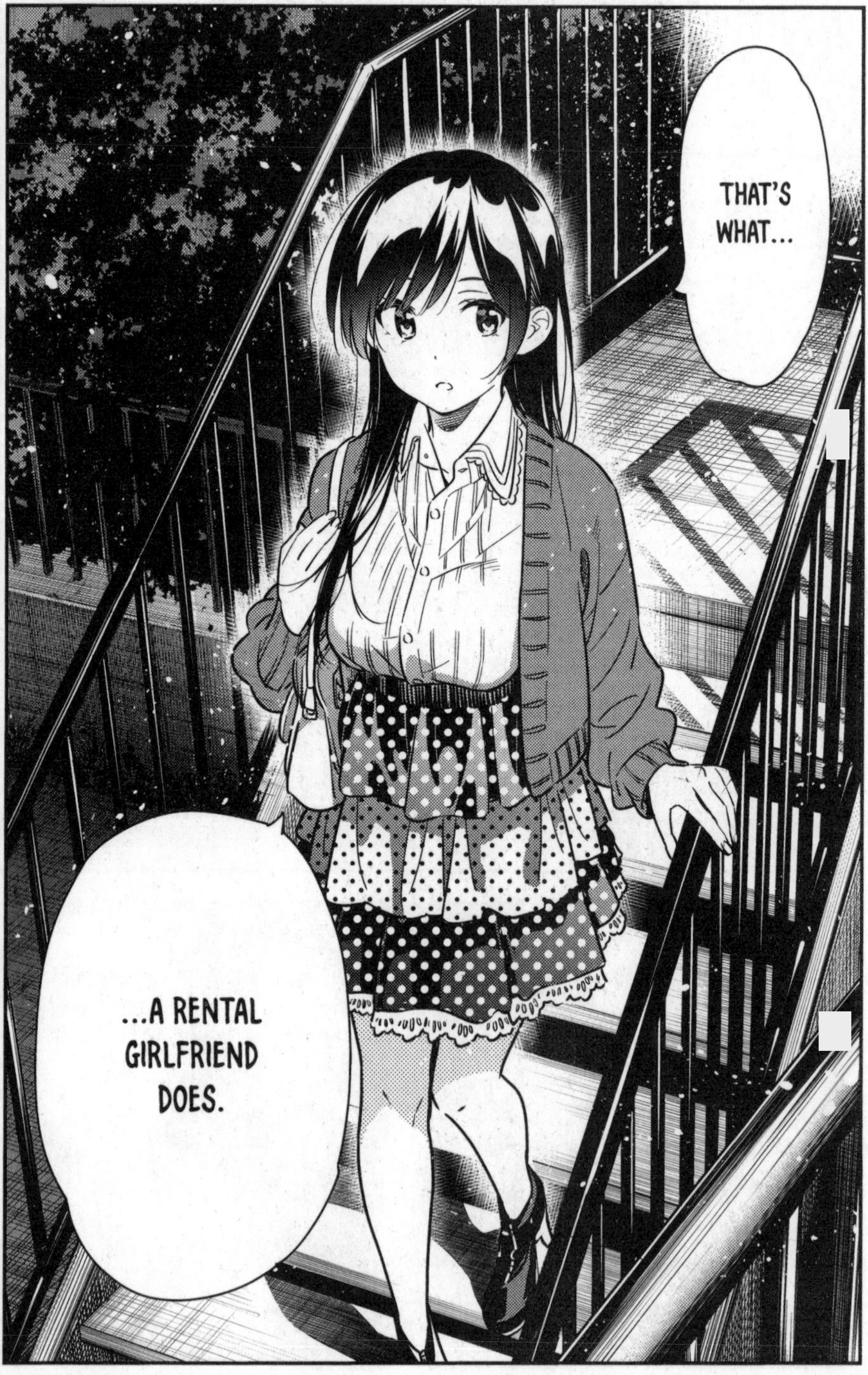
THAT'S WHAT...
...A RENTAL GIRLFRIEND DOES.

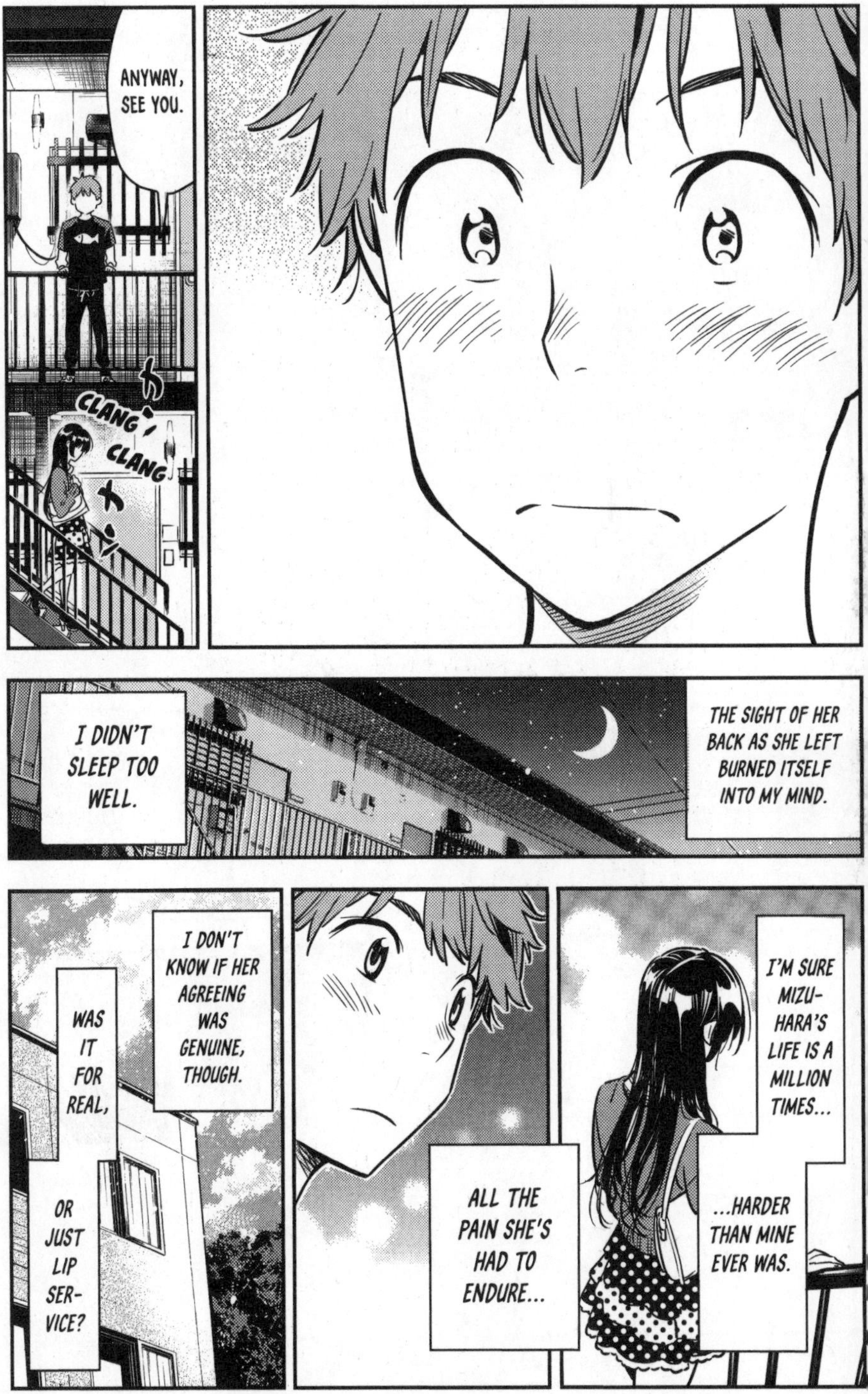
ANYWAY, SEE YOU.
CLANG
CLANG
THE SIGHT OF HER BACK AS SHE LEFT BURNED ITSELF INTO MY MIND.
I DIDN'T SLEEP TOO WELL.
I'M SURE MIZU-HARA'S LIFE IS A MILLION TIMES...
...HARDER THAN MINE EVER WAS.
ALL THE PAIN SHE'S HAD TO ENDURE...
I DON'T KNOW IF HER AGREEING WAS GENUINE, THOUGH.
WAS IT FOR REAL,
OR JUST LIP SER-VICE?

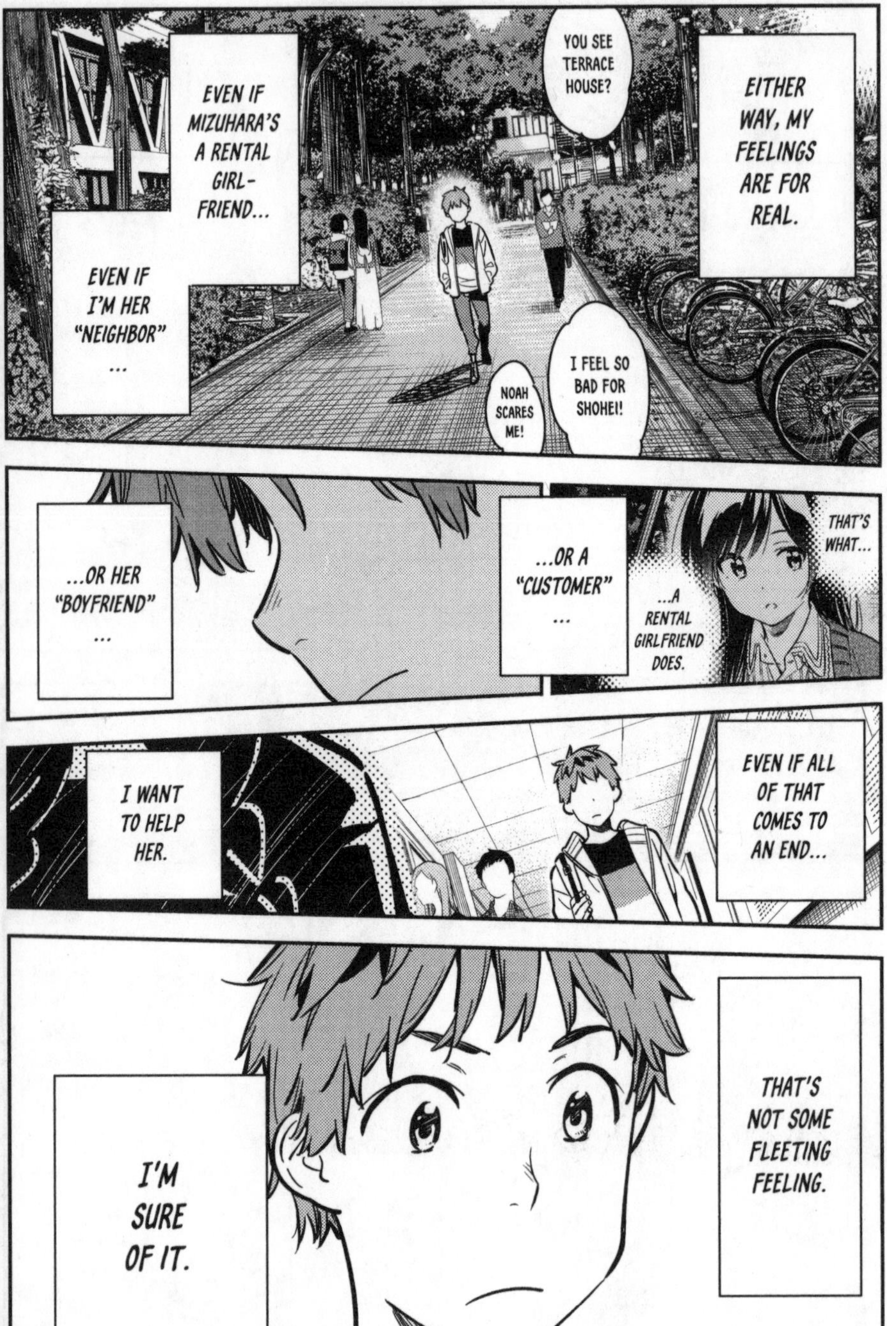
EITHER WAY, MY FEELINGS ARE FOR REAL.
YOU SEE TERRACE HOUSE?
I FEEL SO BAD FOR SHOHEI!
NOAH SCARES ME!
EVEN IF MIZUHARA'S A RENTAL GIRL-FRIEND...
EVEN IF I'M HER "NEIGHBOR"...
THAT'S WHAT...
...A RENTAL GIRLFRIEND DOES.
...OR A "CUSTOMER"...
...OR HER "BOYFRIEND"...
EVEN IF ALL OF THAT COMES TO AN END...
I WANT TO HELP HER.
THAT'S NOT SOME FLEETING FEELING.
I'M SURE OF IT.

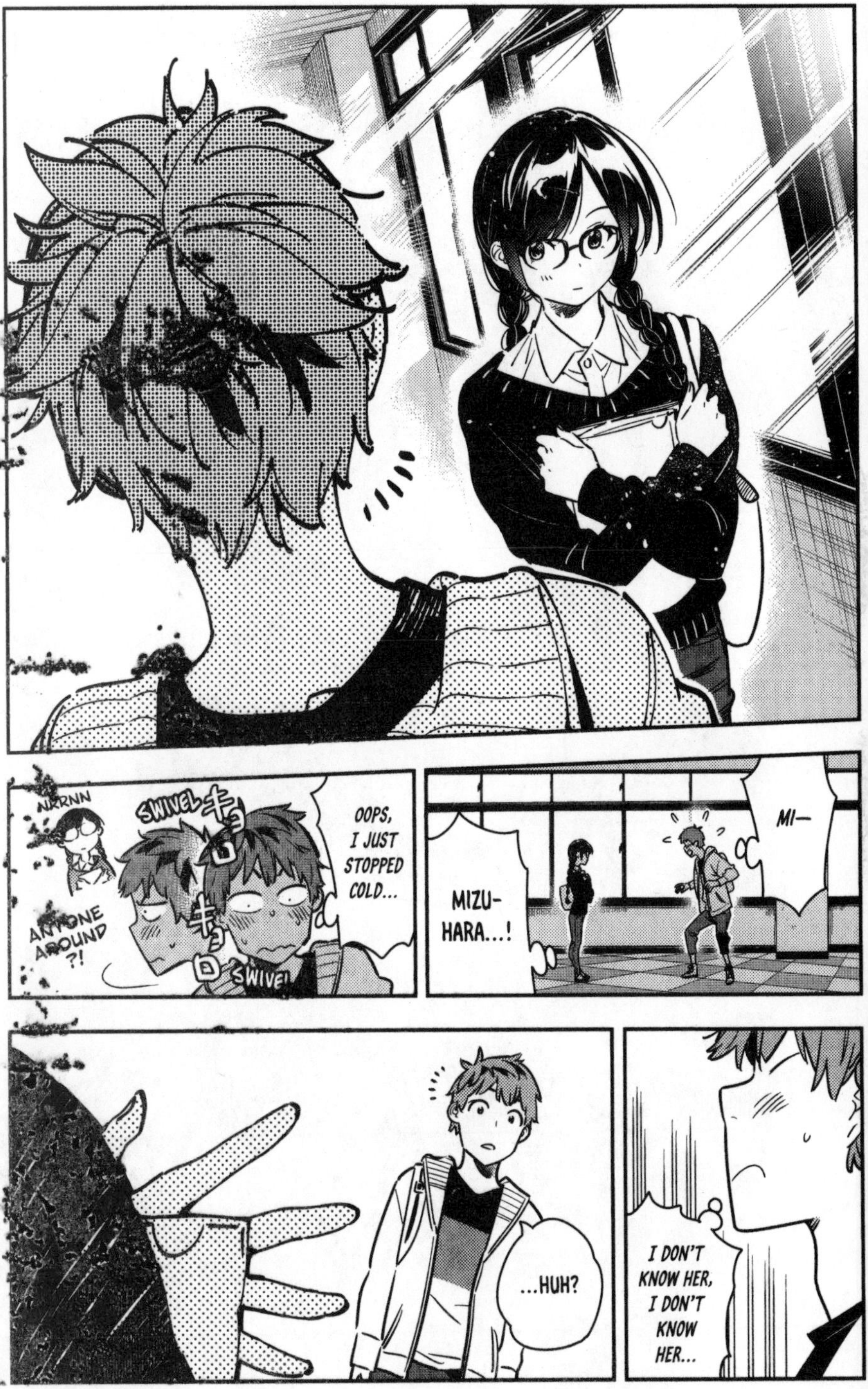
MI—
MIZU-HARA...!
OOPS, I JUST STOPPED COLD...
SWIVEL
キョロ
キョロ
SWIVEL
ANYONE AROUND ?!
I DON'T KNOW HER, I DON'T KNOW HER...
...HUH?

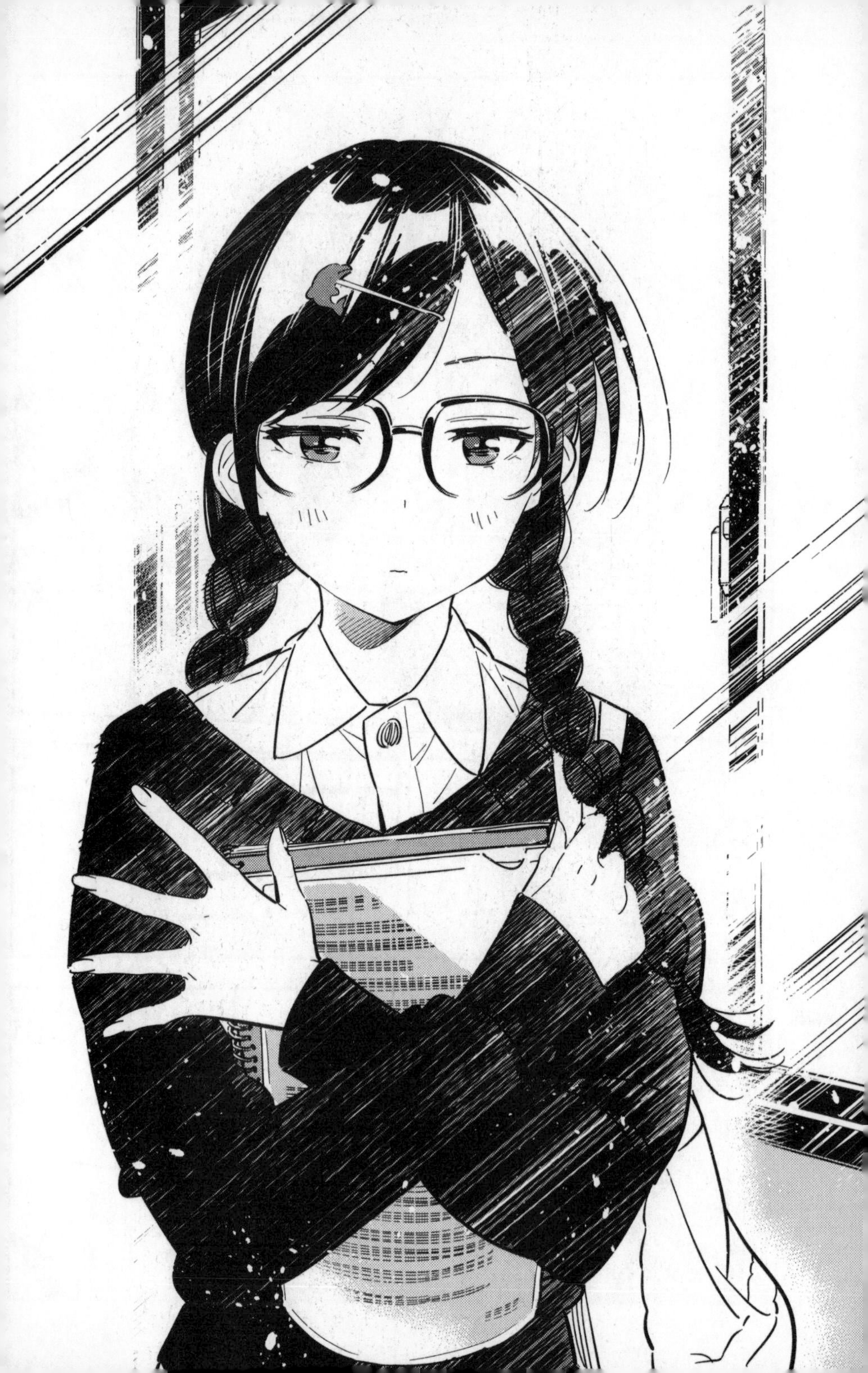

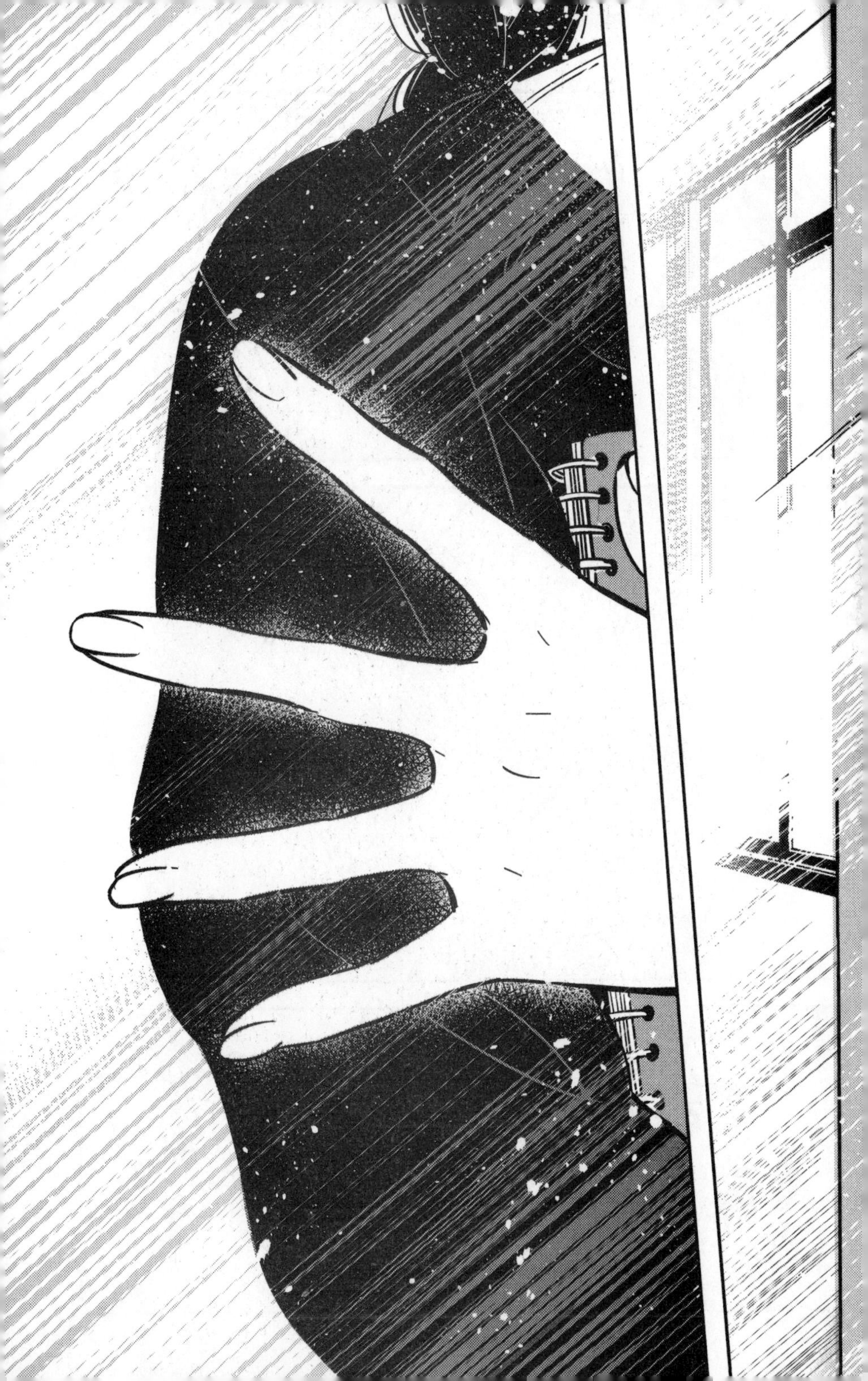

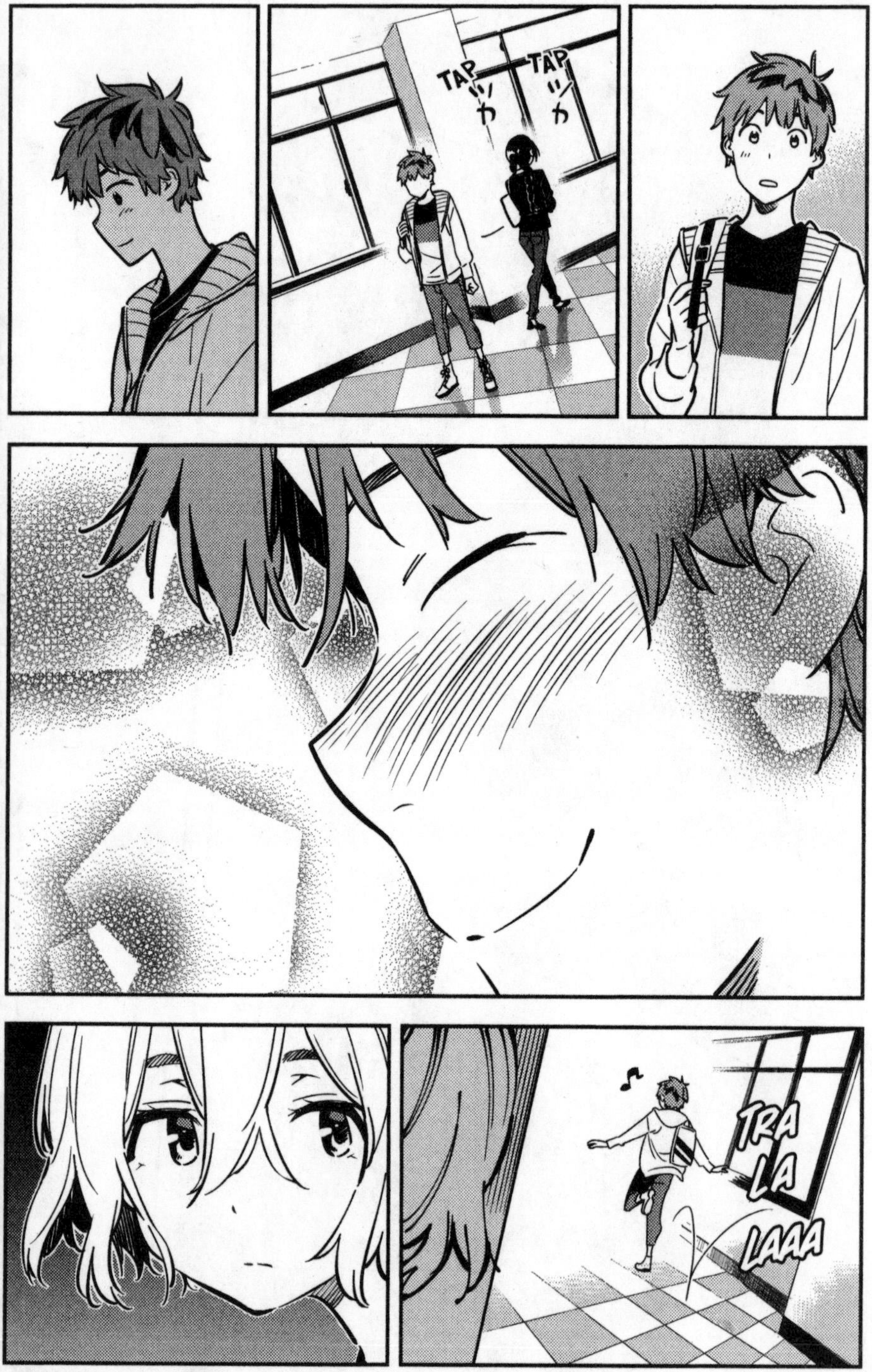
TAP
ッカ
TAP
ッカ
TRA LA LAAA

RATING 62 THAT NIGHT AND MY GIRLFRIEND 1

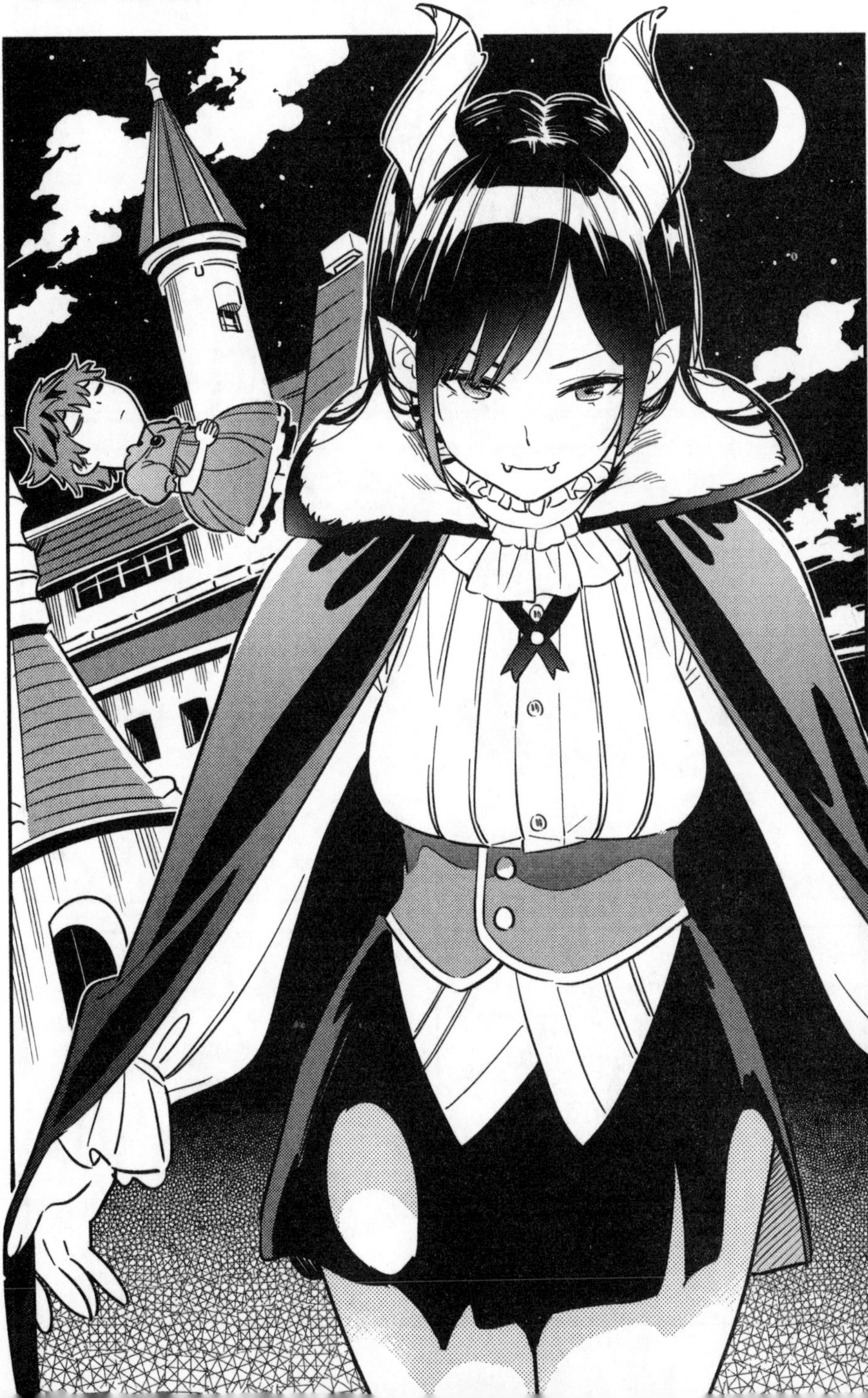

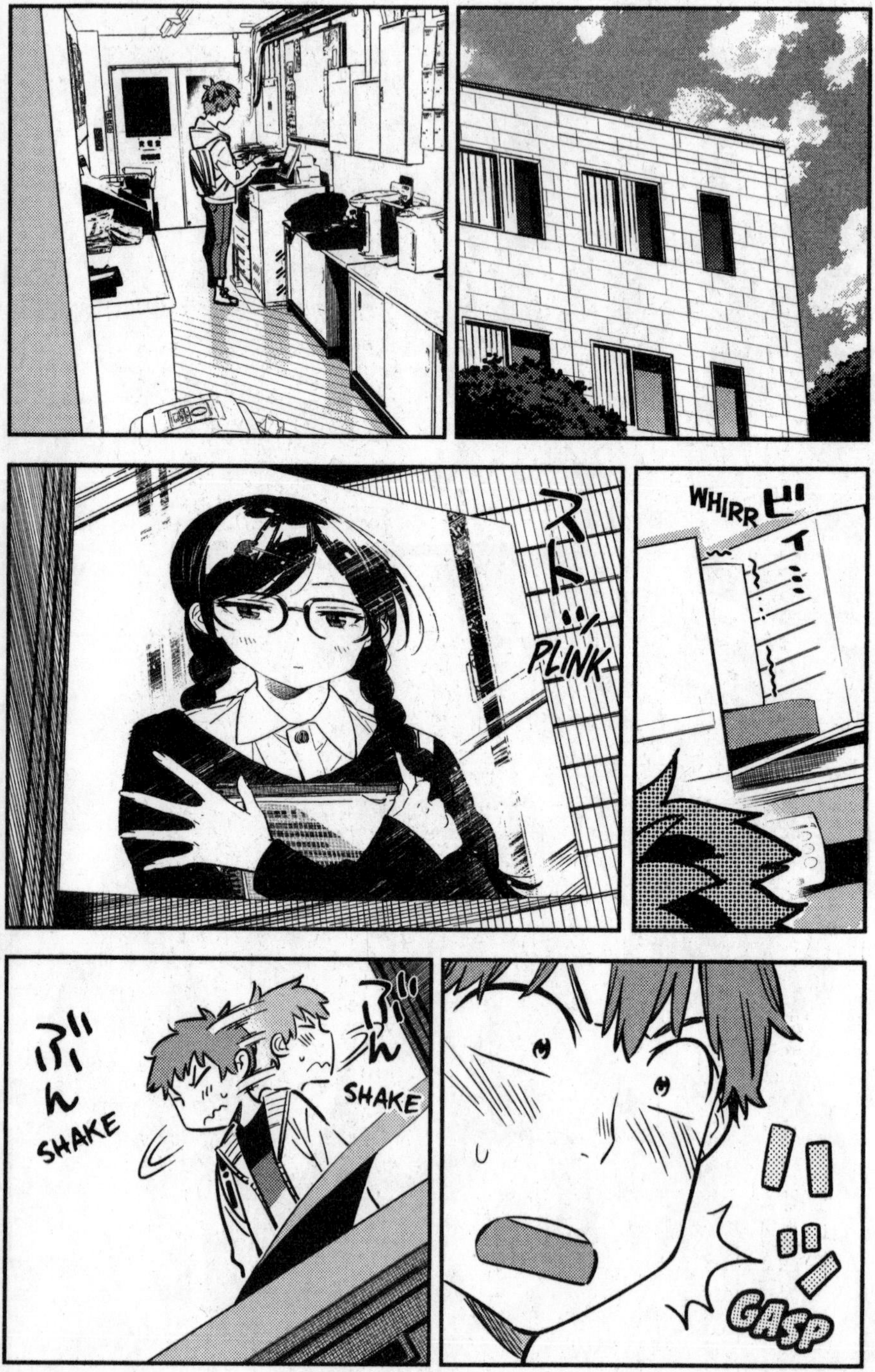
ビイ
WHIRR
ストッ
PLINK
バッ
GASP
ぶん
SHAKE
ぶん
SHAKE

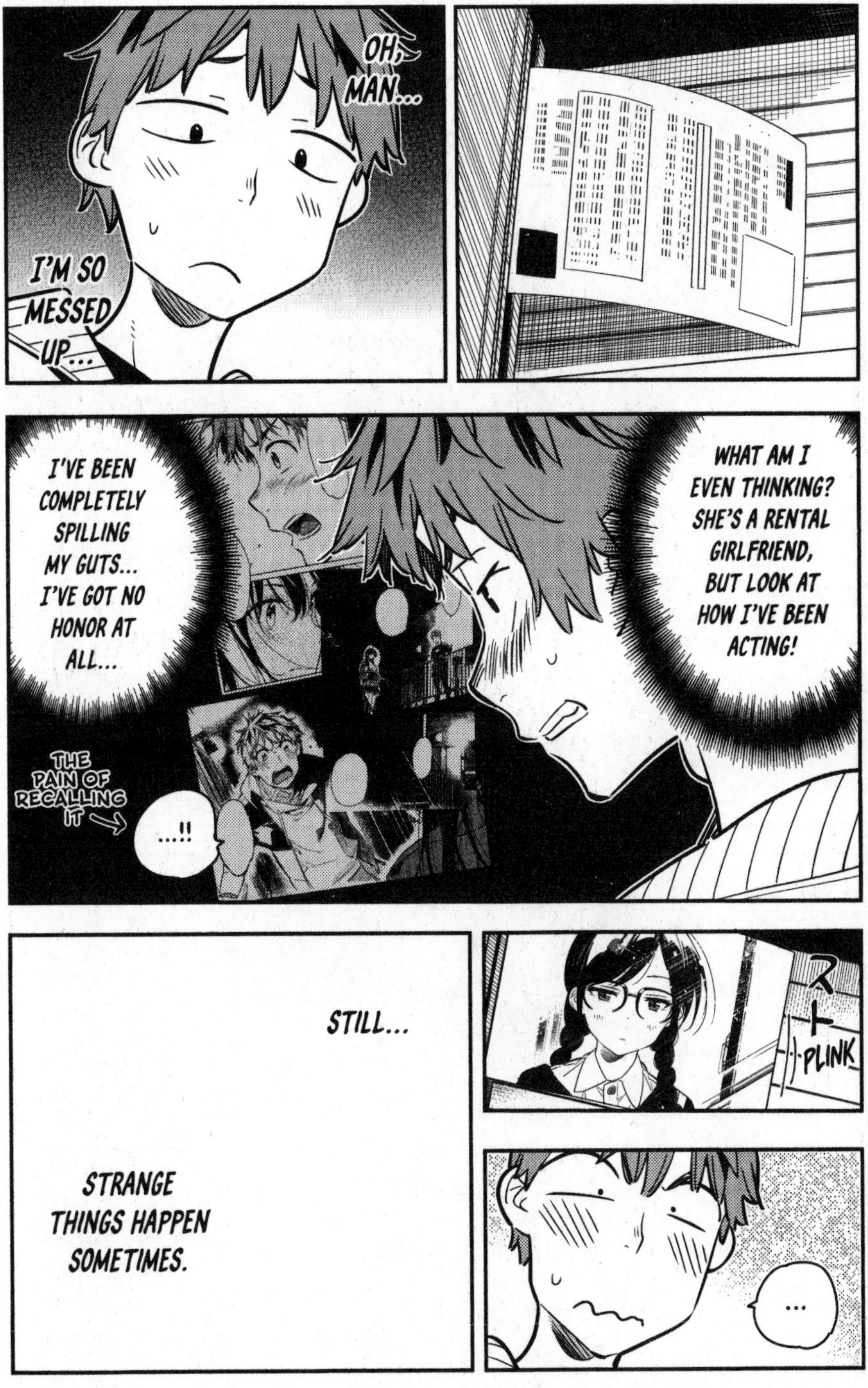
OH, MAN...
I'M SO MESSED UP...
WHAT AM I EVEN THINKING? SHE'S A RENTAL GIRLFRIEND, BUT LOOK AT HOW I'VE BEEN ACTING!
I'VE BEEN COMPLETELY SPILLING MY GUTS... I'VE GOT NO HONOR AT ALL...
THE PAIN OF RECALLING IT
...!!
スト
PLINK
...
STILL...
STRANGE THINGS HAPPEN SOMETIMES.

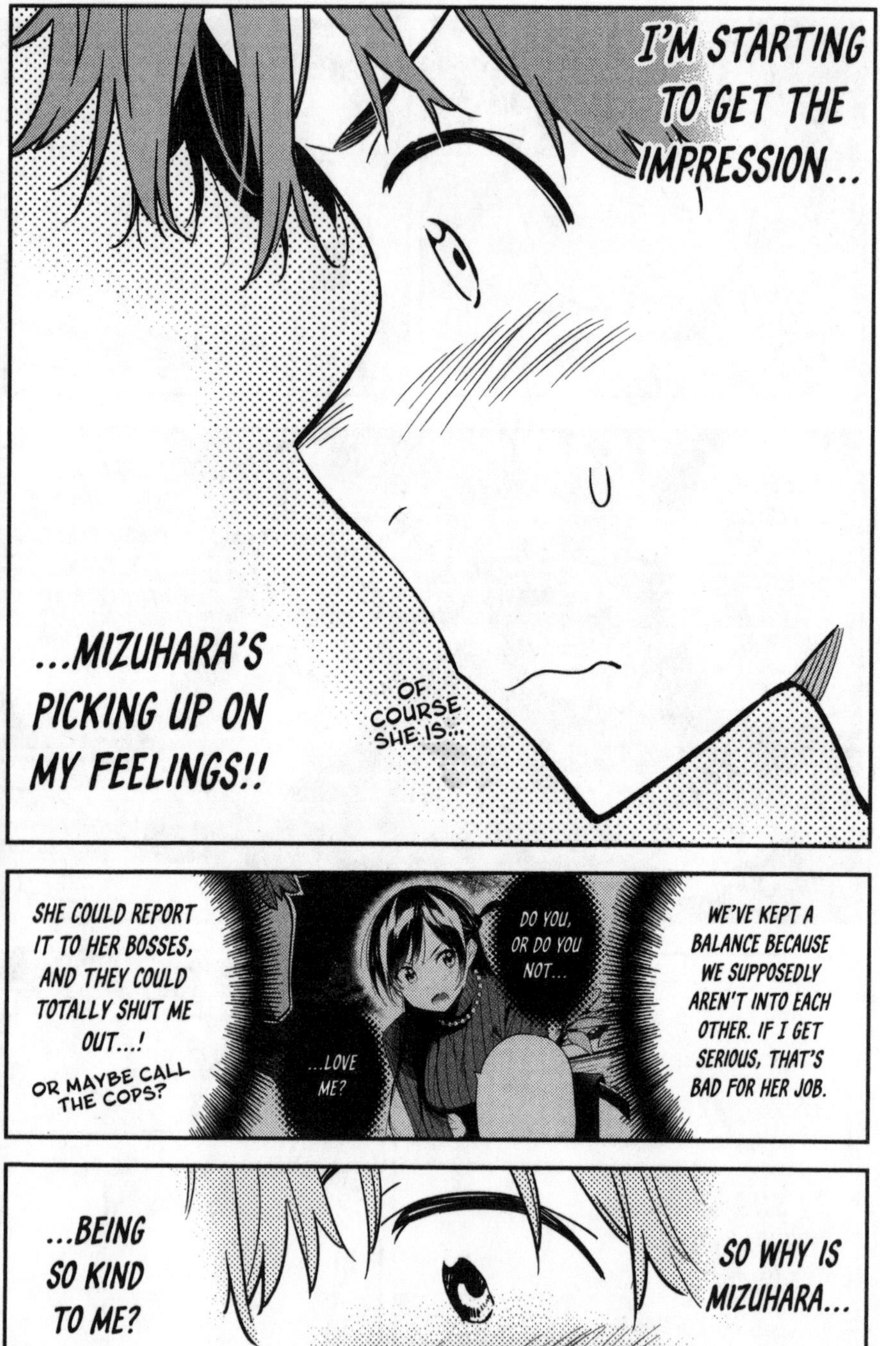
I'M STARTING TO GET THE IMPRESSION...
...MIZUHARA'S PICKING UP ON MY FEELINGS!!
OF COURSE SHE IS...
WE'VE KEPT A BALANCE BECAUSE WE SUPPOSEDLY AREN'T INTO EACH OTHER. IF I GET SERIOUS, THAT'S BAD FOR HER JOB.
DO YOU, OR DO YOU NOT...
...LOVE ME?
SHE COULD REPORT IT TO HER BOSSES, AND THEY COULD TOTALLY SHUT ME OUT...!
OR MAYBE CALL THE COPS?
SO WHY IS MIZUHARA...
...BEING SO KIND TO ME?

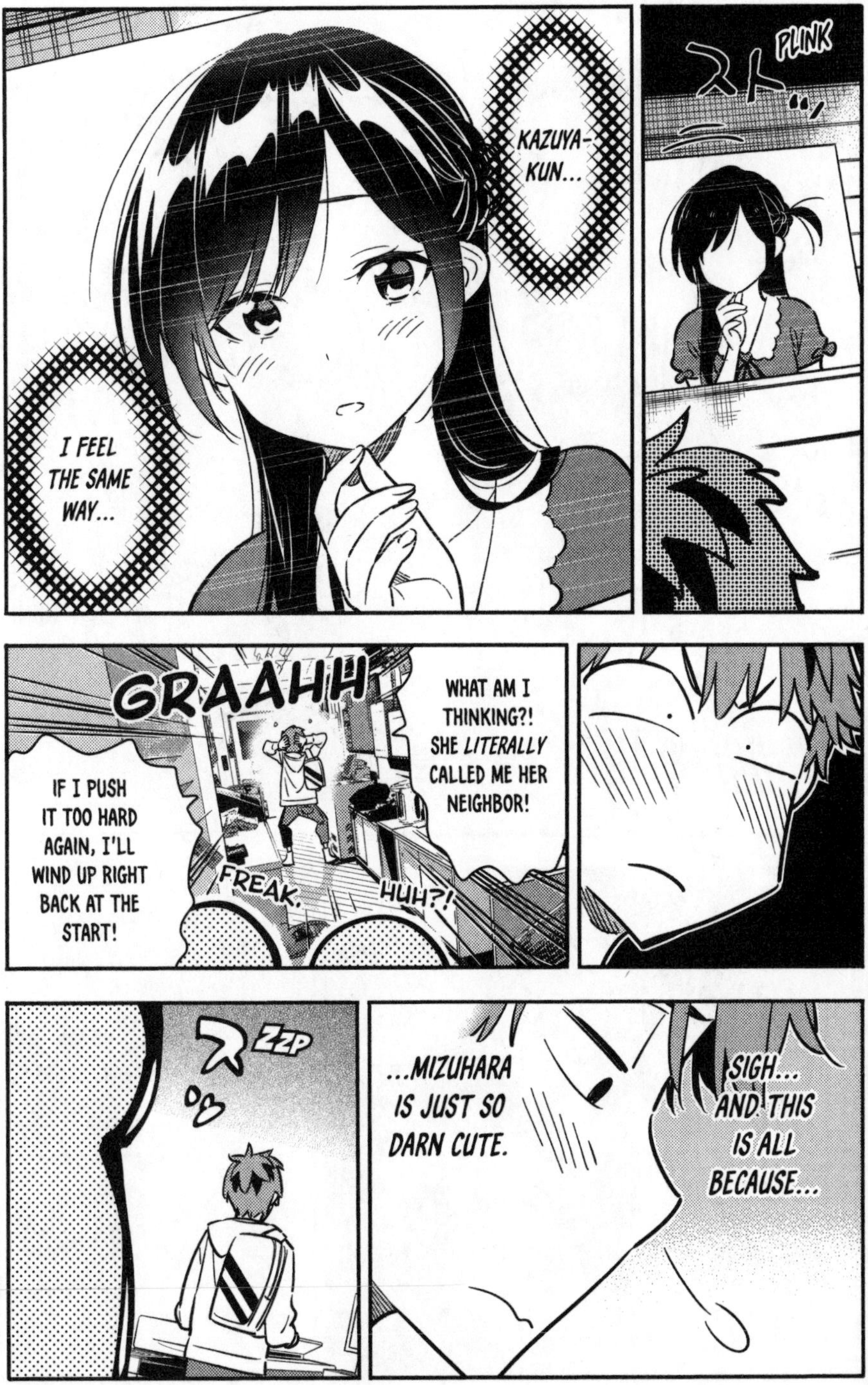
PLINK
KAZUYA-KUN...
I FEEL THE SAME WAY...
WHAT AM I THINKING?! SHE *LITERALLY* CALLED ME HER NEIGHBOR!
GRAAHH
IF I PUSH IT TOO HARD AGAIN, I'LL WIND UP RIGHT BACK AT THE START!
HUH?!
FREAK.
SIGH... AND THIS IS ALL BECAUSE...
...MIZUHARA IS JUST SO DARN CUTE.
ZZP

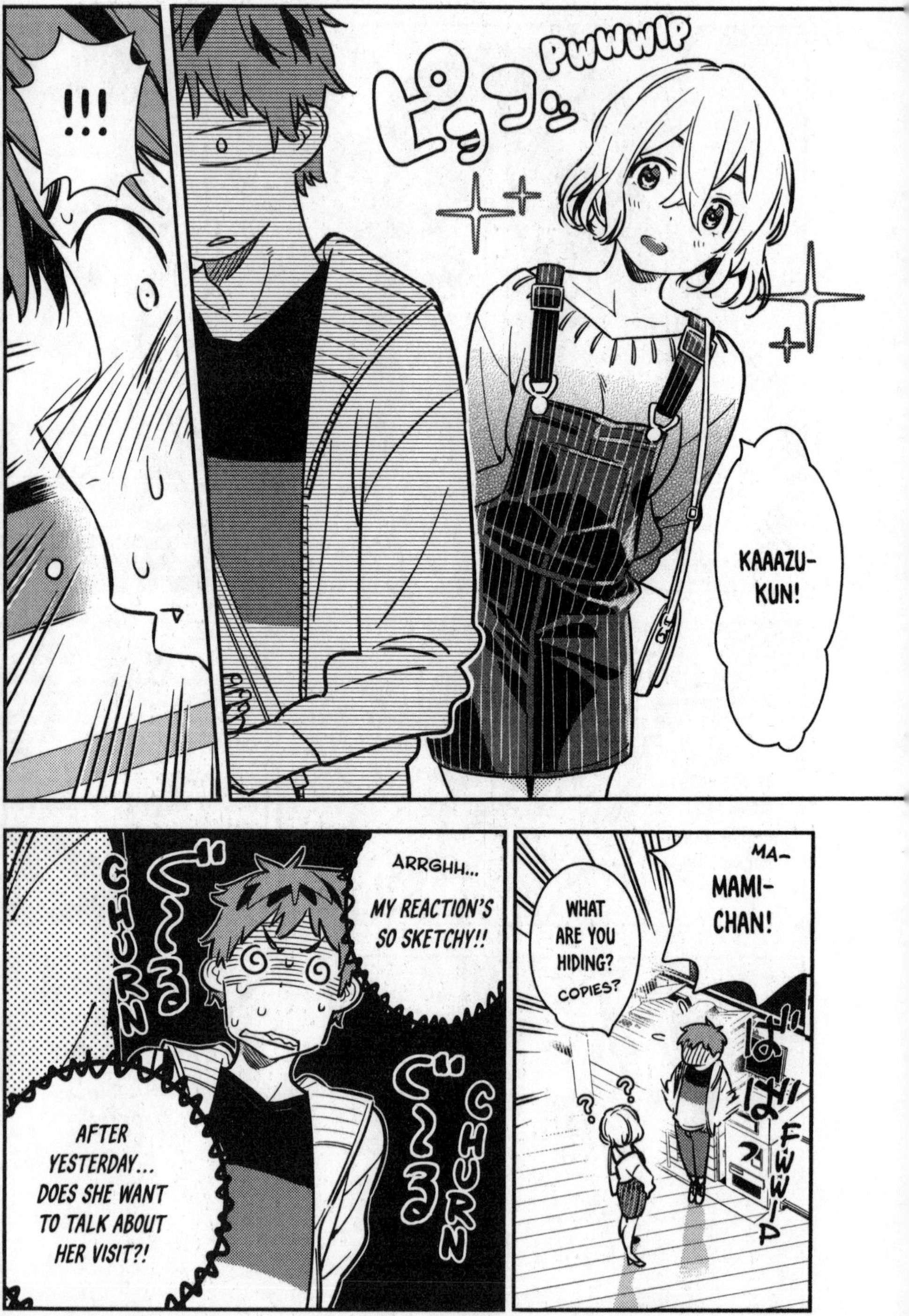
ピョコッ
PWWWIP
KAAAZU-KUN!
!!!
MA-
MAMI-CHAN!
WHAT ARE YOU HIDING? COPIES?
FWWIP
ARRGHH...
MY REACTION'S SO SKETCHY!!
CHURN
CHURN
AFTER YESTERDAY... DOES SHE WANT TO TALK ABOUT HER VISIT?!

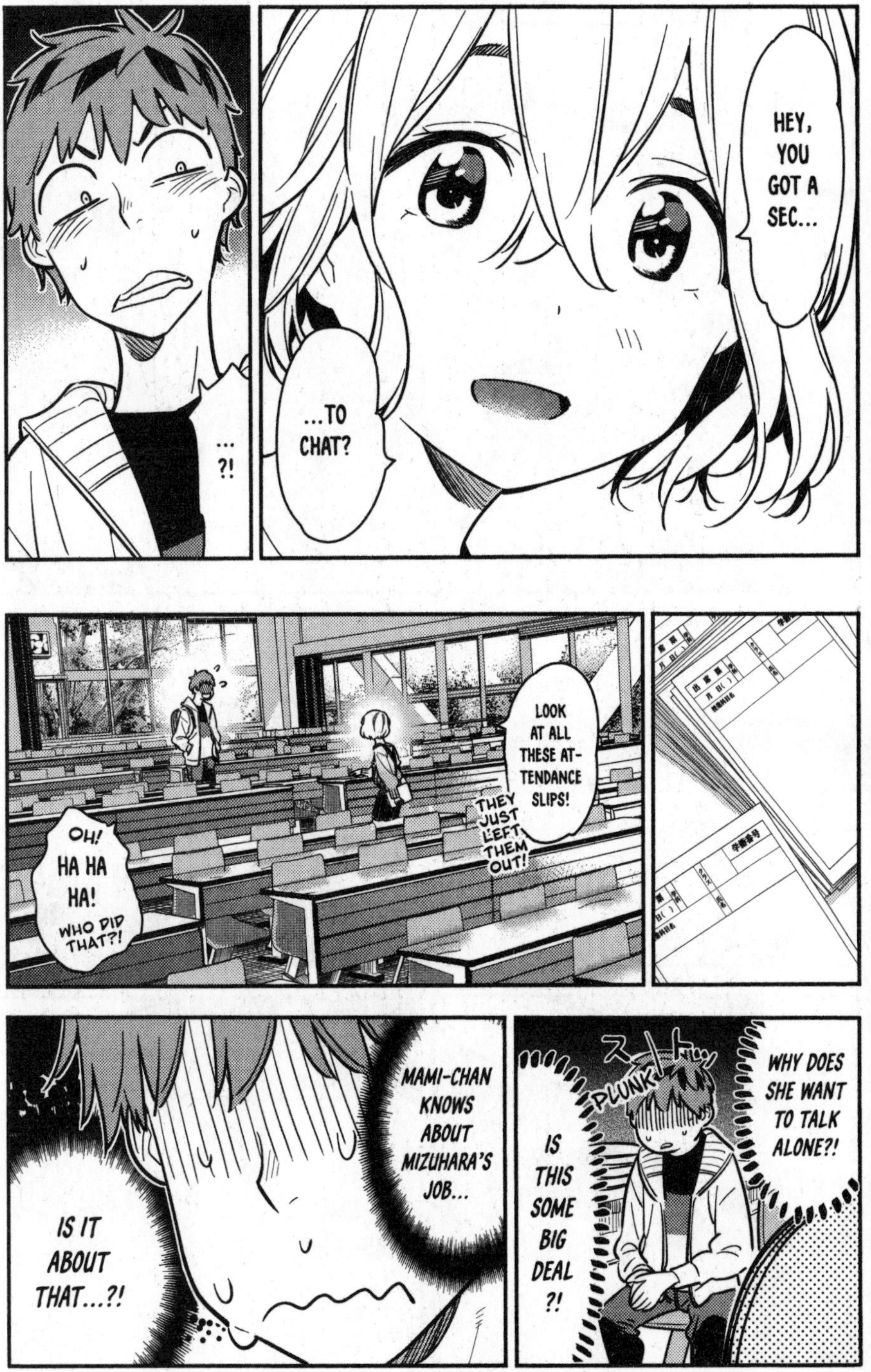
HEY, YOU GOT A SEC...
...TO CHAT?
...?!
LOOK AT ALL THESE AT-TENDANCE SLIPS!
THEY JUST LEFT THEM OUT!
OH! HA HA HA!
WHO DID THAT?!
PLUNK
WHY DOES SHE WANT TO TALK ALONE?!
IS THIS SOME BIG DEAL?!
MAMI-CHAN KNOWS ABOUT MIZUHARA'S JOB...
IS IT ABOUT THAT...?!

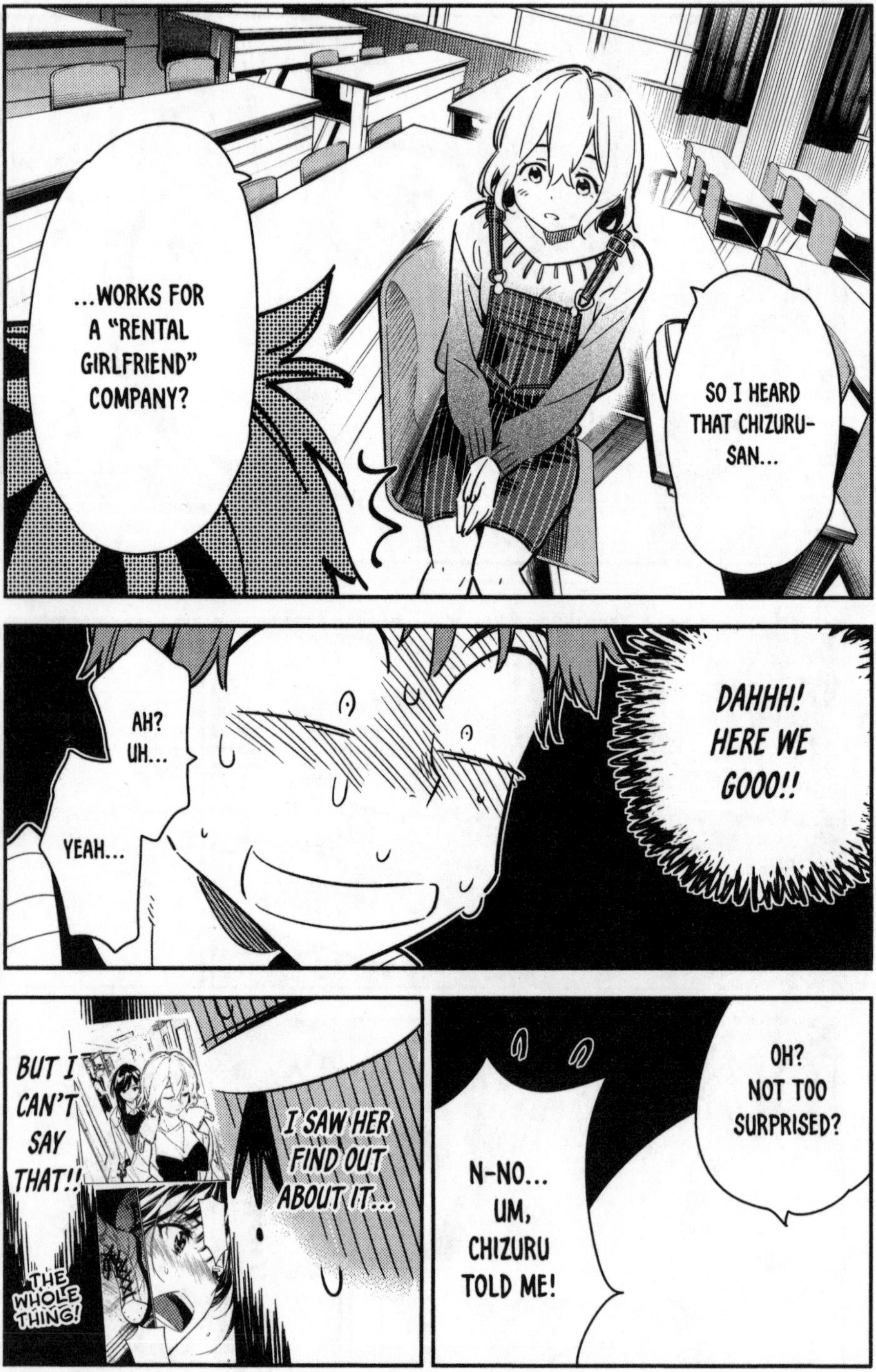
SO I HEARD THAT CHIZURU-SAN...
...WORKS FOR A "RENTAL GIRLFRIEND" COMPANY?
DAHHH! HERE WE GOOO!!
AH? UH...
YEAH...
OH? NOT TOO SURPRISED?
N-NO... UM, CHIZURU TOLD ME!
I SAW HER FIND OUT ABOUT IT...
BUT I CAN'T SAY THAT!!
THE WHOLE THING!

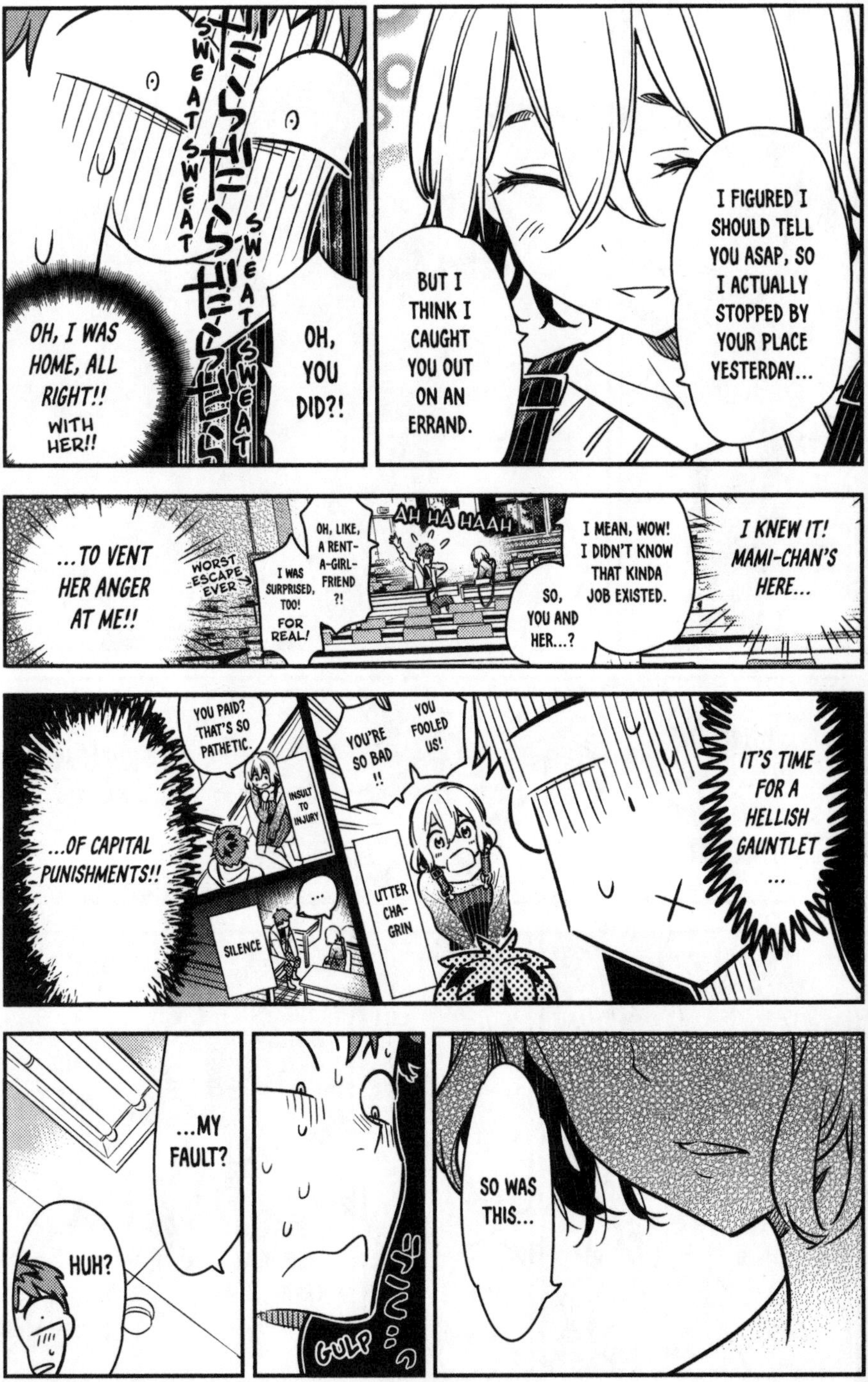
I FIGURED I SHOULD TELL YOU ASAP, SO I ACTUALLY STOPPED BY YOUR PLACE YESTERDAY...
BUT I THINK I CAUGHT YOU OUT ON AN ERRAND.
SWEAT SWEAT
SWEAT SWEAT
SWEAT SWEAT
OH, YOU DID?!
OH, I WAS HOME, ALL RIGHT!! WITH HER!!
I KNEW IT! MAMI-CHAN'S HERE...
I MEAN, WOW! I DIDN'T KNOW THAT KINDA JOB EXISTED.
SO, YOU AND HER...?
AH HA HAAAH
OH, LIKE, A RENT-A-GIRL-FRIEND?!
I WAS SURPRISED, TOO! FOR REAL!
WORST ESCAPE EVER
...TO VENT HER ANGER AT ME!!
IT'S TIME FOR A HELLISH GAUNTLET...
YOU FOOLED US!
YOU'RE SO BAD!!
UTTER CHA-GRIN
YOU PAID? THAT'S SO PATHETIC.
INSULT TO INJURY
...
SILENCE
...OF CAPITAL PUNISHMENTS!!
SO WAS THIS...
GULP
...MY FAULT?
HUH?

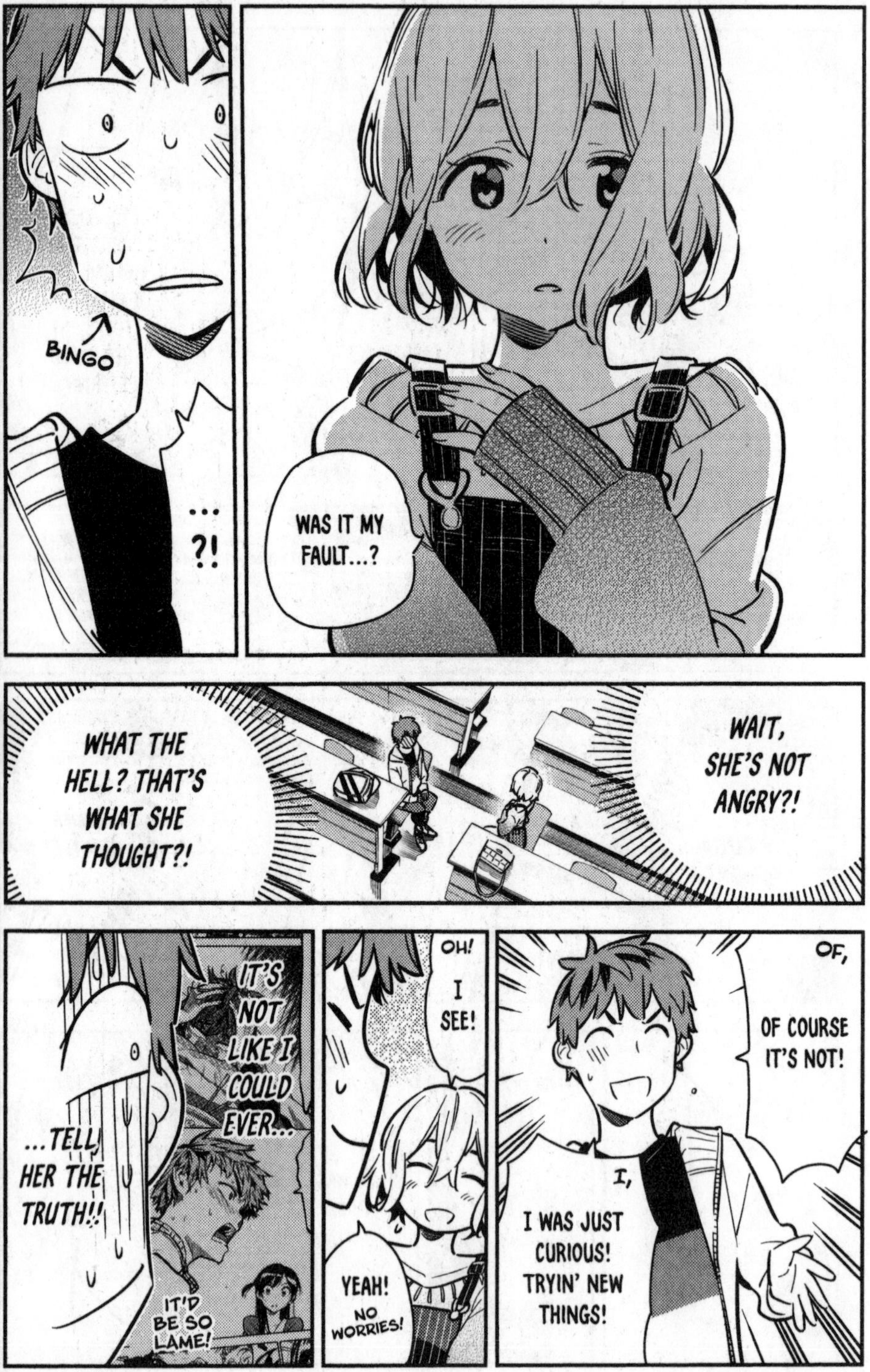
WAS IT MY FAULT...?
BINGO
...
?!
WAIT, SHE'S NOT ANGRY?!
WHAT THE HELL? THAT'S WHAT SHE THOUGHT?!
OF,
OF COURSE IT'S NOT!
I,
I WAS JUST CURIOUS! TRYIN' NEW THINGS!
OH!
I SEE!
YEAH! NO WORRIES!
IT'S NOT LIKE I COULD EVER...
...TELL HER THE TRUTH!!
IT'D BE SO LAME!

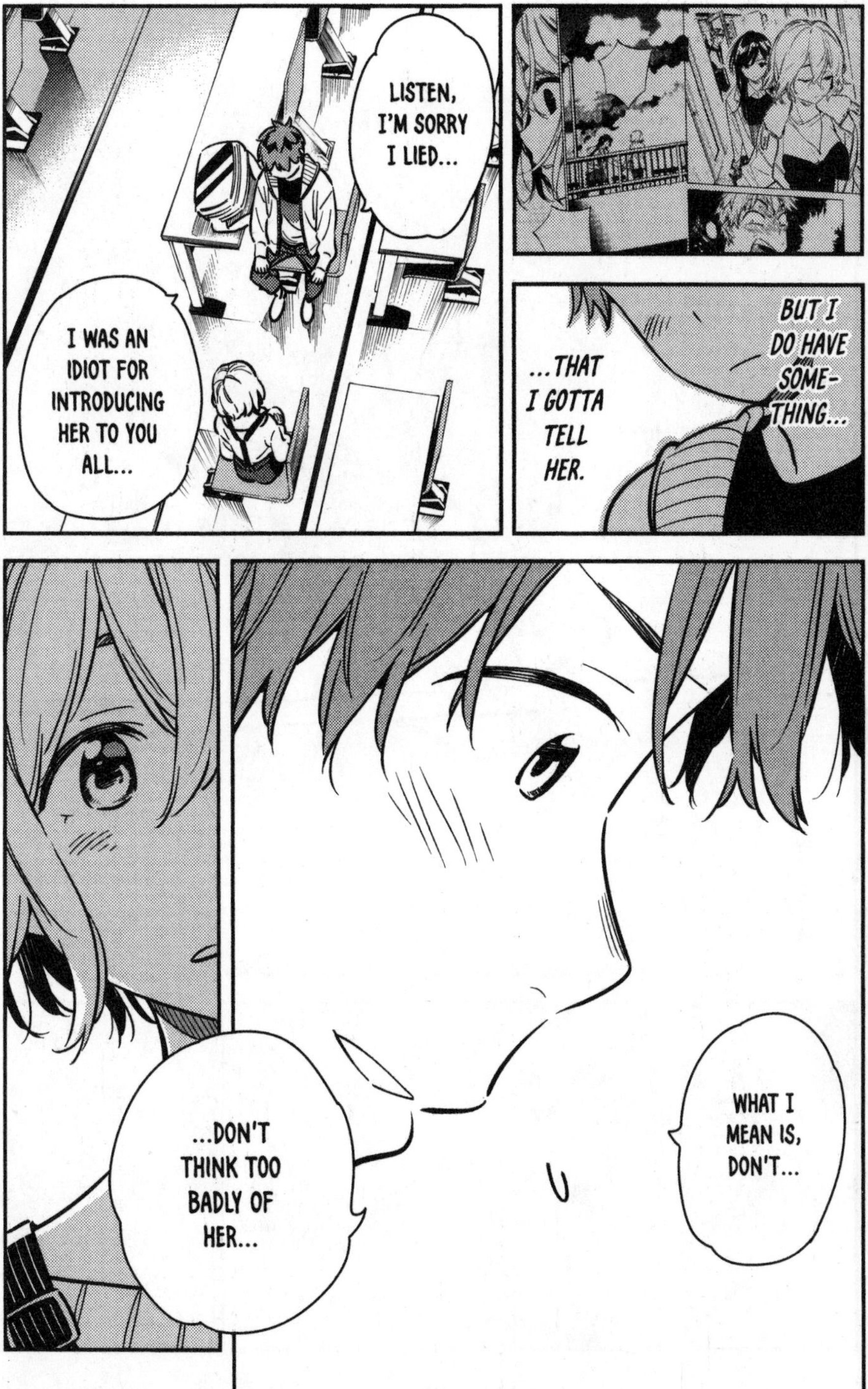
BUT I DO HAVE SOME-THING...
...THAT I GOTTA TELL HER.
LISTEN, I'M SORRY I LIED...
I WAS AN IDIOT FOR INTRODUCING HER TO YOU ALL...
WHAT I MEAN IS, DON'T...
...DON'T THINK TOO BADLY OF HER...

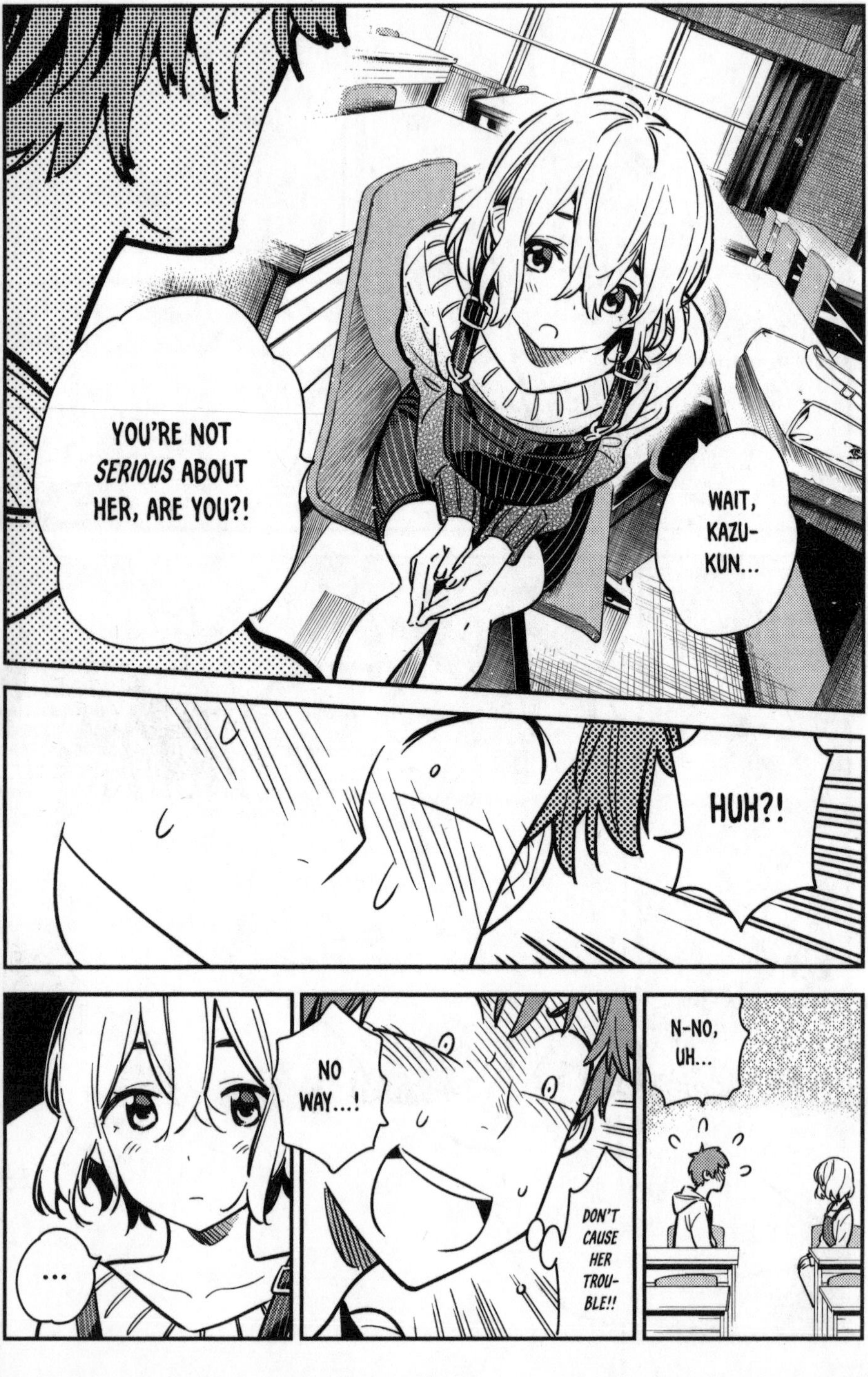
WAIT, KAZU-KUN...
YOU'RE NOT *SERIOUS* ABOUT HER, ARE YOU?!
HUH?!
N-NO, UH...
NO WAY...!
DON'T CAUSE HER TROUBLE!!
...

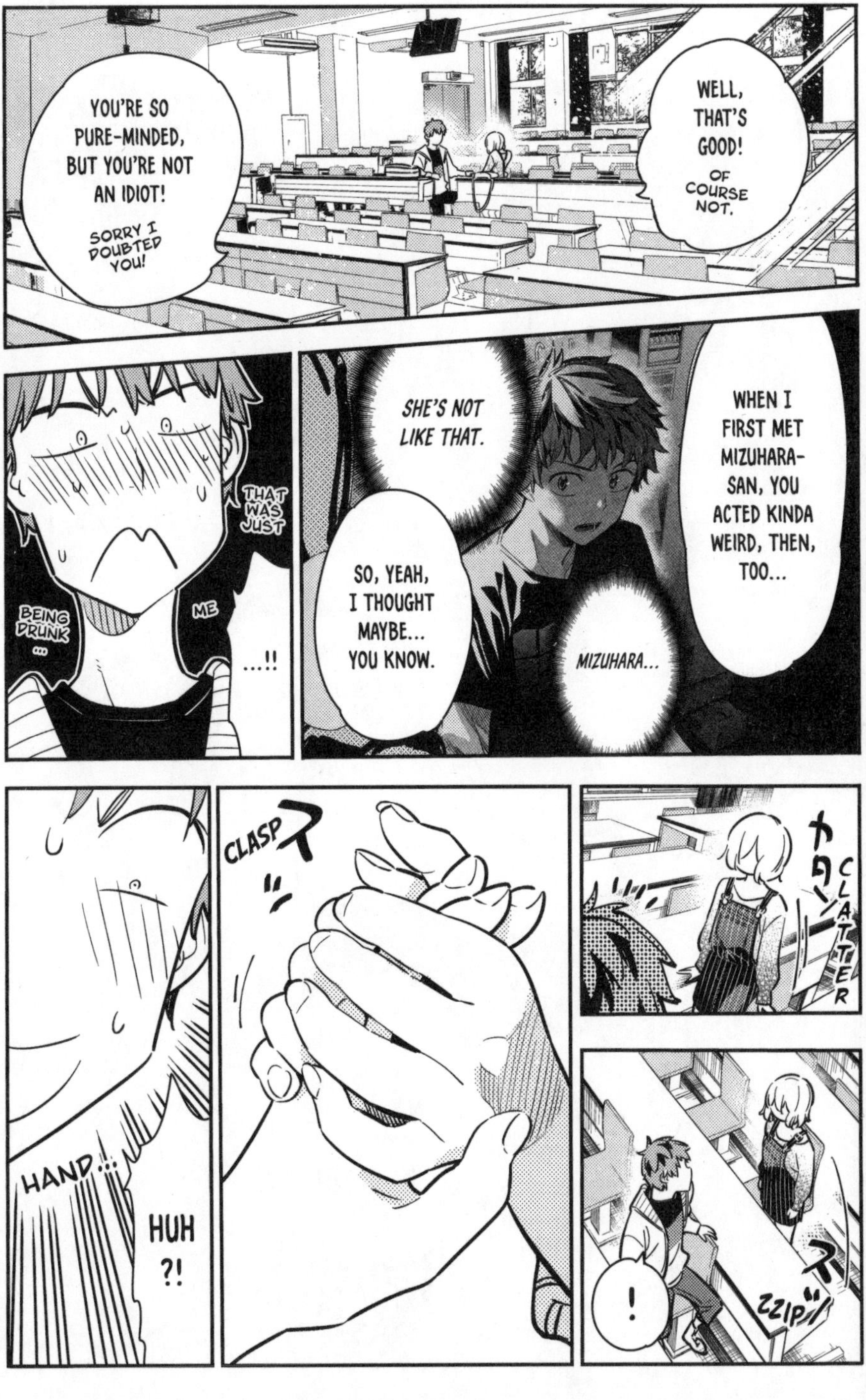
WELL, THAT'S GOOD!
OF COURSE NOT.
YOU'RE SO PURE-MINDED, BUT YOU'RE NOT AN IDIOT!
SORRY I DOUBTED YOU!
WHEN I FIRST MET MIZUHARA-SAN, YOU ACTED KINDA WEIRD, THEN, TOO...
SHE'S NOT LIKE THAT.
SO, YEAH, I THOUGHT MAYBE... YOU KNOW.
MIZUHARA...
THAT WAS JUST
ME
BEING DRUNK...
...!!
カタン
CLATTER
ZZIP
!
CLASP
HAND...
HUH?!

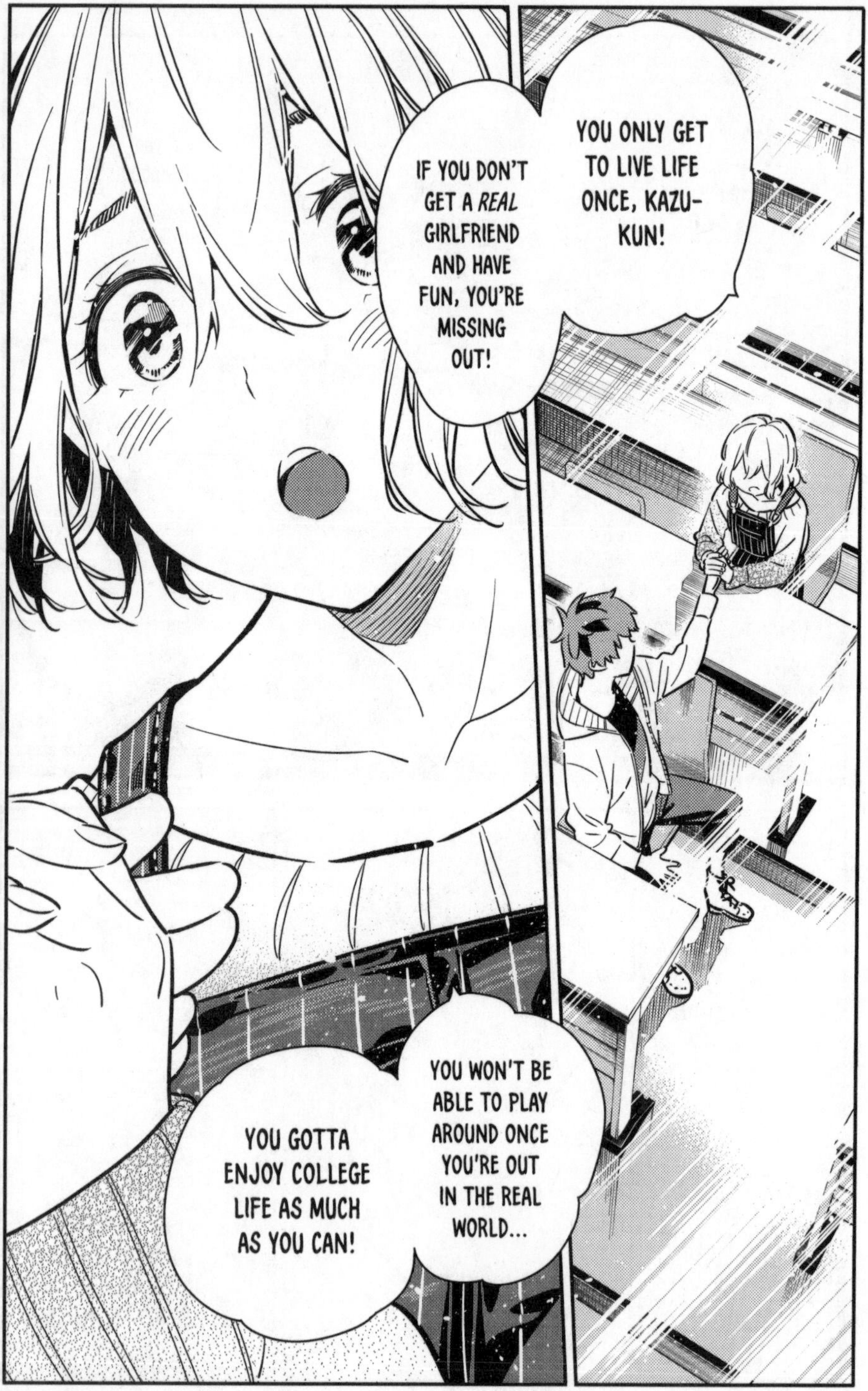
YOU ONLY GET TO LIVE LIFE ONCE, KAZU-KUN!
IF YOU DON'T GET A *REAL* GIRLFRIEND AND HAVE FUN, YOU'RE MISSING OUT!
YOU WON'T BE ABLE TO PLAY AROUND ONCE YOU'RE OUT IN THE REAL WORLD...
YOU GOTTA ENJOY COLLEGE LIFE AS MUCH AS YOU CAN!

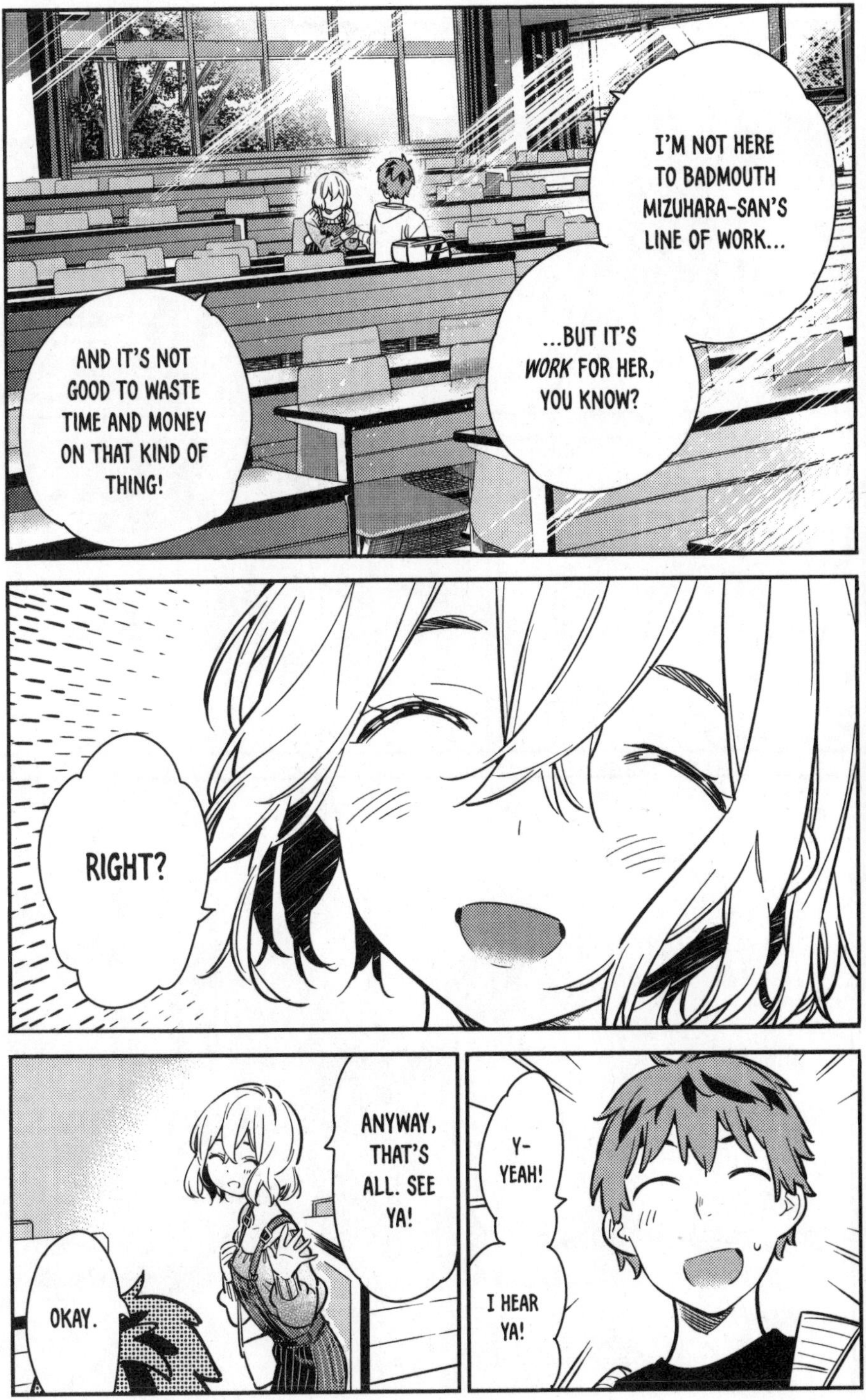
I'M NOT HERE TO BADMOUTH MIZUHARA-SAN'S LINE OF WORK...
...BUT IT'S WORK FOR HER, YOU KNOW?
AND IT'S NOT GOOD TO WASTE TIME AND MONEY ON THAT KIND OF THING!
RIGHT?
Y- YEAH!
I HEAR YA!
ANYWAY, THAT'S ALL. SEE YA!
OKAY.

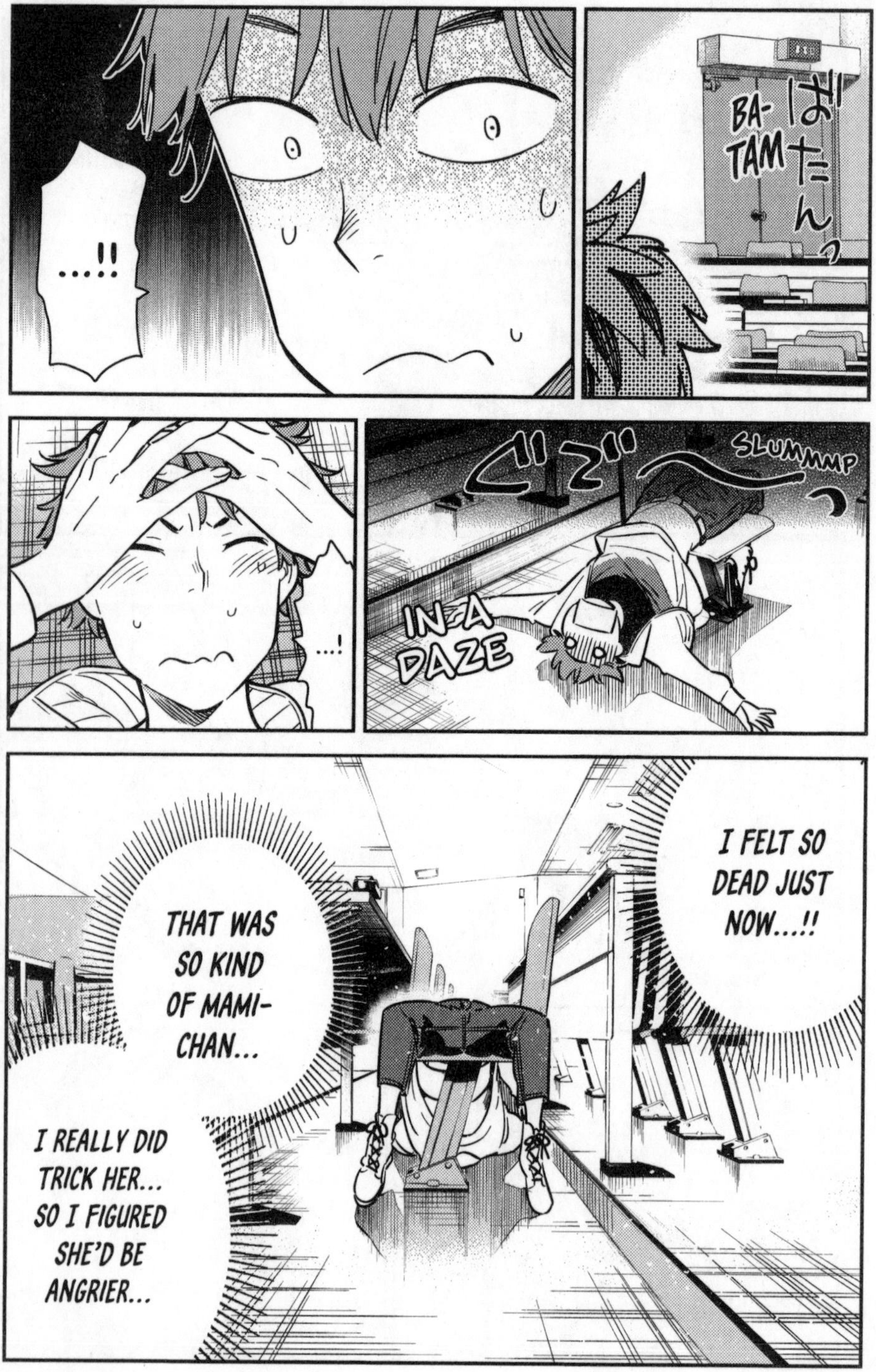
BA-TAM
ばたんっ
...!!
SLUMMMP
IN A DAZE
...!
I FELT SO DEAD JUST NOW...!!
THAT WAS SO KIND OF MAMI-CHAN...
I REALLY DID TRICK HER... SO I FIGURED SHE'D BE ANGRIER...

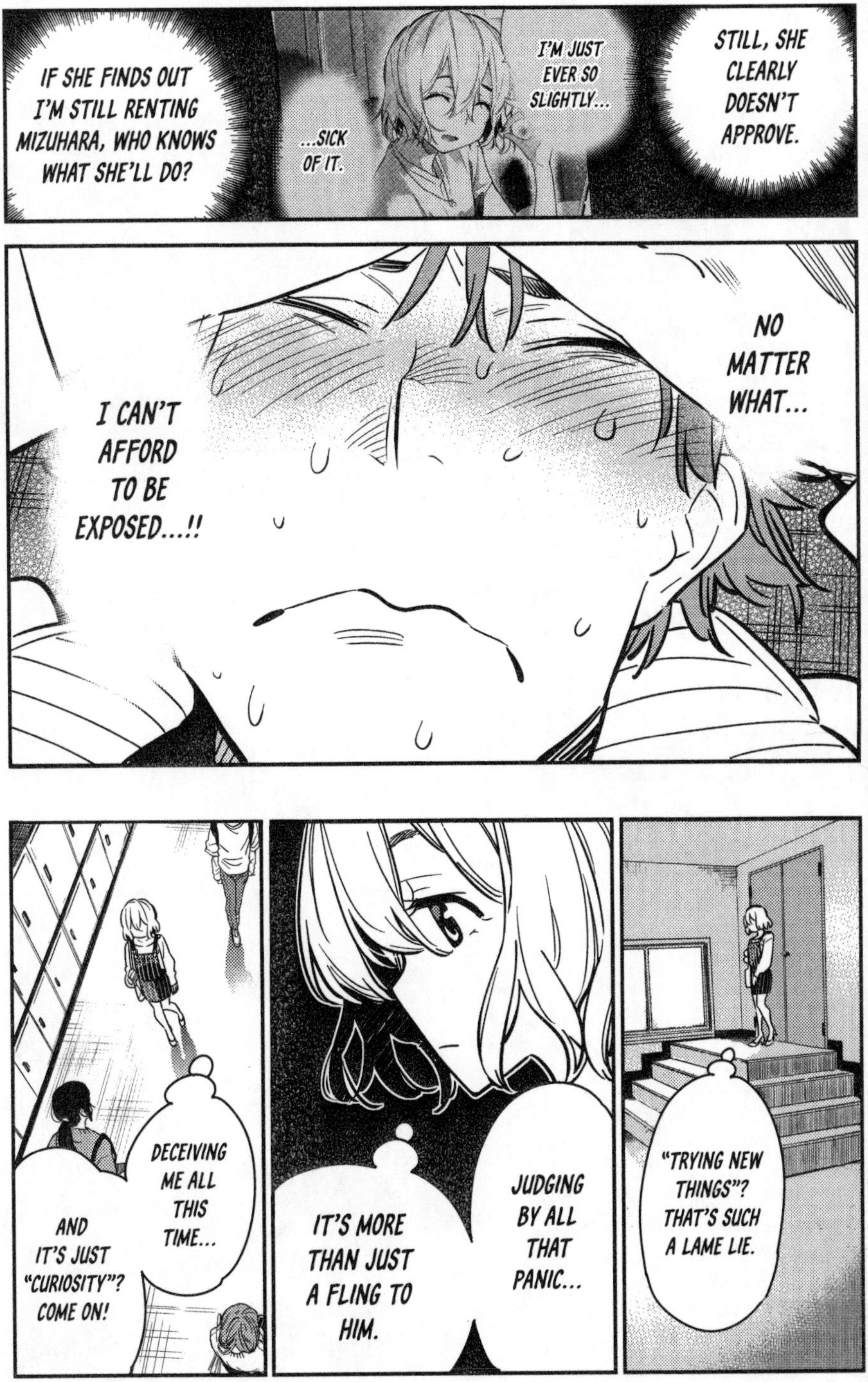
STILL, SHE CLEARLY DOESN'T APPROVE.
I'M JUST EVER SO SLIGHTLY...
...SICK OF IT.
IF SHE FINDS OUT I'M STILL RENTING MIZUHARA, WHO KNOWS WHAT SHE'LL DO?
NO MATTER WHAT...
I CAN'T AFFORD TO BE EXPOSED...!!
"TRYING NEW THINGS"? THAT'S SUCH A LAME LIE.
JUDGING BY ALL THAT PANIC...
IT'S MORE THAN JUST A FLING TO HIM.
DECEIVING ME ALL THIS TIME...
AND IT'S JUST "CURIOSITY"? COME ON!

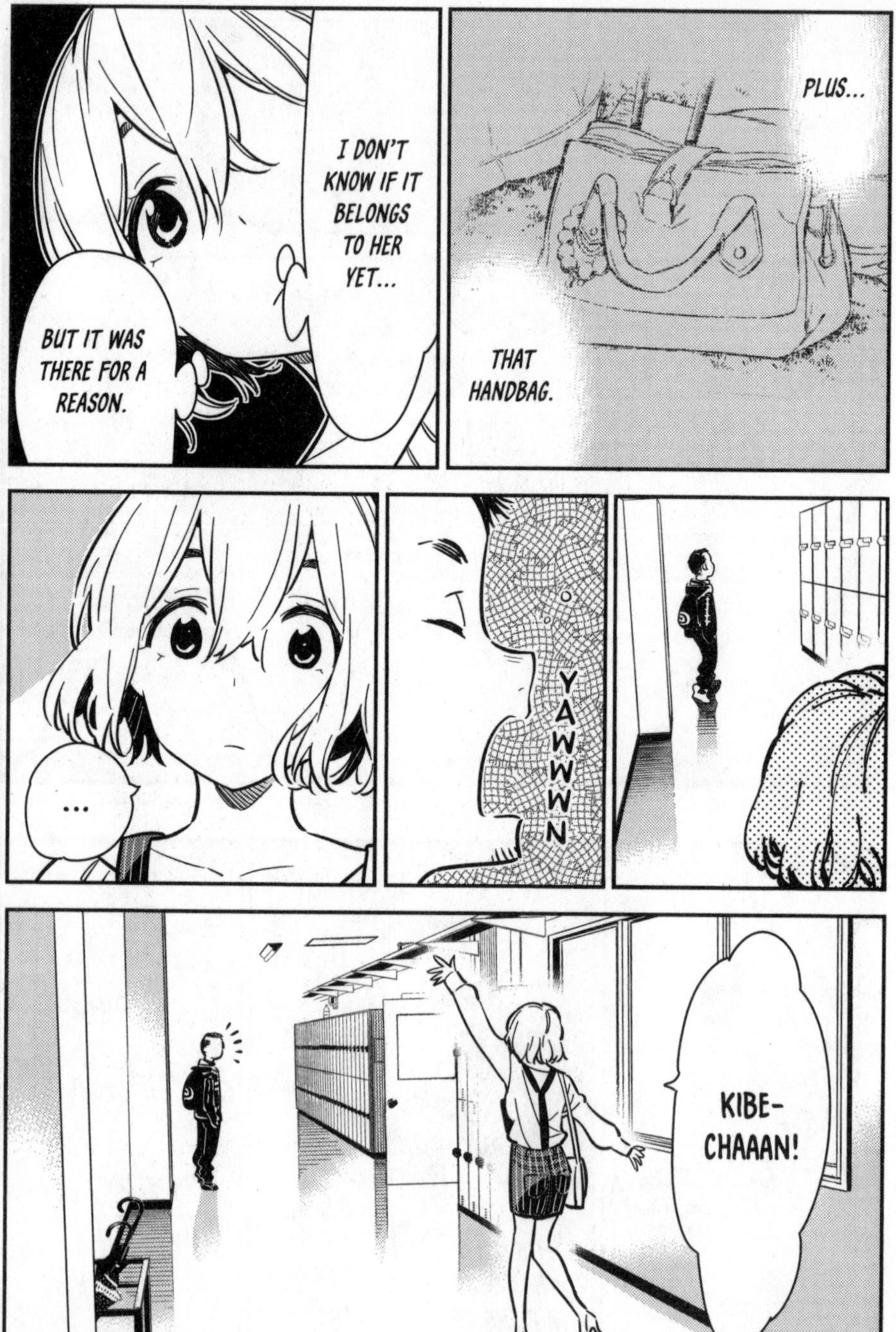
PLUS...
THAT HANDBAG.
I DON'T KNOW IF IT BELONGS TO HER YET...
BUT IT WAS THERE FOR A REASON.
YAWWWN
...
KIBE-CHAAAN!

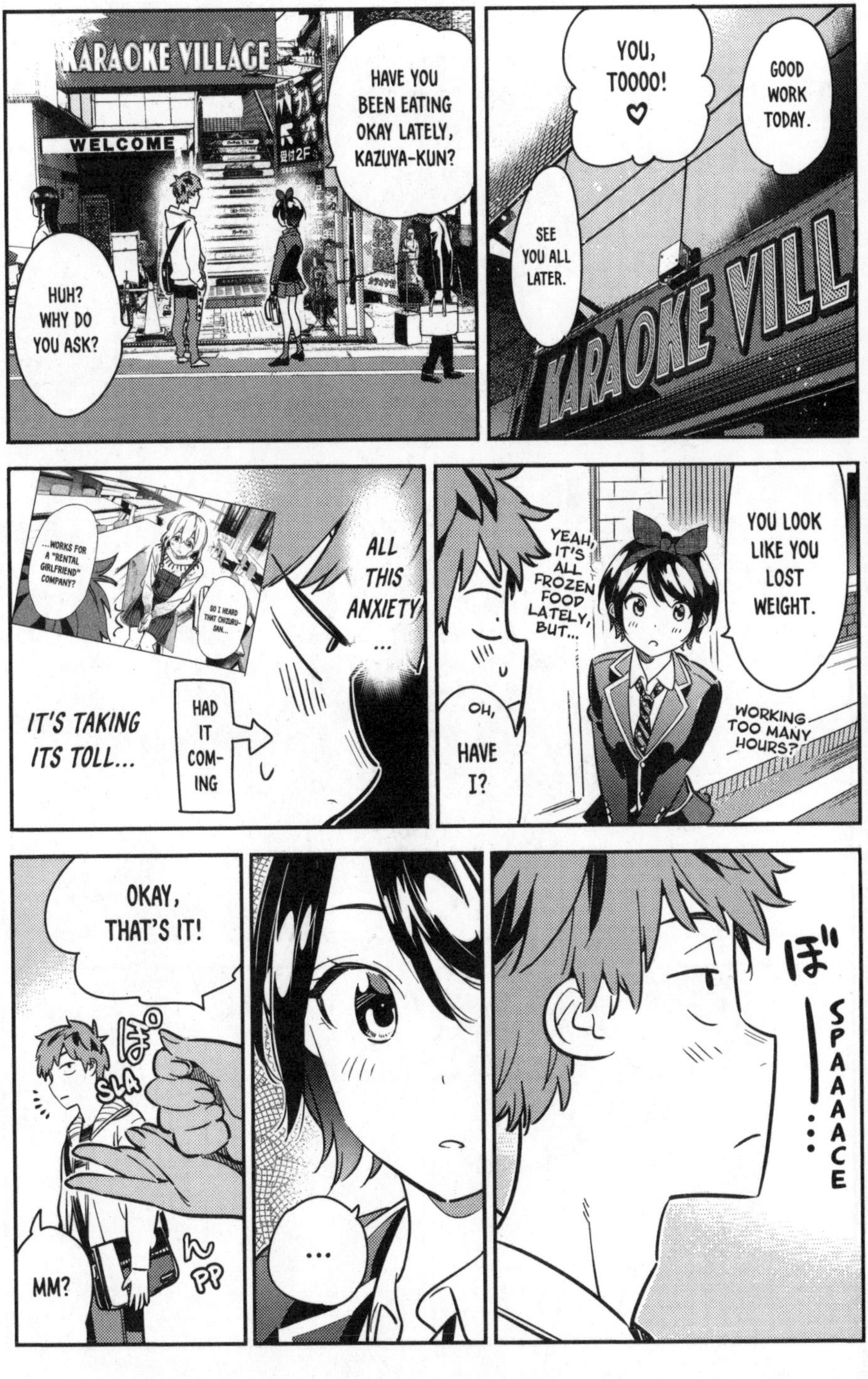
GOOD WORK TODAY.
YOU, TOOOO! ♡
SEE YOU ALL LATER.
KARAOKE VILL
KARAOKE VILLAGE
WELCOME
HAVE YOU BEEN EATING OKAY LATELY, KAZUYA-KUN?
HUH? WHY DO YOU ASK?
YOU LOOK LIKE YOU LOST WEIGHT.
WORKING TOO MANY HOURS?
YEAH, IT'S ALL FROZEN FOOD LATELY, BUT...
OH, HAVE I?
ALL THIS ANXIETY...
SO I HEARD THAT CHIZURU-SAN...
...WORKS FOR A "RENTAL GIRLFRIEND" COMPANY?
HAD IT COMING
IT'S TAKING ITS TOLL...
ぼ
SPAAAACE...
...
OKAY, THAT'S IT!
ぽ
SLA
ん
PP
MM?

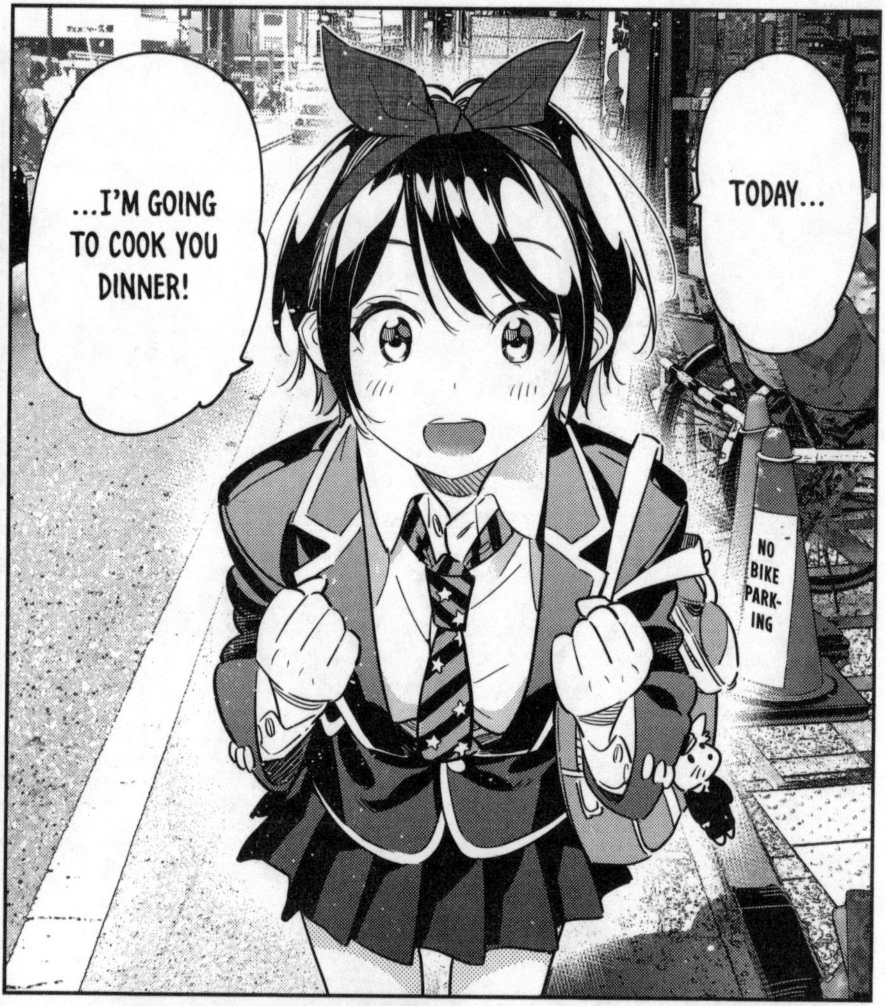
TODAY...
...I'M GOING TO COOK YOU DINNER!
NO BIKE PARK-ING
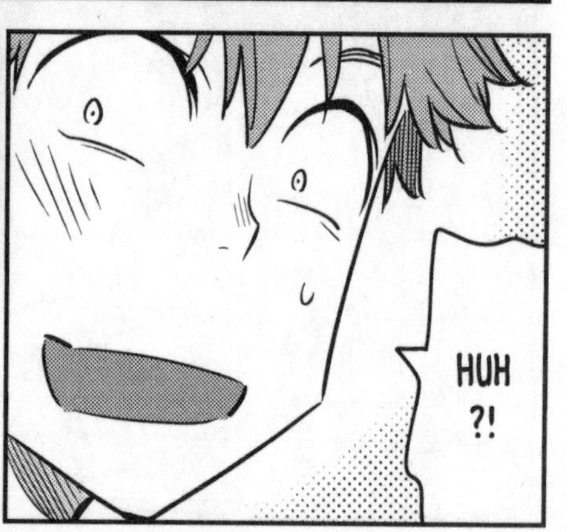
HUH ?!
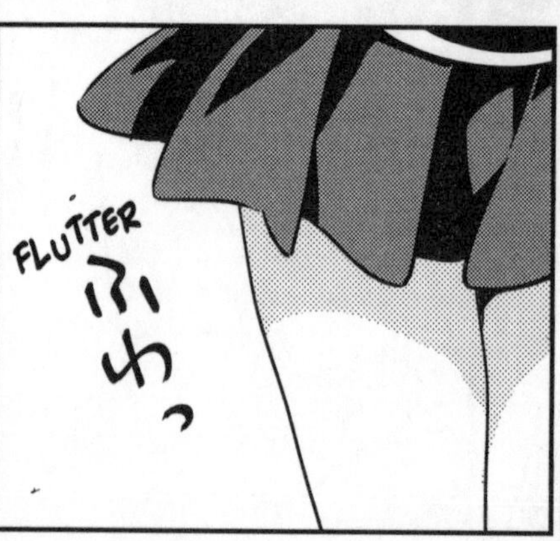
FLUTTER
ふわっ

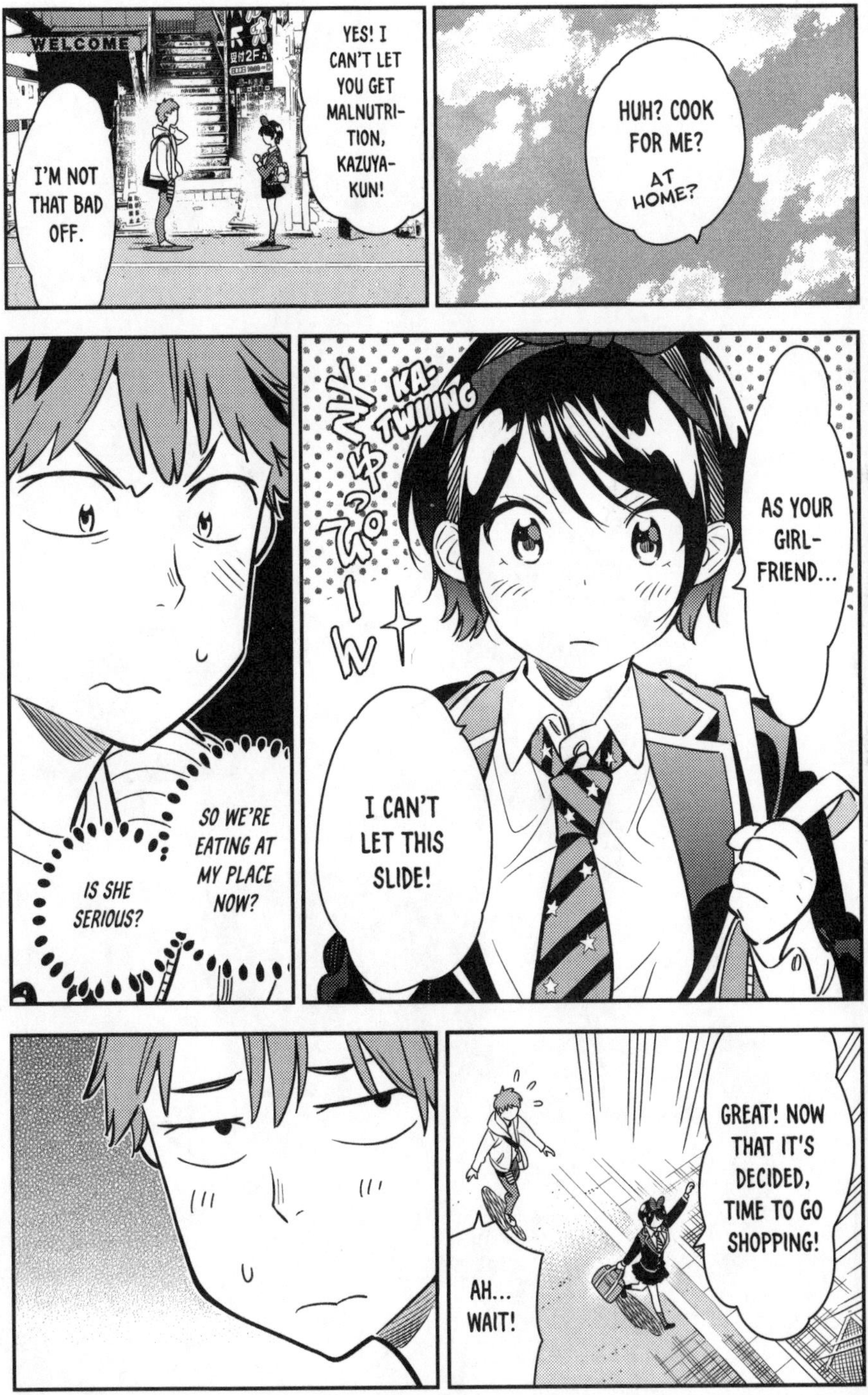
HUH? COOK FOR ME?
AT HOME?
WELCOME
YES! I CAN'T LET YOU GET MALNUTRITION, KAZUYA-KUN!
I'M NOT THAT BAD OFF.
AS YOUR GIRLFRIEND...
I CAN'T LET THIS SLIDE!
KA-TWIIING
ぎゅっぴーん
SO WE'RE EATING AT MY PLACE NOW?
IS SHE SERIOUS?
GREAT! NOW THAT IT'S DECIDED, TIME TO GO SHOPPING!
AH... WAIT!

RATING 63 THAT NIGHT AND MY GIRLFRIEND 2

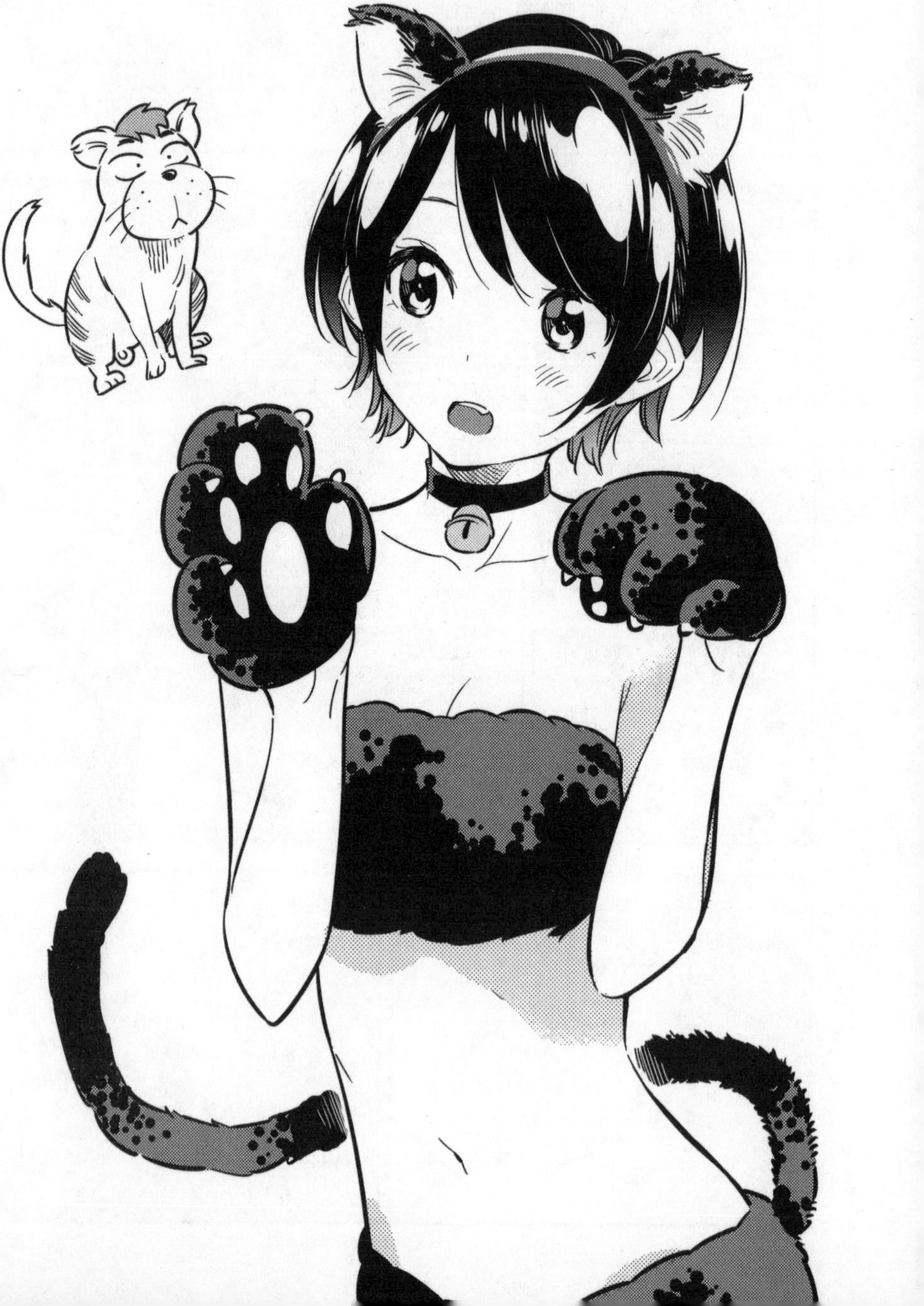

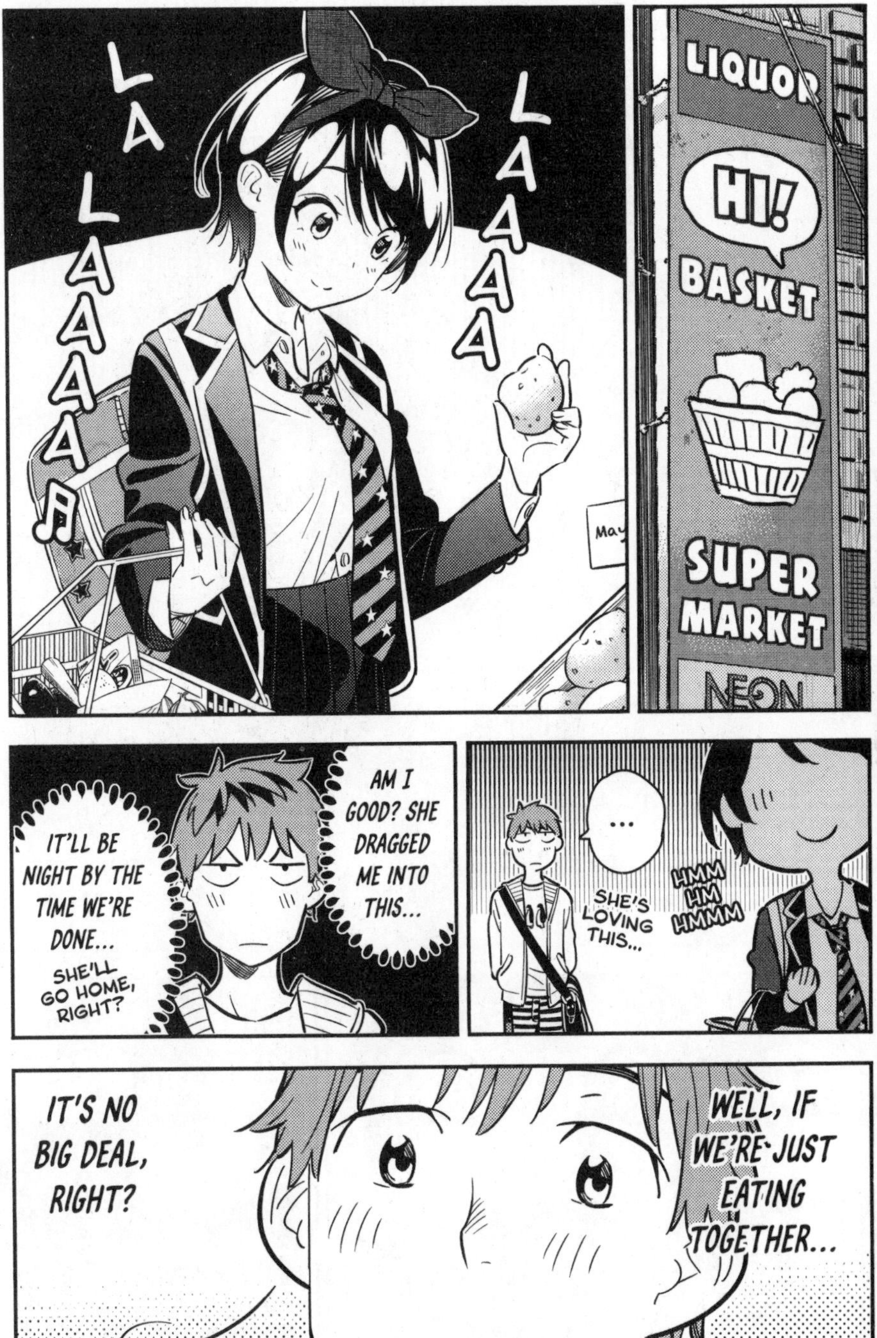
LIQUOR
HI!
BASKET
SUPER MARKET
NEON
LAAAAA
LA LAAAAAA♪
May
...
HMM HM HMMM
SHE'S LOVING THIS...
AM I GOOD? SHE DRAGGED ME INTO THIS...
IT'LL BE NIGHT BY THE TIME WE'RE DONE...
SHE'LL GO HOME, RIGHT?
WELL, IF WE'RE JUST EATING TOGETHER...
IT'S NO BIG DEAL, RIGHT?

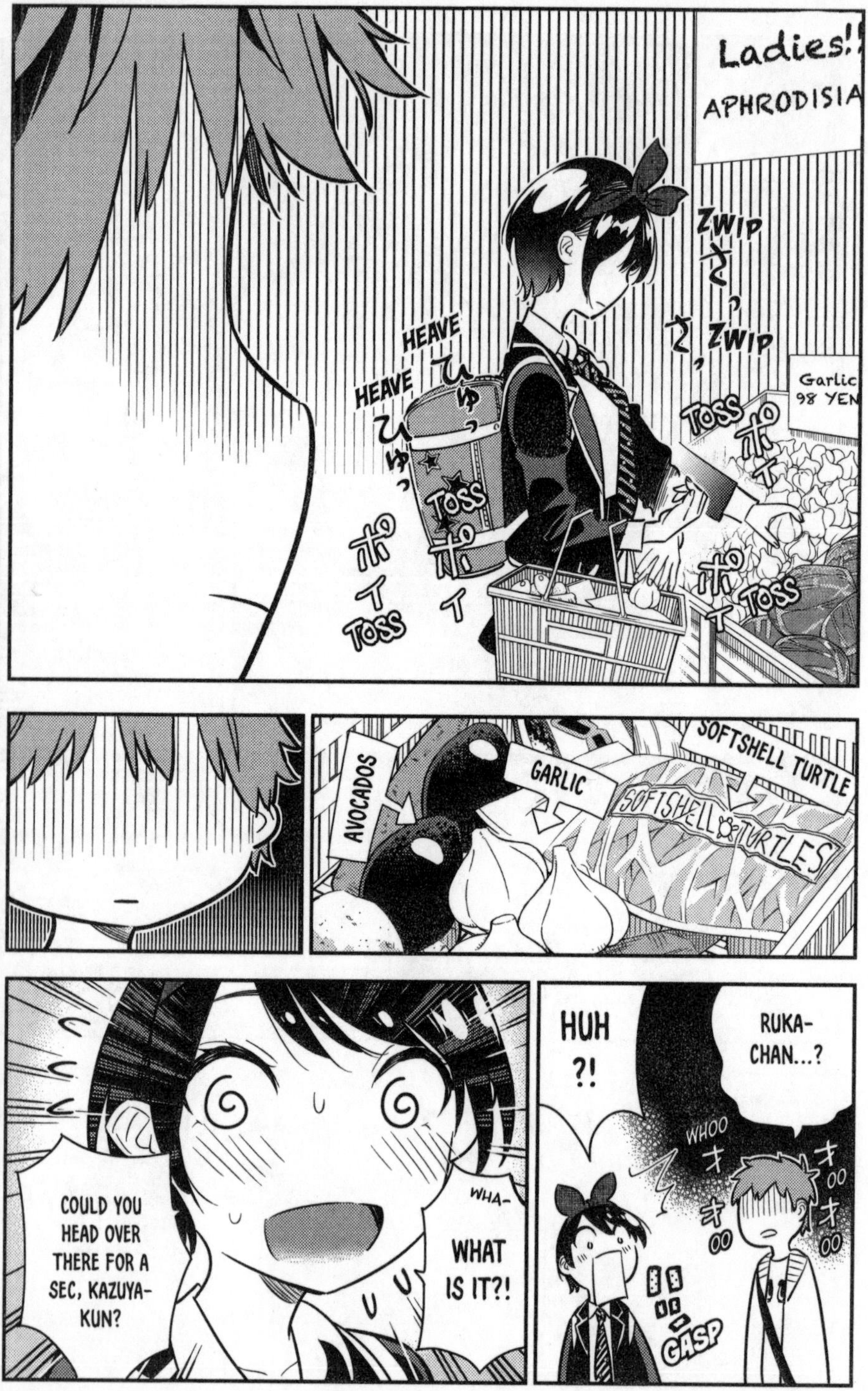

Ladies!!
APHRODISIA
ZWIP さ,
さ, ZWIP
Garlic 98 YEN
TOSS ポイ
TOSS ポイ
HEAVE ひゅっ
HEAVE ひゅっ
TOSS ポイ
ポイ TOSS
SOFTSHELL TURTLE
SOFTSHELL TURTLES
GARLIC
AVOCADOS
RUKA-CHAN...?
HUH ?!
WHOO オオオオ OO
GASP
WHA-
WHAT IS IT?!
COULD YOU HEAD OVER THERE FOR A SEC, KAZUYA-KUN?

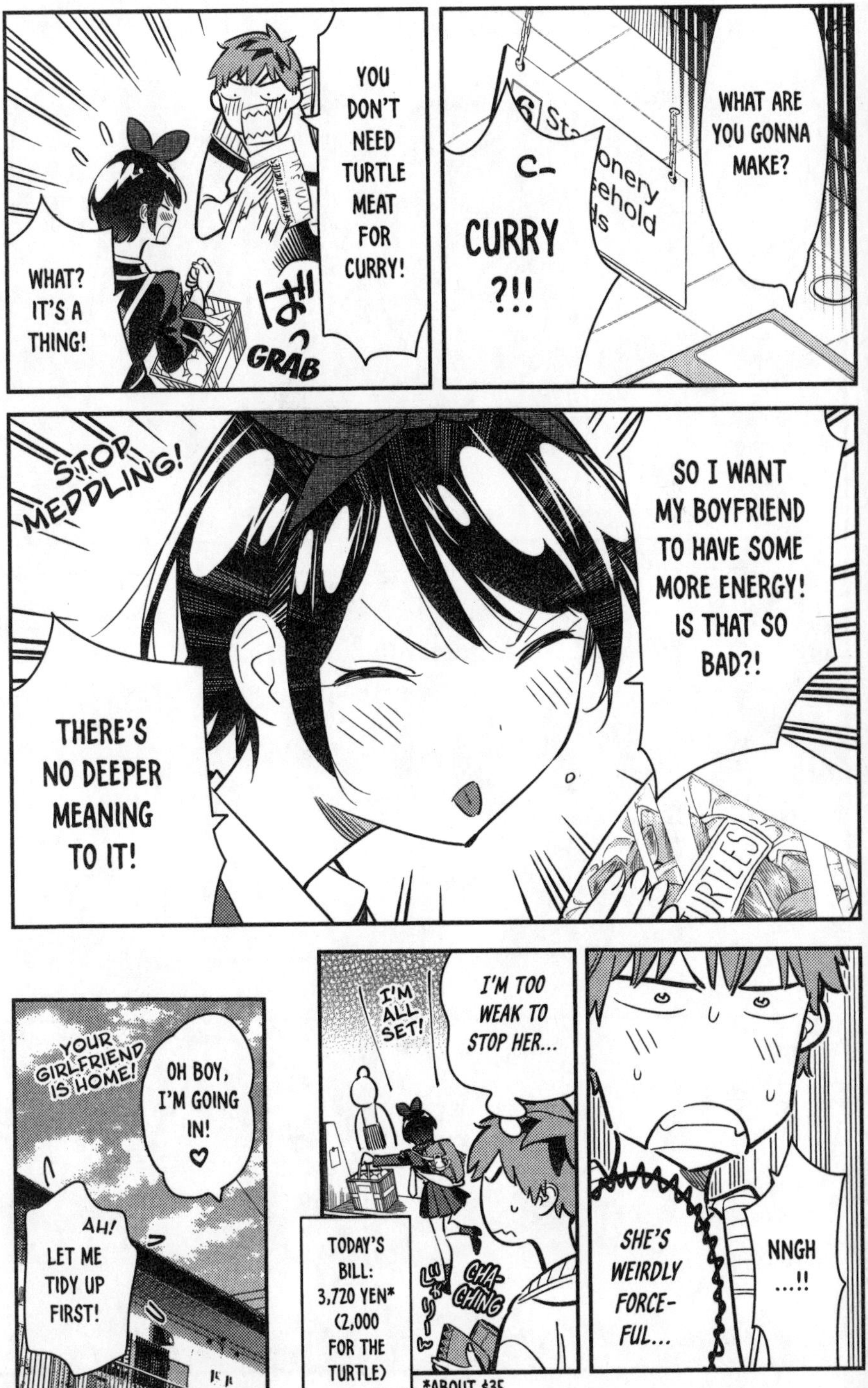
WHAT ARE YOU GONNA MAKE?
C-
CURRY ?!!
YOU DON'T NEED TURTLE MEAT FOR CURRY!
GRAB
WHAT? IT'S A THING!
SO I WANT MY BOYFRIEND TO HAVE SOME MORE ENERGY! IS THAT SO BAD?!
THERE'S NO DEEPER MEANING TO IT!
STOP MEDDLING!
TURTLES
NNGH ...!!
SHE'S WEIRDLY FORCE-FUL...
I'M TOO WEAK TO STOP HER...
I'M ALL SET!
CHA-CHING
TODAY'S BILL: 3,720 YEN* (2,000 FOR THE TURTLE)
YOUR GIRLFRIEND IS HOME!
OH BOY, I'M GOING IN! ♡
AH! LET ME TIDY UP FIRST!

*ABOUT $35.

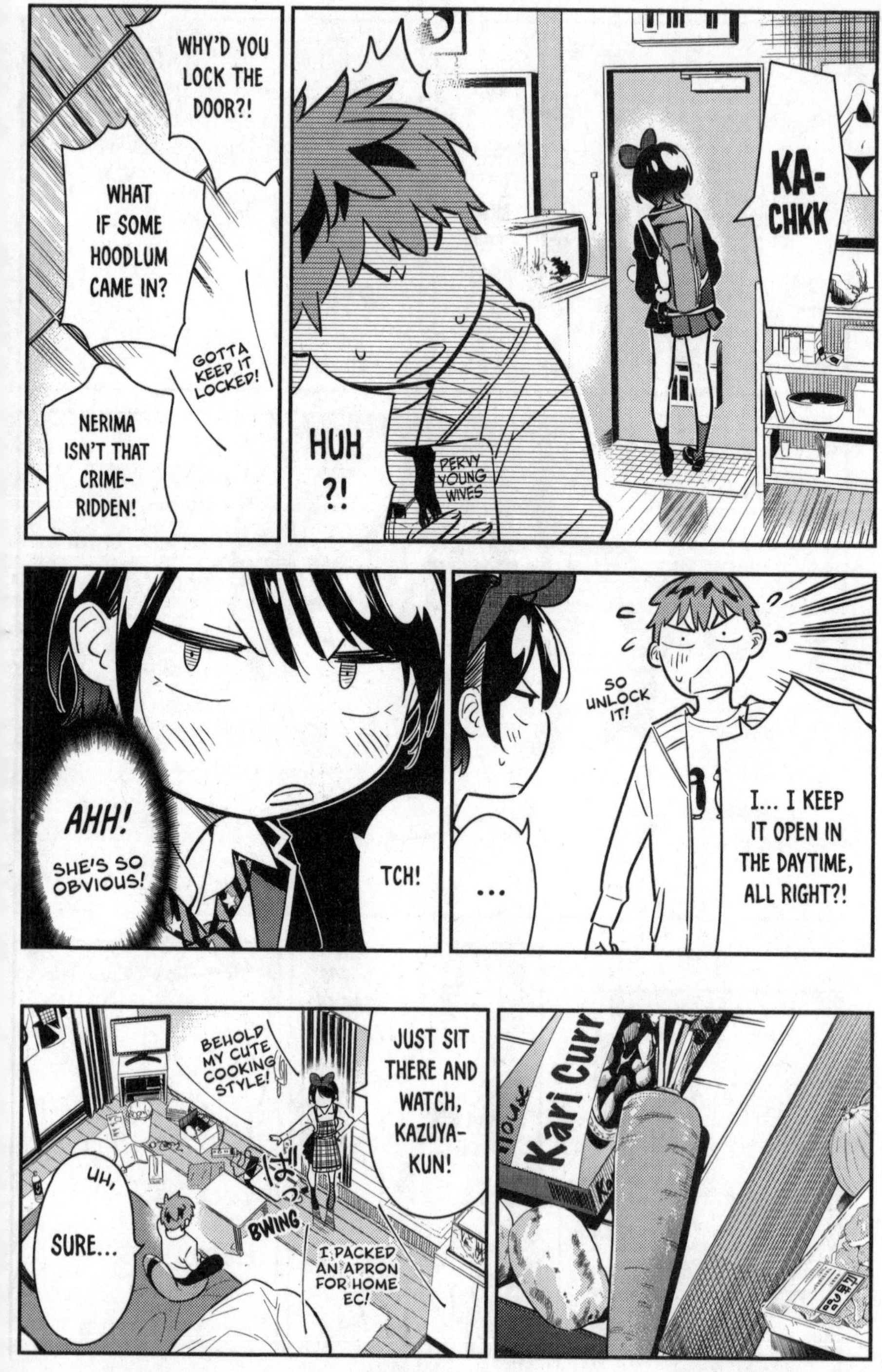
KA-CHKK
PERVY YOUNG WIVES
HUH ?!
WHY'D YOU LOCK THE DOOR?!
WHAT IF SOME HOODLUM CAME IN?
GOTTA KEEP IT LOCKED!
NERIMA ISN'T THAT CRIME-RIDDEN!
SO UNLOCK IT!
I... I KEEP IT OPEN IN THE DAYTIME, ALL RIGHT?!
...
TCH!
AHH!
SHE'S SO OBVIOUS!
Kari Curr
JUST SIT THERE AND WATCH, KAZUYA-KUN!
BEHOLD MY CUTE COOKING STYLE!
BWING
I PACKED AN APRON FOR HOME EC!
UH,
SURE...

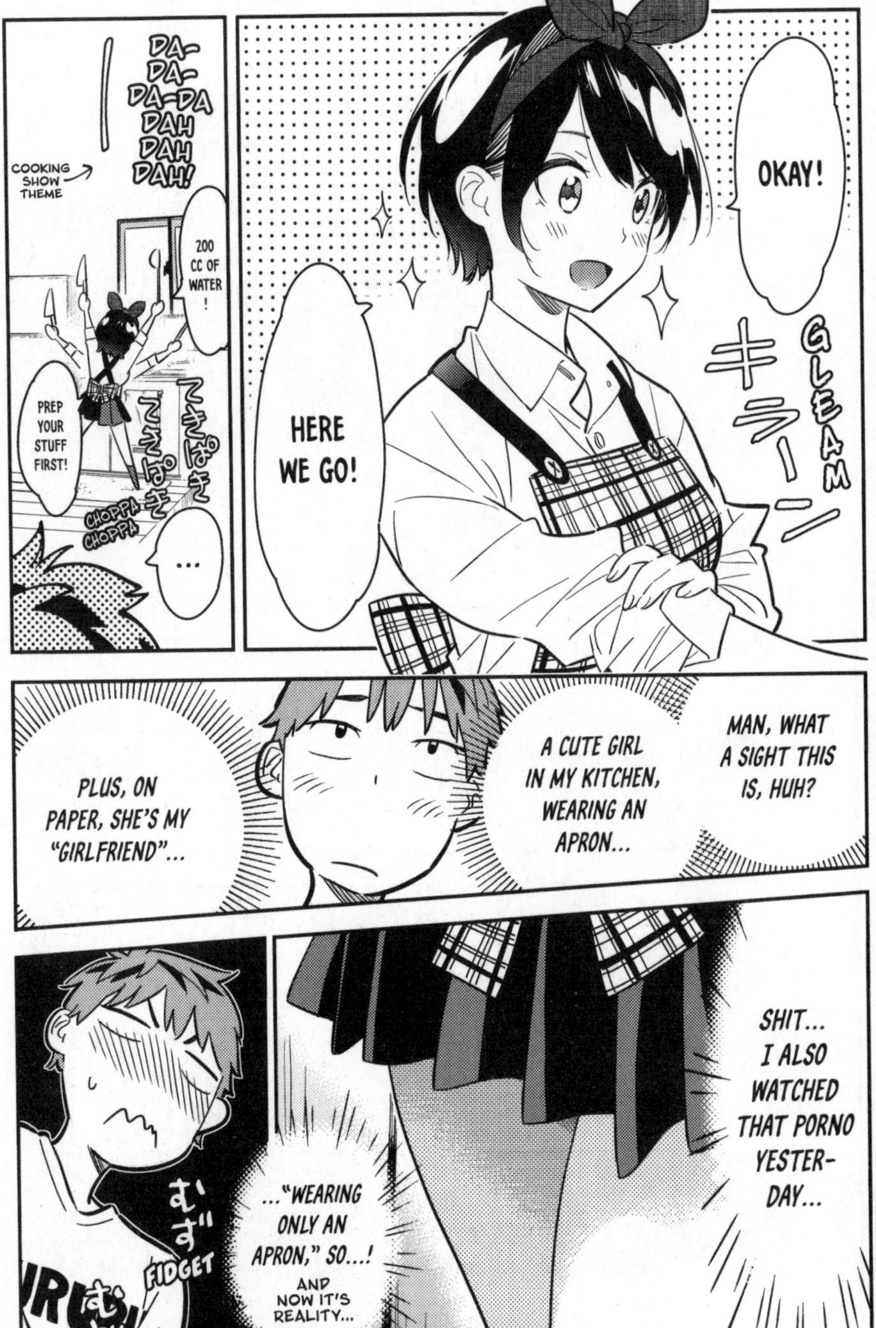
OKAY!
GLEAM
キラーン
HERE WE GO!
DA-DA-DA-DA DAH DAH DAH!
COOKING SHOW THEME
200 CC OF WATER!
PREP YOUR STUFF FIRST!
てきぱき てきぱき
CHOPPA CHOPPA
...
MAN, WHAT A SIGHT THIS IS, HUH?
A CUTE GIRL IN MY KITCHEN, WEARING AN APRON...
PLUS, ON PAPER, SHE'S MY "GIRLFRIEND"...
SHIT... I ALSO WATCHED THAT PORNO YESTER-DAY...
..."WEARING ONLY AN APRON," SO...!
AND NOW IT'S REALITY...
むず
FIDGET
むず
FIDGET

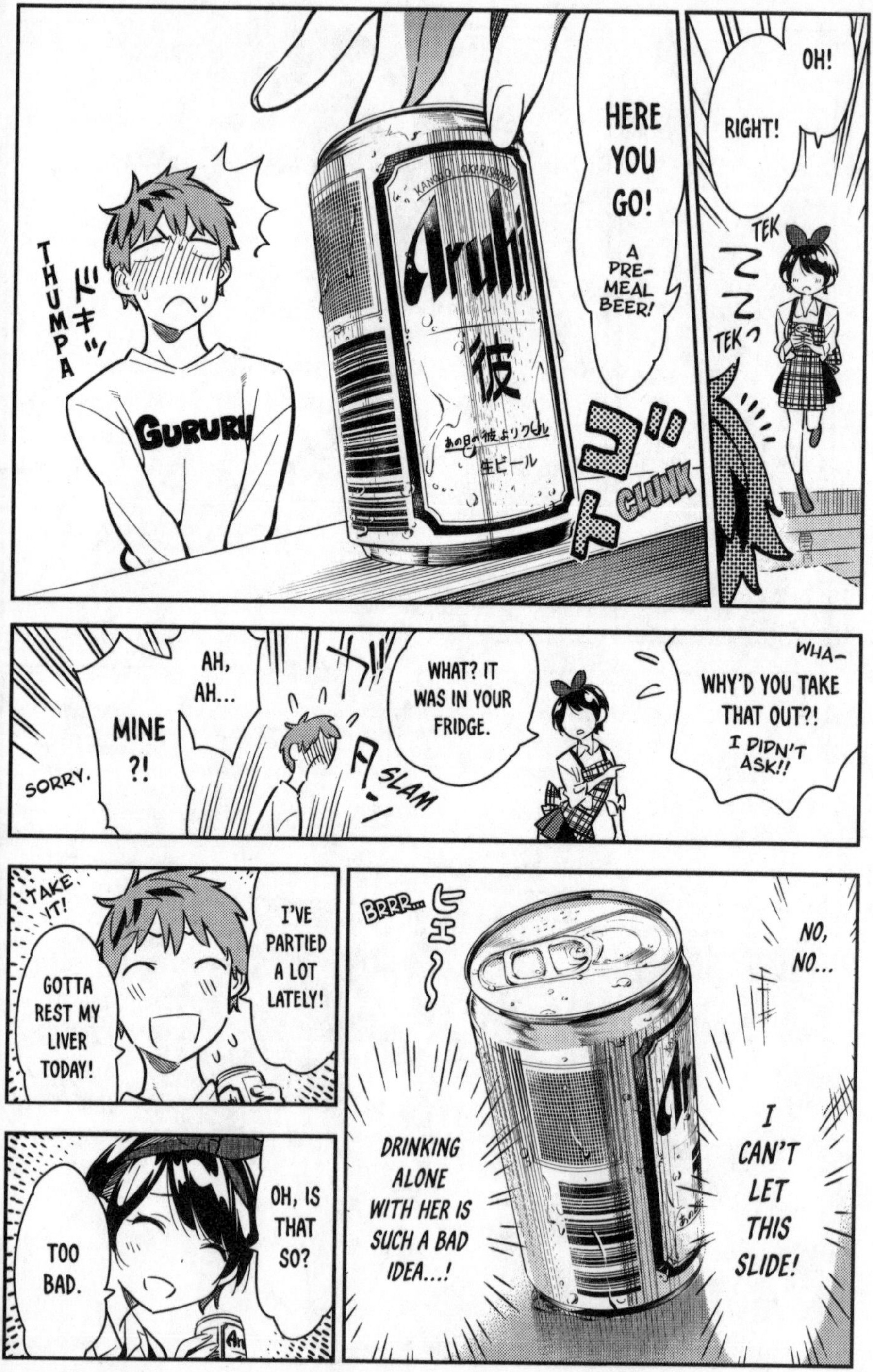
OH!
RIGHT!
TEK
TEK
HERE YOU GO!
A PRE-MEAL BEER!
ゴトッ CLUNK
Aruhi
彼
あの日の彼よりクール
生ビール
ドキッ THUMPA
GURURU
WHA-
WHY'D YOU TAKE THAT OUT?!
I DIDN'T ASK!!
WHAT? IT WAS IN YOUR FRIDGE.
SLAM
AH, AH...
MINE ?!
SORRY.
NO, NO...
I CAN'T LET THIS SLIDE!
DRINKING ALONE WITH HER IS SUCH A BAD IDEA...!
BRRR... ヒェ〜
I'VE PARTIED A LOT LATELY!
TAKE IT!
GOTTA REST MY LIVER TODAY!
OH, IS THAT SO?
TOO BAD.

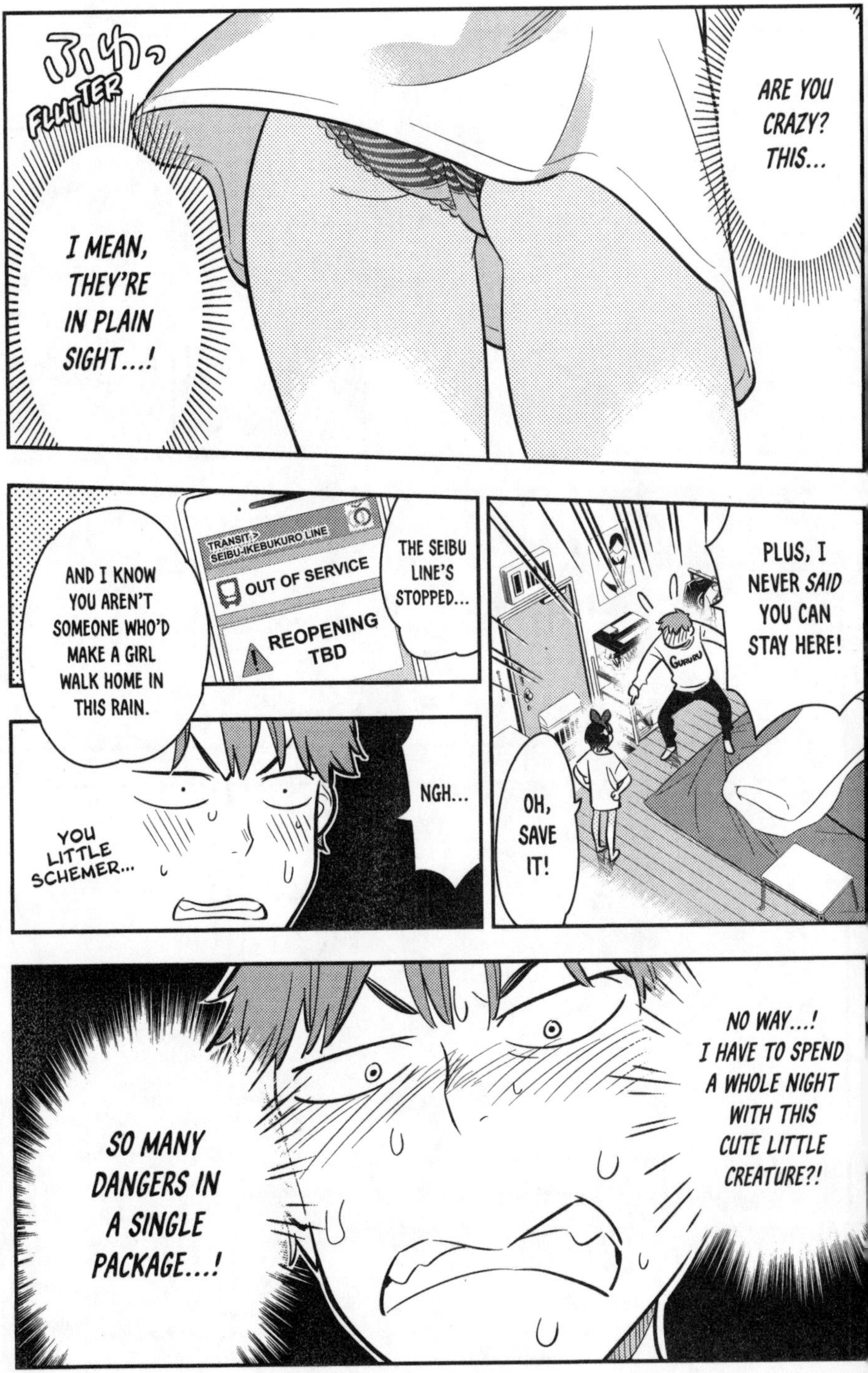
ARE YOU CRAZY? THIS...
ふわっ
FLUTTER
I MEAN, THEY'RE IN PLAIN SIGHT...!
PLUS, I NEVER SAID YOU CAN STAY HERE!
OH, SAVE IT!
THE SEIBU LINE'S STOPPED...
TRANSIT > SEIBU-IKEBUKURO LINE
OUT OF SERVICE
REOPENING TBD
AND I KNOW YOU AREN'T SOMEONE WHO'D MAKE A GIRL WALK HOME IN THIS RAIN.
NGH...
YOU LITTLE SCHEMER...
NO WAY...! I HAVE TO SPEND A WHOLE NIGHT WITH THIS CUTE LITTLE CREATURE?!
SO MANY DANGERS IN A SINGLE PACKAGE...!

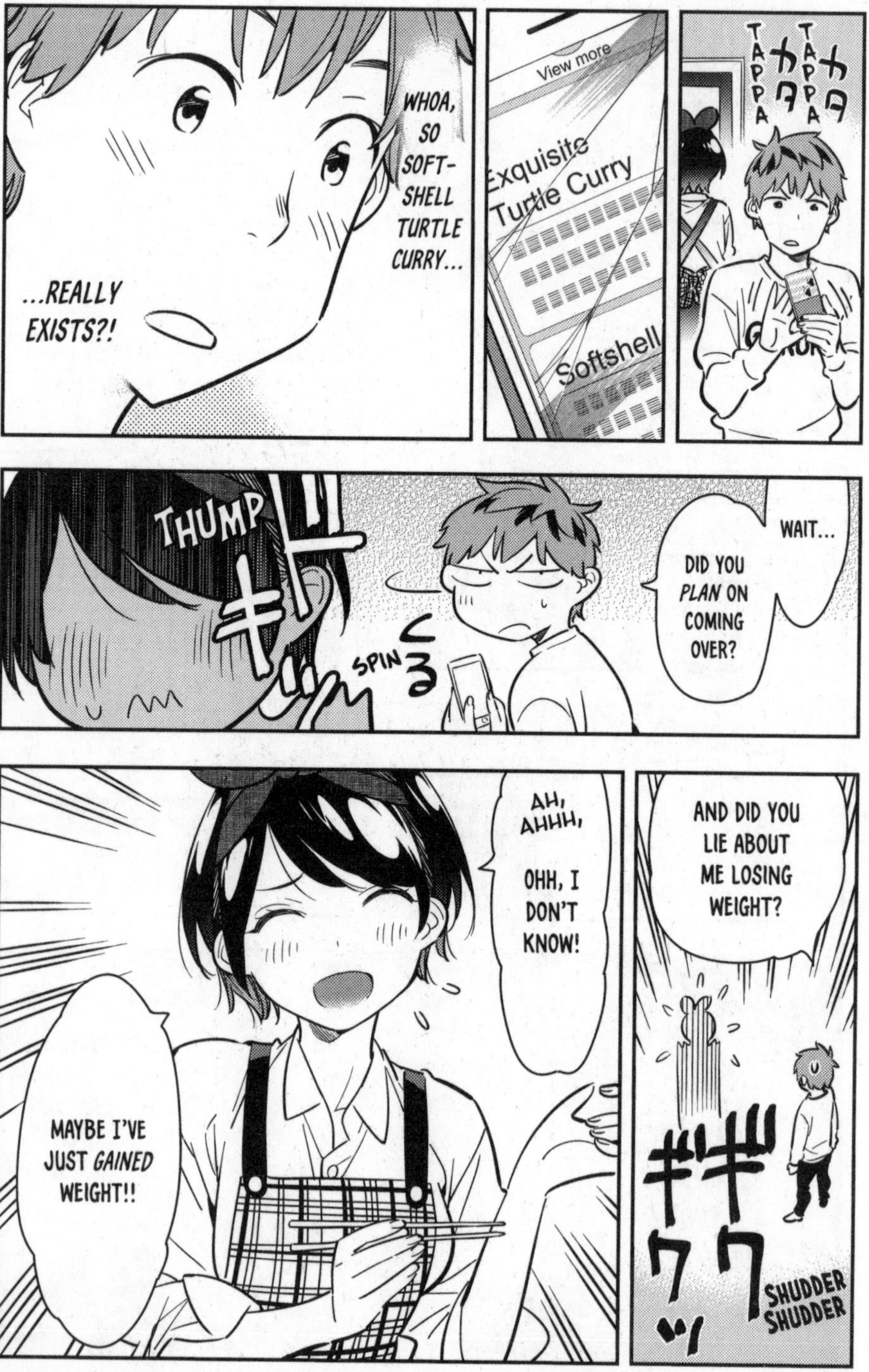
TAPPA TAPPA
View more
Exquisite Turtle Curry
Softshell
WHOA, SO SOFT-SHELL TURTLE CURRY...
...REALLY EXISTS?!
WAIT...
DID YOU PLAN ON COMING OVER?
THUMP
SPIN
AND DID YOU LIE ABOUT ME LOSING WEIGHT?
SHUDDER SHUDDER
AH, AHHH,
OHH, I DON'T KNOW!
MAYBE I'VE JUST GAINED WEIGHT!!

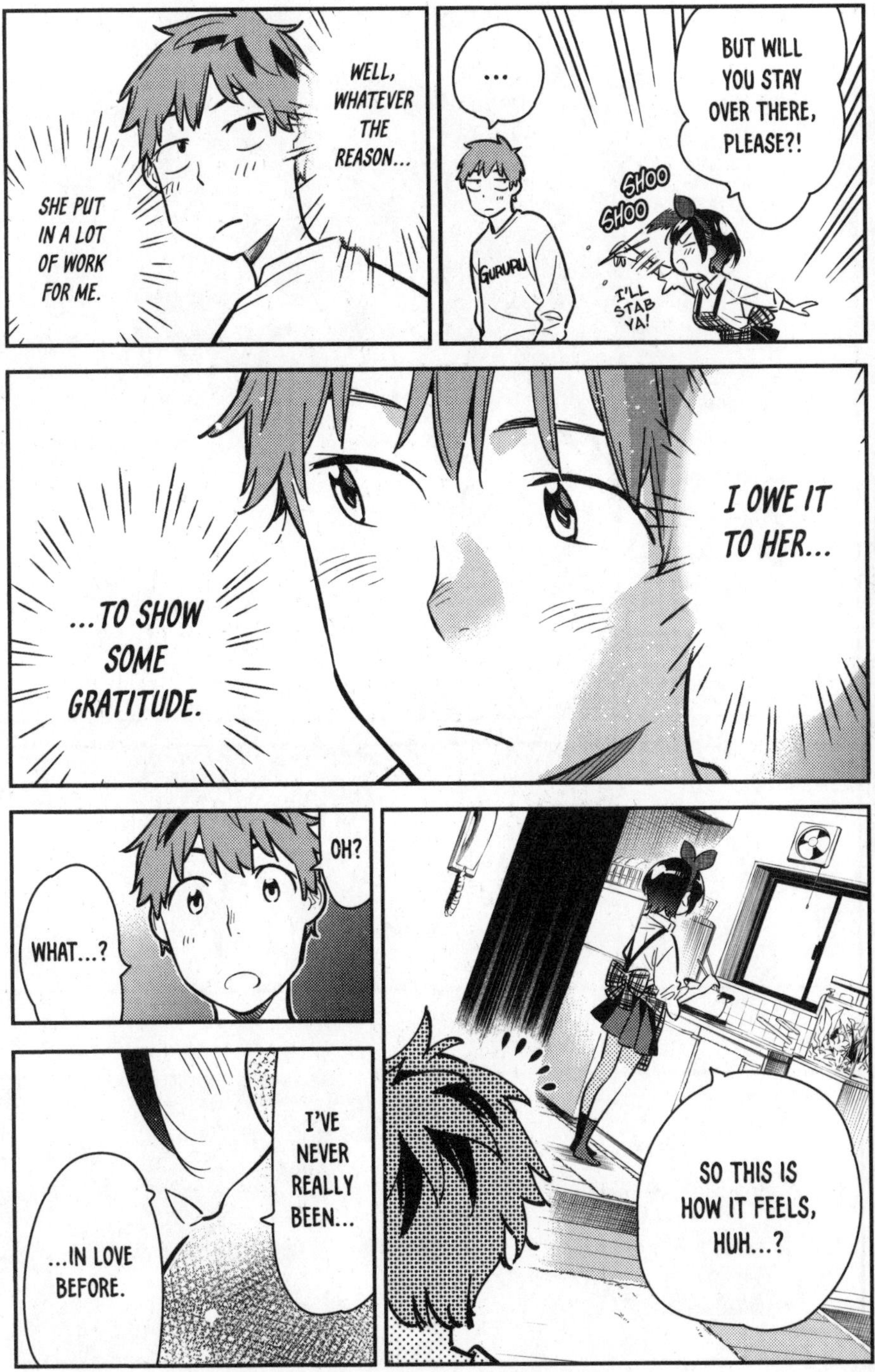
BUT WILL YOU STAY OVER THERE, PLEASE?!
...
SHOO SHOO
I'LL STAB YA!
GURUPU
WELL, WHATEVER THE REASON...
SHE PUT IN A LOT OF WORK FOR ME.
I OWE IT TO HER...
...TO SHOW SOME GRATITUDE.
SO THIS IS HOW IT FEELS, HUH...?
OH?
WHAT...?
I'VE NEVER REALLY BEEN...
...IN LOVE BEFORE.

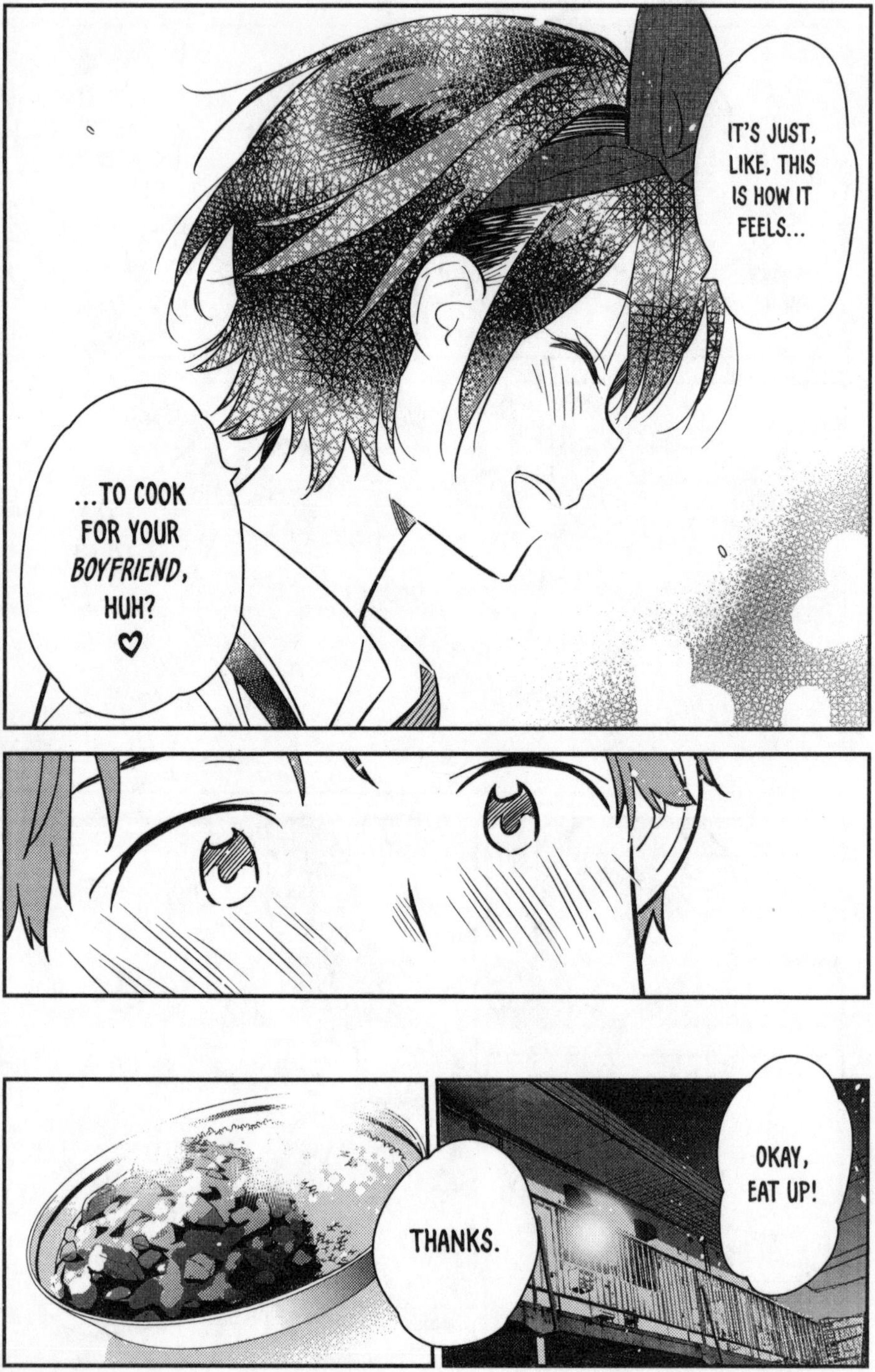
IT'S JUST, LIKE, THIS IS HOW IT FEELS...
...TO COOK FOR YOUR *BOYFRIEND*, HUH? ♡
OKAY, EAT UP!
THANKS.

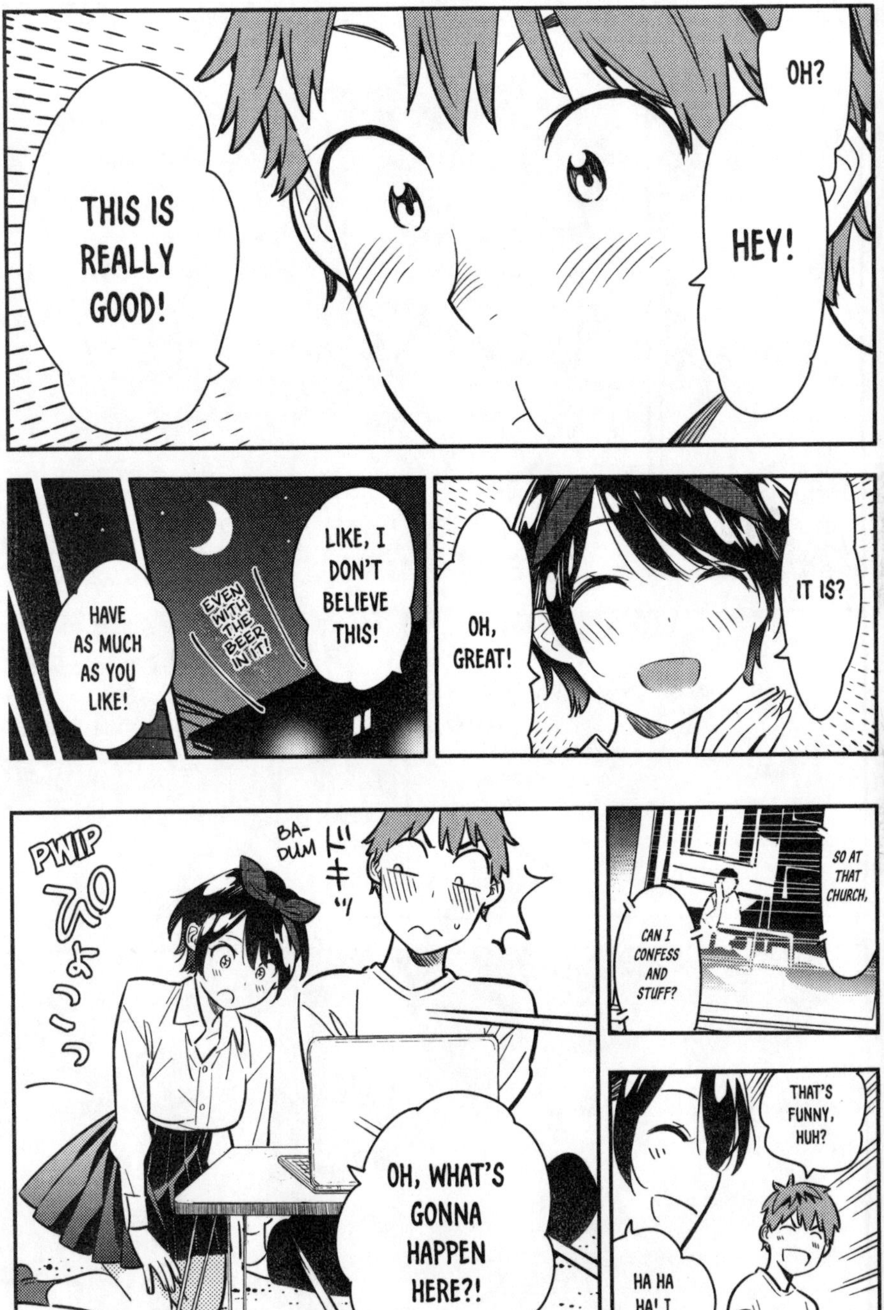
OH?
HEY!
THIS IS REALLY GOOD!
IT IS?
OH, GREAT!
LIKE, I DON'T BELIEVE THIS!
EVEN WITH THE BEER IN IT!
HAVE AS MUCH AS YOU LIKE!
SO AT THAT CHURCH,
CAN I CONFESS AND STUFF?
THAT'S FUNNY, HUH?
HA HA HA! I LIKE IT!
BA-DUM
ドキッ
PWIP
ぴょこっ
OH, WHAT'S GONNA HAPPEN HERE?!

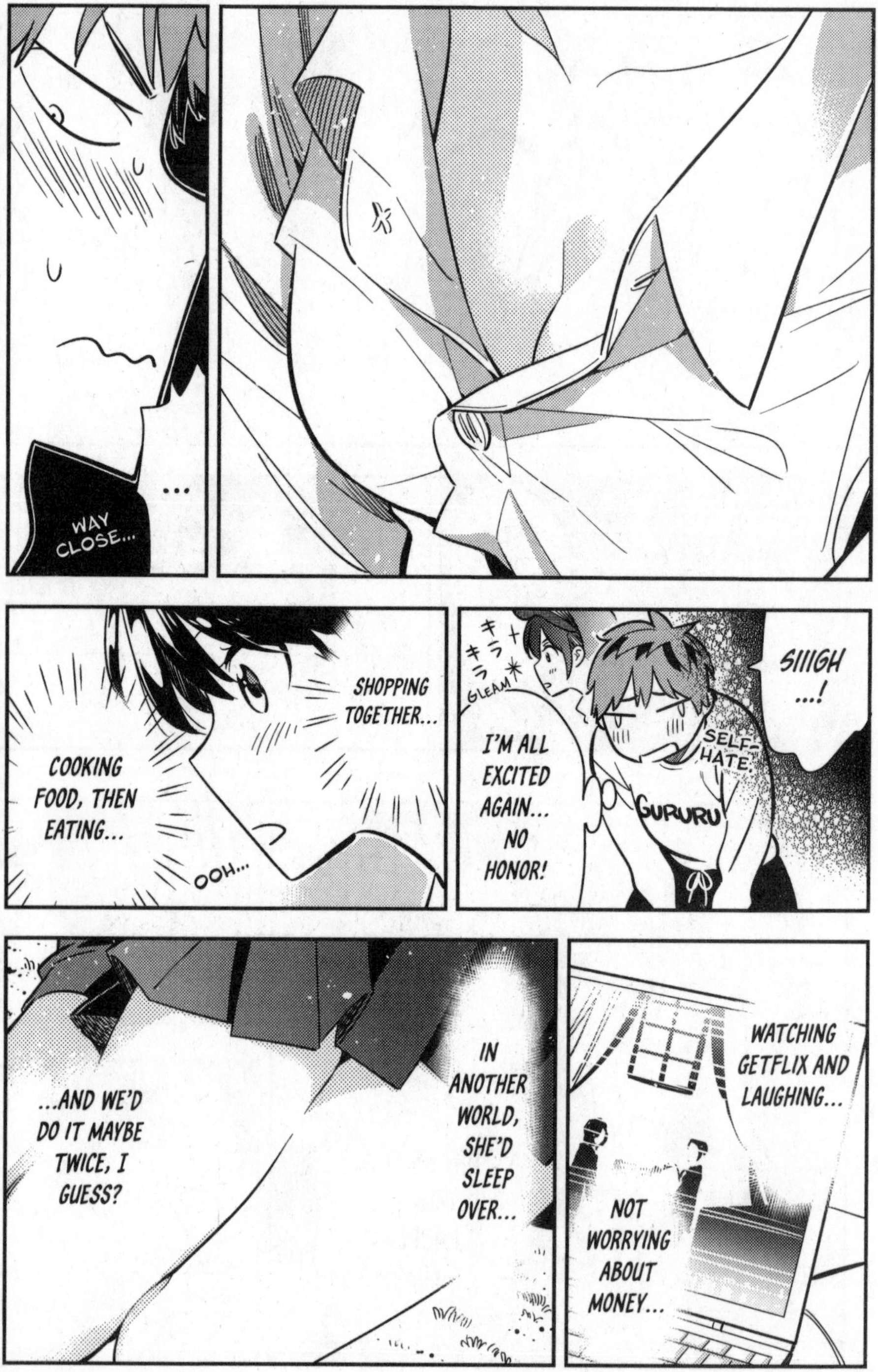
...
WAY CLOSE...
SIIIGH ...!
キラキラ
GLEAM
I'M ALL EXCITED AGAIN... NO HONOR!
SELF-HATE.
GURURU
SHOPPING TOGETHER...
COOKING FOOD, THEN EATING...
OOH...
WATCHING GETFLIX AND LAUGHING...
NOT WORRYING ABOUT MONEY...
IN ANOTHER WORLD, SHE'D SLEEP OVER...
...AND WE'D DO IT MAYBE TWICE, I GUESS?

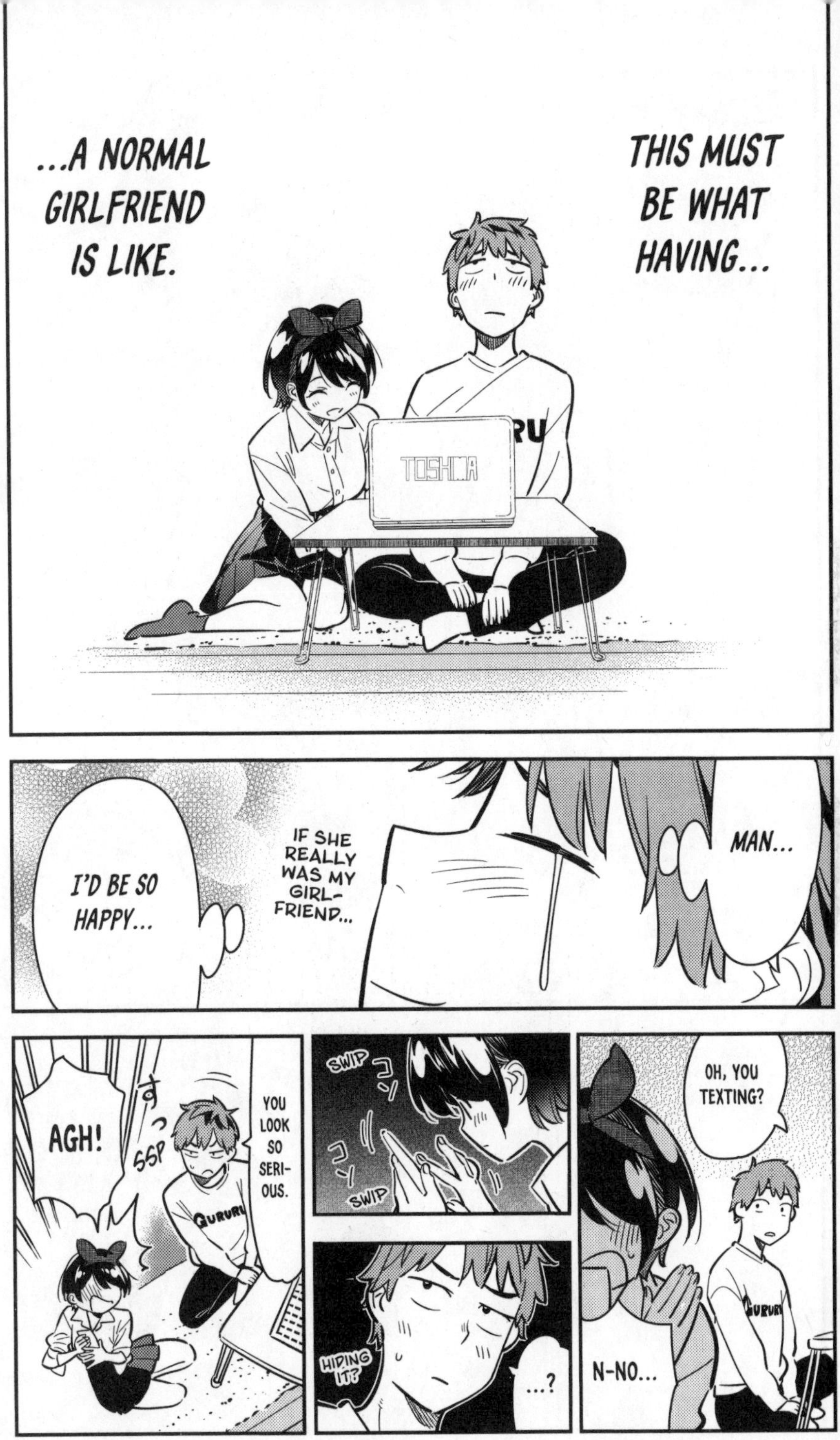

THIS MUST BE WHAT HAVING...
...A NORMAL GIRLFRIEND IS LIKE.
MAN...
IF SHE REALLY WAS MY GIRL-FRIEND...
I'D BE SO HAPPY...
OH, YOU TEXTING?
N-NO...
SWIP
SWIP
...?
HIDING IT?
YOU LOOK SO SERI-OUS.
SSP
AGH!

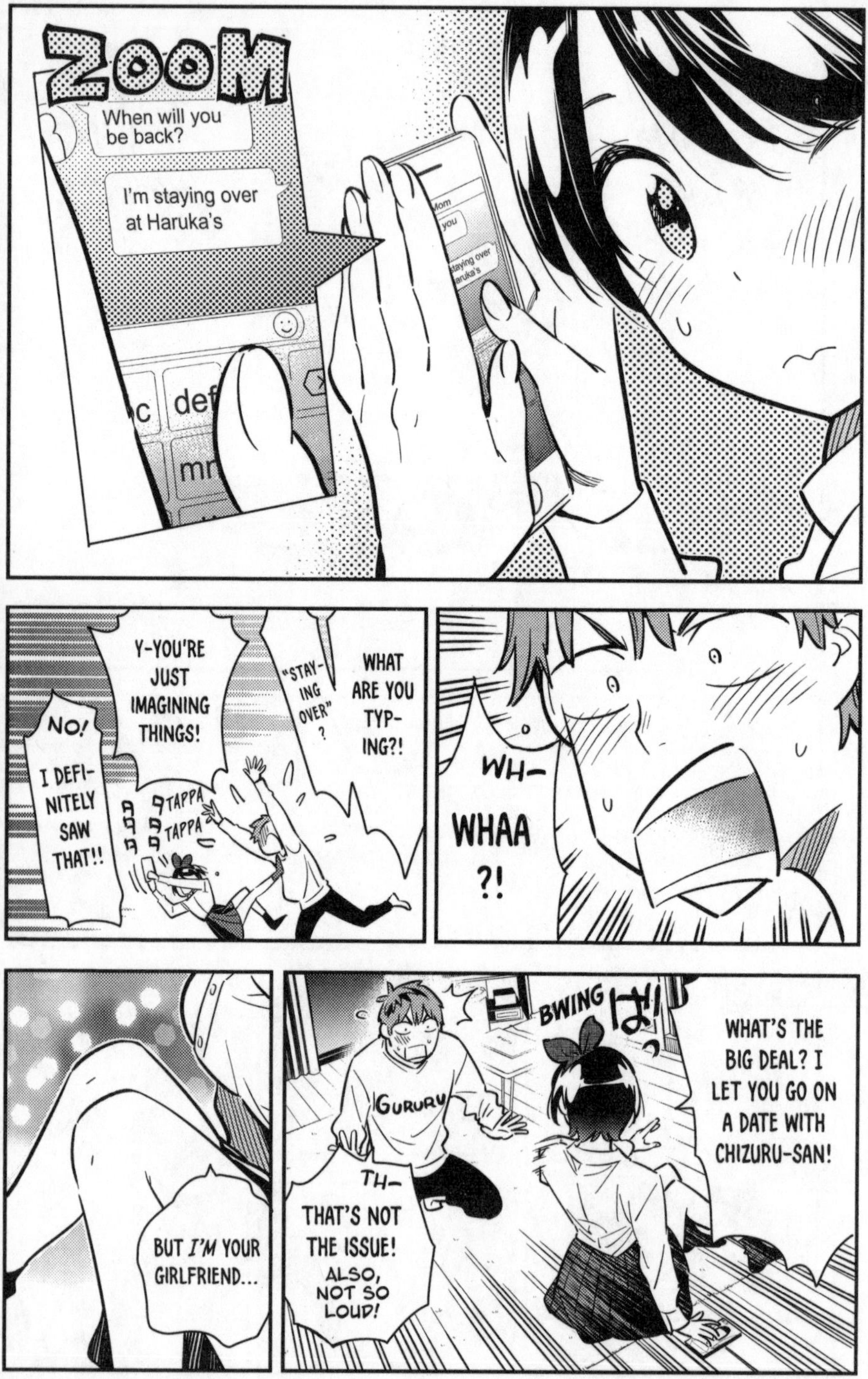
ZOOM
When will you be back?
I'm staying over at Haruka's
WH- WHAA ?!
WHAT ARE YOU TYP- ING?!
"STAY- ING OVER" ?
Y-YOU'RE JUST IMAGINING THINGS!
NO! I DEFI- NITELY SAW THAT!!
TAPPA TAPPA
WHAT'S THE BIG DEAL? I LET YOU GO ON A DATE WITH CHIZURU-SAN!
BWING
GURURU
TH- THAT'S NOT THE ISSUE!
ALSO, NOT SO LOUD!
BUT *I'M* YOUR GIRLFRIEND...

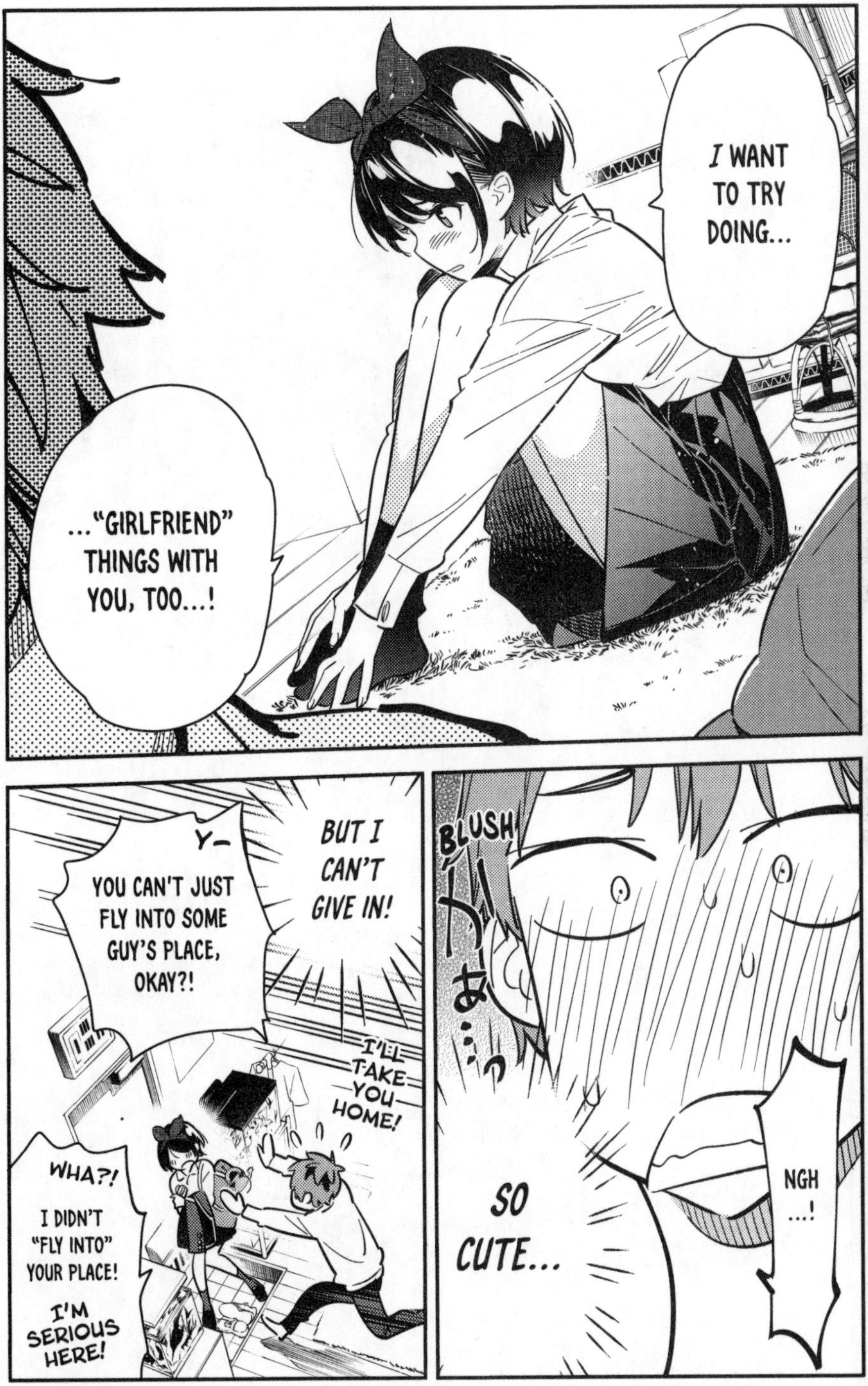
I WANT TO TRY DOING...
..."GIRLFRIEND" THINGS WITH YOU, TOO...!
BLUSH
かあ…っ
NGH ...!
SO CUTE...
BUT I CAN'T GIVE IN!
Y— YOU CAN'T JUST FLY INTO SOME GUY'S PLACE, OKAY?!
I'LL TAKE YOU HOME!
WHA?!
I DIDN'T "FLY INTO" YOUR PLACE!
I'M SERIOUS HERE!

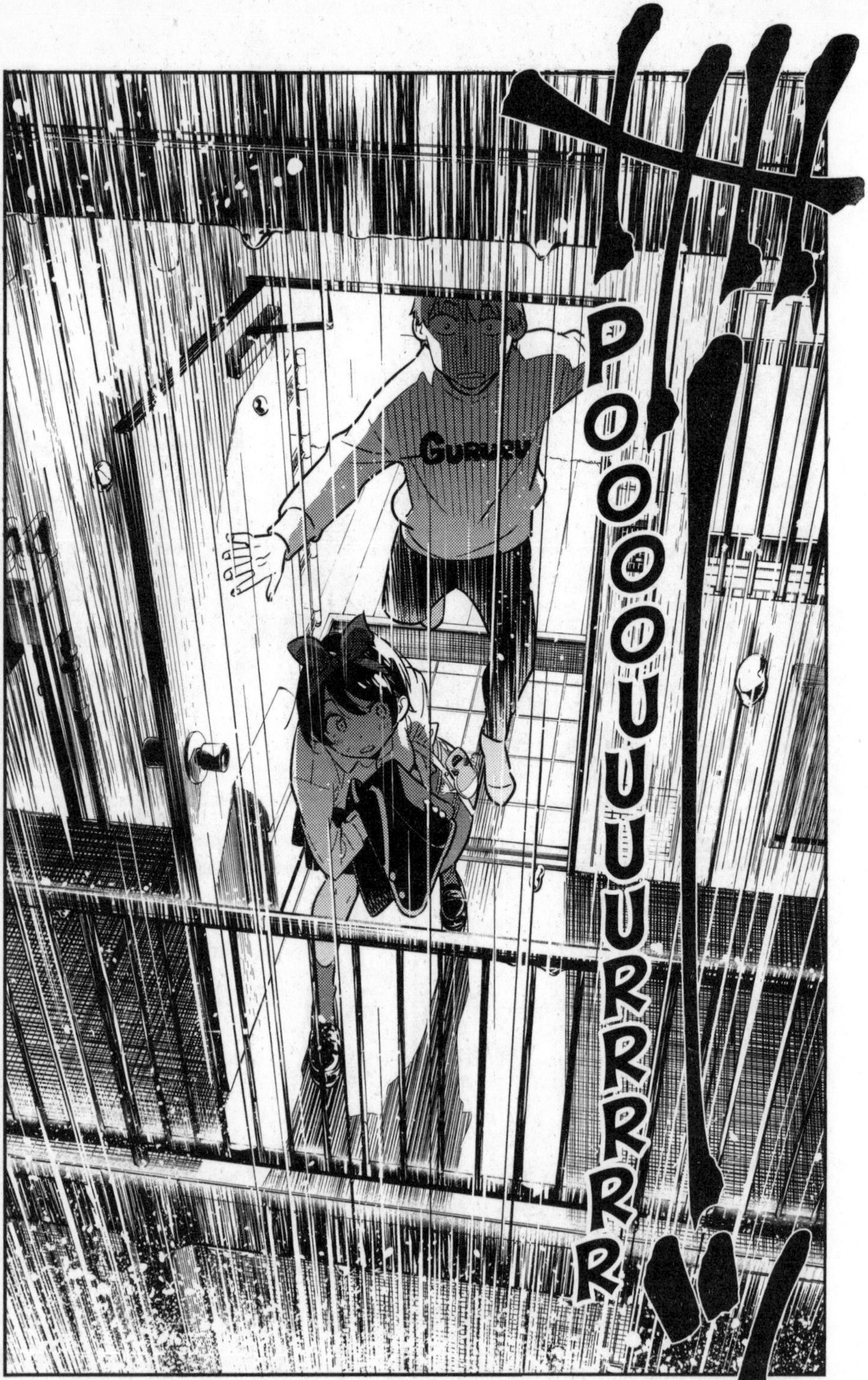
POOOOOUUURRRRR
GURURU

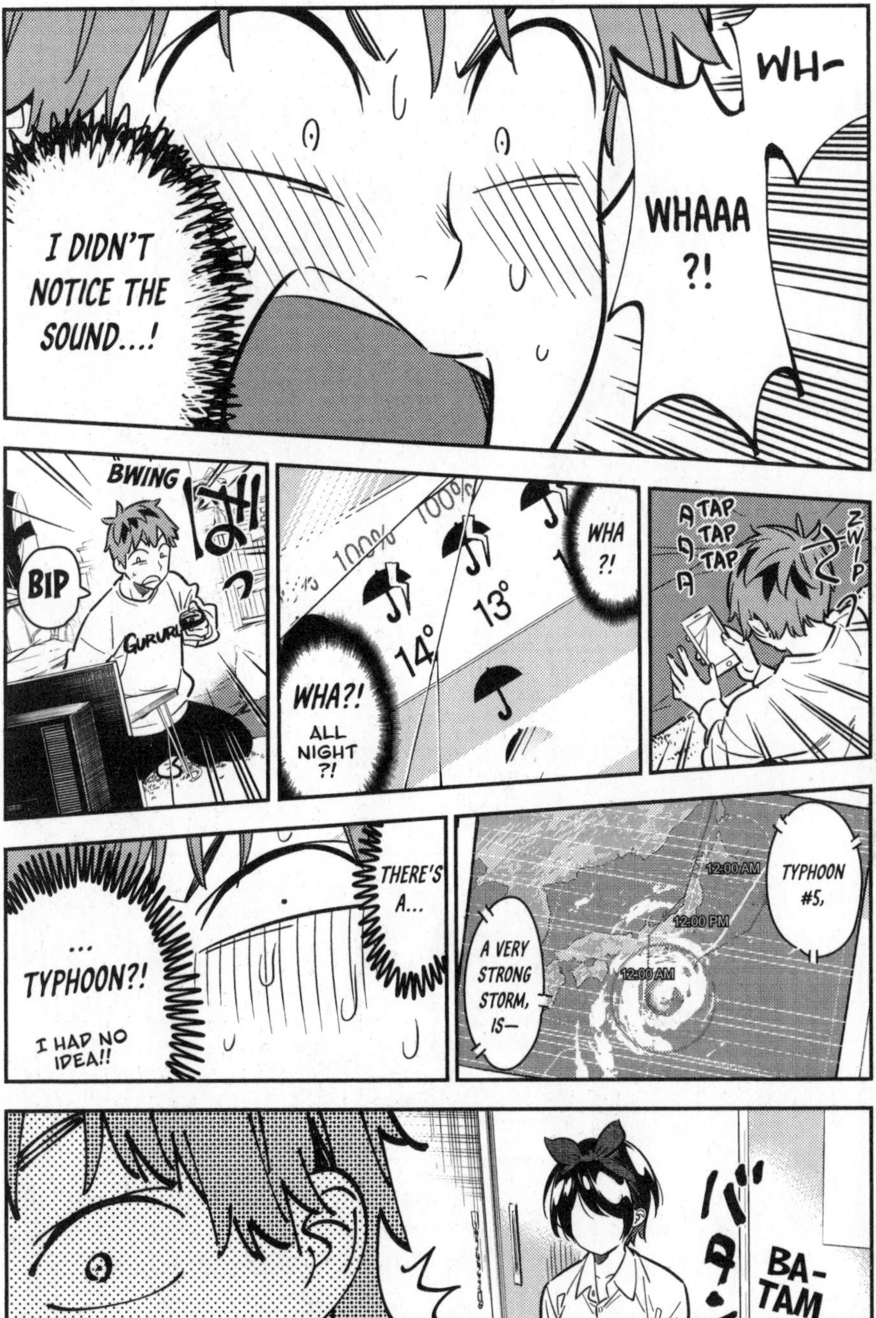
WH-
WHAAA ?!
I DIDN'T NOTICE THE SOUND...!
TAP TAP TAP
ZWIP
WHA ?!
100%
100%
13°
14°
WHA?!
ALL NIGHT ?!
BWING
はっ
BIP
GURURU
TYPHOON #5,
12:00 AM
12:00 PM
12:00 AM
A VERY STRONG STORM, IS—
THERE'S A...
... TYPHOON?!
I HAD NO IDEA!!
バタン
BA-TAM

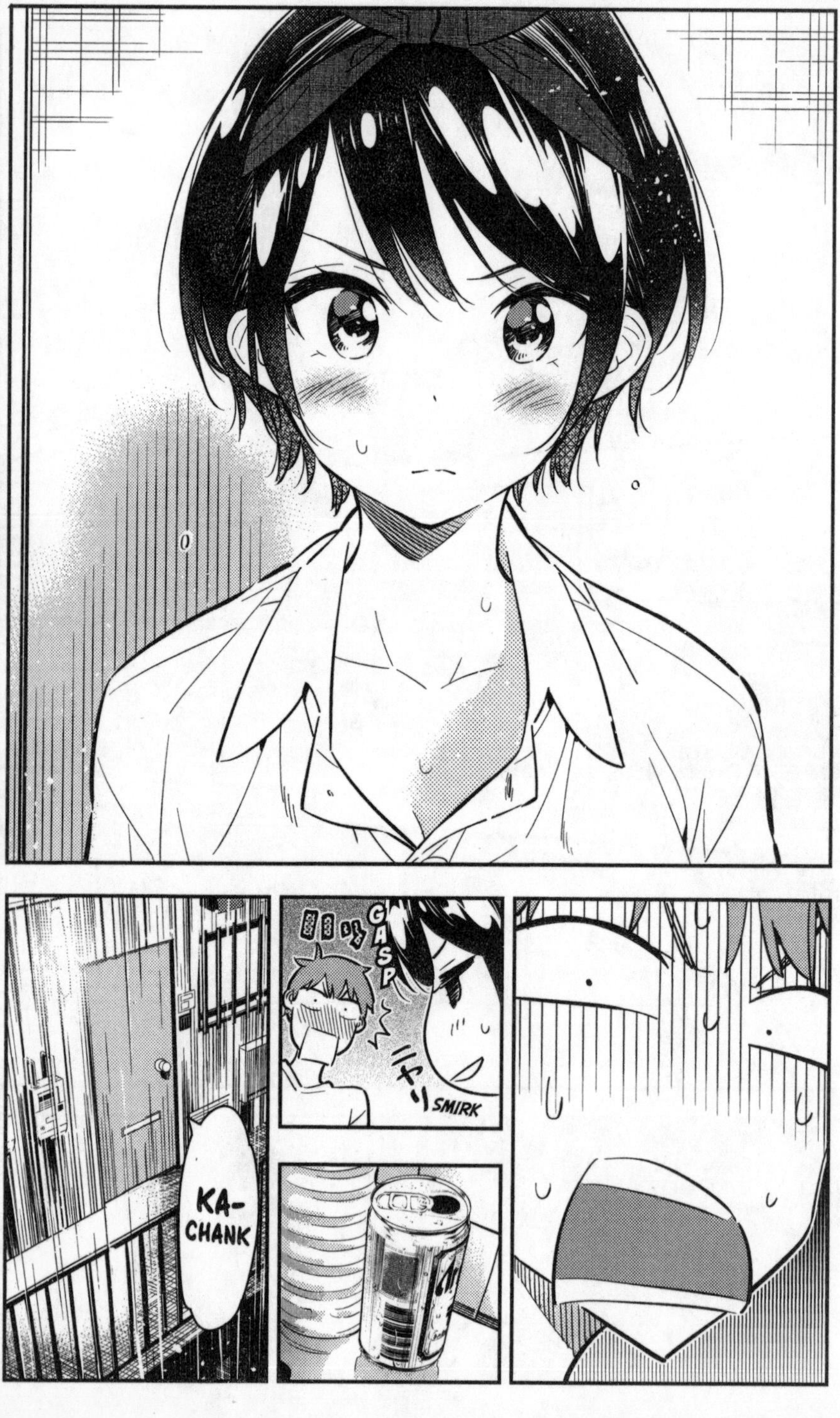
GASP
SMIRK
KA-
CHANK

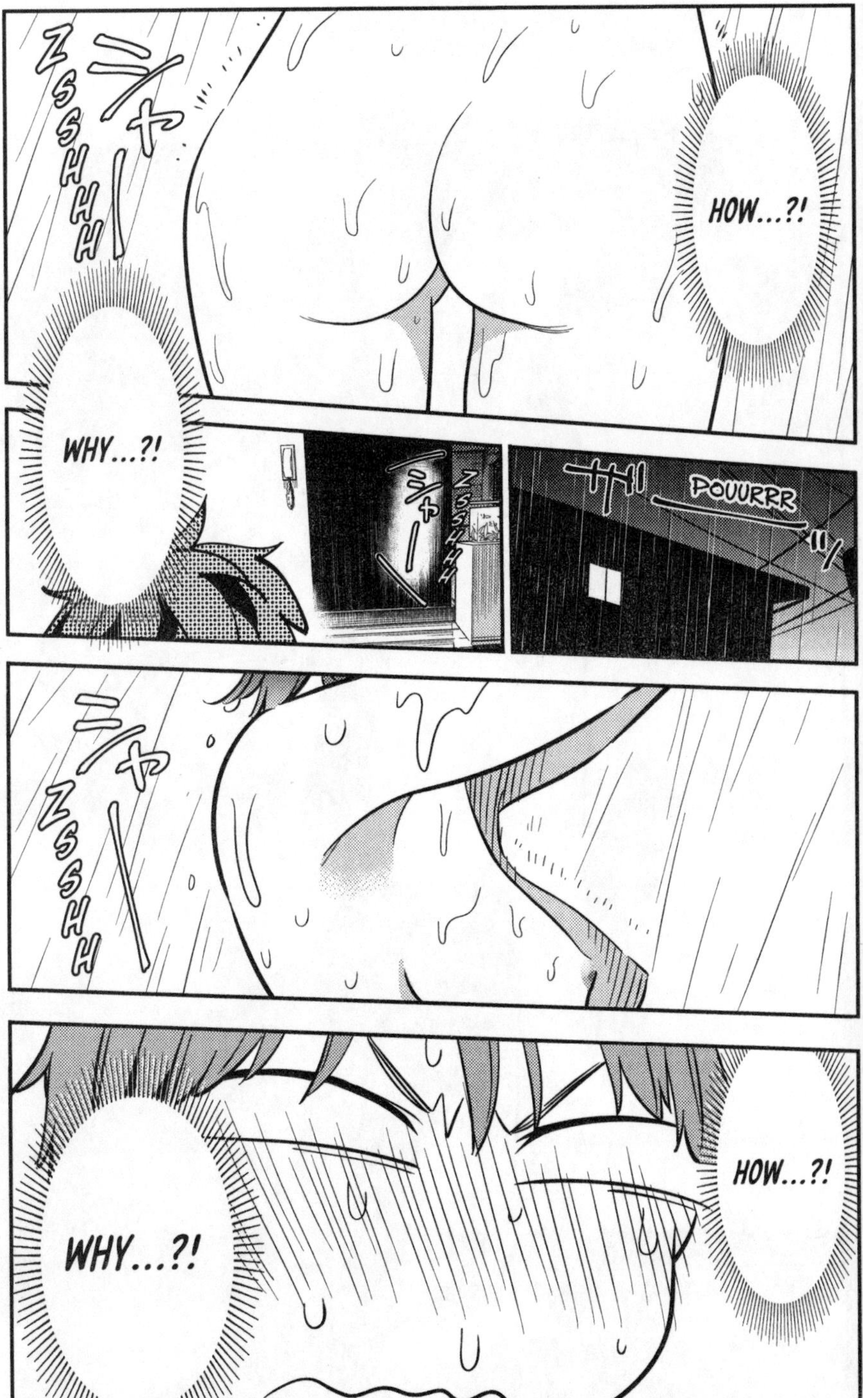
HOW...?!
ZSSHHH
WHY...?!
POUURRR
ZSSHHH
ZSSHHH
HOW...?!
WHY...?!

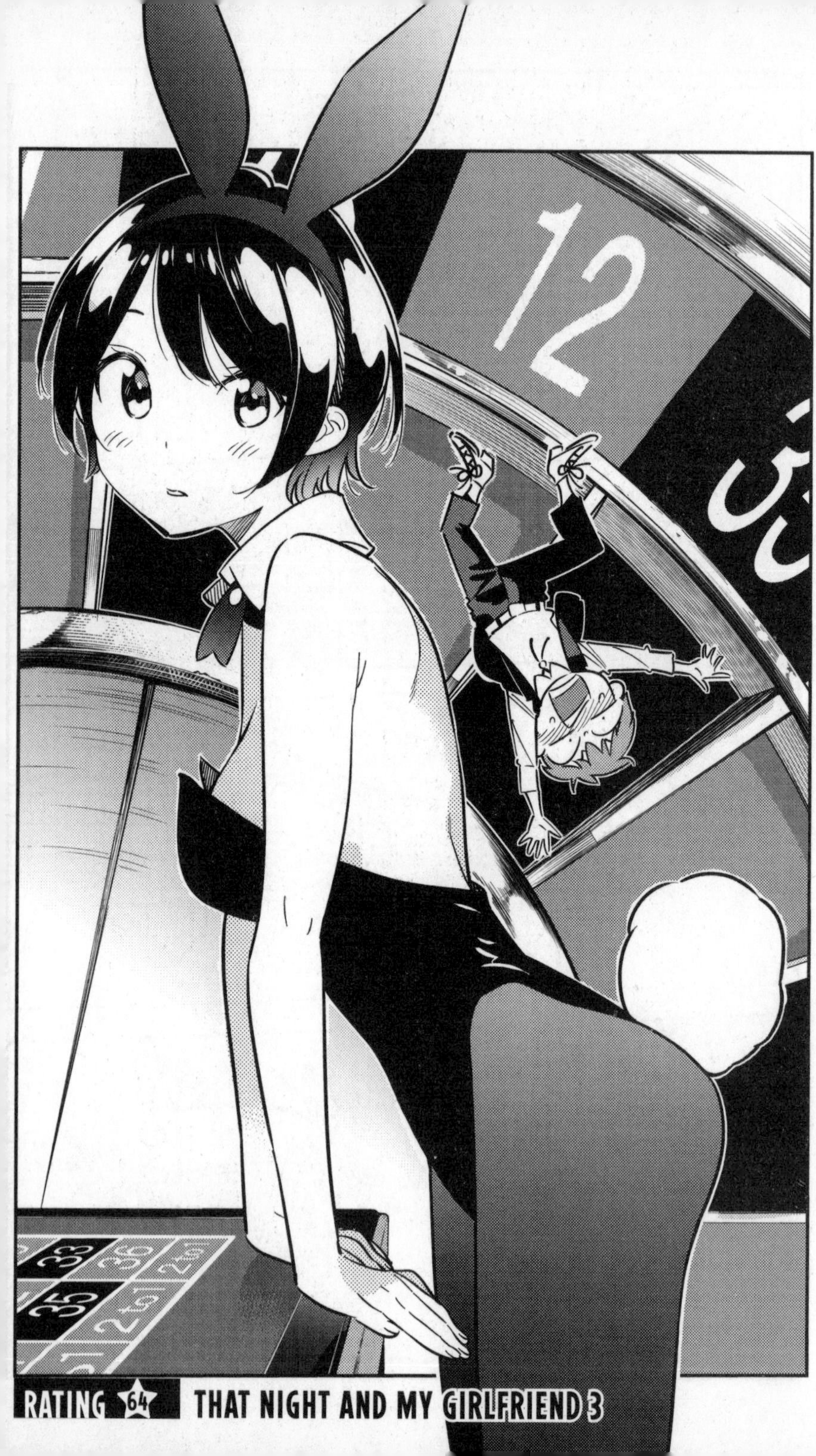
12

RATING 64 THAT NIGHT AND MY GIRLFRIEND 3

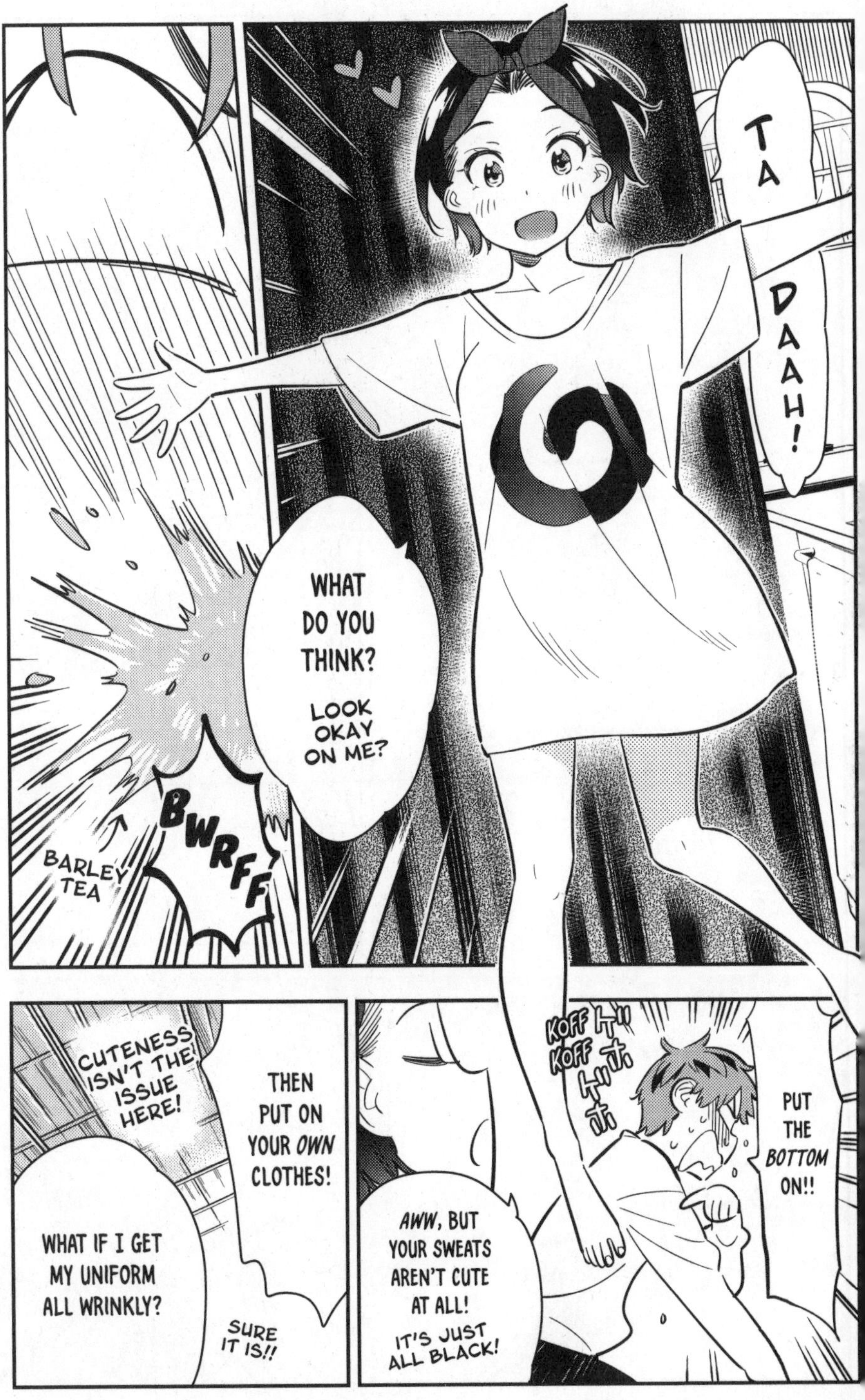

TA DAAH!
WHAT DO YOU THINK?
LOOK OKAY ON ME?
BWRFFF
BARLEY TEA
KOFF KOFF
PUT THE *BOTTOM* ON!!
AWW, BUT YOUR SWEATS AREN'T CUTE AT ALL!
IT'S JUST ALL BLACK!
THEN PUT ON YOUR *OWN* CLOTHES!
CUTENESS ISN'T THE ISSUE HERE!
WHAT IF I GET MY UNIFORM ALL WRINKLY?
SURE IT IS!!

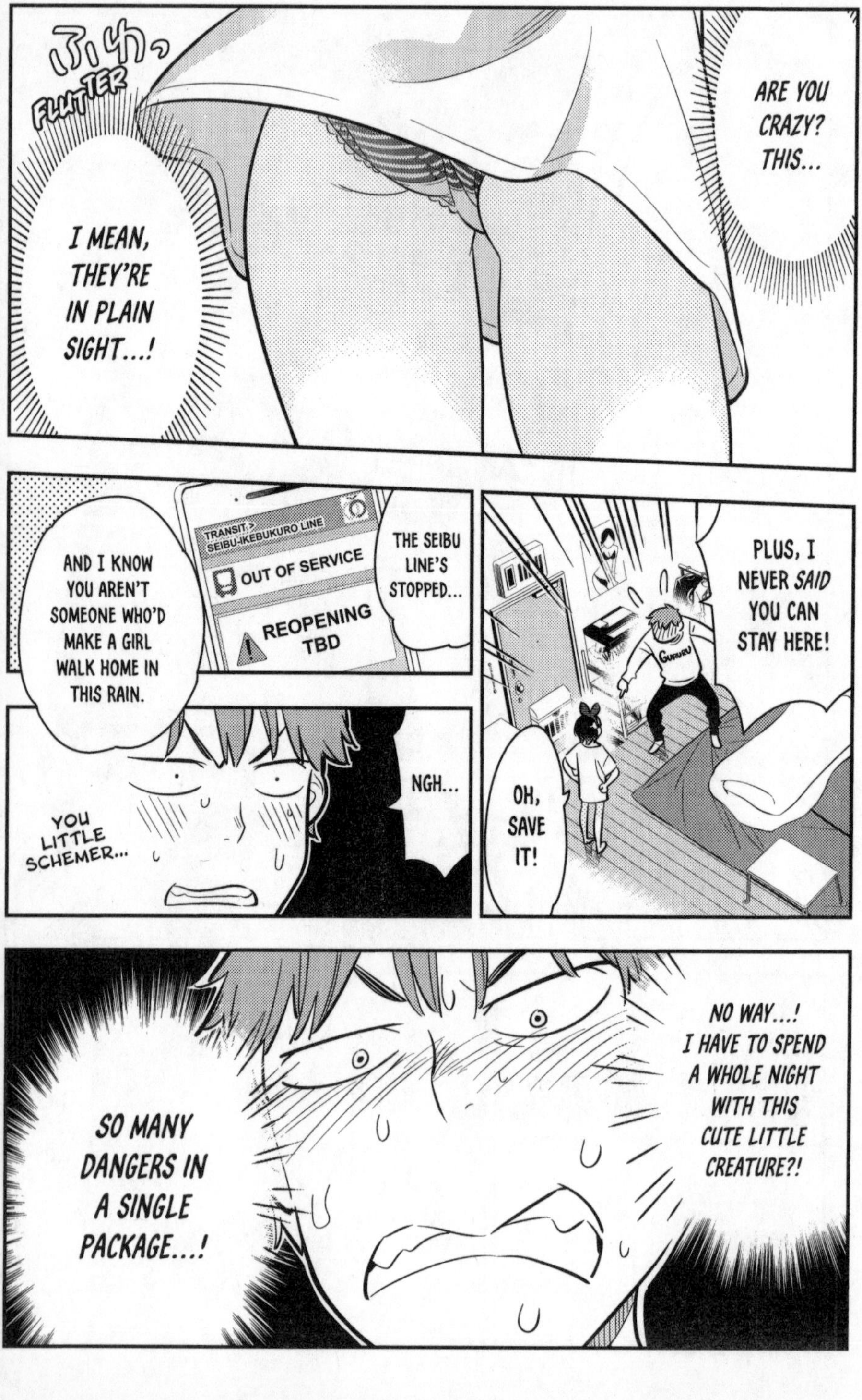
ARE YOU CRAZY? THIS...
ふわっ
FLUTTER
I MEAN, THEY'RE IN PLAIN SIGHT...!
PLUS, I NEVER *SAID* YOU CAN STAY HERE!
GURURU
OH, SAVE IT!
THE SEIBU LINE'S STOPPED...
TRANSIT > SEIBU-IKEBUKURO LINE
OUT OF SERVICE
REOPENING TBD
AND I KNOW YOU AREN'T SOMEONE WHO'D MAKE A GIRL WALK HOME IN THIS RAIN.
NGH...
YOU LITTLE SCHEMER...
NO WAY...! I HAVE TO SPEND A WHOLE NIGHT WITH THIS CUTE LITTLE CREATURE?!
SO MANY DANGERS IN A SINGLE PACKAGE...!

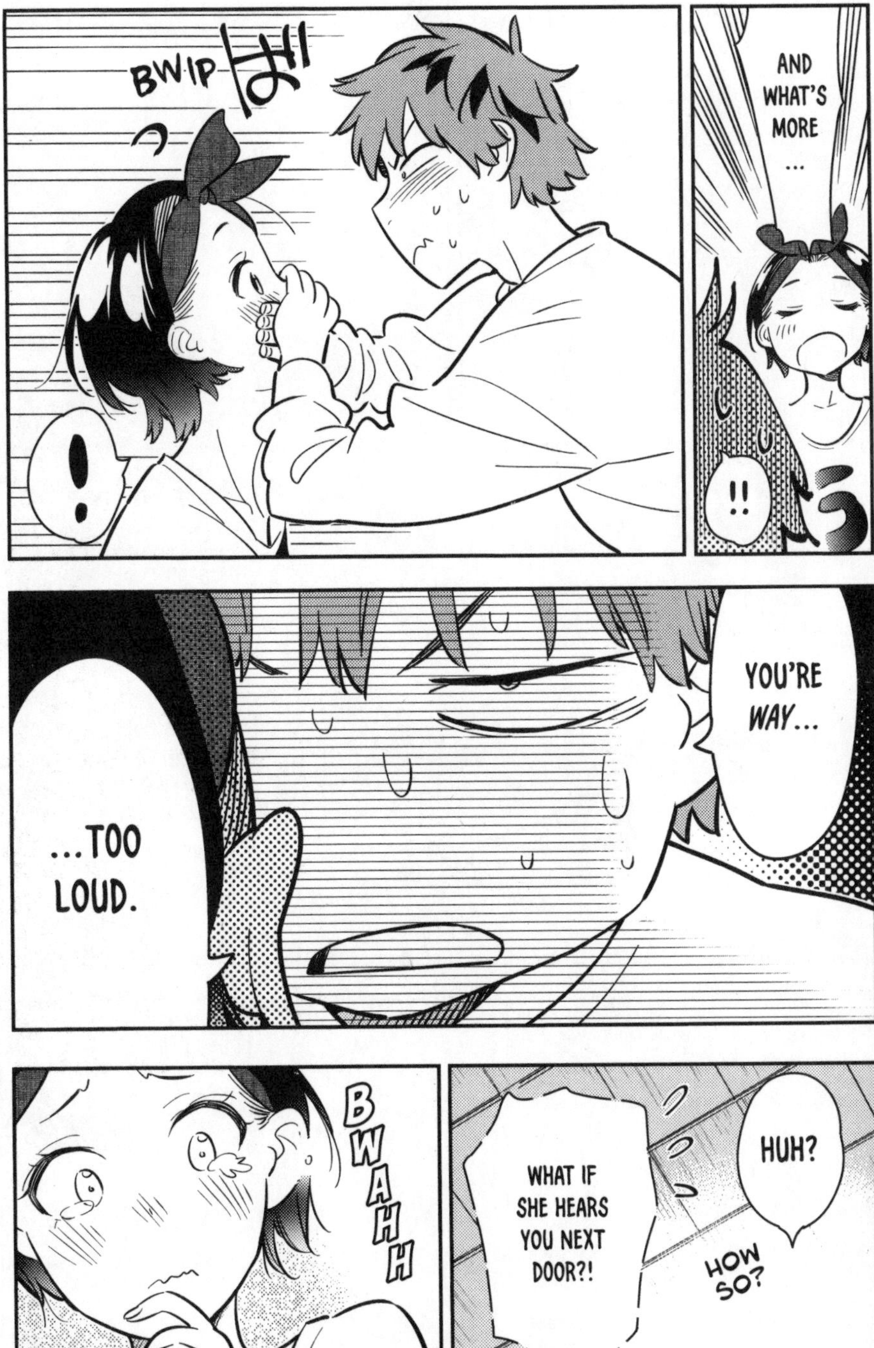
AND WHAT'S MORE ...
!!
BWIP
!
YOU'RE *WAY*...
...TOO LOUD.
HUH?
HOW SO?
WHAT IF SHE HEARS YOU NEXT DOOR?!
BWAHH

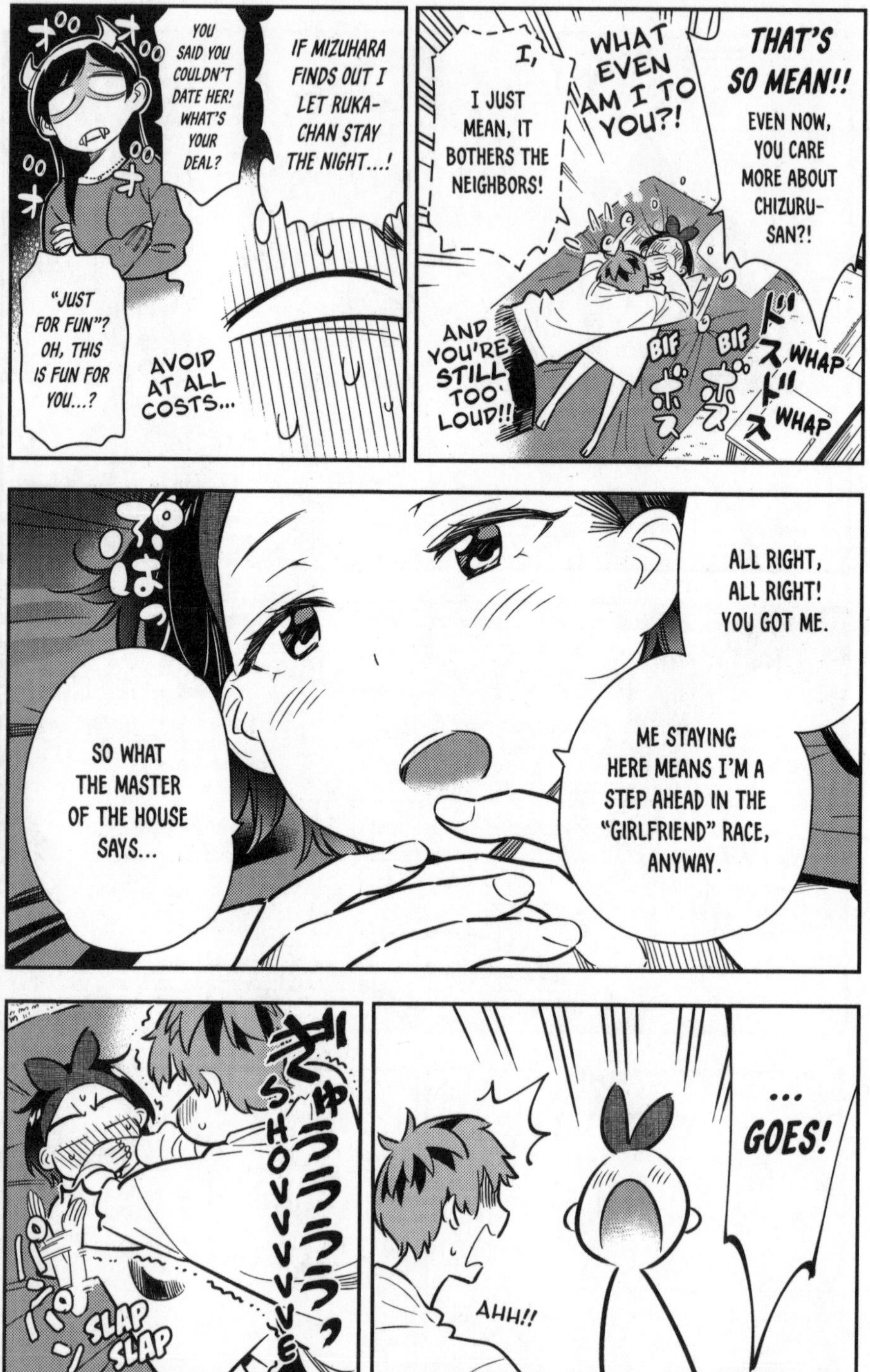
THAT'S SO MEAN!!
EVEN NOW, YOU CARE MORE ABOUT CHIZURU-SAN?!
WHAT EVEN AM I TO YOU?!
I, I JUST MEAN, IT BOTHERS THE NEIGHBORS!
AND YOU'RE STILL TOO LOUD!!
BIF
BIF
WHAP
WHAP
IF MIZUHARA FINDS OUT I LET RUKA-CHAN STAY THE NIGHT...!
YOU SAID YOU COULDN'T DATE HER! WHAT'S YOUR DEAL?
"JUST FOR FUN"? OH, THIS IS FUN FOR YOU...?
AVOID AT ALL COSTS...
ALL RIGHT, ALL RIGHT! YOU GOT ME.
ME STAYING HERE MEANS I'M A STEP AHEAD IN THE "GIRLFRIEND" RACE, ANYWAY.
SO WHAT THE MASTER OF THE HOUSE SAYS...
...GOES!
AHH!!
SHOVVVVVE
SLAP
SLAP

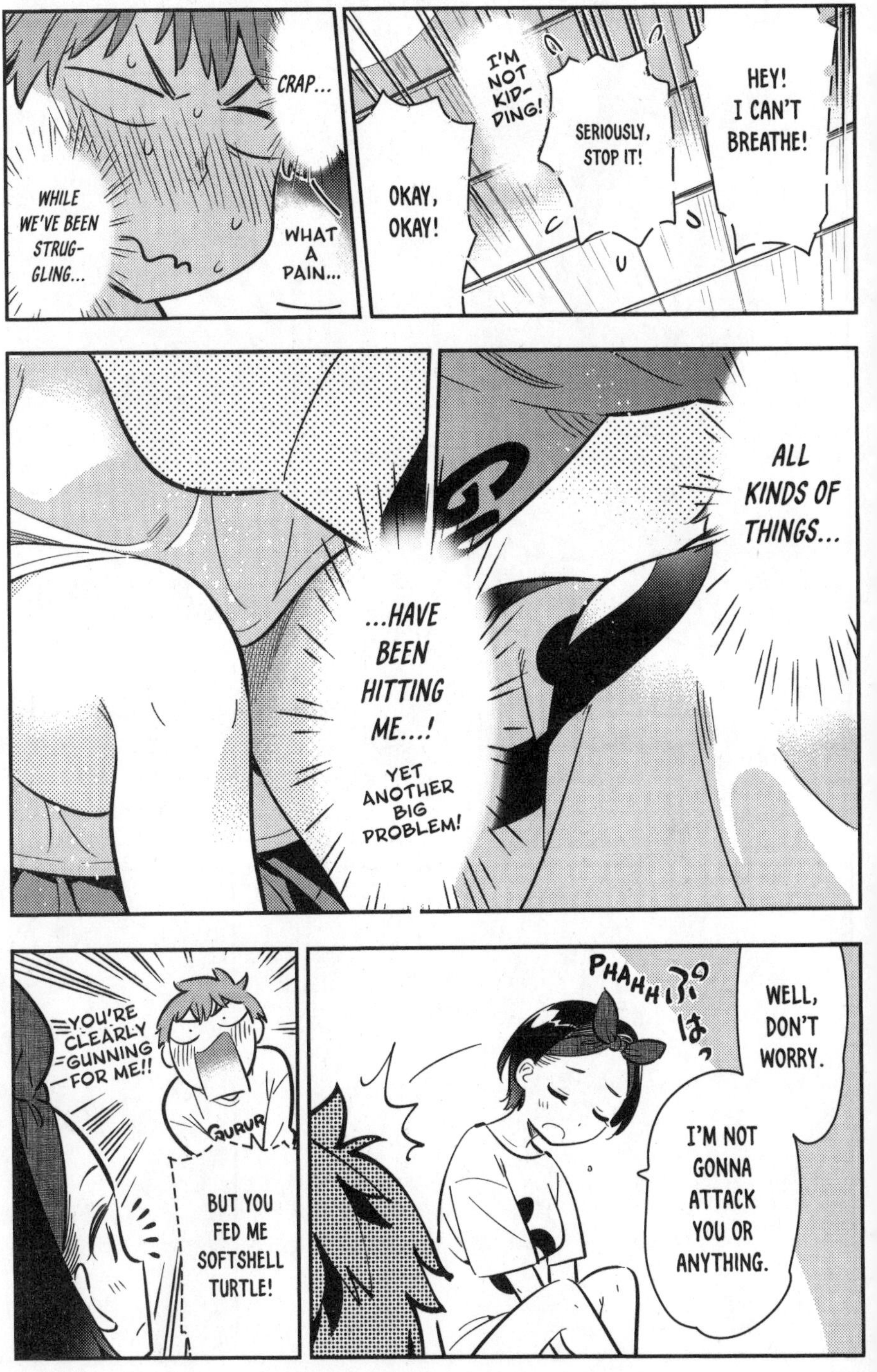
HEY! I CAN'T BREATHE!
I'M NOT KID-DING!
SERIOUSLY, STOP IT!
OKAY, OKAY!
CRAP...
WHAT A PAIN...
WHILE WE'VE BEEN STRUG-GLING...
ALL KINDS OF THINGS...
...HAVE BEEN HITTING ME...!
YET ANOTHER BIG PROBLEM!
PHAHH ぷは
WELL, DON'T WORRY.
I'M NOT GONNA ATTACK YOU OR ANYTHING.
YOU'RE CLEARLY GUNNING FOR ME!!
GURUR
BUT YOU FED ME SOFTSHELL TURTLE!

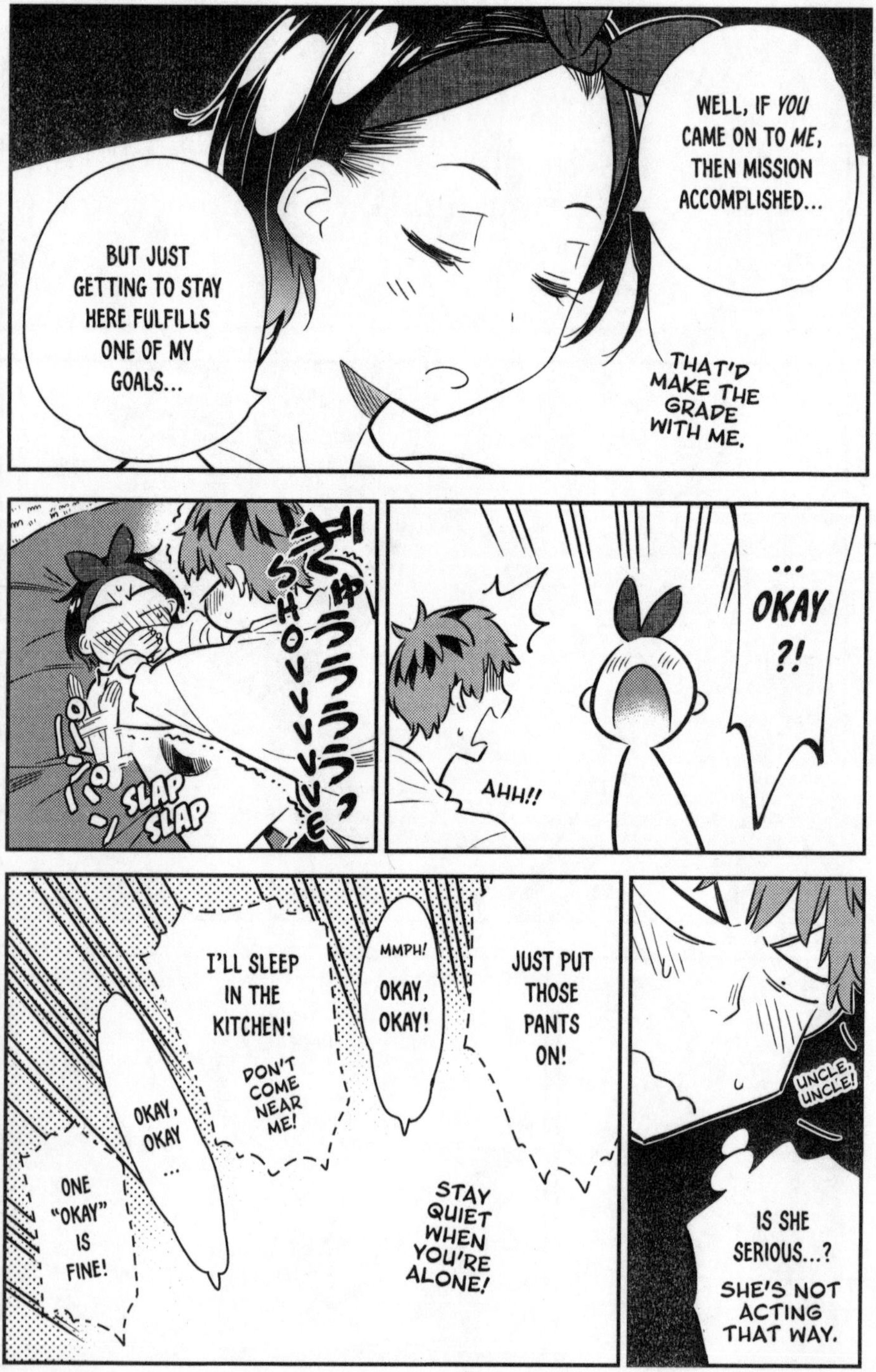
WELL, IF YOU CAME ON TO ME, THEN MISSION ACCOMPLISHED...
THAT'D MAKE THE GRADE WITH ME.
BUT JUST GETTING TO STAY HERE FULFILLS ONE OF MY GOALS...
...OKAY?!
AHH!!
SHOVVVVVVE
SLAP SLAP
UNCLE, UNCLE!
IS SHE SERIOUS...?
SHE'S NOT ACTING THAT WAY.
JUST PUT THOSE PANTS ON!
MMPH!
OKAY, OKAY!
STAY QUIET WHEN YOU'RE ALONE!
I'LL SLEEP IN THE KITCHEN!
DON'T COME NEAR ME!
OKAY, OKAY...
ONE "OKAY" IS FINE!

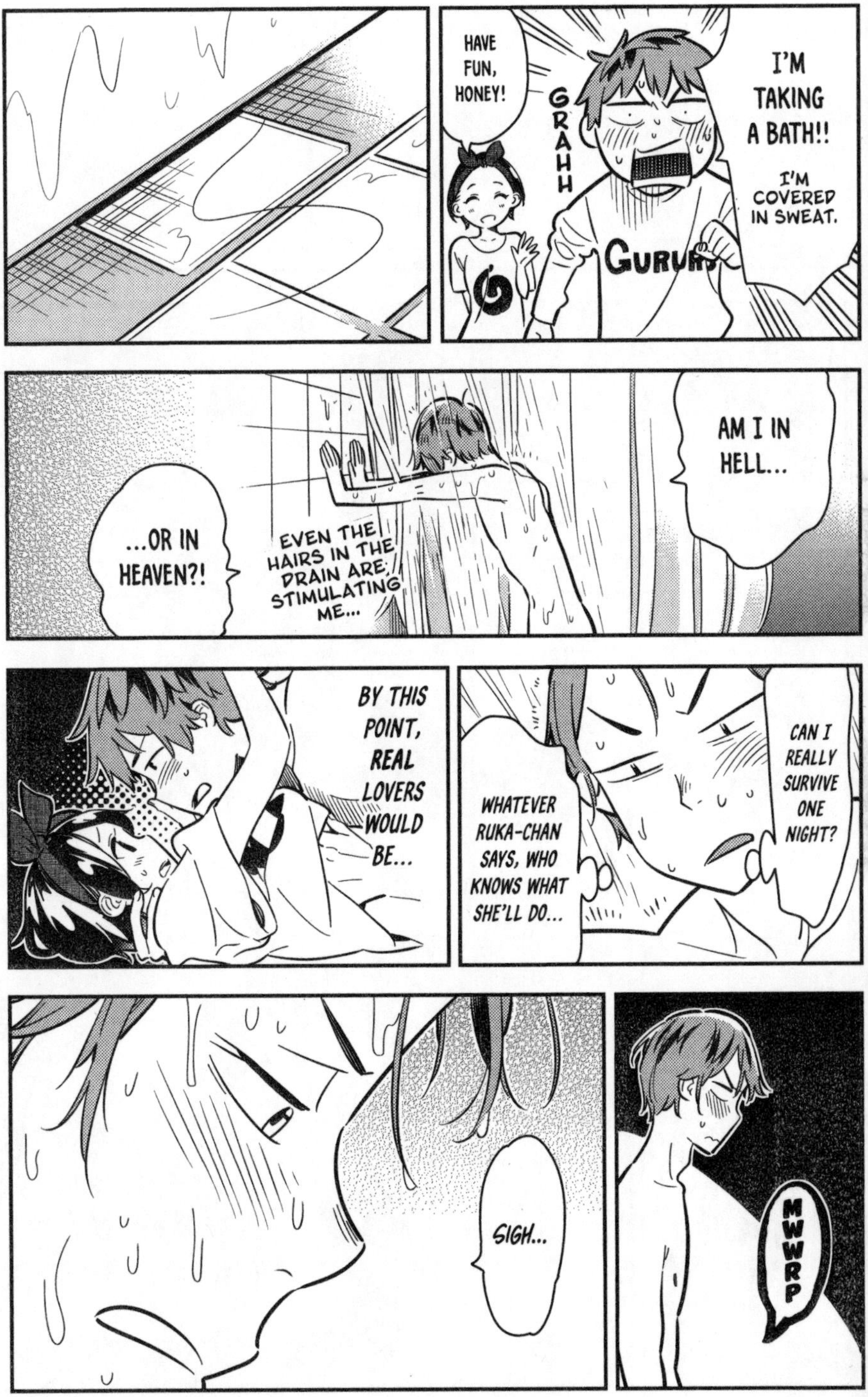
I'M TAKING A BATH!!
I'M COVERED IN SWEAT.
GRAHH
HAVE FUN, HONEY!
GURUR
AM I IN HELL...
EVEN THE HAIRS IN THE DRAIN ARE STIMULATING ME...
...OR IN HEAVEN?!
CAN I REALLY SURVIVE ONE NIGHT?
WHATEVER RUKA-CHAN SAYS, WHO KNOWS WHAT SHE'LL DO...
BY THIS POINT, REAL LOVERS WOULD BE...
MWWRP
SIGH...

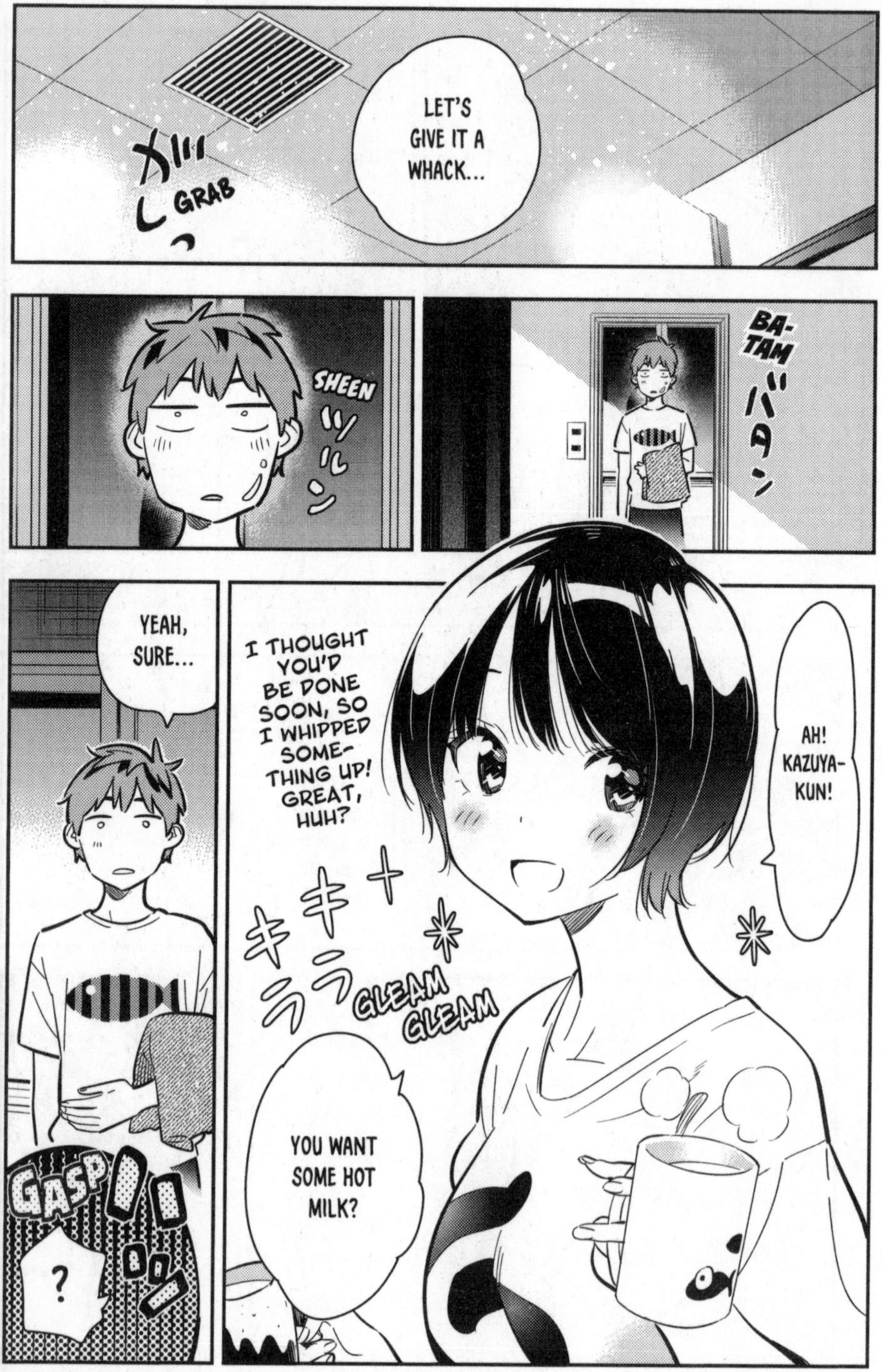
LET'S GIVE IT A WHACK...
ガシッ
GRAB
BA-TAM
バタン
SHEEN
ツルン
AH! KAZUYA-KUN!
I THOUGHT YOU'D BE DONE SOON, SO I WHIPPED SOME-THING UP! GREAT, HUH?
キラキラ
GLEAM GLEAM
YOU WANT SOME HOT MILK?
YEAH, SURE...
GASP!!!
?

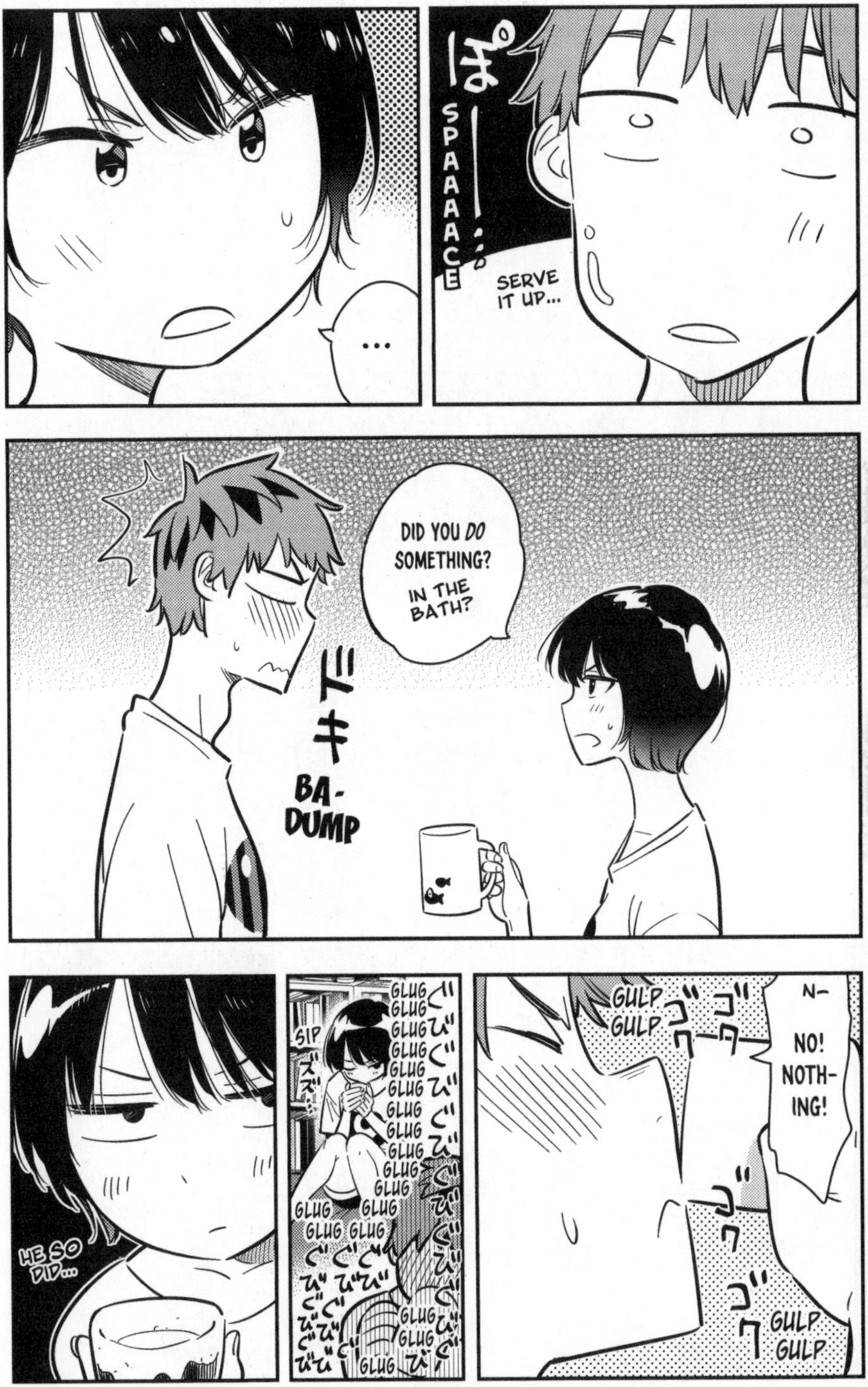

ぽー
SPAAAACE
SERVE IT UP...
...
DID YOU *DO* SOMETHING? IN THE BATH?
ドキ
BA-DUMP
N—
NO! NOTHING!
ゴクゴク
GULP GULP
ゴクゴク
GULP GULP
ぐびぐび
GLUG GLUG
SIP
ズズ…
HE SO DID...

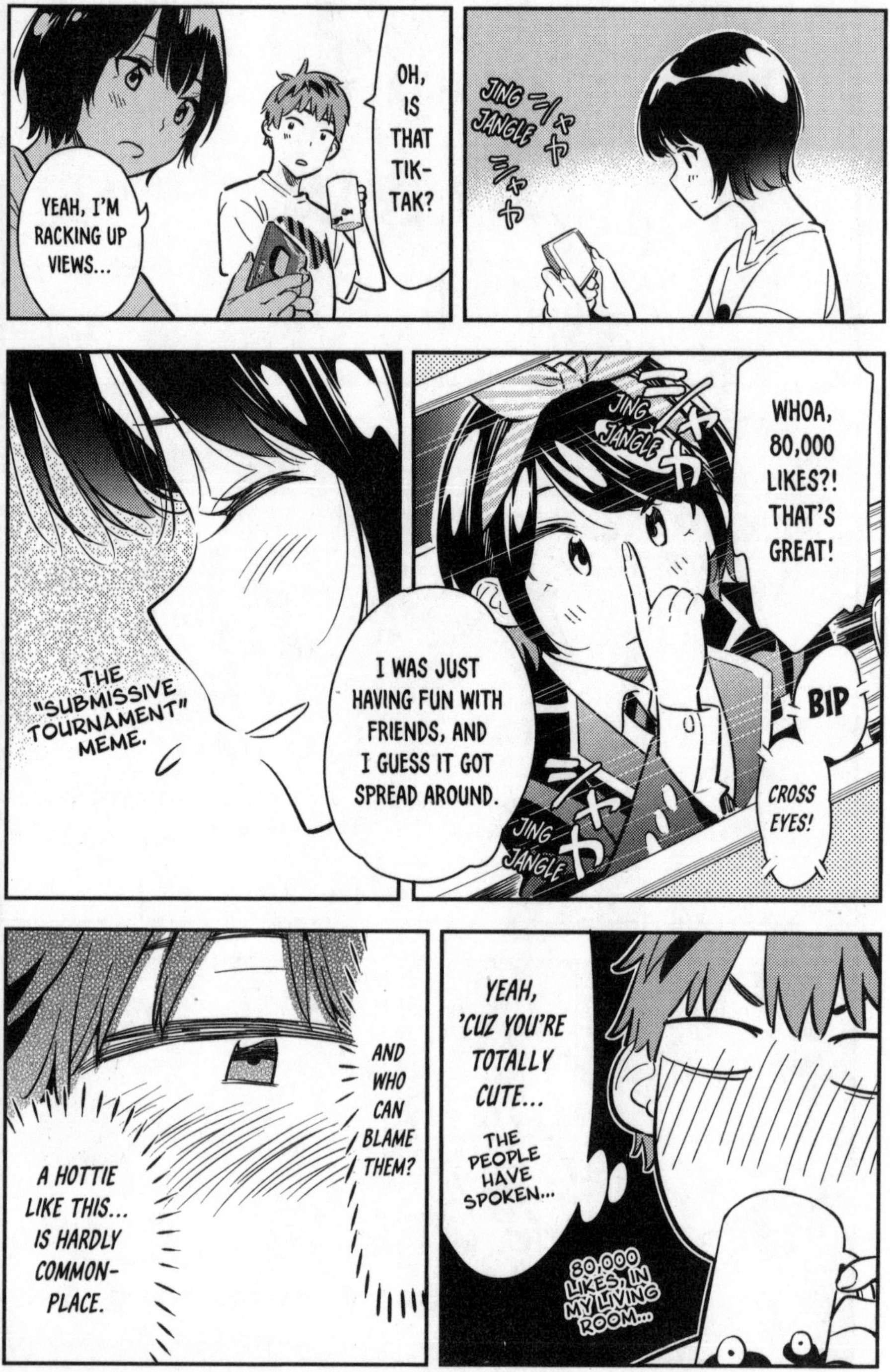
JING JANGLE
OH, IS THAT TIK-TAK?
YEAH, I'M RACKING UP VIEWS...
WHOA, 80,000 LIKES?! THAT'S GREAT!
JING JANGLE
BIP
CROSS EYES!
I WAS JUST HAVING FUN WITH FRIENDS, AND I GUESS IT GOT SPREAD AROUND.
JING JANGLE
THE "SUBMISSIVE TOURNAMENT" MEME.
YEAH, 'CUZ YOU'RE TOTALLY CUTE...
THE PEOPLE HAVE SPOKEN...
80,000 LIKES, IN MY LIVING ROOM...
AND WHO CAN BLAME THEM?
A HOTTIE LIKE THIS... IS HARDLY COMMON-PLACE.

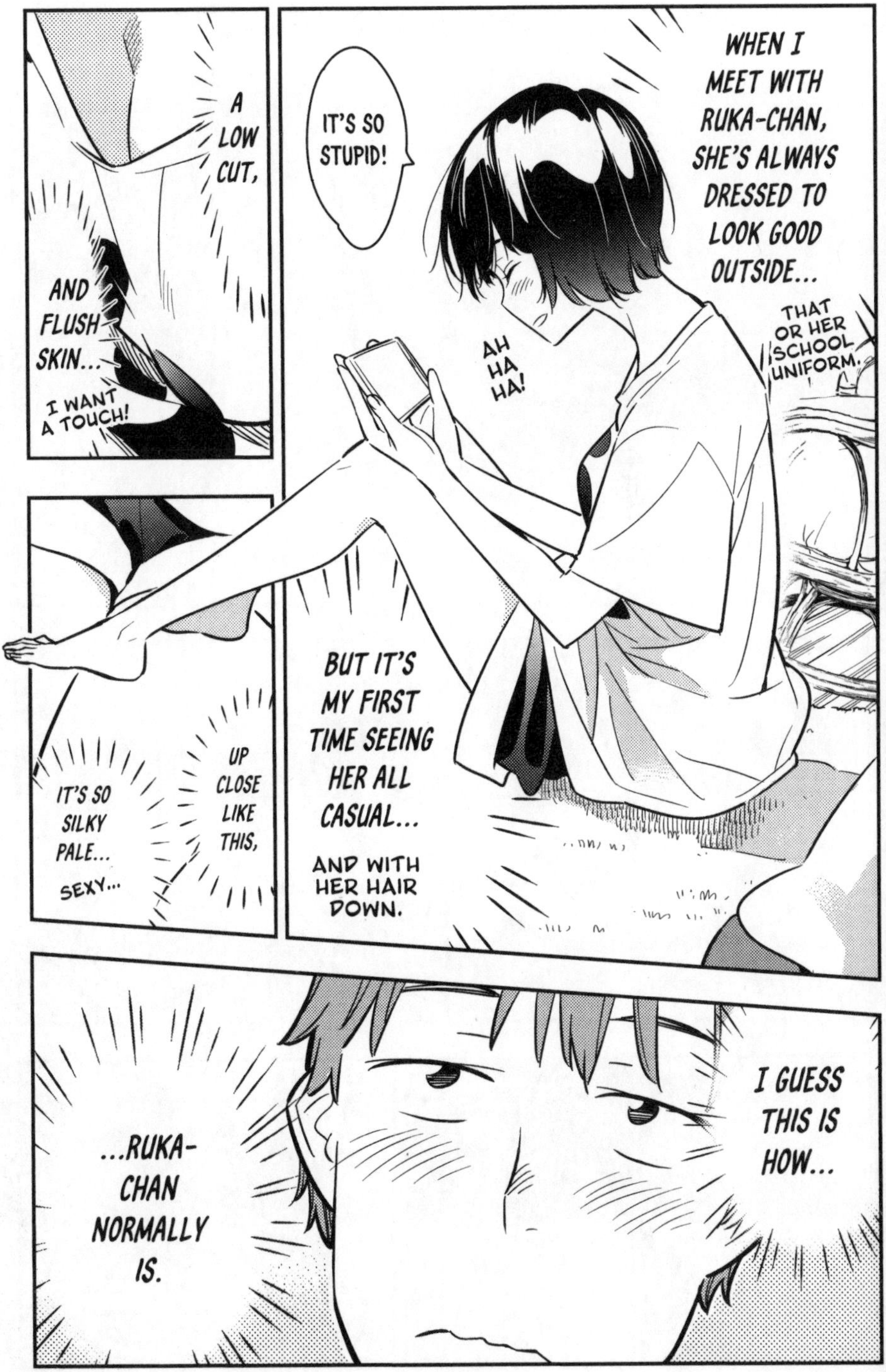
WHEN I MEET WITH RUKA-CHAN, SHE'S ALWAYS DRESSED TO LOOK GOOD OUTSIDE...
THAT OR HER SCHOOL UNIFORM.
IT'S SO STUPID!
AH HA HA!
BUT IT'S MY FIRST TIME SEEING HER ALL CASUAL...
AND WITH HER HAIR DOWN.
A LOW CUT,
AND FLUSH SKIN...
I WANT A TOUCH!
UP CLOSE LIKE THIS,
IT'S SO SILKY PALE...
SEXY...
I GUESS THIS IS HOW...
...RUKA-CHAN NORMALLY IS.

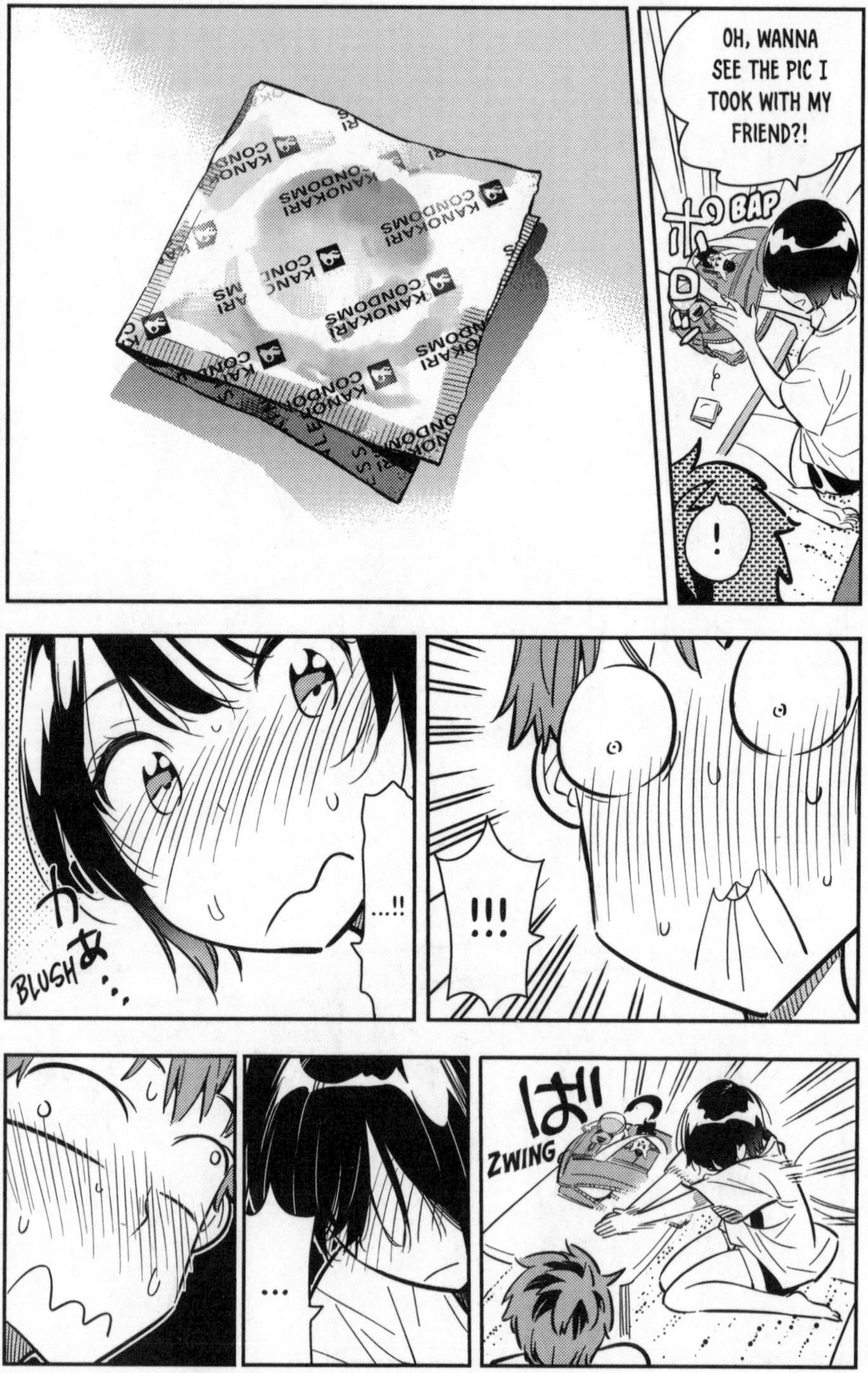
OH, WANNA SEE THE PIC I TOOK WITH MY FRIEND?!
BAP
!
KANOKARI CONDOMS
!!!
...!!
BLUSH...
ZWING
...

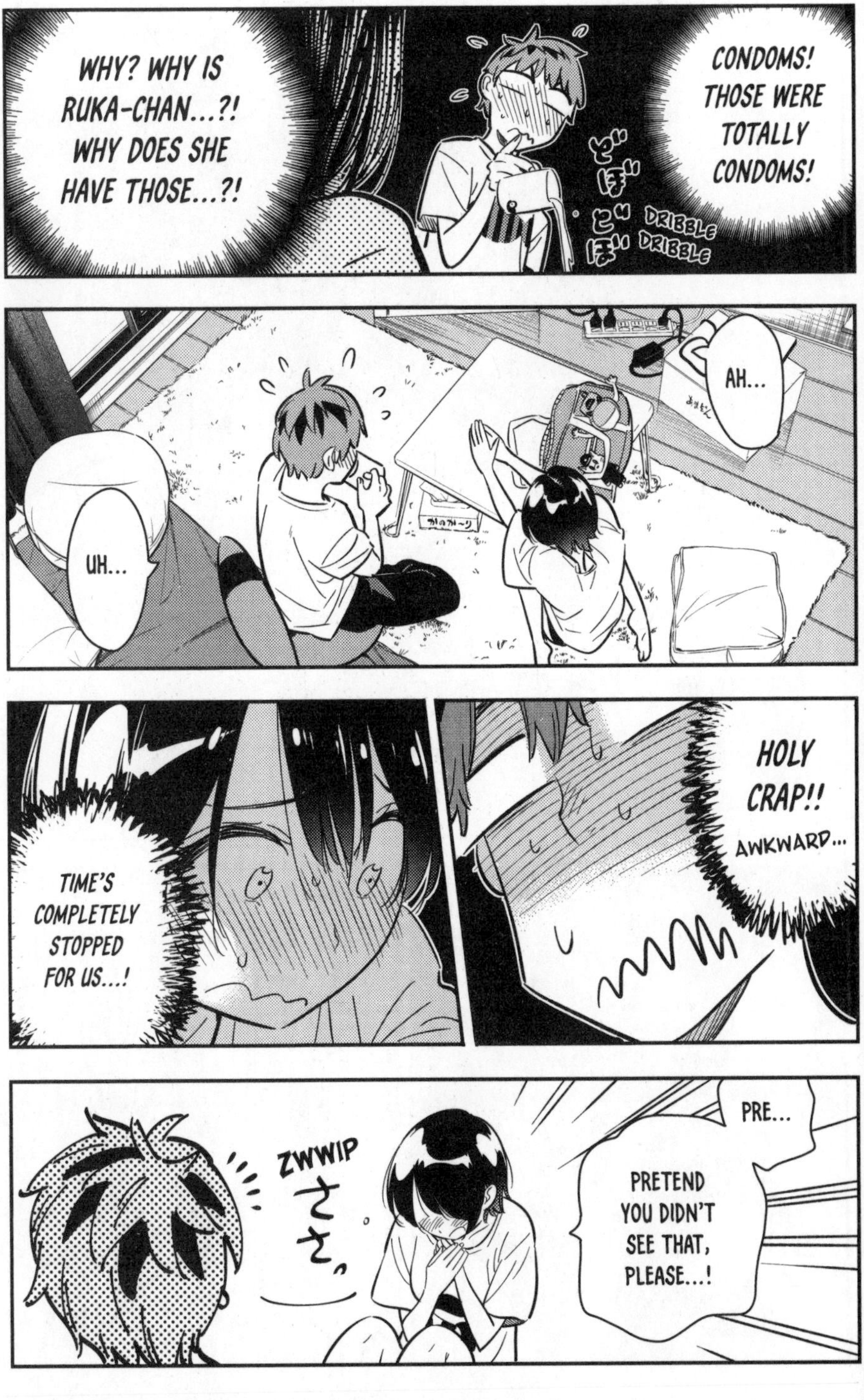
CONDOMS! THOSE WERE TOTALLY CONDOMS!
DRIBBLE DRIBBLE
WHY? WHY IS RUKA-CHAN...?! WHY DOES SHE HAVE THOSE...?!
AH...
UH...
HOLY CRAP!!
AWKWARD...
TIME'S COMPLETELY STOPPED FOR US...!
PRE...
PRETEND YOU DIDN'T SEE THAT, PLEASE...!
ZWWIP

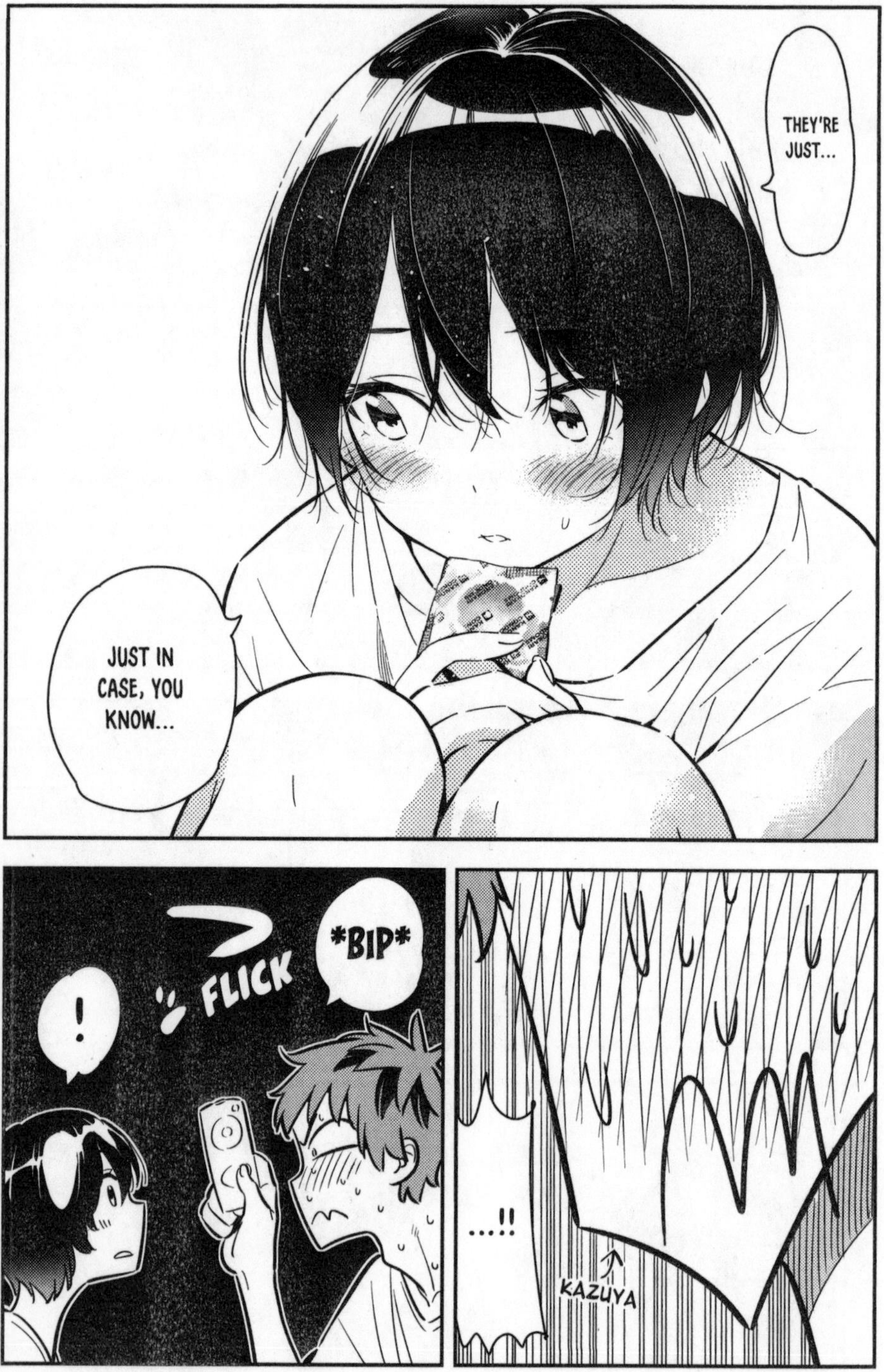
THEY'RE JUST...
JUST IN CASE, YOU KNOW...
...!!
KAZUYA
BIP
FLICK
!

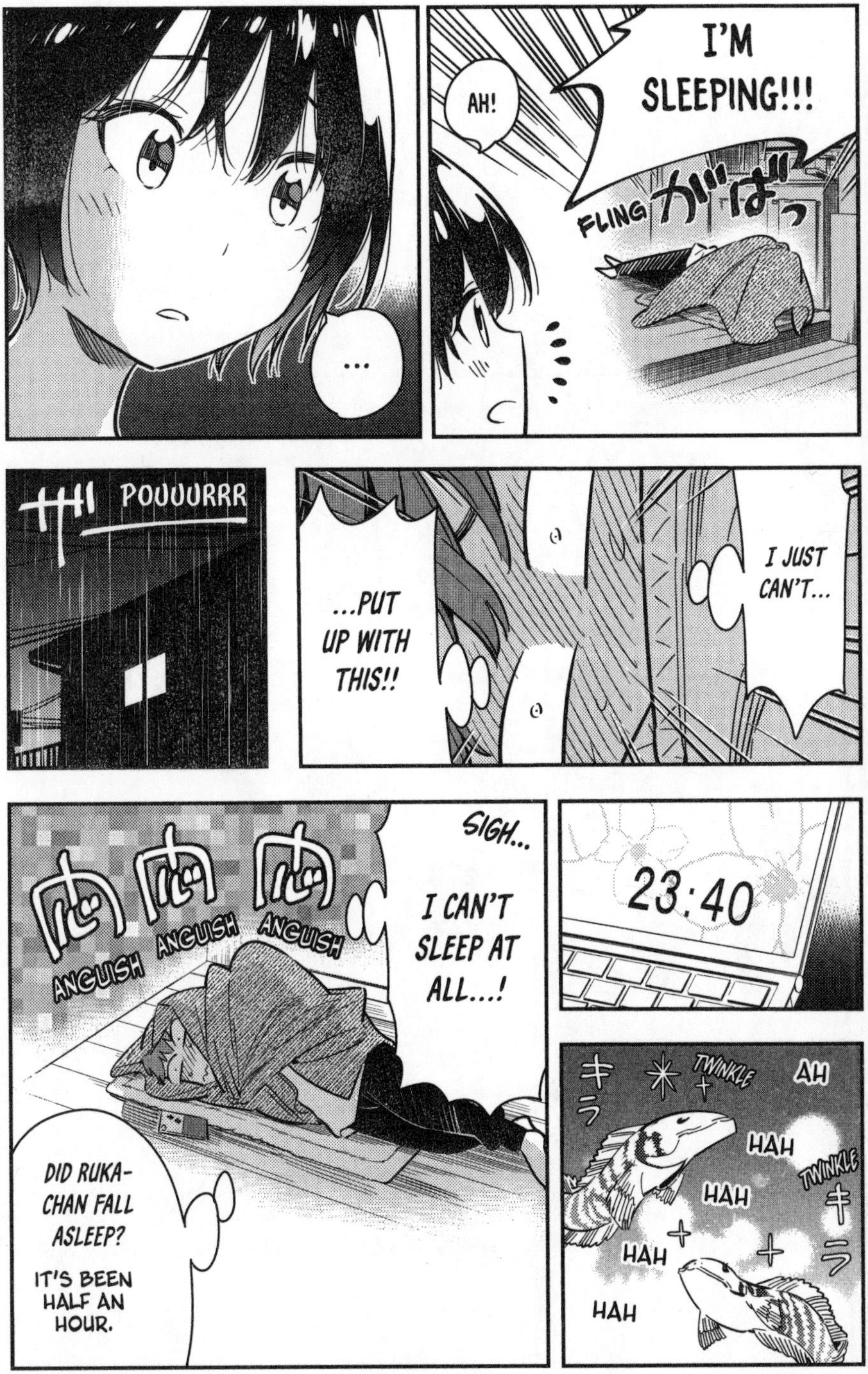
I'M SLEEPING!!!
AH!
FLING がばっ
...
I JUST CAN'T...
...PUT UP WITH THIS!!
POUUURRR
23:40
AH
TWINKLE キラ
HAH
HAH
TWINKLE キラ
HAH
HAH
SIGH...
I CAN'T SLEEP AT ALL...!
悶 ANGUISH
悶 ANGUISH
悶 ANGUISH
DID RUKA-CHAN FALL ASLEEP?
IT'S BEEN HALF AN HOUR.

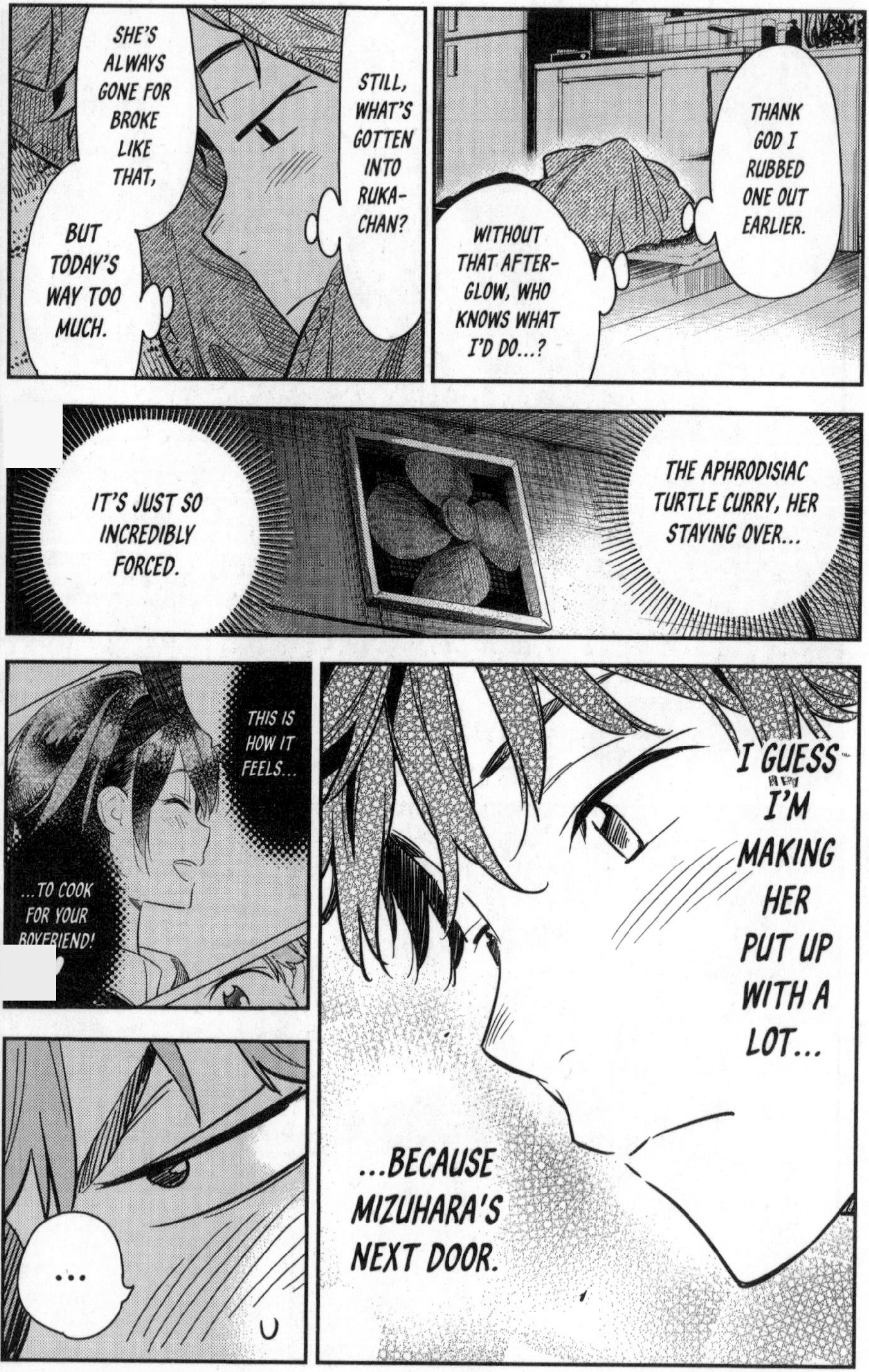
THANK GOD I RUBBED ONE OUT EARLIER.
WITHOUT THAT AFTER-GLOW, WHO KNOWS WHAT I'D DO...?
STILL, WHAT'S GOTTEN INTO RUKA-CHAN?
SHE'S ALWAYS GONE FOR BROKE LIKE THAT,
BUT TODAY'S WAY TOO MUCH.
THE APHRODISIAC TURTLE CURRY, HER STAYING OVER...
IT'S JUST SO INCREDIBLY FORCED.
I GUESS I'M MAKING HER PUT UP WITH A LOT...
...BECAUSE MIZUHARA'S NEXT DOOR.
THIS IS HOW IT FEELS...
...TO COOK FOR YOUR BOYFRIEND!
...

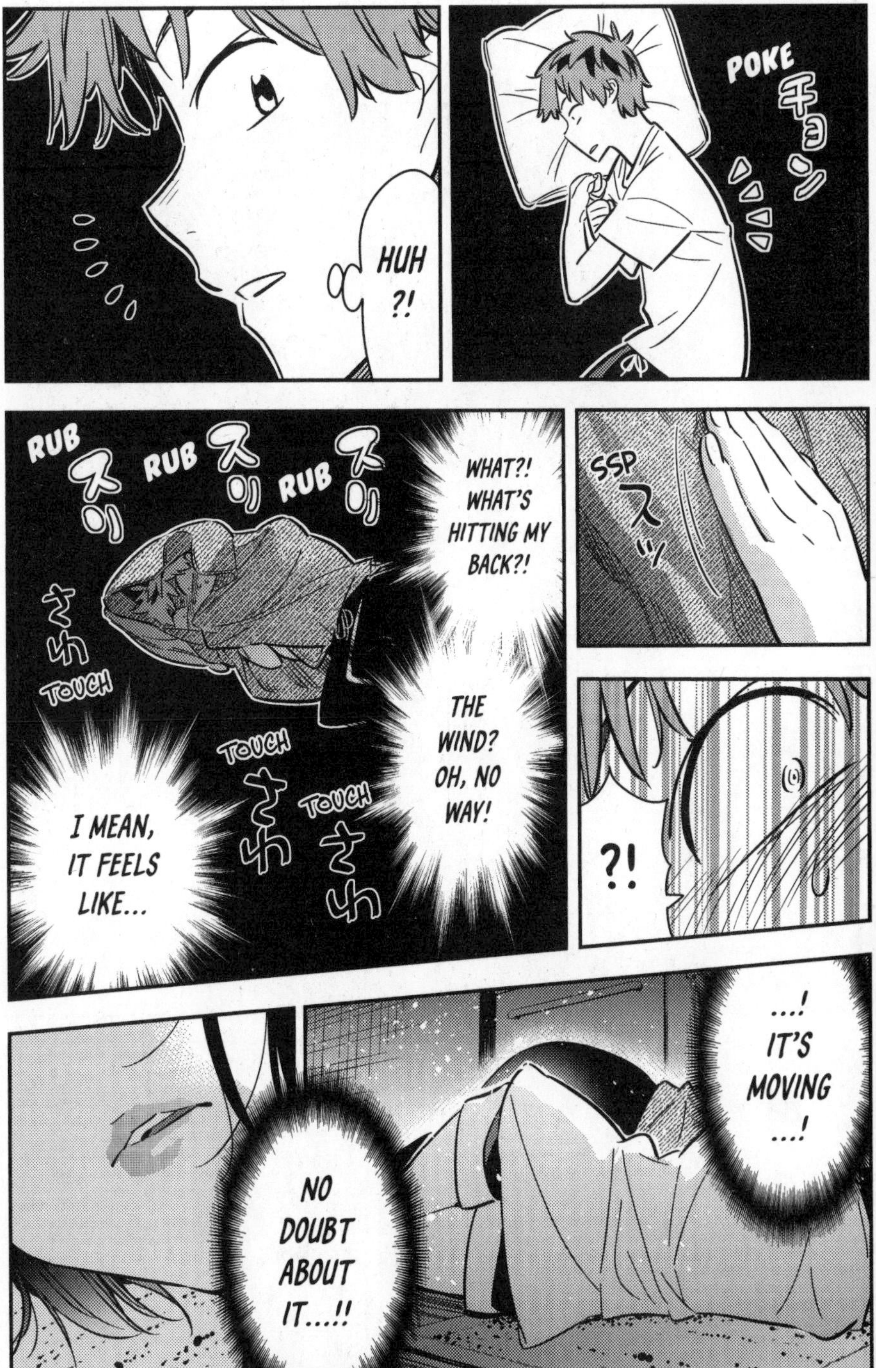
POKE
チョン
HUH ?!
SSP
スッ
?!
WHAT?! WHAT'S HITTING MY BACK?!
RUB
スリ
RUB
スリ
RUB
スリ
THE WIND? OH, NO WAY!
TOUCH
さわ
TOUCH
さわ
さわ
TOUCH
I MEAN, IT FEELS LIKE...
...! IT'S MOVING ...!
NO DOUBT ABOUT IT...!!

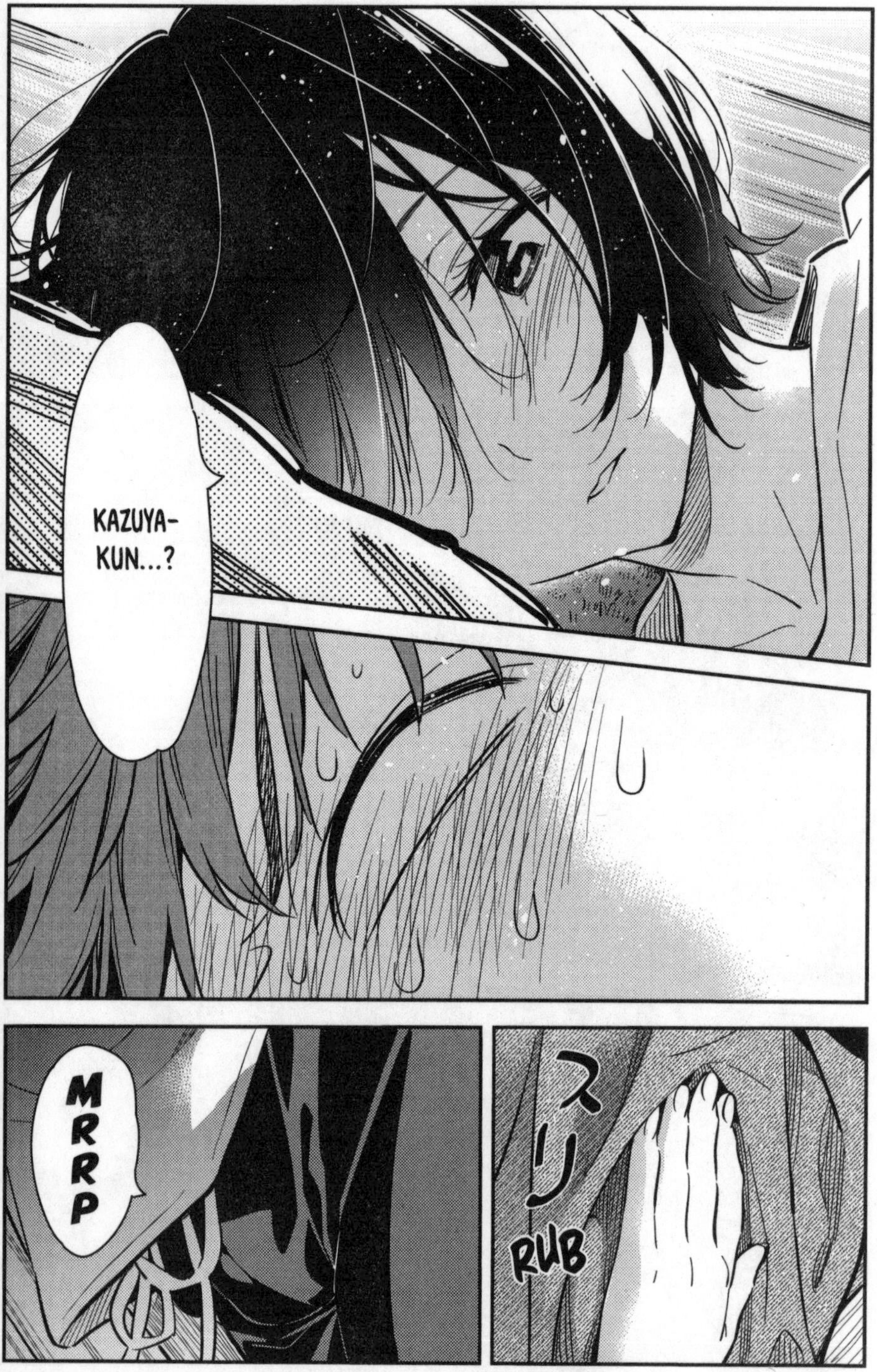
KAZUYA-KUN...?
スリ
RUB
MRRP

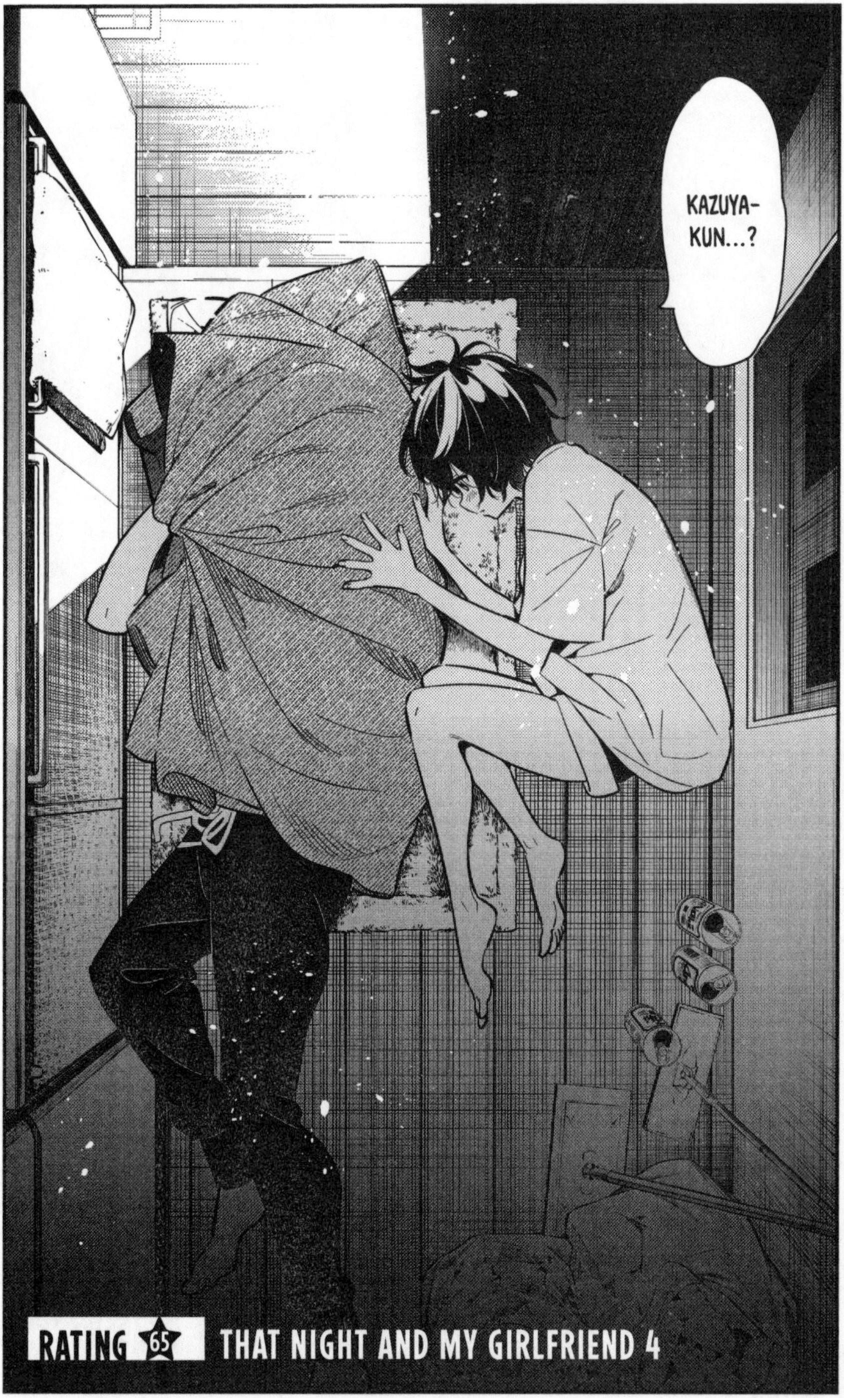
KAZUYA-KUN...?
RATING 65 THAT NIGHT AND MY GIRLFRIEND 4

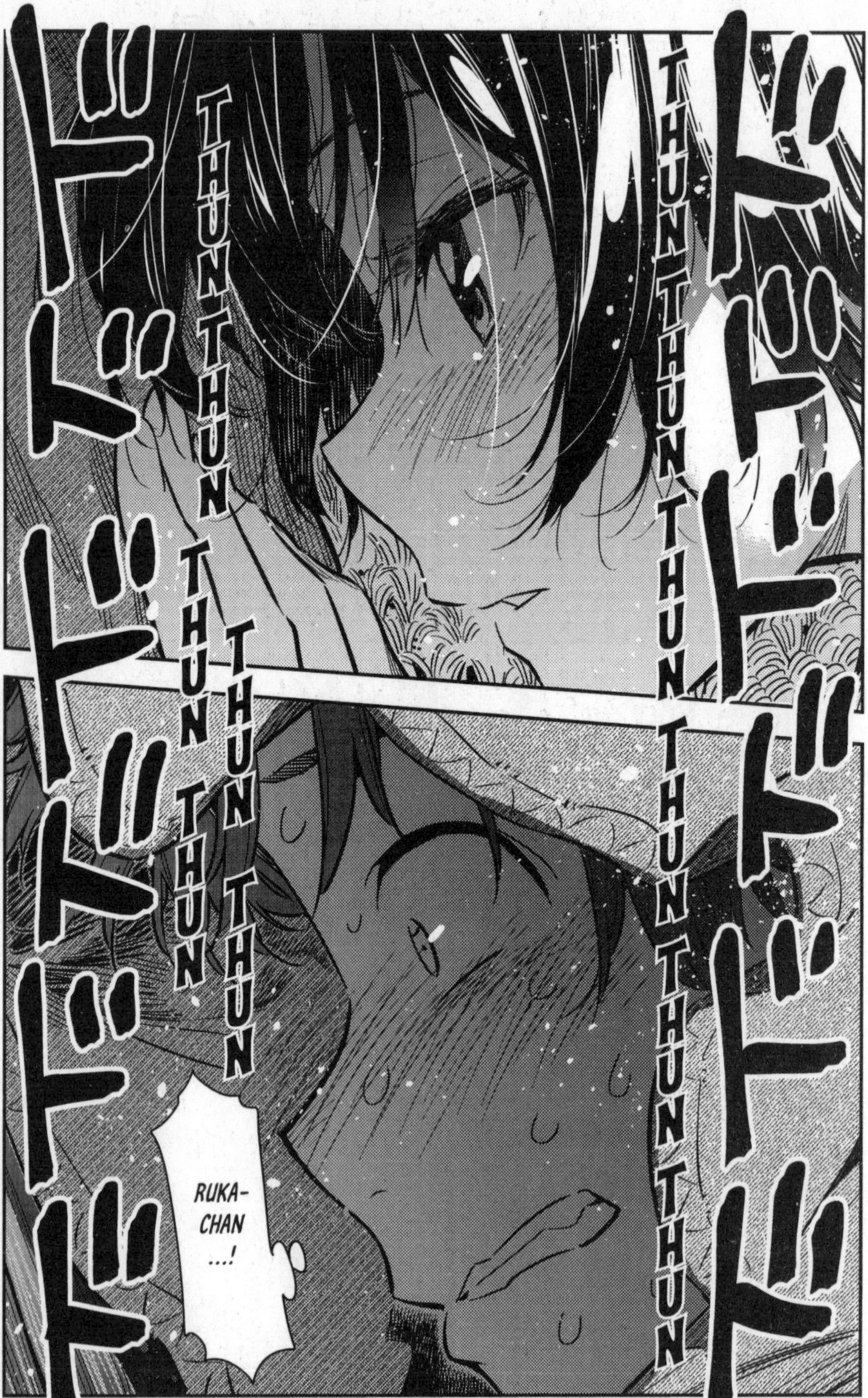
ドドドド
THUN THUN THUN THUN THUN THUN
ドドドド
THUN THUN THUN THUN
RUKA-CHAN ...!

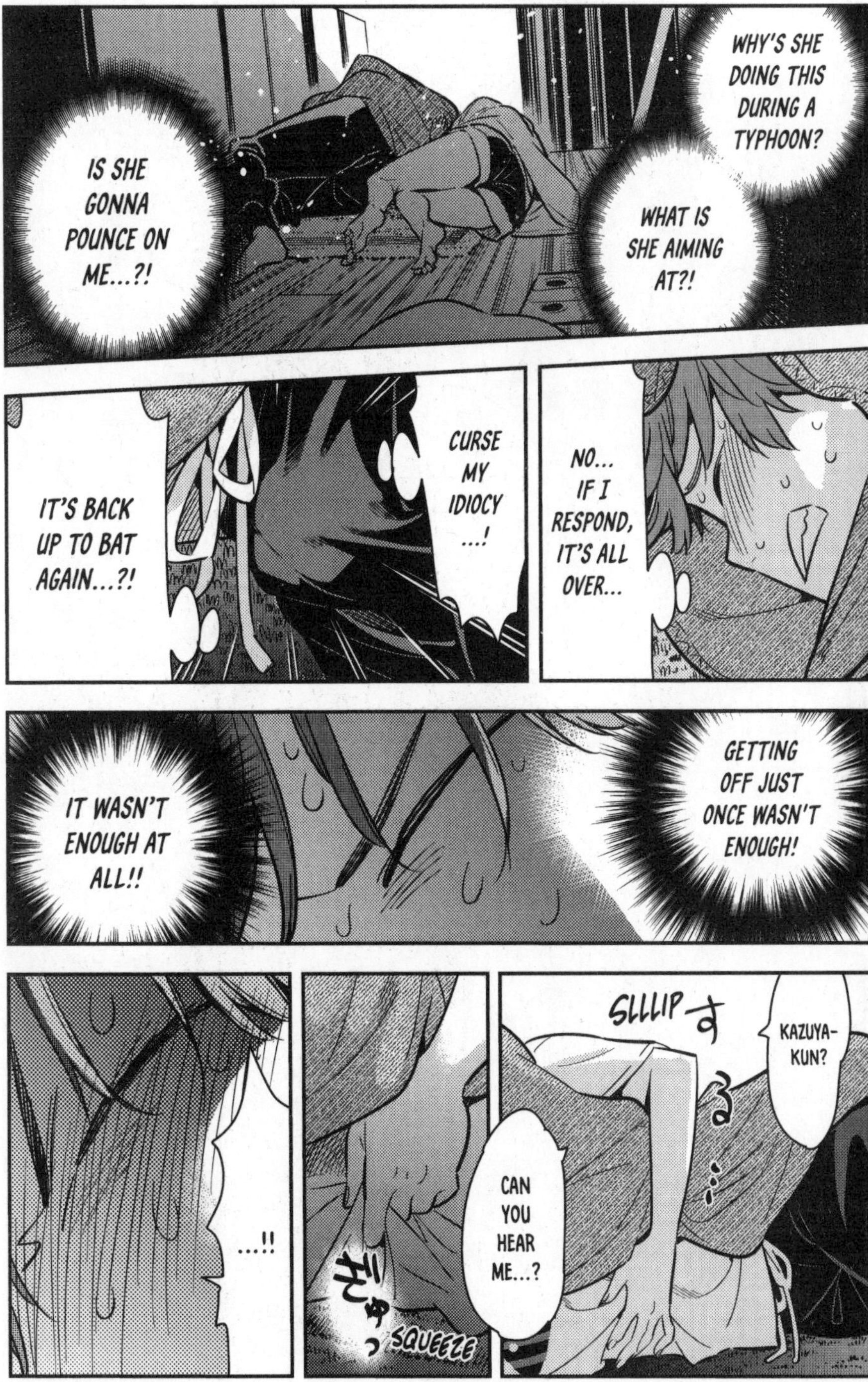
WHY'S SHE DOING THIS DURING A TYPHOON?
WHAT IS SHE AIMING AT?!
IS SHE GONNA POUNCE ON ME...?!
NO... IF I RESPOND, IT'S ALL OVER...
CURSE MY IDIOCY ...!
IT'S BACK UP TO BAT AGAIN...?!
GETTING OFF JUST ONCE WASN'T ENOUGH!
IT WASN'T ENOUGH AT ALL!!
KAZUYA-KUN?
SLLLIP
する...
CAN YOU HEAR ME...?
ぎゅっ
SQUEEZE
...!!

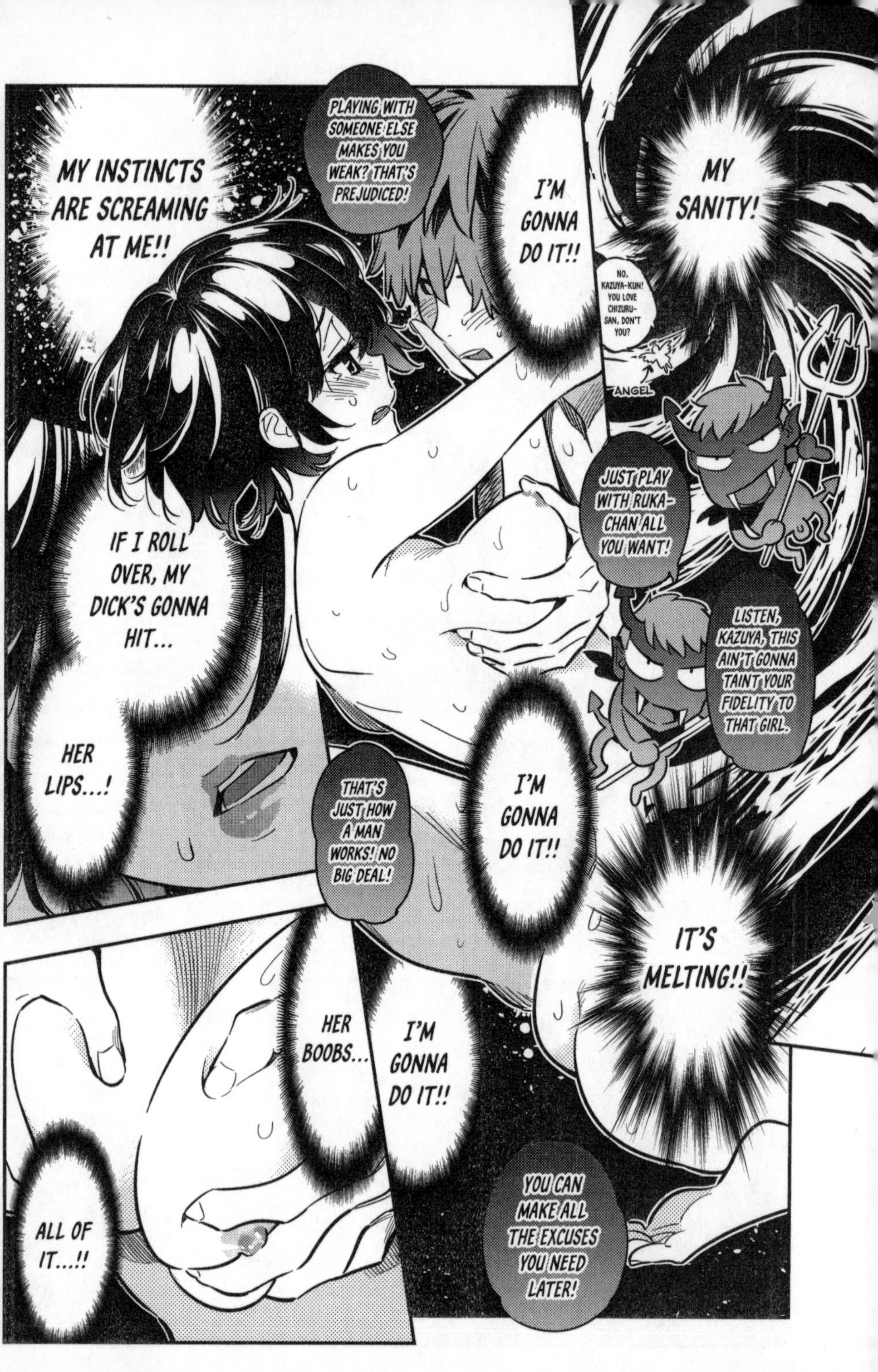
MY SANITY!
NO, KAZUYA-KUN! YOU LOVE CHIZURU-SAN, DON'T YOU?
ANGEL
JUST PLAY WITH RUKA-CHAN ALL YOU WANT!
LISTEN, KAZUYA, THIS AIN'T GONNA TAINT YOUR FIDELITY TO THAT GIRL.
IT'S MELTING!!
PLAYING WITH SOMEONE ELSE MAKES YOU WEAK? THAT'S PREJUDICED!
I'M GONNA DO IT!!
MY INSTINCTS ARE SCREAMING AT ME!!
IF I ROLL OVER, MY DICK'S GONNA HIT...
I'M GONNA DO IT!!
THAT'S JUST HOW A MAN WORKS! NO BIG DEAL!
HER LIPS...!
YOU CAN MAKE ALL THE EXCUSES YOU NEED LATER!
I'M GONNA DO IT!!
HER BOOBS...
ALL OF IT...!!

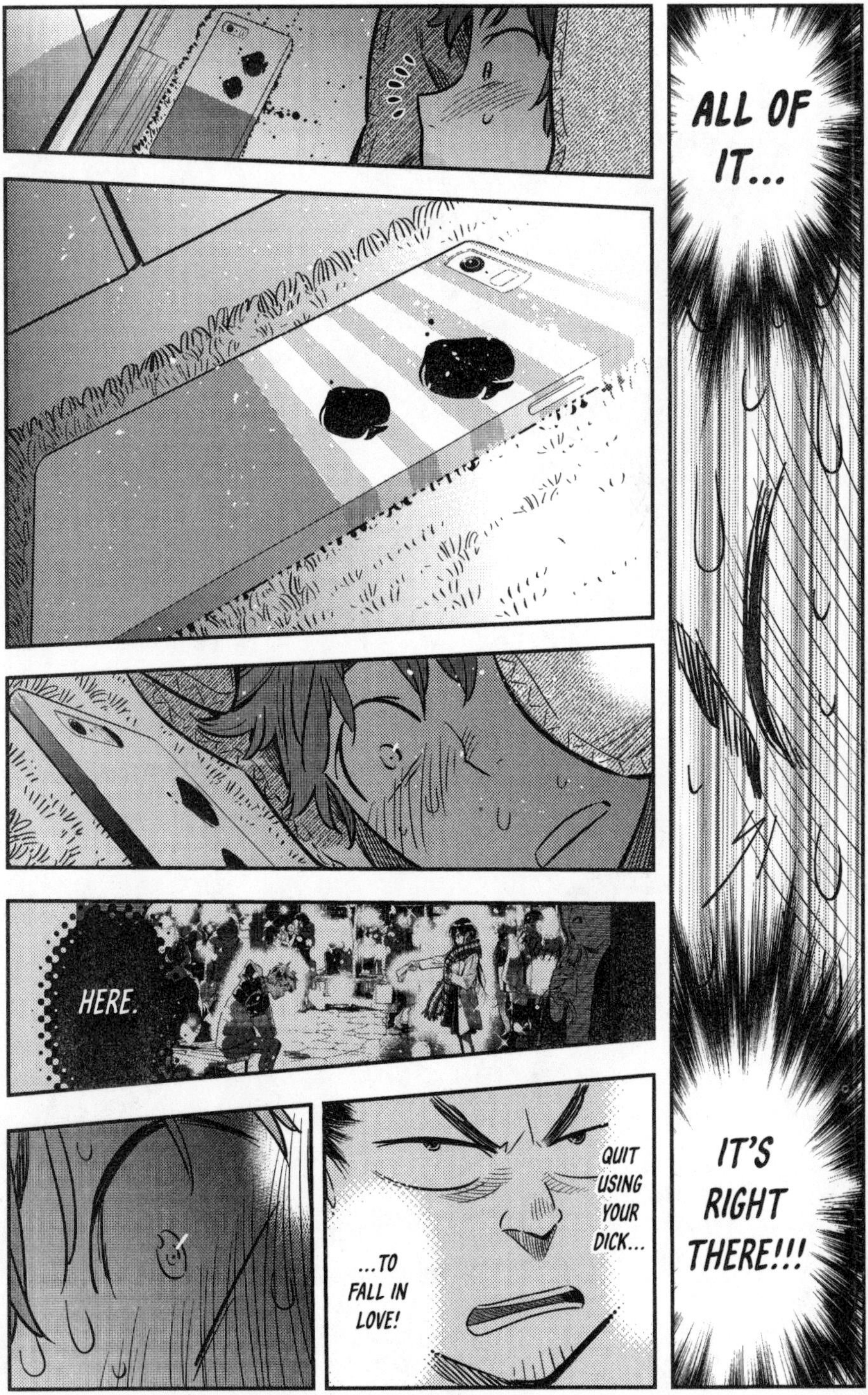
ALL OF IT...
IT'S RIGHT THERE!!!
HERE.
QUIT USING YOUR DICK...
...TO FALL IN LOVE!

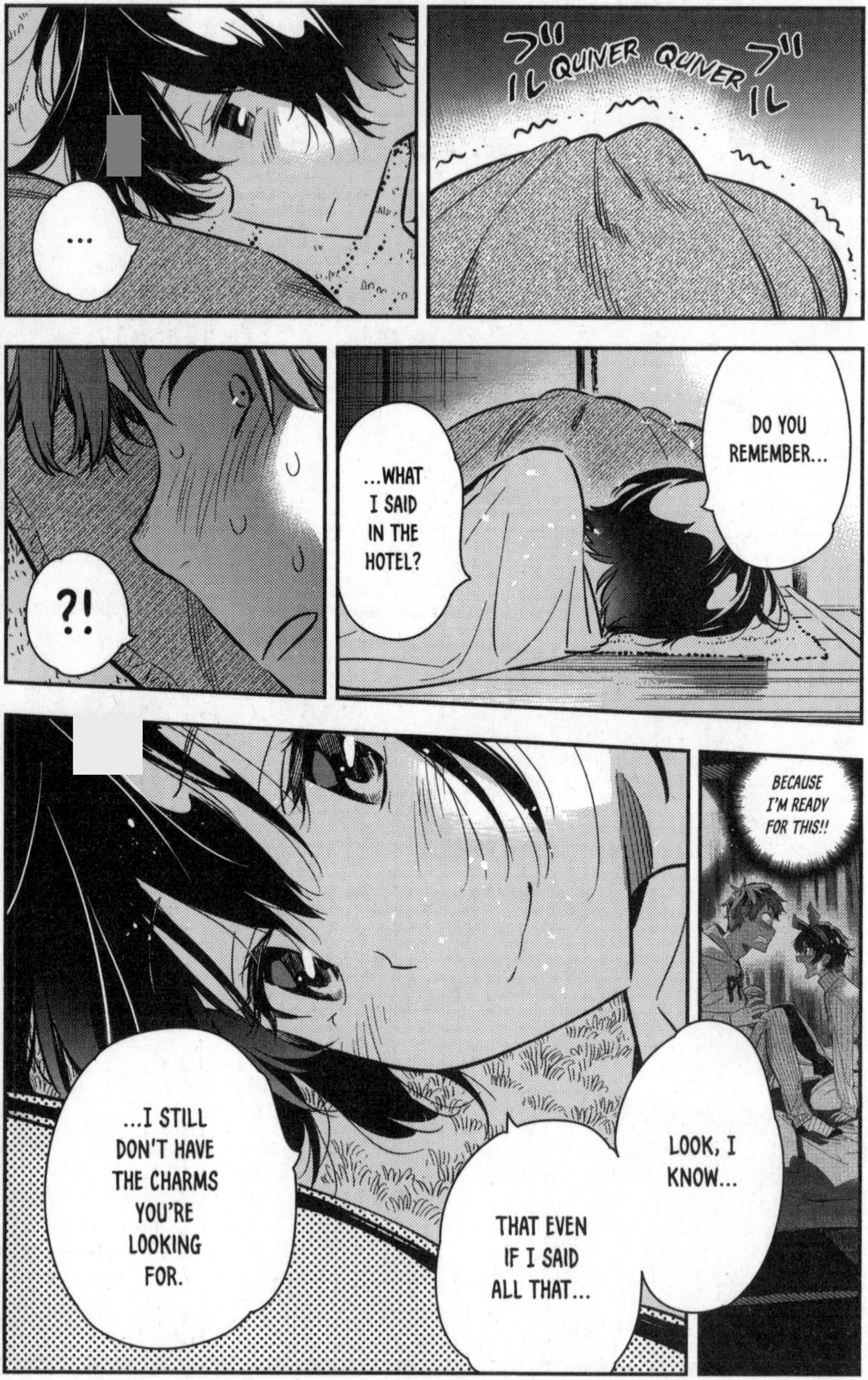
ブル QUIVER QUIVER ブル
...
DO YOU REMEMBER...
...WHAT I SAID IN THE HOTEL?
?!
BECAUSE I'M READY FOR THIS!!
LOOK, I KNOW...
THAT EVEN IF I SAID ALL THAT...
...I STILL DON'T HAVE THE CHARMS YOU'RE LOOKING FOR.

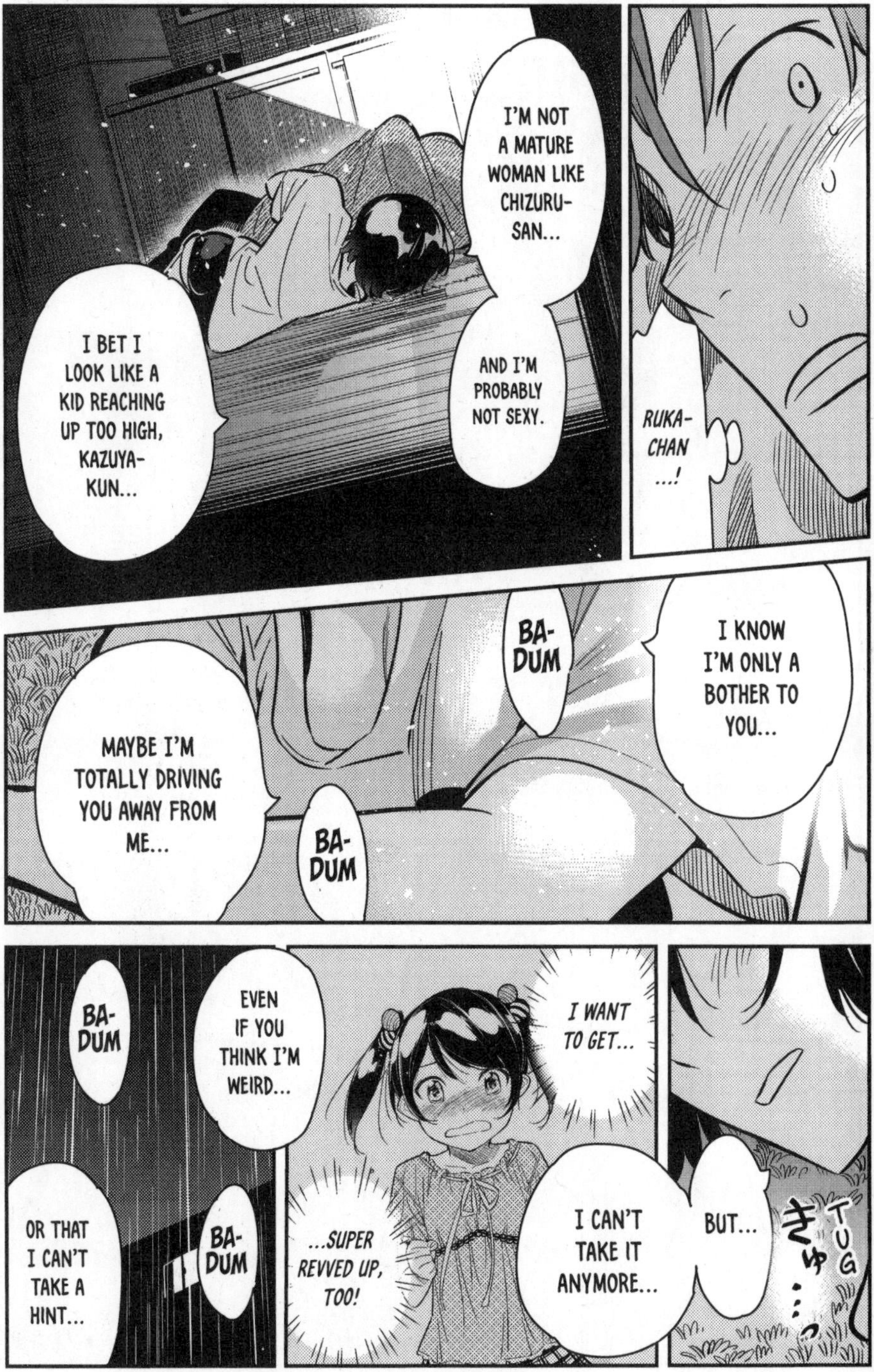
RUKA-CHAN...!
I'M NOT A MATURE WOMAN LIKE CHIZURU-SAN...
AND I'M PROBABLY NOT SEXY.
I BET I LOOK LIKE A KID REACHING UP TOO HIGH, KAZUYA-KUN...
I KNOW I'M ONLY A BOTHER TO YOU...
BA-DUM
BA-DUM
MAYBE I'M TOTALLY DRIVING YOU AWAY FROM ME...
きゅ…っ TUG
BUT...
I WANT TO GET...
EVEN IF YOU THINK I'M WEIRD...
I CAN'T TAKE IT ANYMORE...
...SUPER REVVED UP, TOO!
BA-DUM
BA-DUM
OR THAT I CAN'T TAKE A HINT...

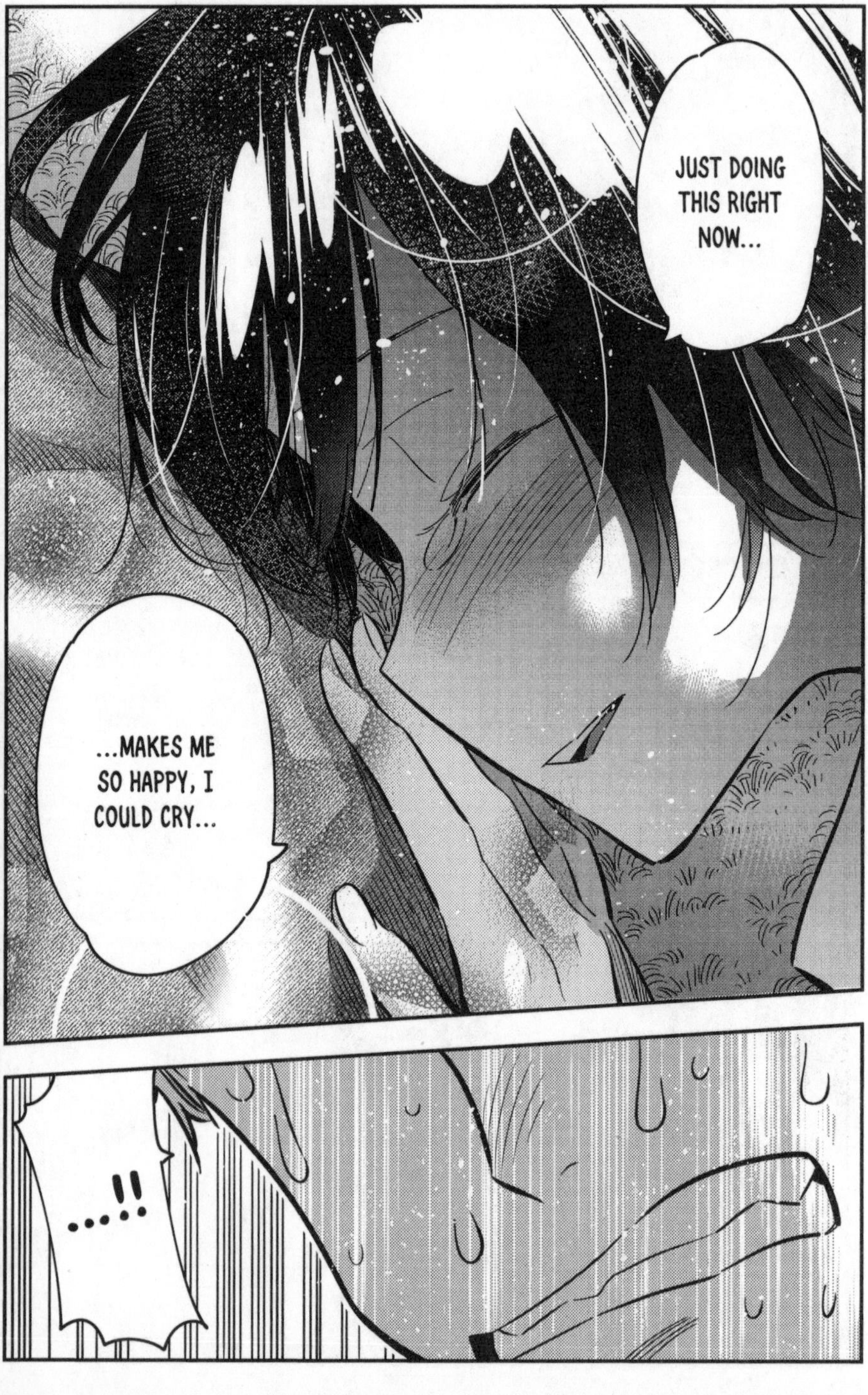
JUST DOING THIS RIGHT NOW...
...MAKES ME SO HAPPY, I COULD CRY...
...!!

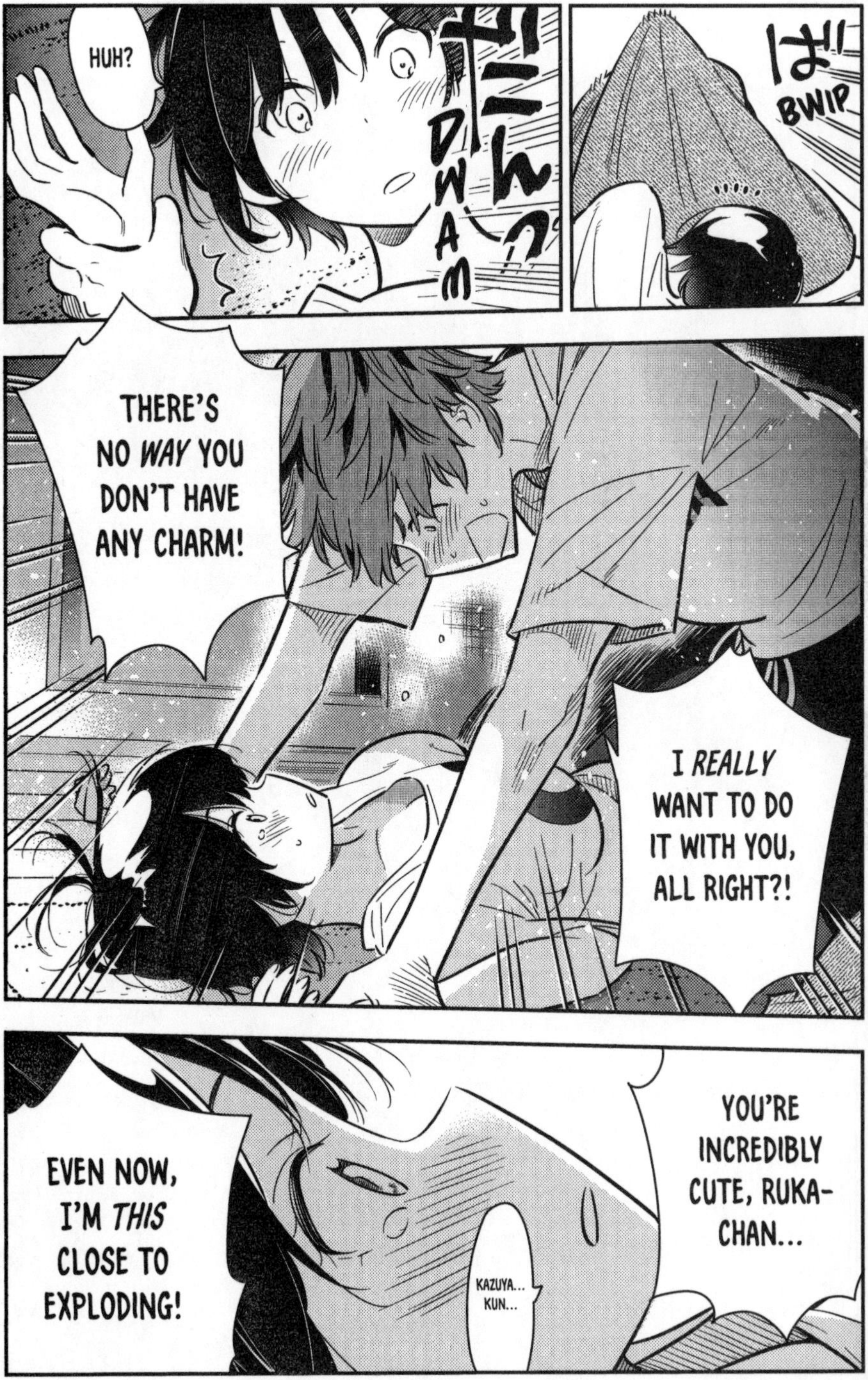

ば!!
BWIP
HUH?
DWAM
THERE'S NO *WAY* YOU DON'T HAVE ANY CHARM!
I *REALLY* WANT TO DO IT WITH YOU, ALL RIGHT?!
YOU'RE INCREDIBLY CUTE, RUKA-CHAN...
KAZUYA... KUN...
EVEN NOW, I'M *THIS* CLOSE TO EXPLODING!

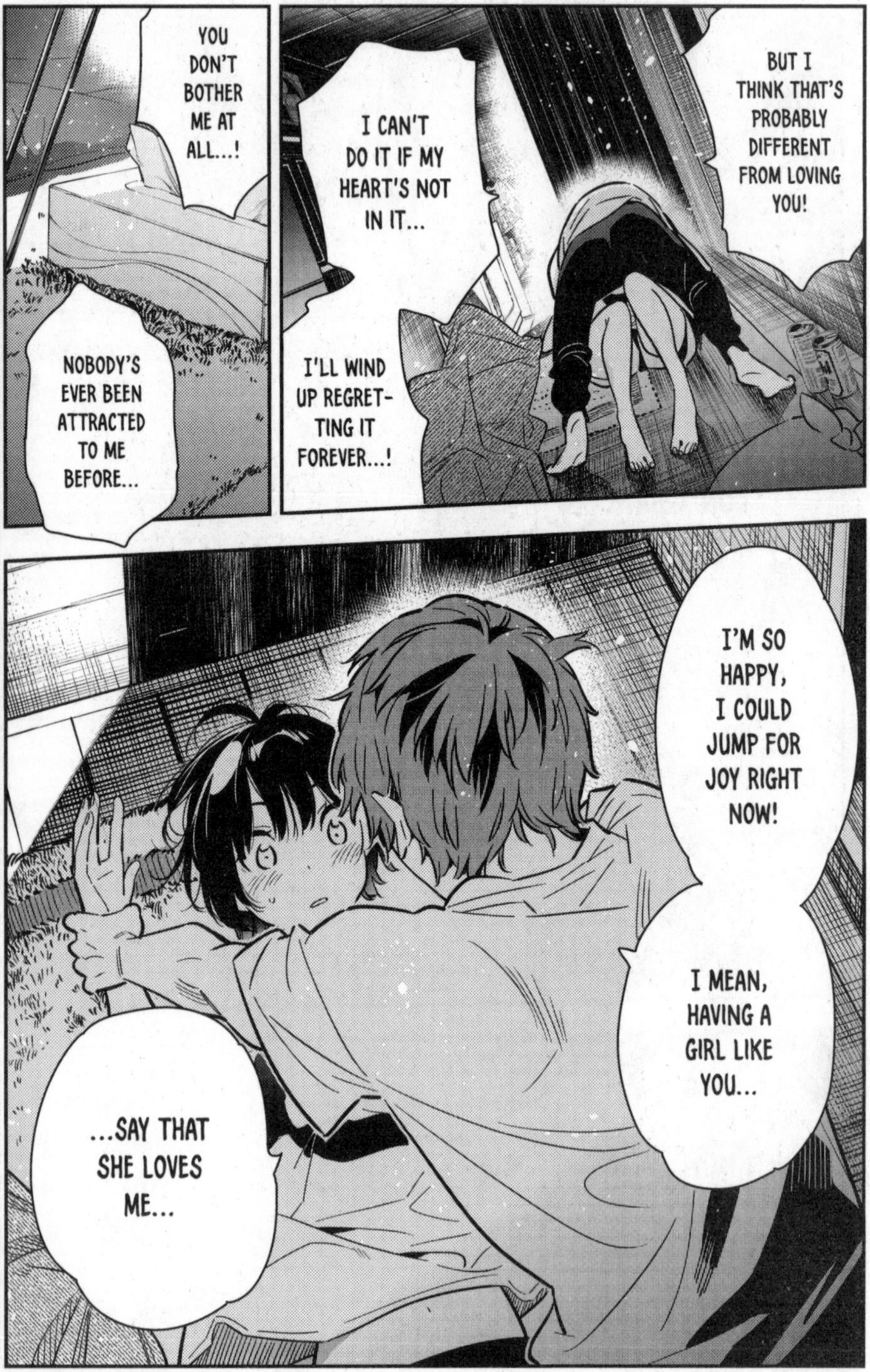
BUT I THINK THAT'S PROBABLY DIFFERENT FROM LOVING YOU!
I CAN'T DO IT IF MY HEART'S NOT IN IT...
I'LL WIND UP REGRET-TING IT FOREVER...!
YOU DON'T BOTHER ME AT ALL...!
NOBODY'S EVER BEEN ATTRACTED TO ME BEFORE...
I'M SO HAPPY, I COULD JUMP FOR JOY RIGHT NOW!
I MEAN, HAVING A GIRL LIKE YOU...
...SAY THAT SHE LOVES ME...

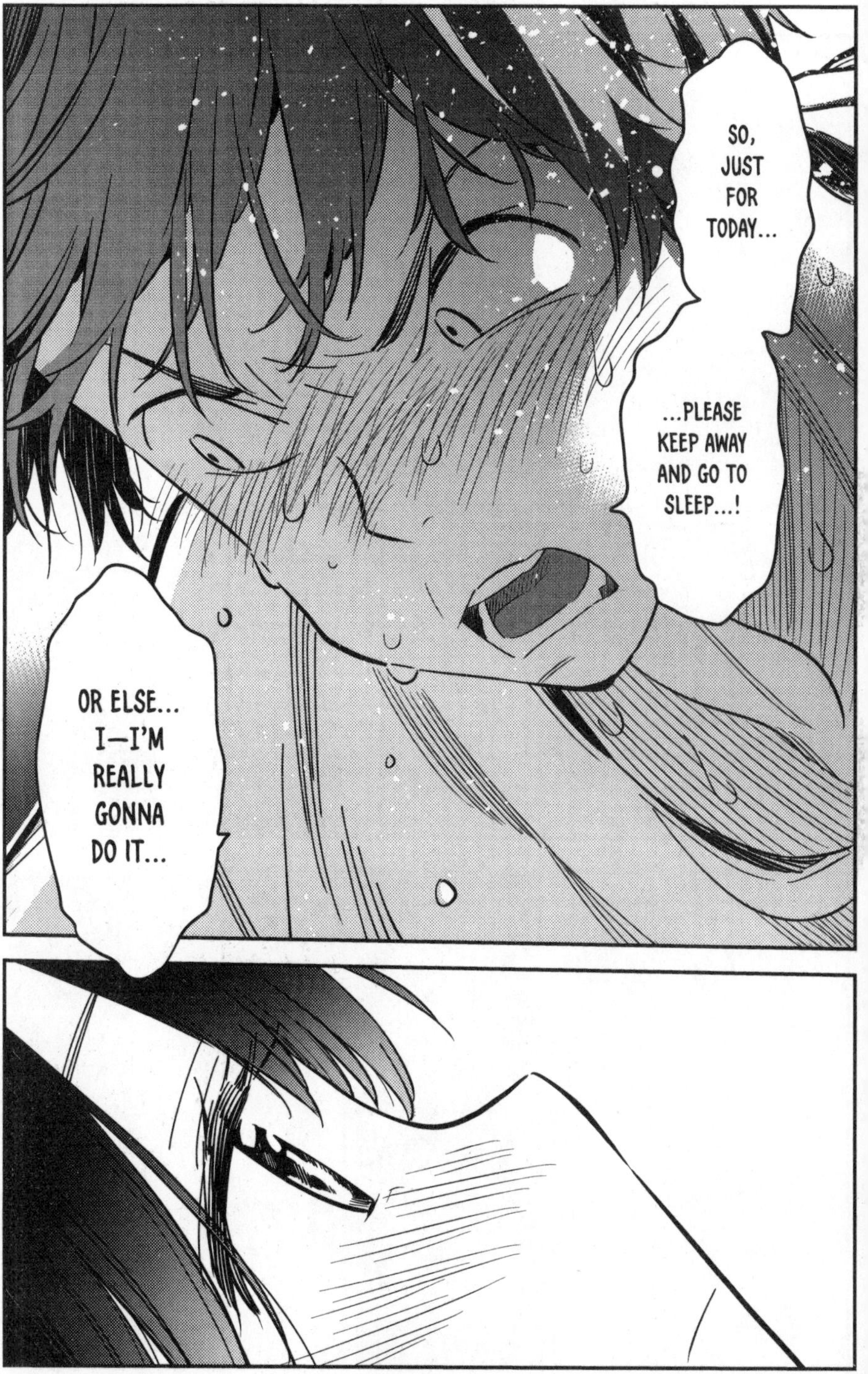
SO, JUST FOR TODAY...
...PLEASE KEEP AWAY AND GO TO SLEEP...!
OR ELSE... I—I'M REALLY GONNA DO IT...

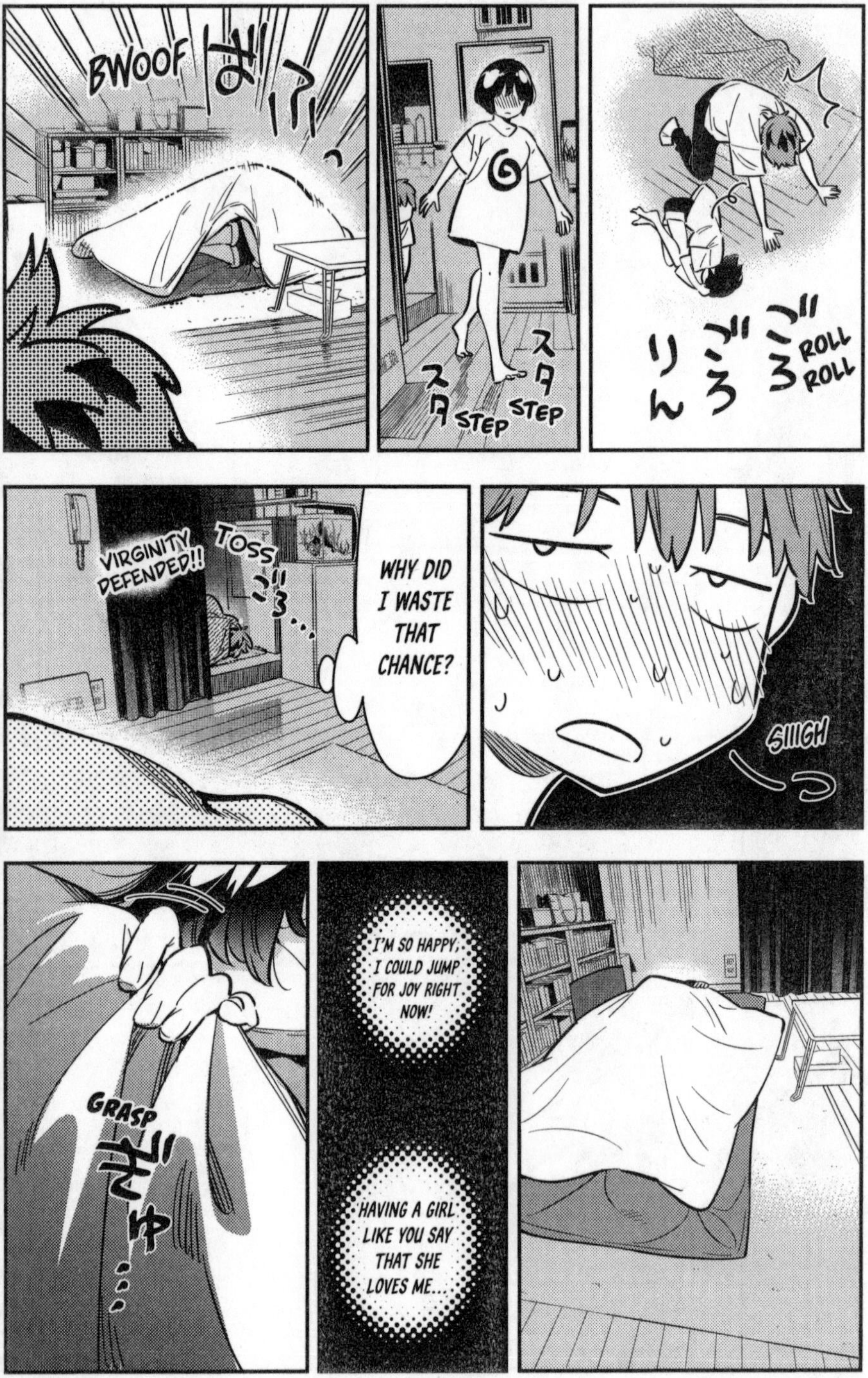

ごろ
ごろ
りん
ROLL ROLL
スタ
スタ
STEP STEP
BWOOF
SIIIGH
WHY DID I WASTE THAT CHANCE?
TOSS
ごろ...
VIRGINITY DEFENDED!!
I'M SO HAPPY, I COULD JUMP FOR JOY RIGHT NOW!
HAVING A GIRL LIKE YOU SAY THAT SHE LOVES ME...
GRASP
ぎゅ...

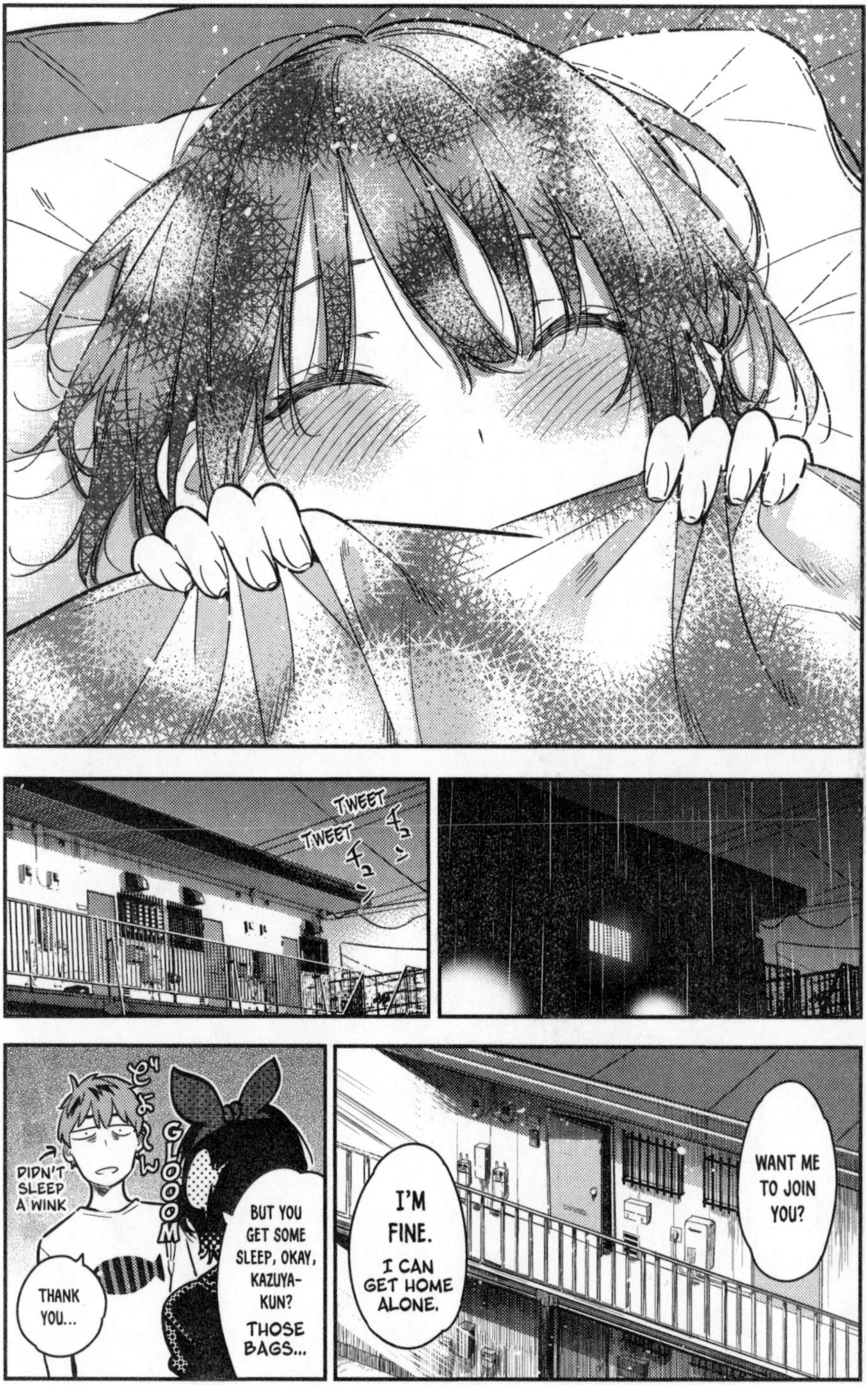
TWEET
TWEET
チュン
チュン
WANT ME TO JOIN YOU?
I'M FINE. I CAN GET HOME ALONE.
BUT YOU GET SOME SLEEP, OKAY, KAZUYA-KUN? THOSE BAGS...
GLOOOM
DIDN'T SLEEP A WINK
THANK YOU...

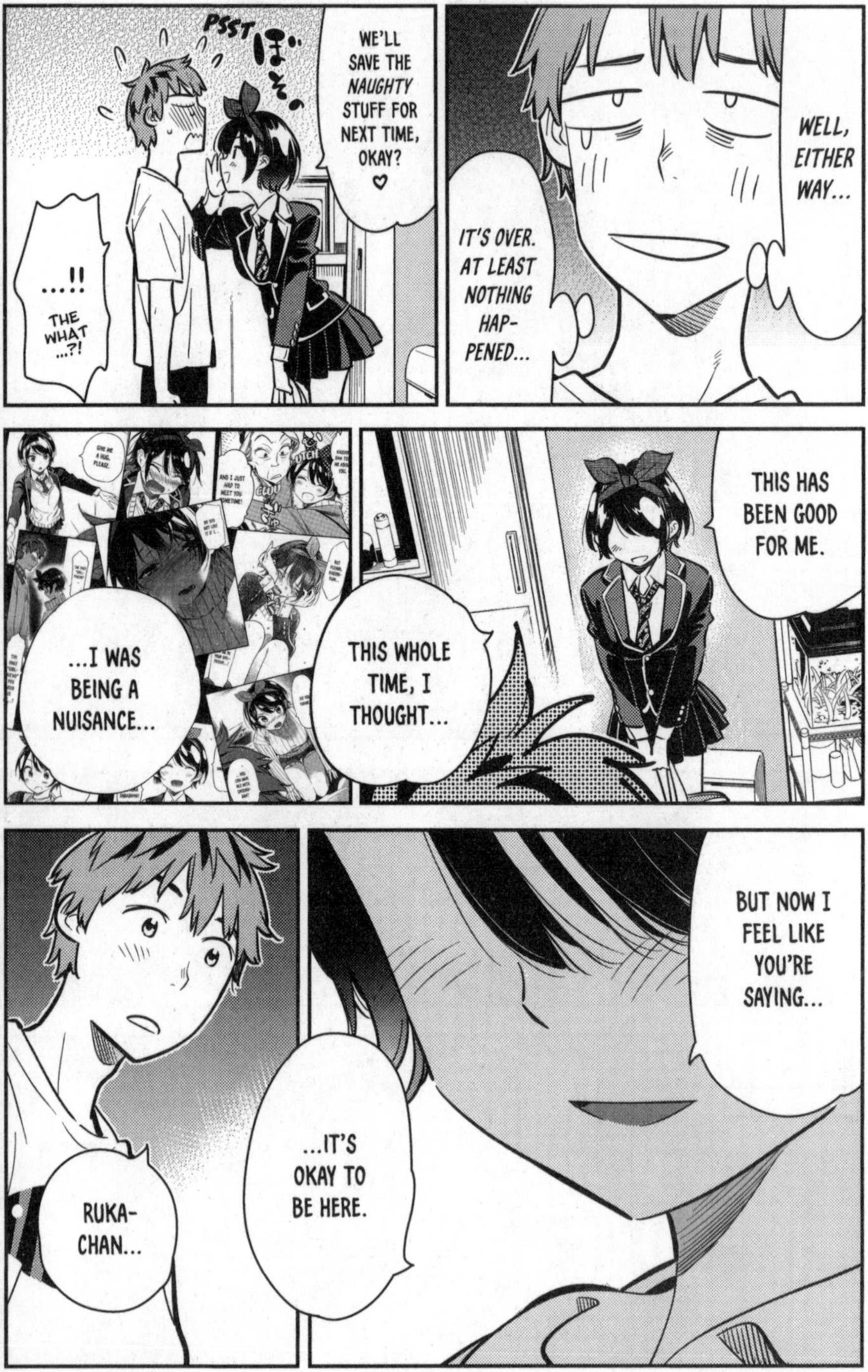
WELL, EITHER WAY...
IT'S OVER. AT LEAST NOTHING HAP-PENED...
PSST
ぼそっ
WE'LL SAVE THE *NAUGHTY* STUFF FOR NEXT TIME, OKAY? ♡
...!!
THE WHAT ...?!
THIS HAS BEEN GOOD FOR ME.
THIS WHOLE TIME, I THOUGHT...
...I WAS BEING A NUISANCE...
BUT NOW I FEEL LIKE YOU'RE SAYING...
...IT'S OKAY TO BE HERE.
RUKA-CHAN...

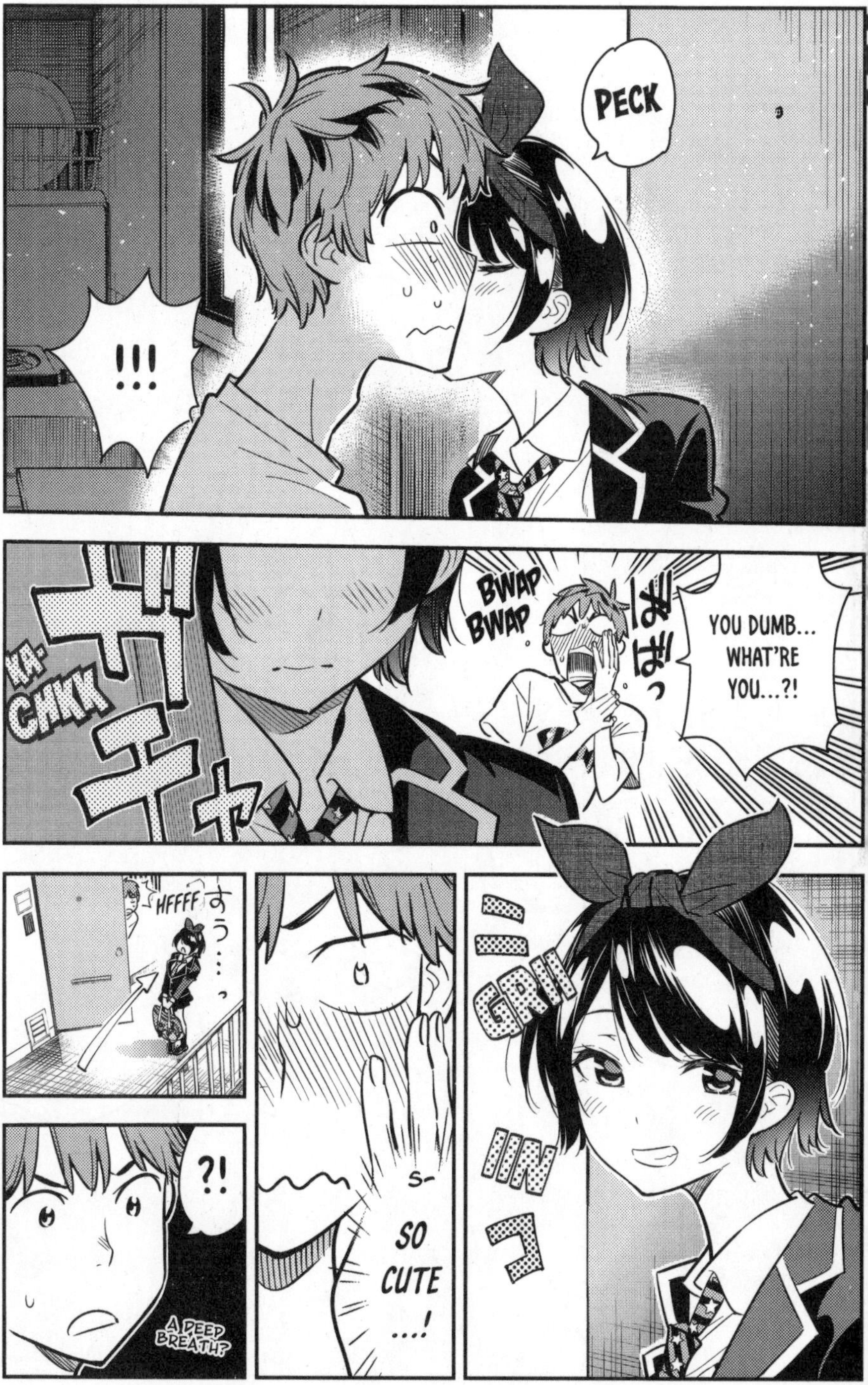
PECK
!!!
YOU DUMB... WHAT'RE YOU...?!
BWAP BWAP
KA-CHKK
GRIIIN
S-
SO CUTE ...!
HFFFF
すう…っ
?!
A DEEP BREATH?

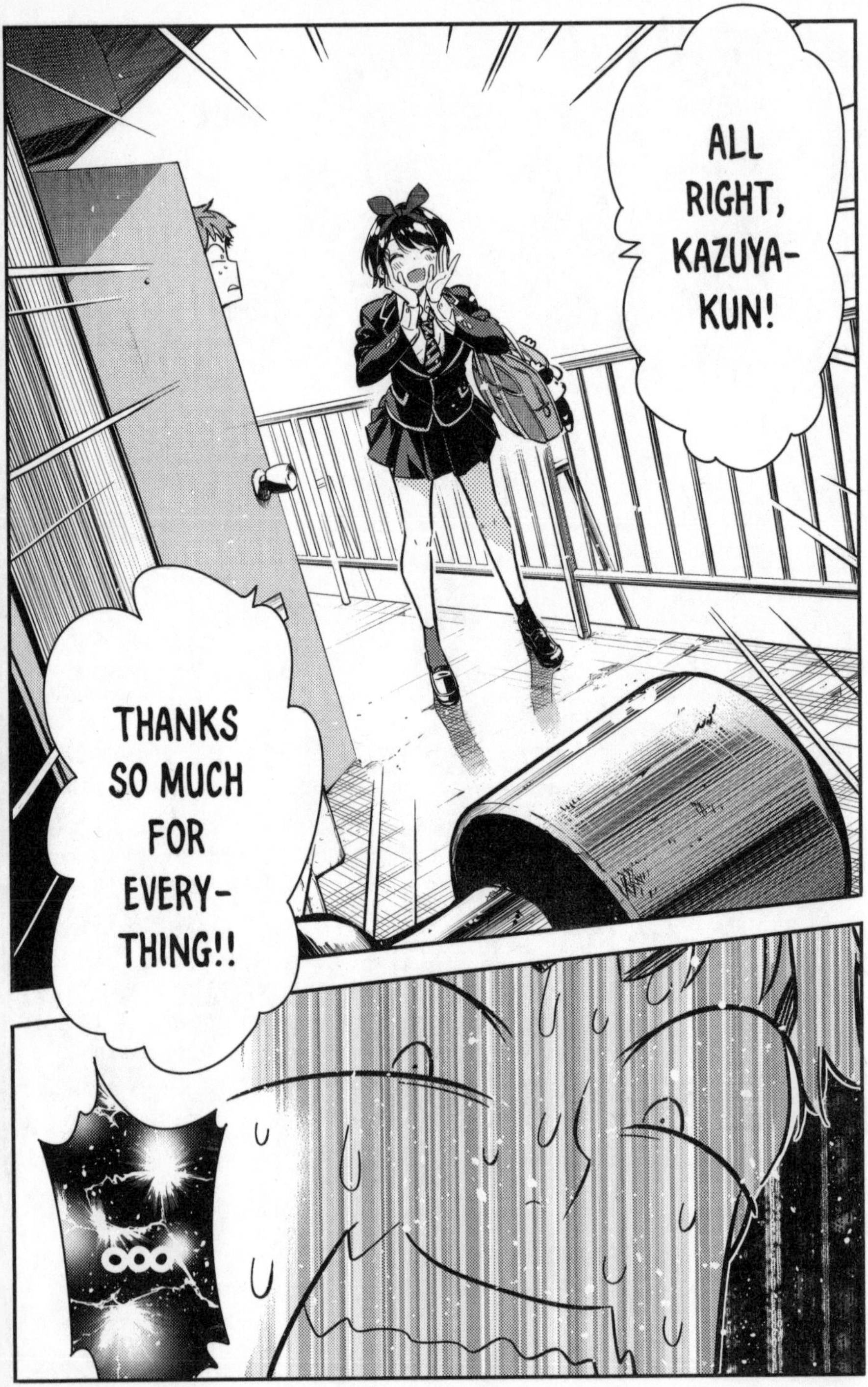
ALL RIGHT, KAZUYA-KUN!
THANKS SO MUCH FOR EVERY-THING!!

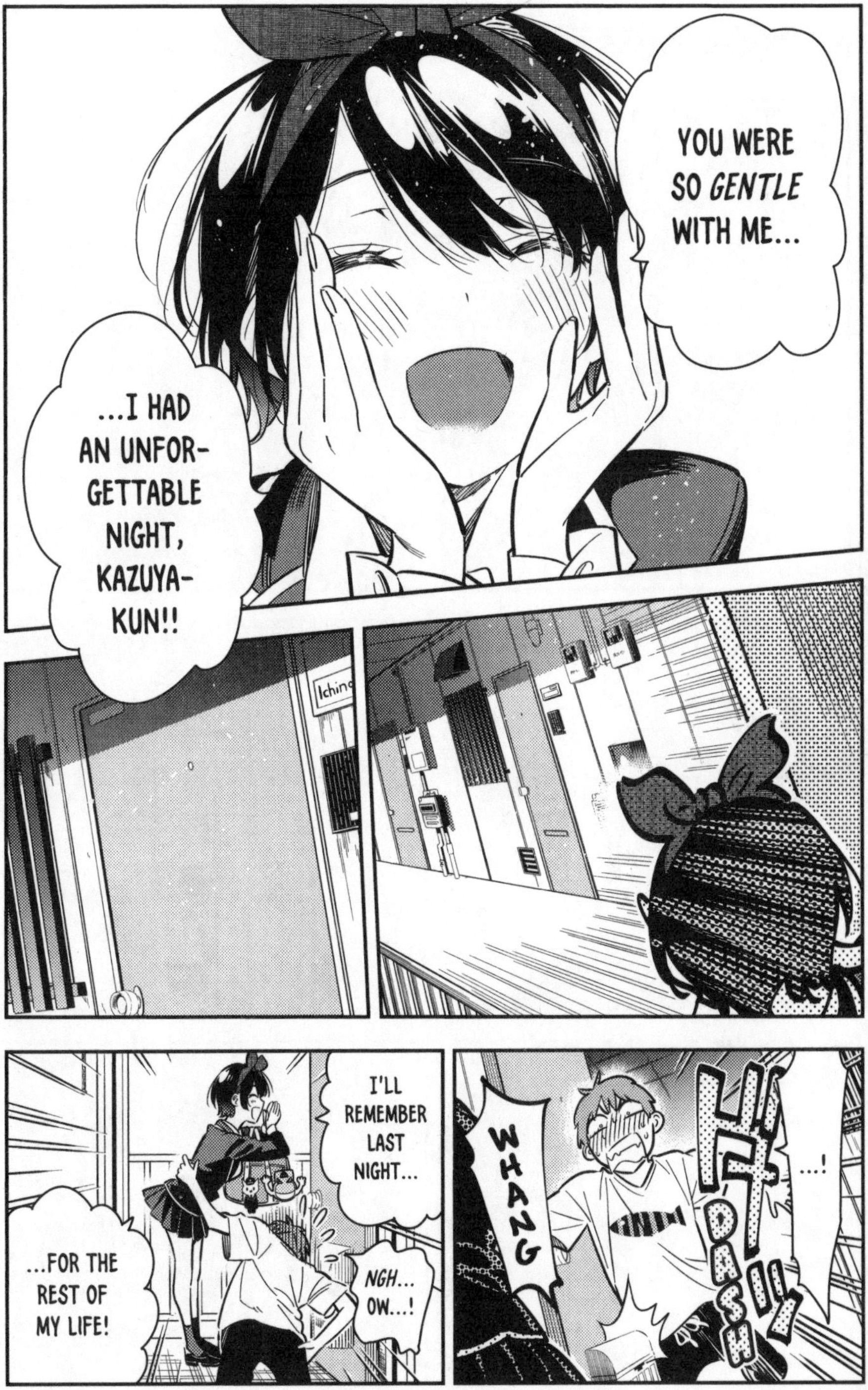
YOU WERE SO *GENTLE* WITH ME...
...I HAD AN UNFOR-GETTABLE NIGHT, KAZUYA-KUN!!
HIT
DASH!!
...!
WHANG
I'LL REMEMBER LAST NIGHT...
...FOR THE REST OF MY LIFE!
NGH... OW...!

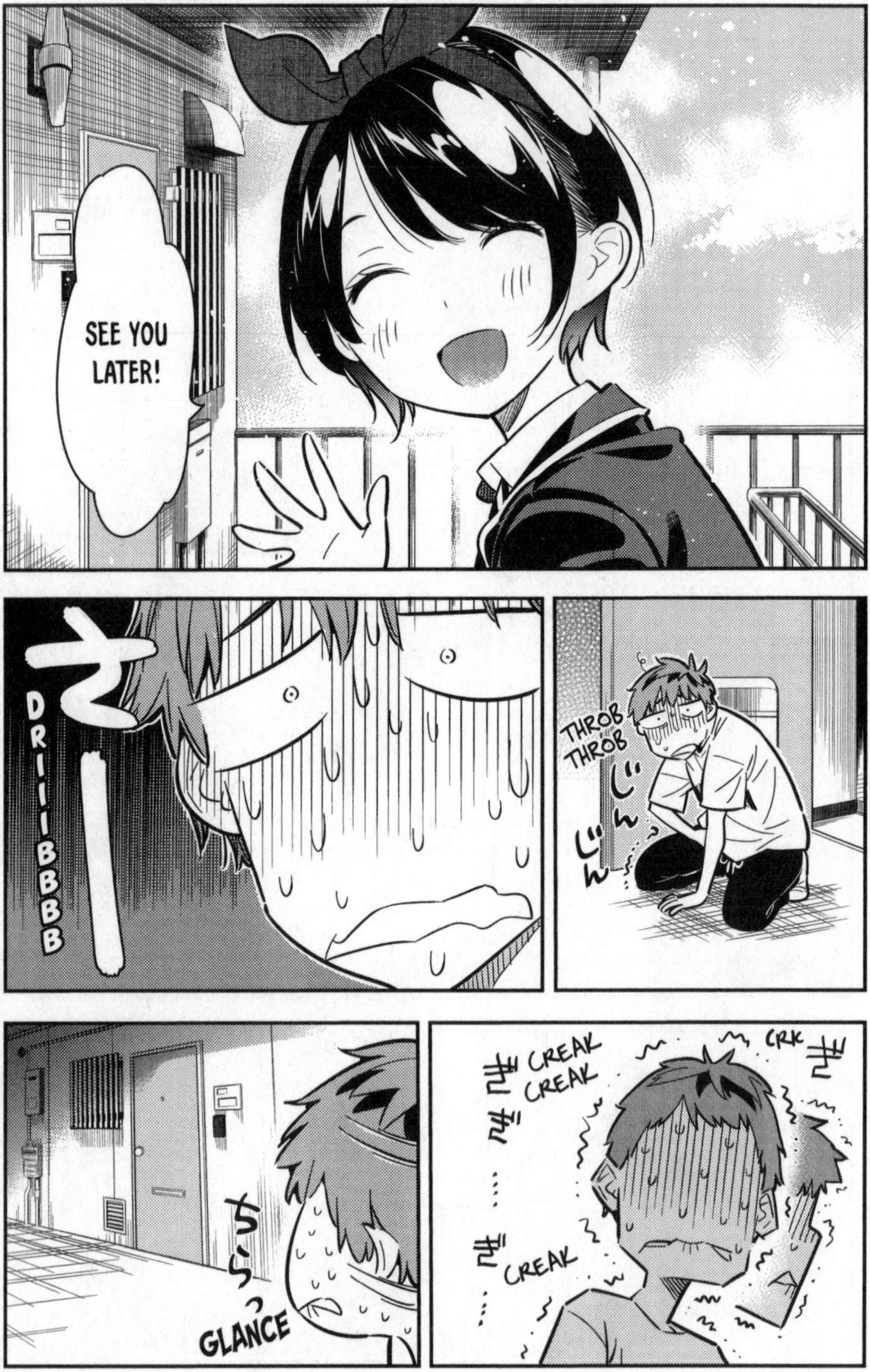
SEE YOU LATER!
THROB THROB
じん じん
ざー
DRIIIIBBBBB
CRK
ぎ
CREAK CREAK
ぎ ぎ
CREAK
ぎ
ちらっ
GLANCE

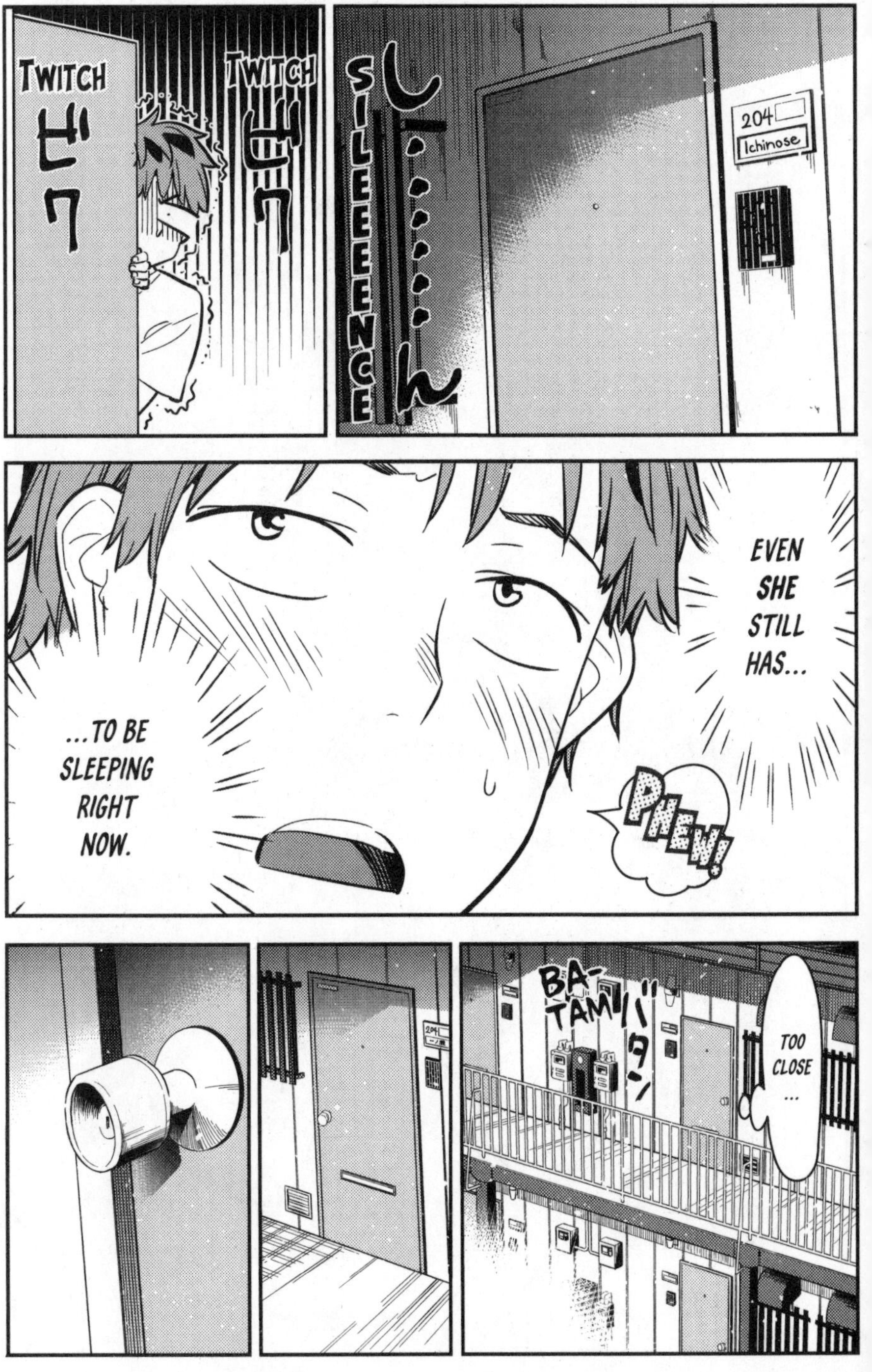

SILEEEENCE
し……ん
204
Ichinose
TWITCH
ビク
TWITCH
ビク
EVEN SHE STILL HAS...
PHEW!
...TO BE SLEEPING RIGHT NOW.
BA-TAM
バタン
TOO CLOSE ...

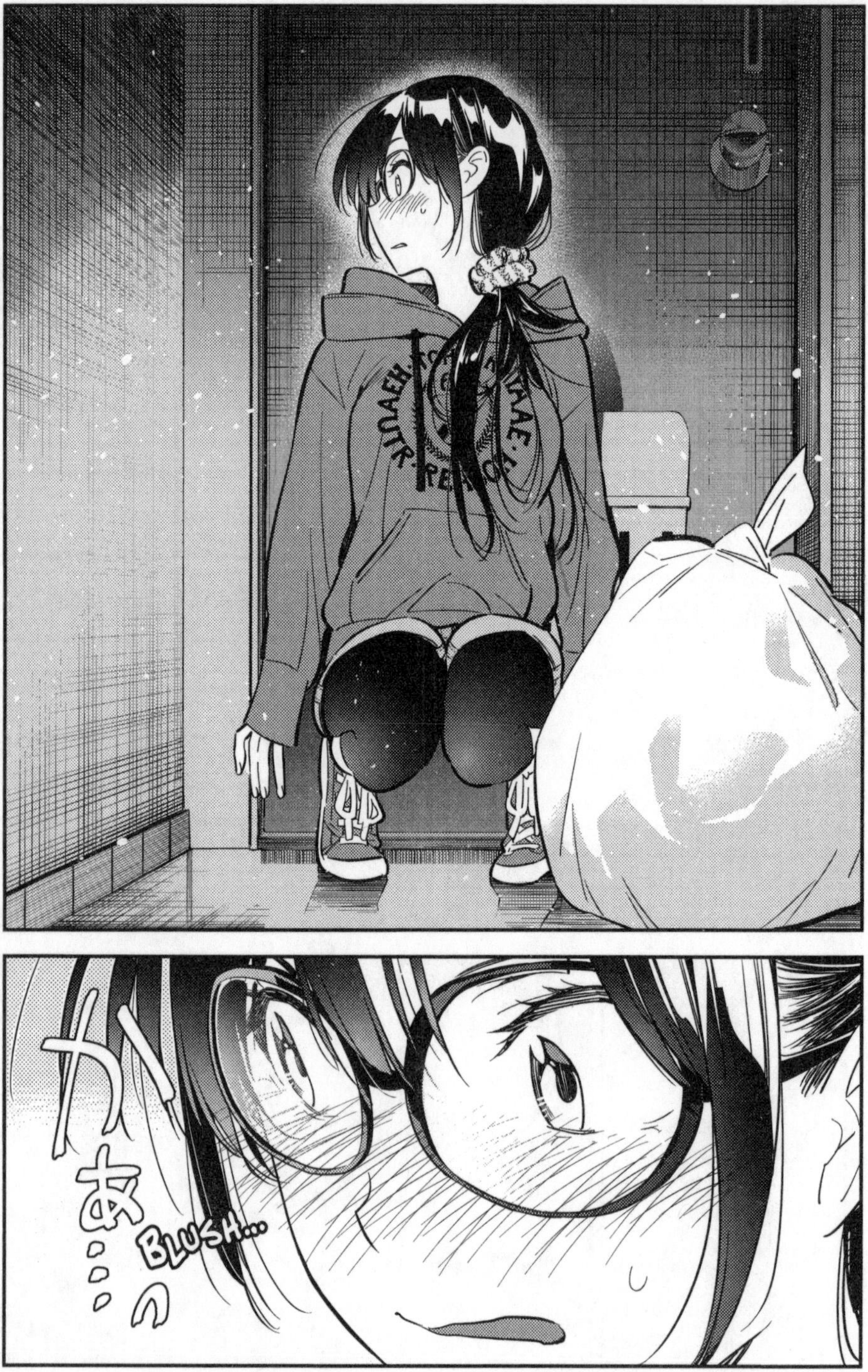
かぁ…っ
BLUSH...

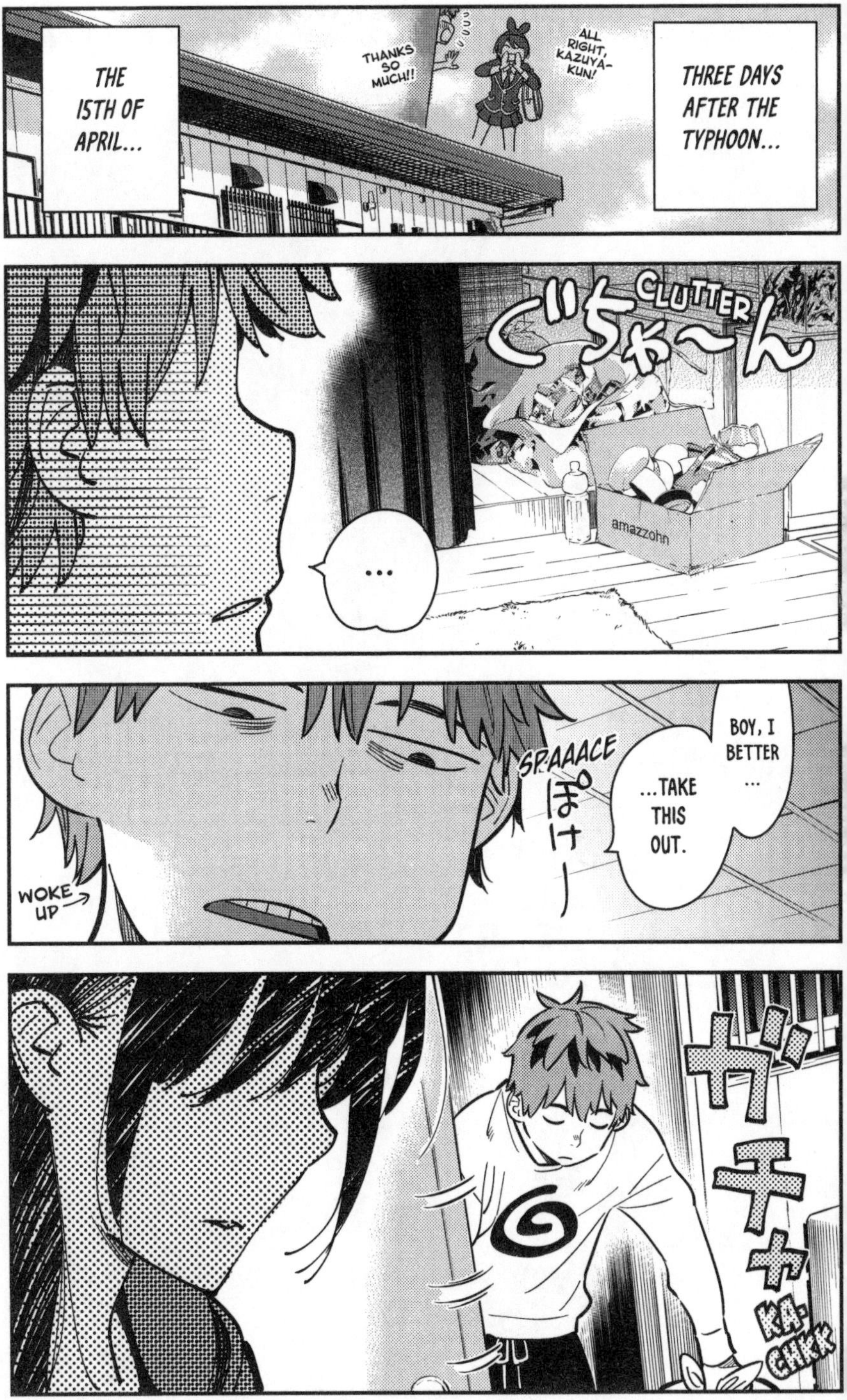
THREE DAYS AFTER THE TYPHOON...
ALL RIGHT, KAZUYA-KUN!
THANKS SO MUCH!!
THE 15TH OF APRIL...
CLUTTER
ぐちゃ〜ん
amazzohn
...
BOY, I BETTER ...
...TAKE THIS OUT.
SPAAACE
ぽけー
WOKE UP
ガチャ
KA-CHKK

RATING 66 THE BIRTHDAY AND MY GIRLFRIEND 1

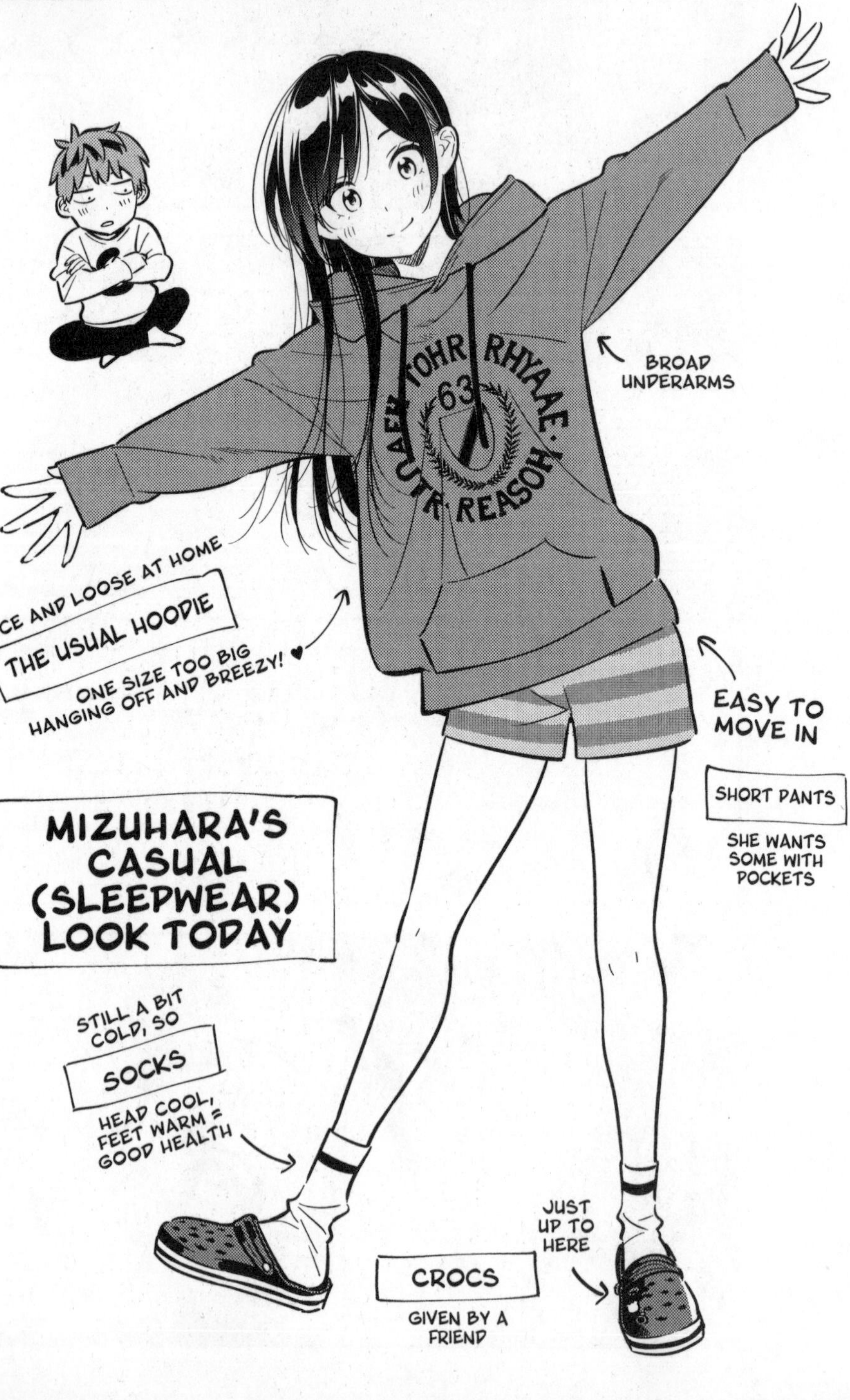
BROAD UNDERARMS
NICE AND LOOSE AT HOME
THE USUAL HOODIE
ONE SIZE TOO BIG HANGING OFF AND BREEZY! ♥
EASY TO MOVE IN
SHORT PANTS
SHE WANTS SOME WITH POCKETS
MIZUHARA'S CASUAL (SLEEPWEAR) LOOK TODAY
STILL A BIT COLD, SO
SOCKS
HEAD COOL, FEET WARM = GOOD HEALTH
JUST UP TO HERE
CROCS
GIVEN BY A FRIEND

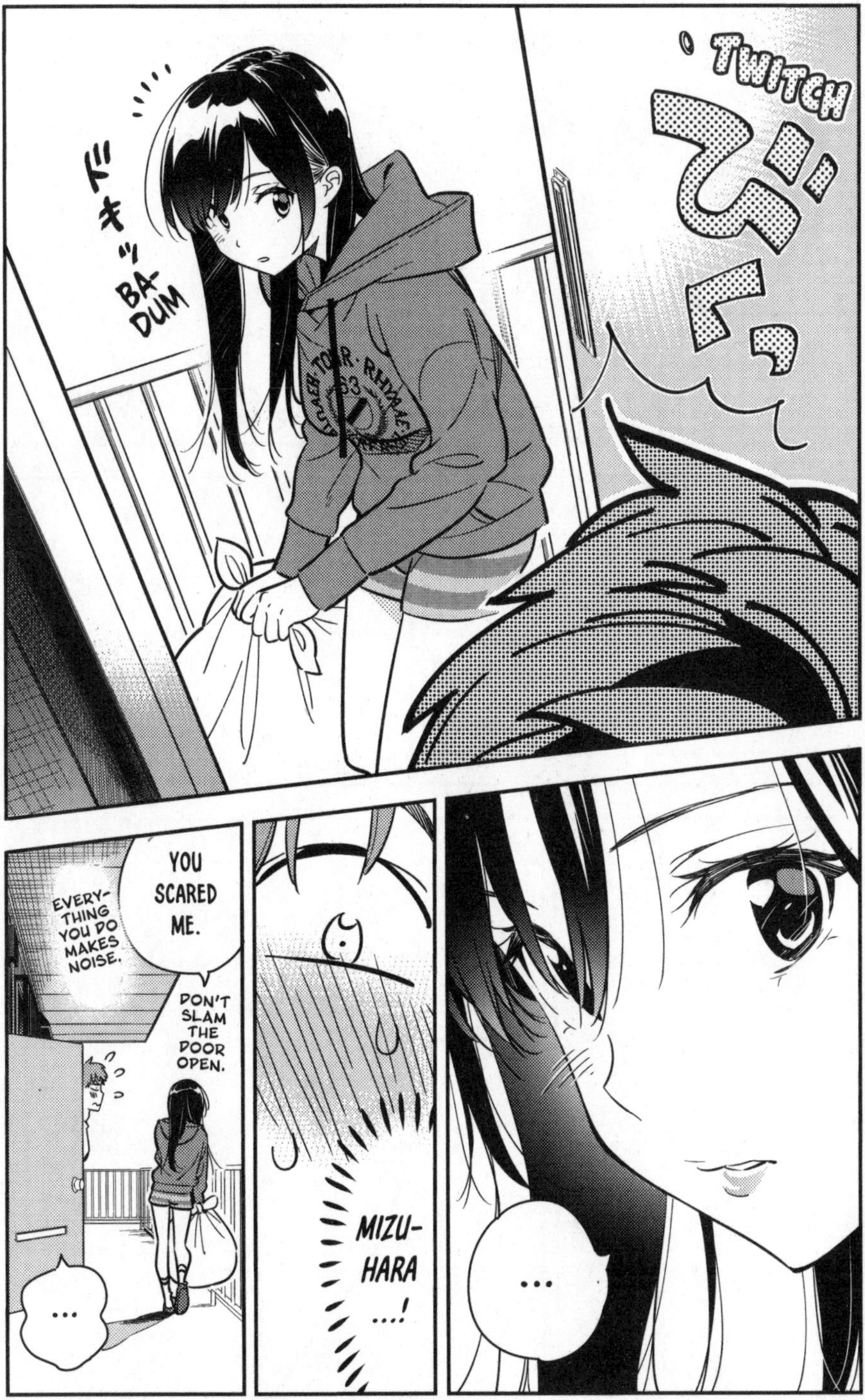
TWITCH
びくっ
ドキッ
BA-DUM
...
MIZU-HARA ...!
YOU SCARED ME.
DON'T SLAM THE DOOR OPEN.
EVERY-THING YOU DO MAKES NOISE.
...

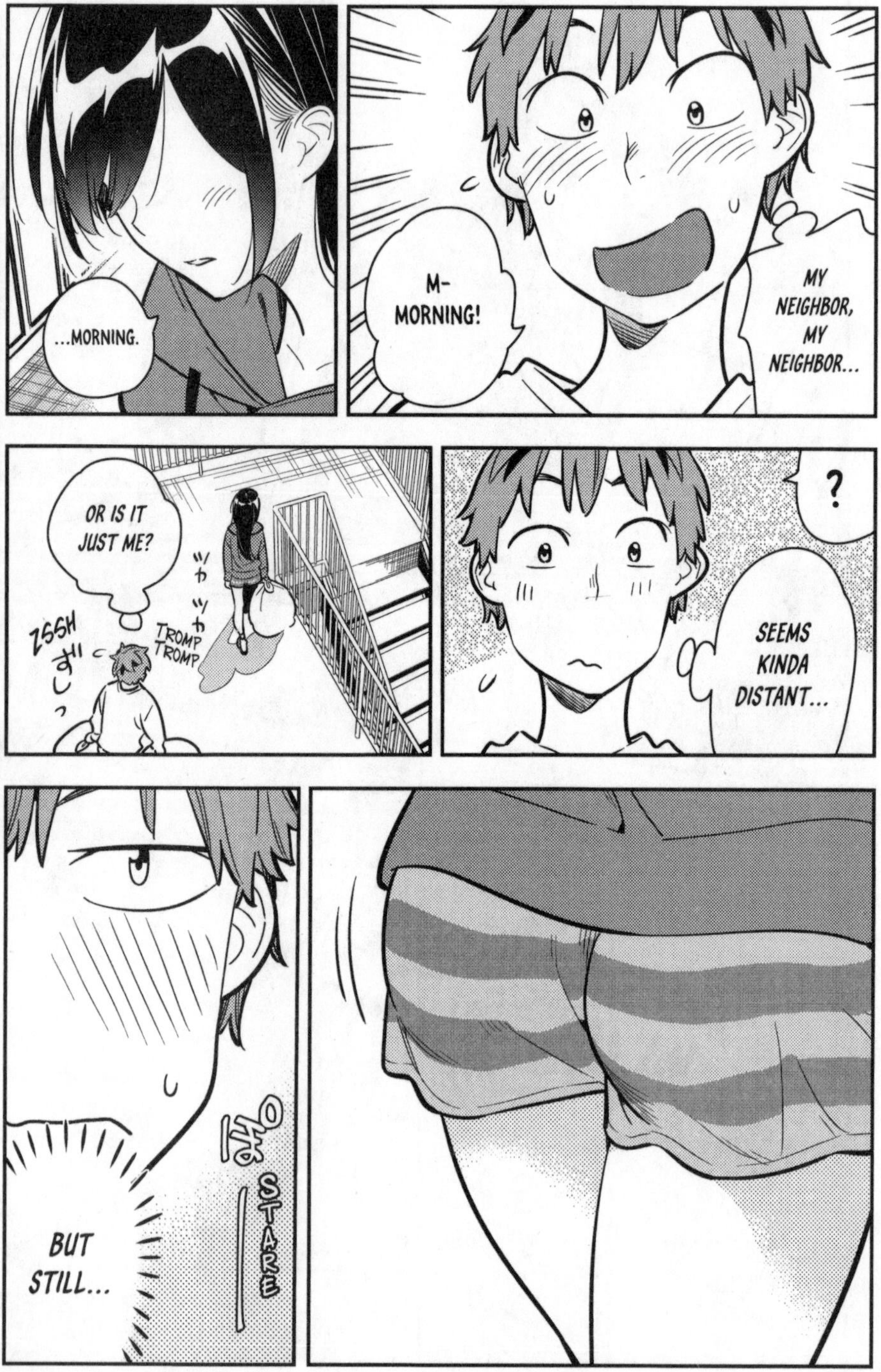
MY NEIGHBOR, MY NEIGHBOR...
M- MORNING!
...MORNING.
?
SEEMS KINDA DISTANT...
OR IS IT JUST ME?
ツカ ツカ
TROMP TROMP
ZSSH
ずしっ
じー
STARE
BUT STILL...

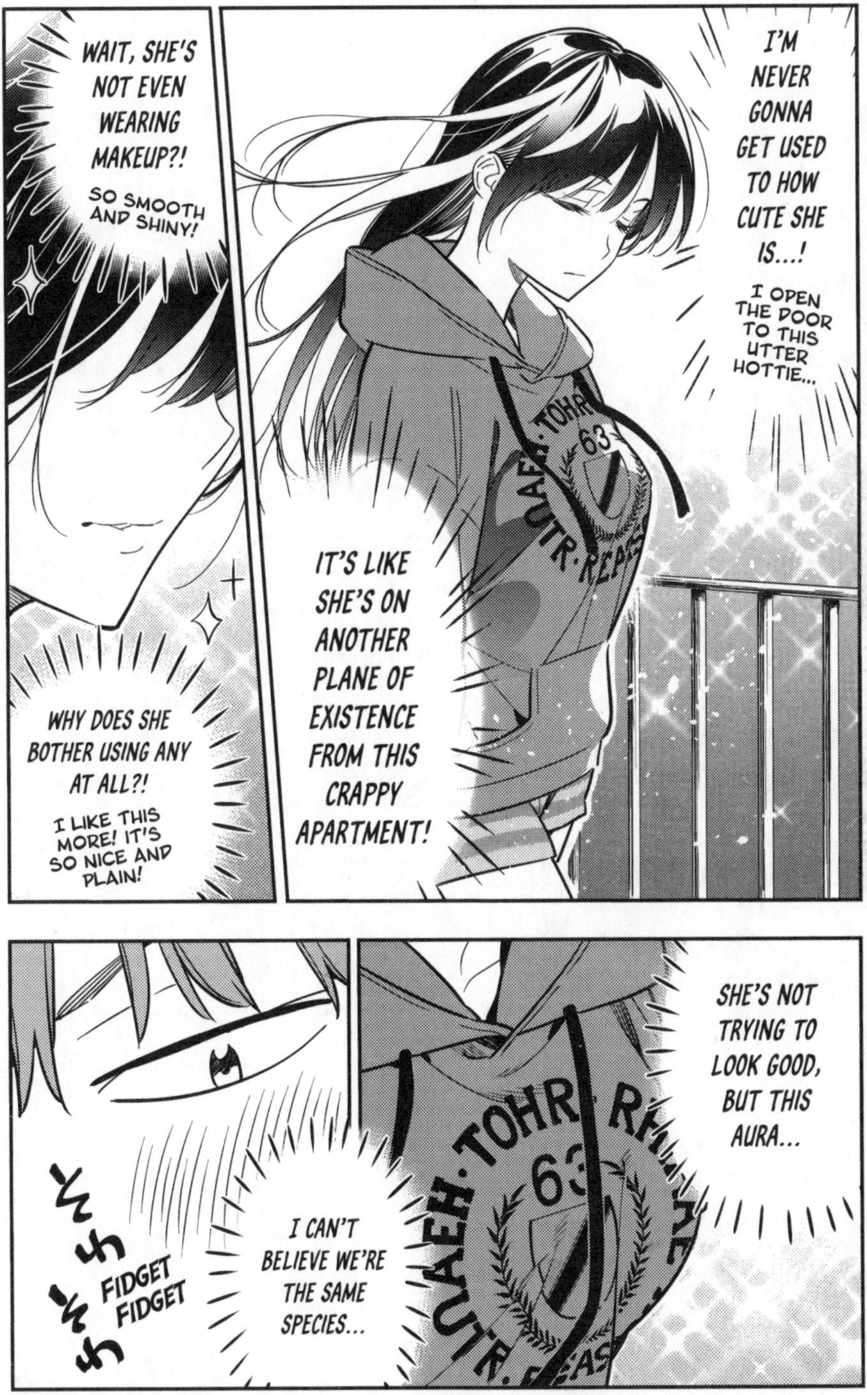
I'M NEVER GONNA GET USED TO HOW CUTE SHE IS...!
I OPEN THE DOOR TO THIS UTTER HOTTIE...
IT'S LIKE SHE'S ON ANOTHER PLANE OF EXISTENCE FROM THIS CRAPPY APARTMENT!
WAIT, SHE'S NOT EVEN WEARING MAKEUP?!
SO SMOOTH AND SHINY!
WHY DOES SHE BOTHER USING ANY AT ALL?!
I LIKE THIS MORE! IT'S SO NICE AND PLAIN!
SHE'S NOT TRYING TO LOOK GOOD, BUT THIS AURA...
I CAN'T BELIEVE WE'RE THE SAME SPECIES...
FIDGET FIDGET

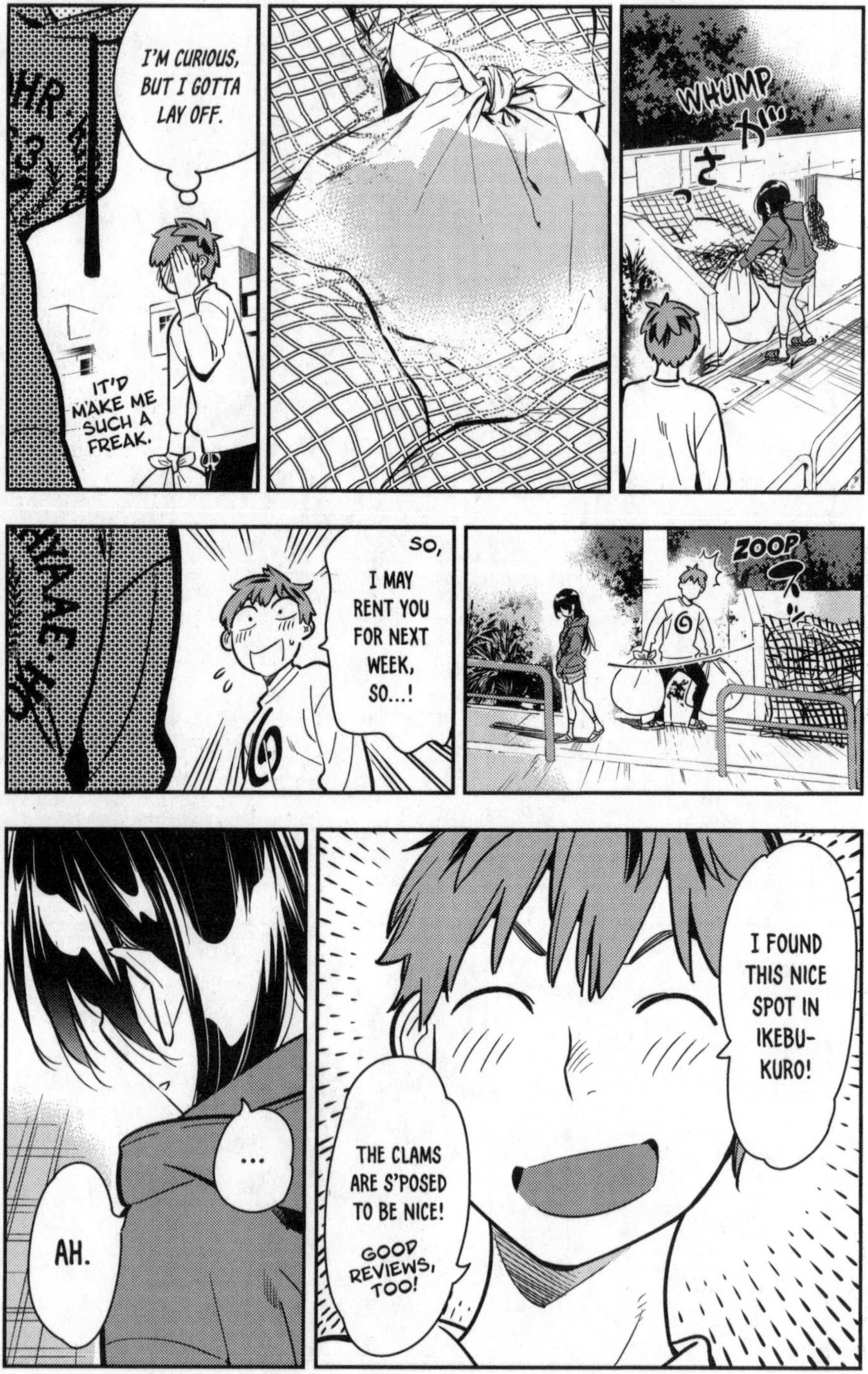
WHUMP
I'M CURIOUS, BUT I GOTTA LAY OFF.
IT'D MAKE ME SUCH A FREAK.
ZOOP
SO, I MAY RENT YOU FOR NEXT WEEK, SO...!
I FOUND THIS NICE SPOT IN IKEBU-KURO!
THE CLAMS ARE S'POSED TO BE NICE!
GOOD REVIEWS, TOO!
...
AH.

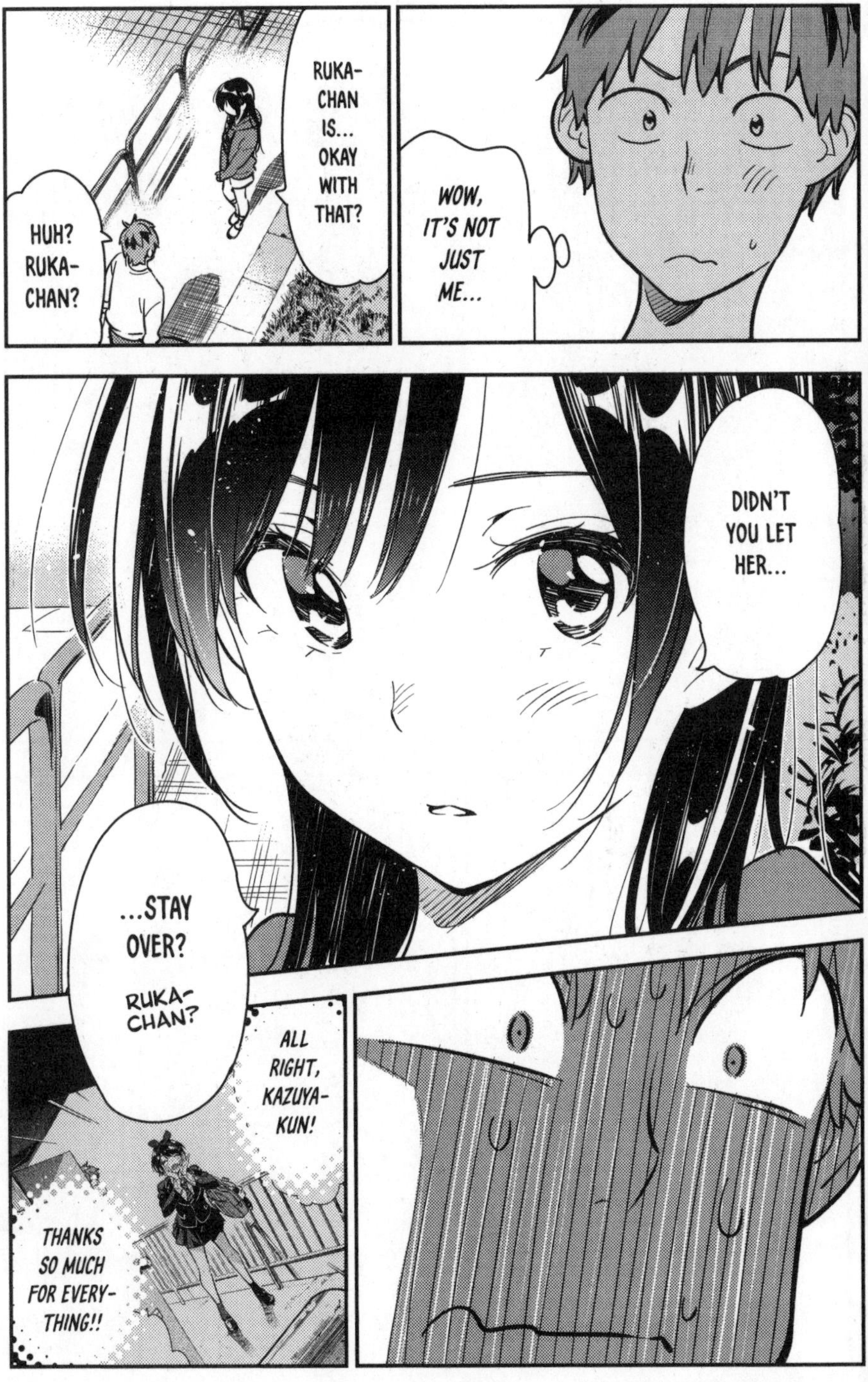
WOW, IT'S NOT JUST ME...
RUKA-CHAN IS... OKAY WITH THAT?
HUH? RUKA-CHAN?
DIDN'T YOU LET HER...
...STAY OVER?
RUKA-CHAN?
ALL RIGHT, KAZUYA-KUN!
THANKS SO MUCH FOR EVERYTHING!!

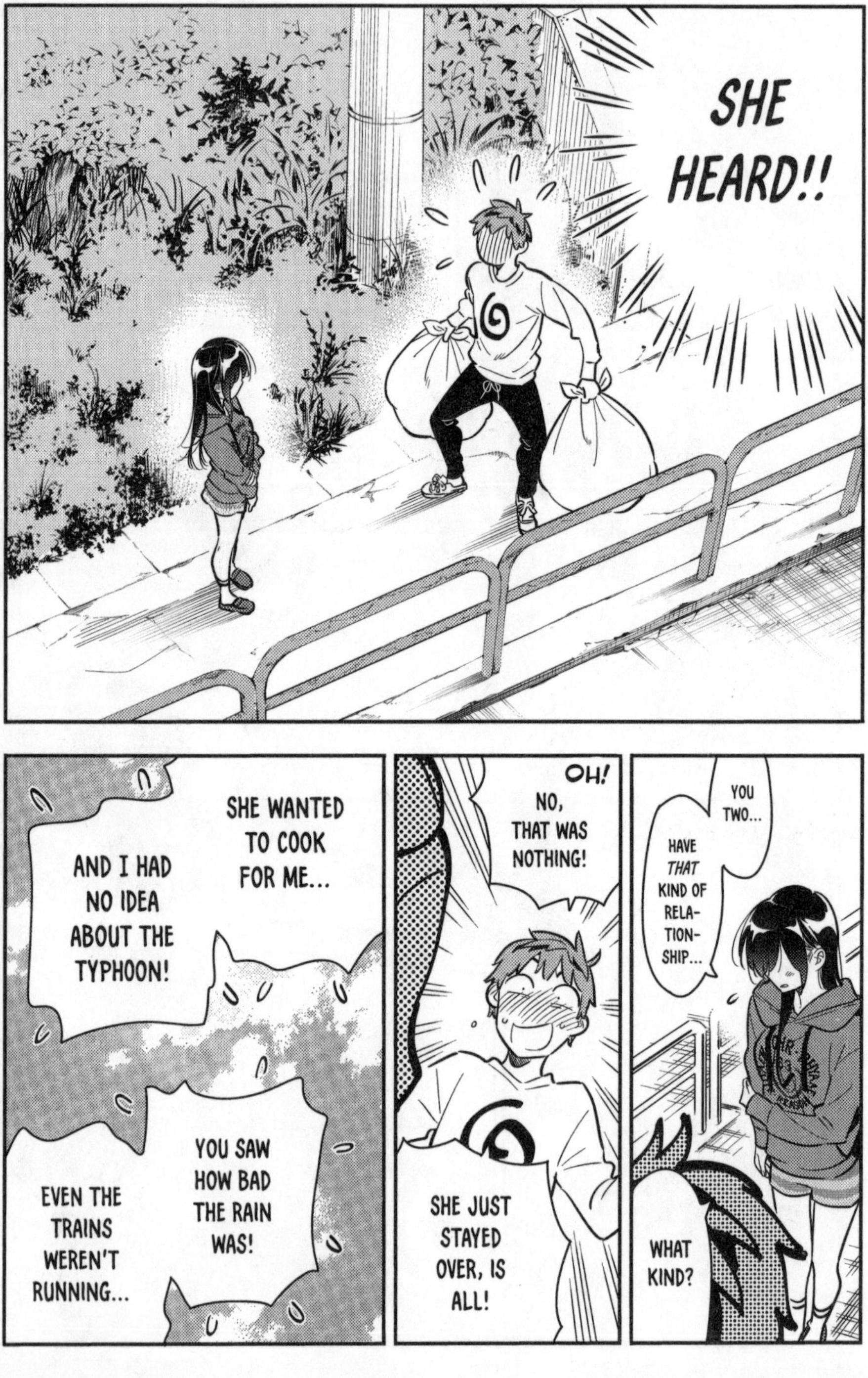
SHE HEARD!!
YOU TWO... HAVE *THAT* KIND OF RELATIONSHIP...
WHAT KIND?
OH!
NO, THAT WAS NOTHING!
SHE JUST STAYED OVER, IS ALL!
SHE WANTED TO COOK FOR ME...
AND I HAD NO IDEA ABOUT THE TYPHOON!
YOU SAW HOW BAD THE RAIN WAS!
EVEN THE TRAINS WEREN'T RUNNING...

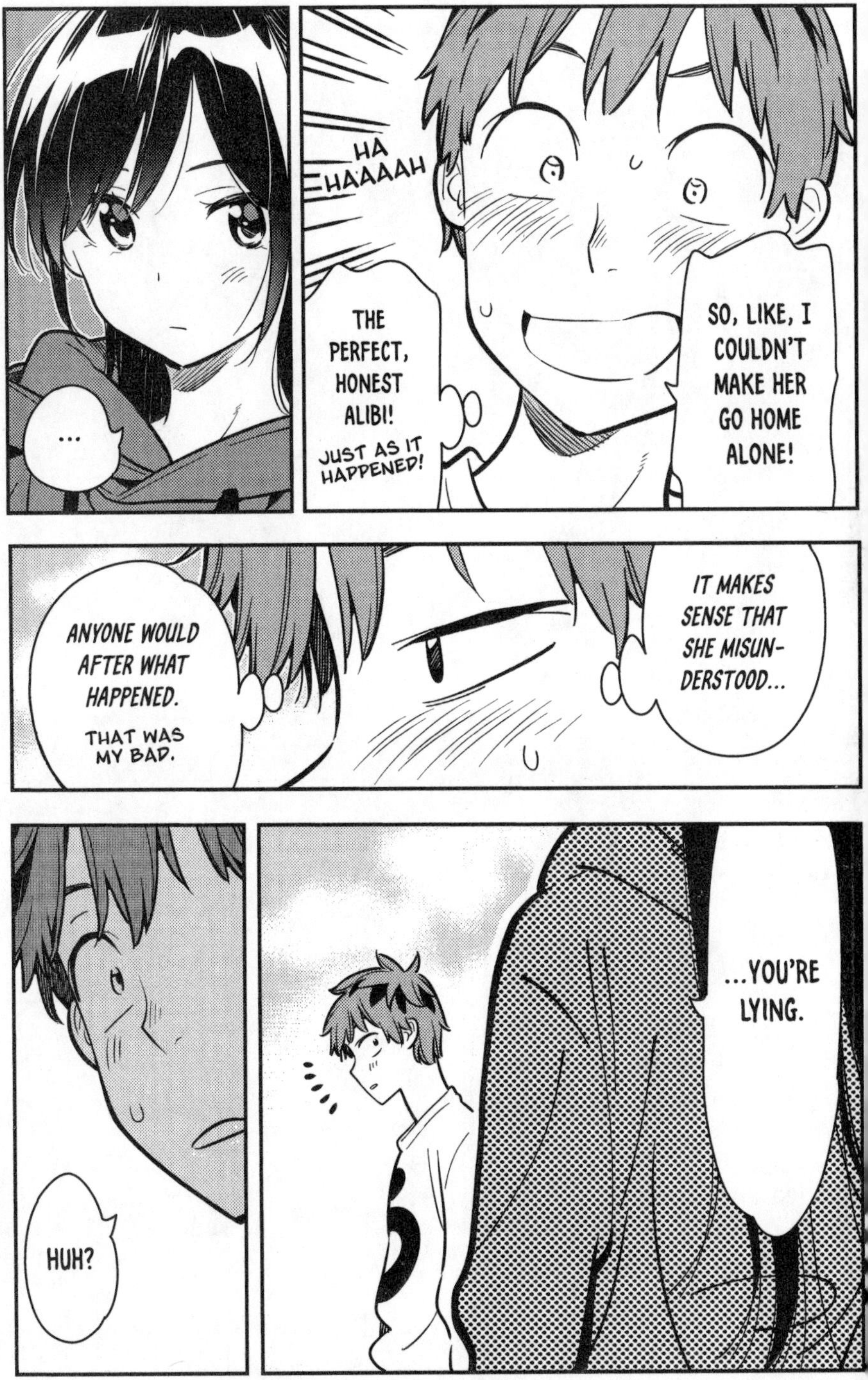
HA HAAAAH
SO, LIKE, I COULDN'T MAKE HER GO HOME ALONE!
THE PERFECT, HONEST ALIBI! JUST AS IT HAPPENED!
...
IT MAKES SENSE THAT SHE MISUNDERSTOOD...
ANYONE WOULD AFTER WHAT HAPPENED. THAT WAS MY BAD.
...YOU'RE LYING.
HUH?

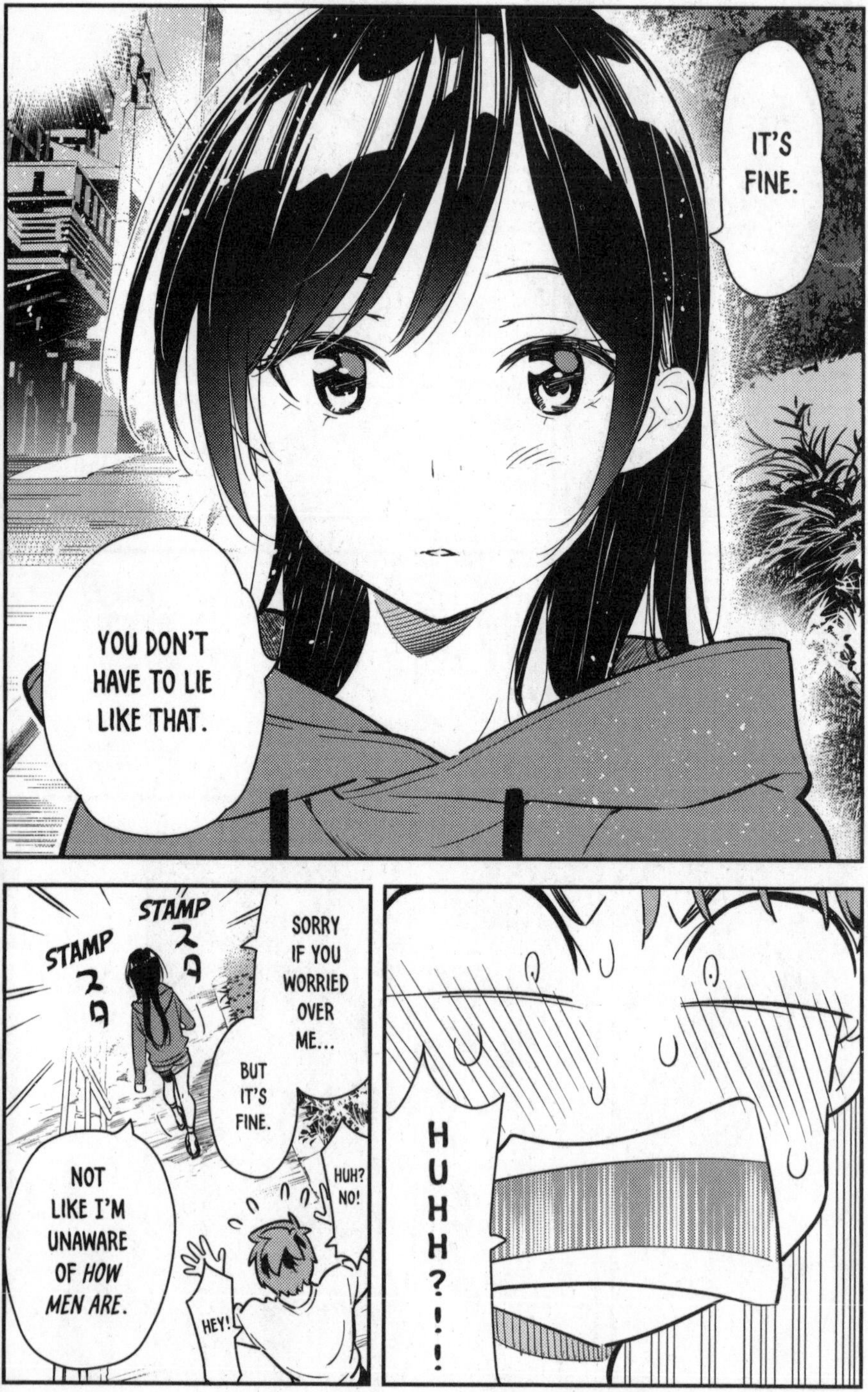
IT'S FINE.
YOU DON'T HAVE TO LIE LIKE THAT.
HUHH?!!
SORRY IF YOU WORRIED OVER ME...
BUT IT'S FINE.
STAMP スタ
STAMP スタ
HUH? NO!
NOT LIKE I'M UNAWARE OF *HOW MEN ARE*.
HEY!

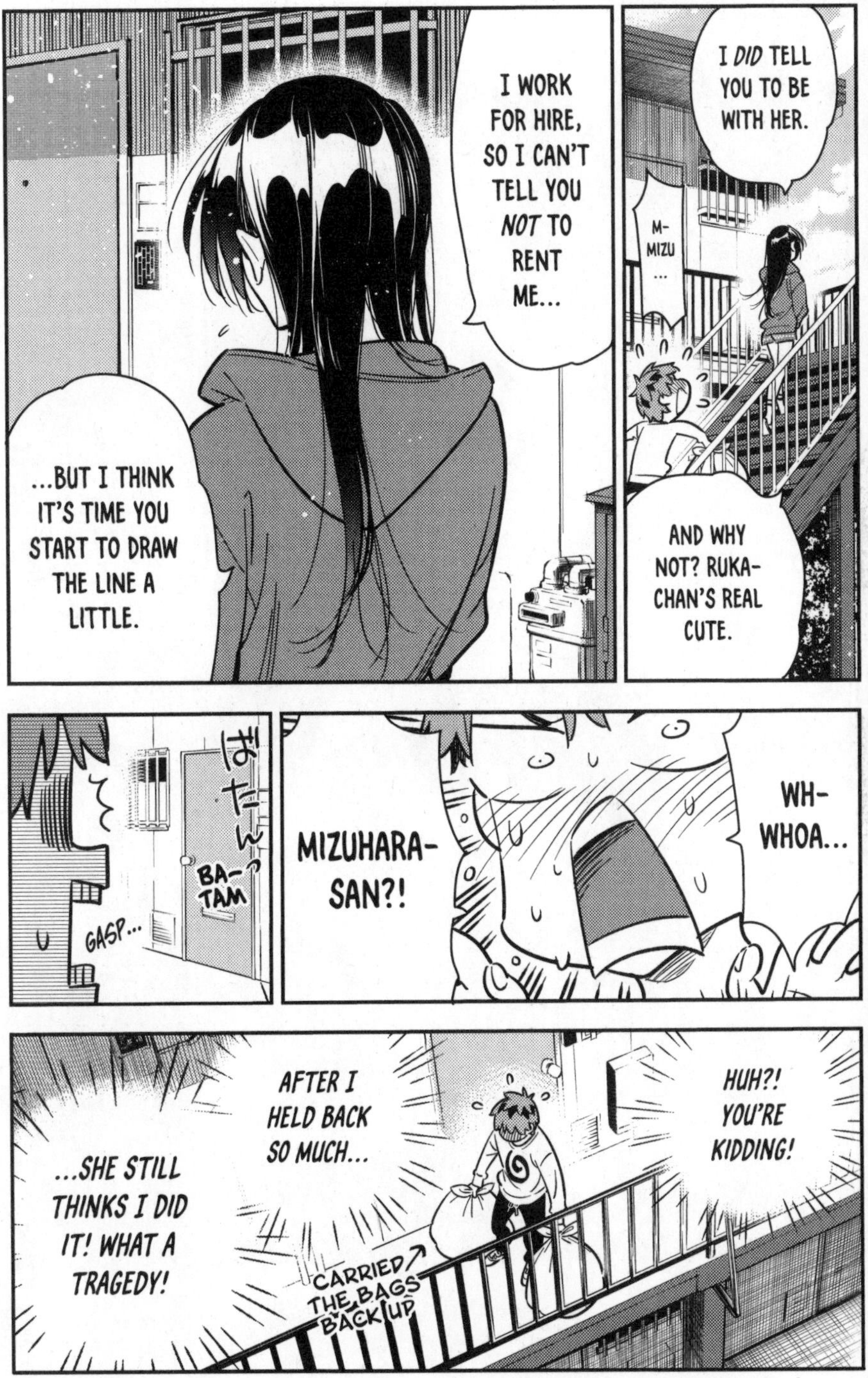
I DID TELL YOU TO BE WITH HER.
M-MIZU...
AND WHY NOT? RUKA-CHAN'S REAL CUTE.
I WORK FOR HIRE, SO I CAN'T TELL YOU NOT TO RENT ME...
...BUT I THINK IT'S TIME YOU START TO DRAW THE LINE A LITTLE.
WH-WHOA...
MIZUHARA-SAN?!
ばたんっ
BA-TAM
GASP...
HUH?! YOU'RE KIDDING!
AFTER I HELD BACK SO MUCH...
...SHE STILL THINKS I DID IT! WHAT A TRAGEDY!
CARRIED THE BAGS BACK UP

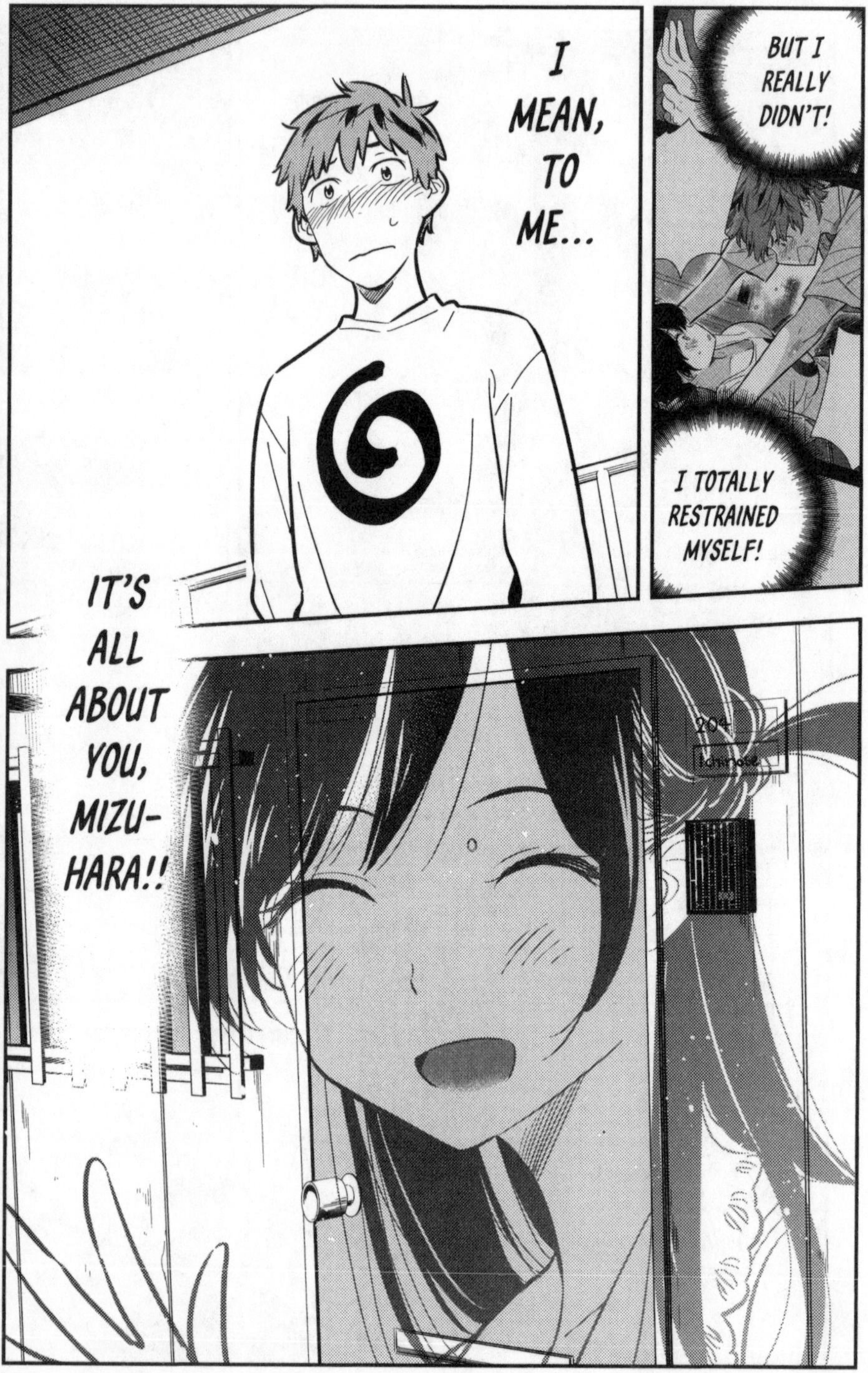
BUT I REALLY DIDN'T!
I TOTALLY RESTRAINED MYSELF!
I MEAN, TO ME...
IT'S ALL ABOUT YOU, MIZUHARA!!
204
Ichinose

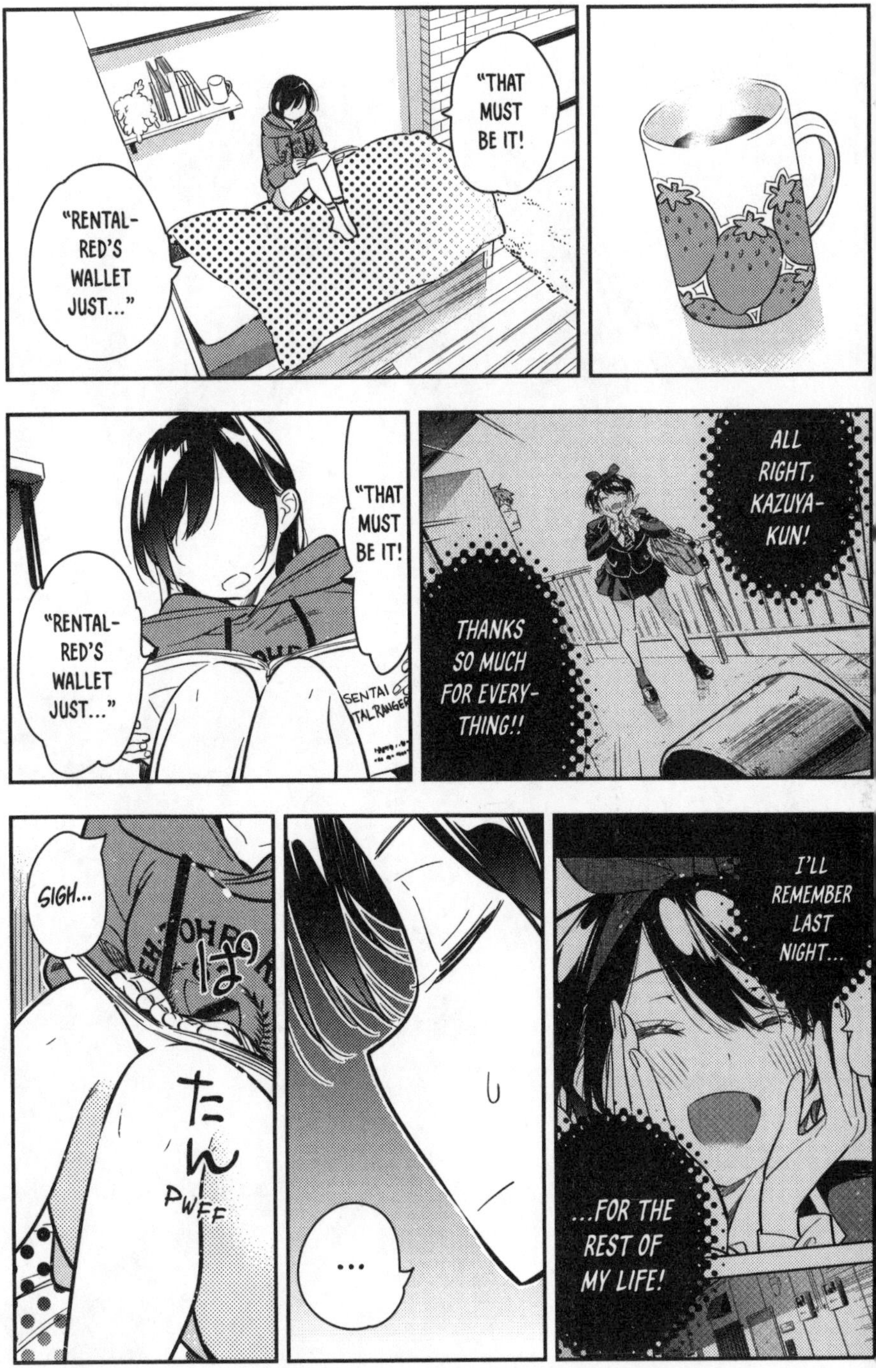
"THAT MUST BE IT!
"RENTAL-RED'S WALLET JUST..."
ALL RIGHT, KAZUYA-KUN!
THANKS SO MUCH FOR EVERYTHING!!
"THAT MUST BE IT!
"RENTAL-RED'S WALLET JUST..."
I'LL REMEMBER LAST NIGHT...
...FOR THE REST OF MY LIFE!
...
SIGH...
たん
PWFF

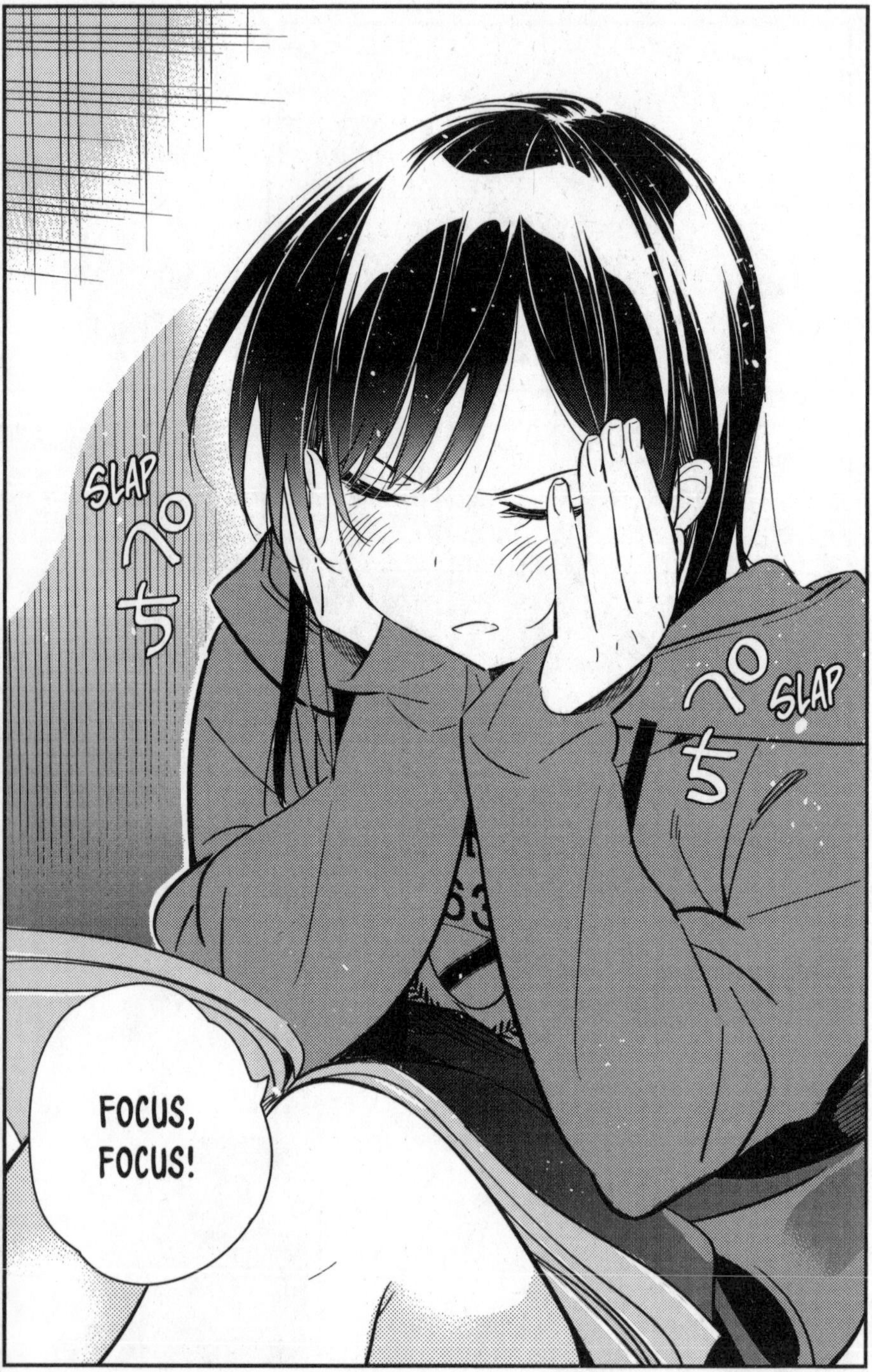
SLAP
ぺち
ぺち
SLAP
FOCUS, FOCUS!

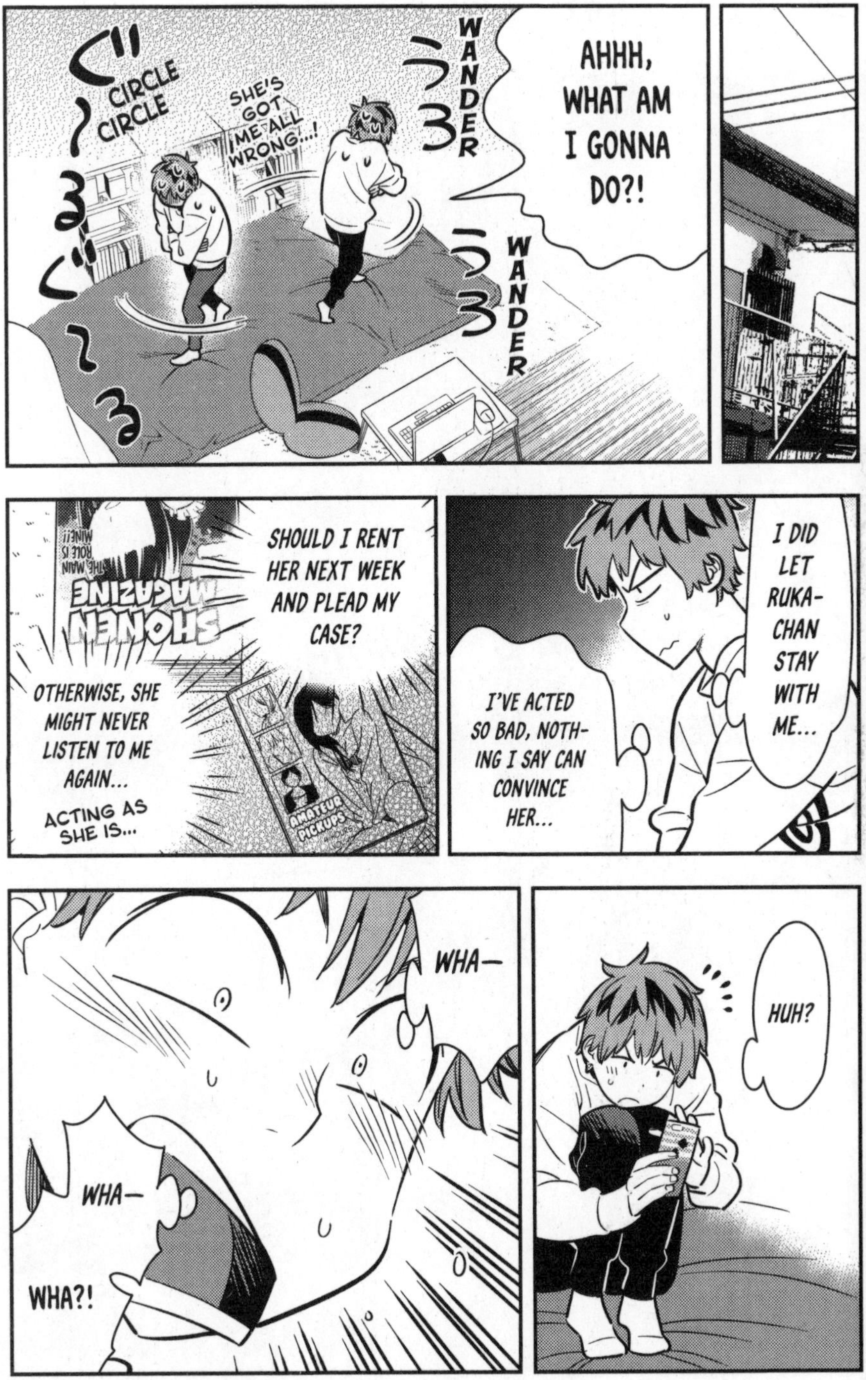
AHHH, WHAT AM I GONNA DO?!
WANDER
WANDER
SHE'S GOT ME ALL WRONG...!
CIRCLE CIRCLE
I DID LET RUKA-CHAN STAY WITH ME...
I'VE ACTED SO BAD, NOTHING I SAY CAN CONVINCE HER...
SHOULD I RENT HER NEXT WEEK AND PLEAD MY CASE?
SHONEN MAGAZINE
THE MAIN ROLE IS MINE!!
OTHERWISE, SHE MIGHT NEVER LISTEN TO ME AGAIN...
ACTING AS SHE IS...
AMATEUR PICKUPS
HUH?
WHA—
WHA—
WHA?!

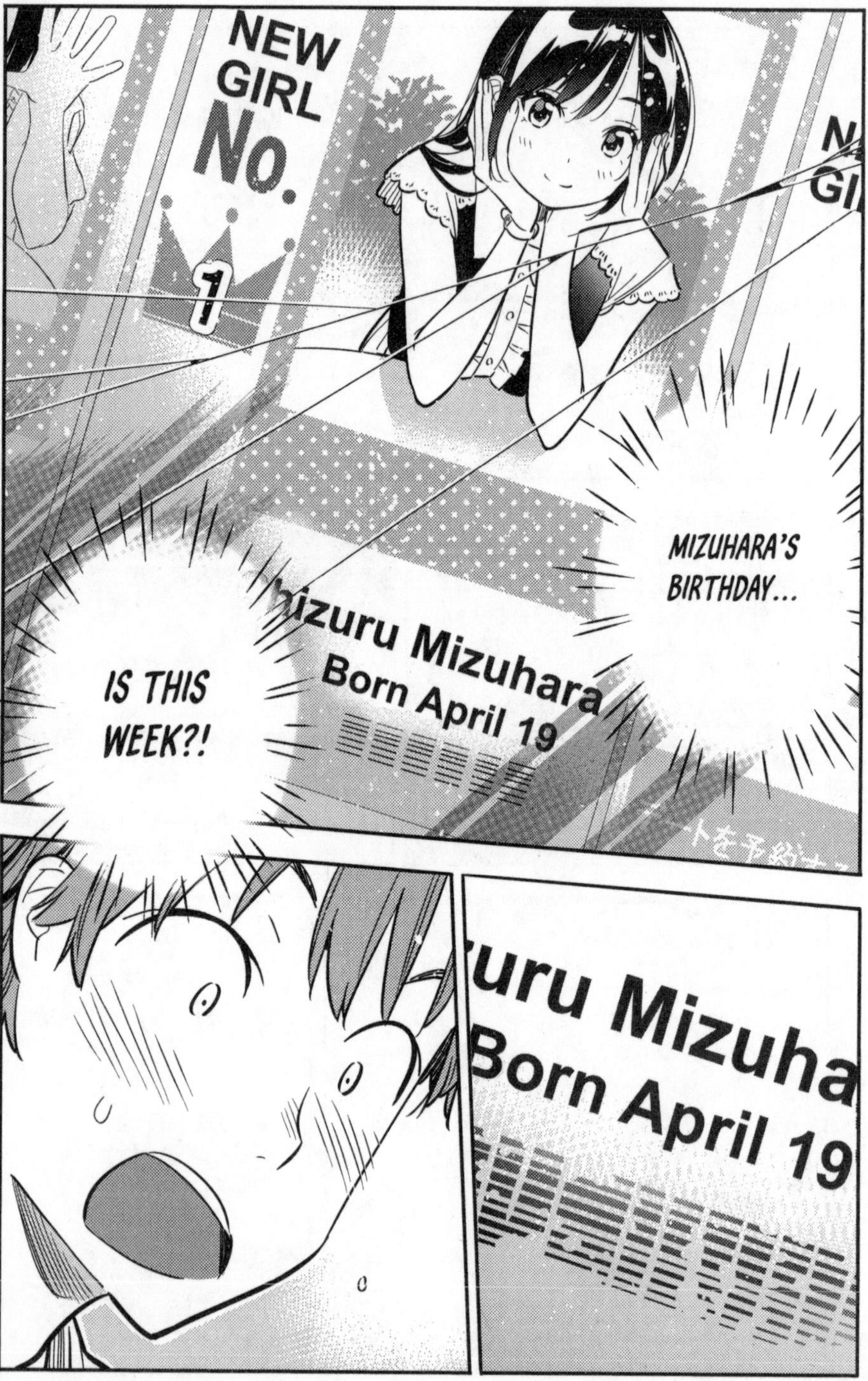
NEW GIRL No. 1
MIZUHARA'S BIRTHDAY...
izuru Mizuhara Born April 19
IS THIS WEEK?!
zuru Mizuha Born April 19

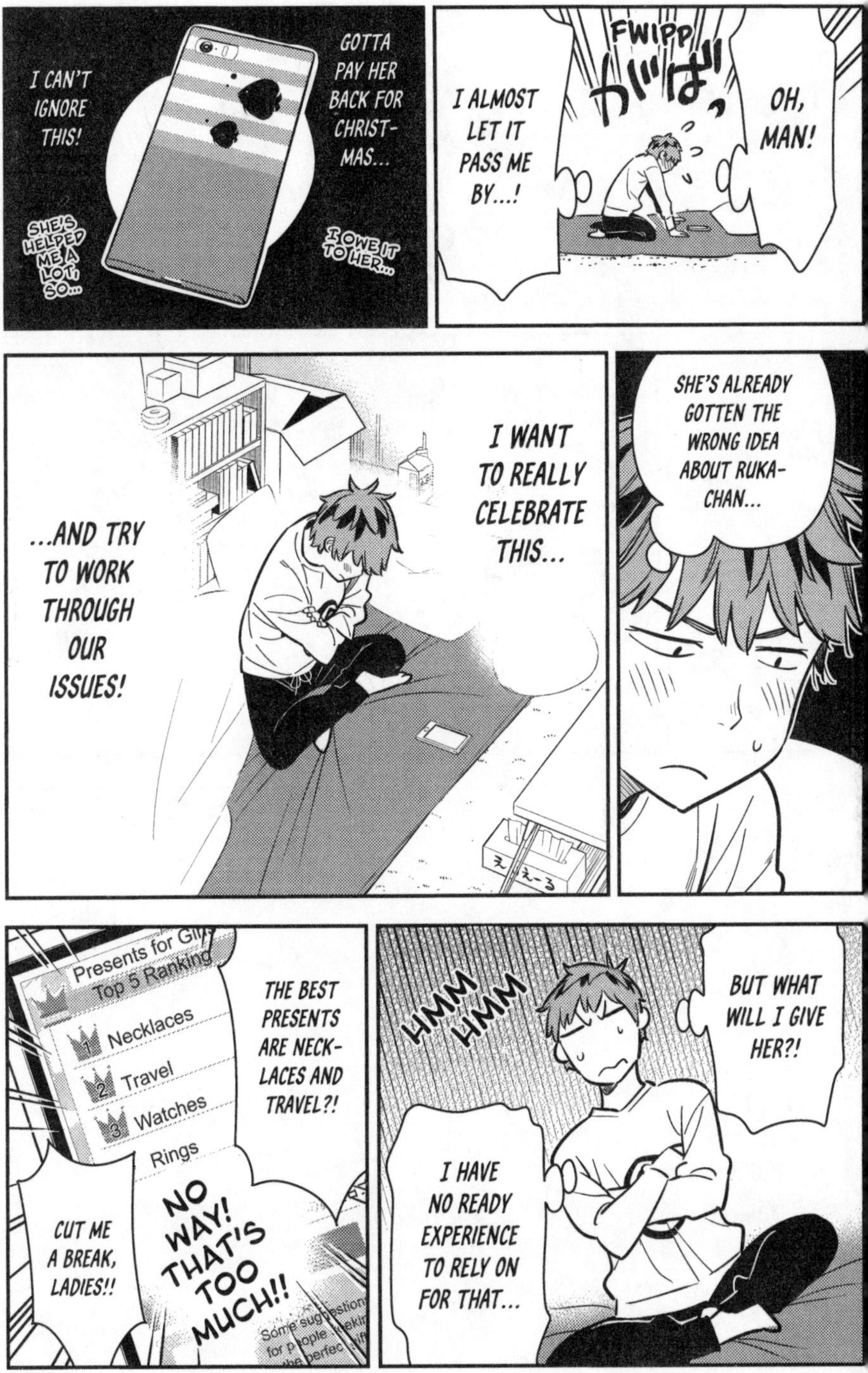
OH, MAN!
FWIPP
I ALMOST LET IT PASS ME BY...!
GOTTA PAY HER BACK FOR CHRISTMAS...
I OWE IT TO HER...
I CAN'T IGNORE THIS!
SHE'S HELPED ME A LOT, SO...
SHE'S ALREADY GOTTEN THE WRONG IDEA ABOUT RUKA-CHAN...
I WANT TO REALLY CELEBRATE THIS...
...AND TRY TO WORK THROUGH OUR ISSUES!
BUT WHAT WILL I GIVE HER?!
HMM HMM
I HAVE NO READY EXPERIENCE TO RELY ON FOR THAT...
Top 5 Ranking
1 Necklaces
2 Travel
3 Watches
Rings
THE BEST PRESENTS ARE NECKLACES AND TRAVEL?!
NO WAY! THAT'S TOO MUCH!!
CUT ME A BREAK, LADIES!!

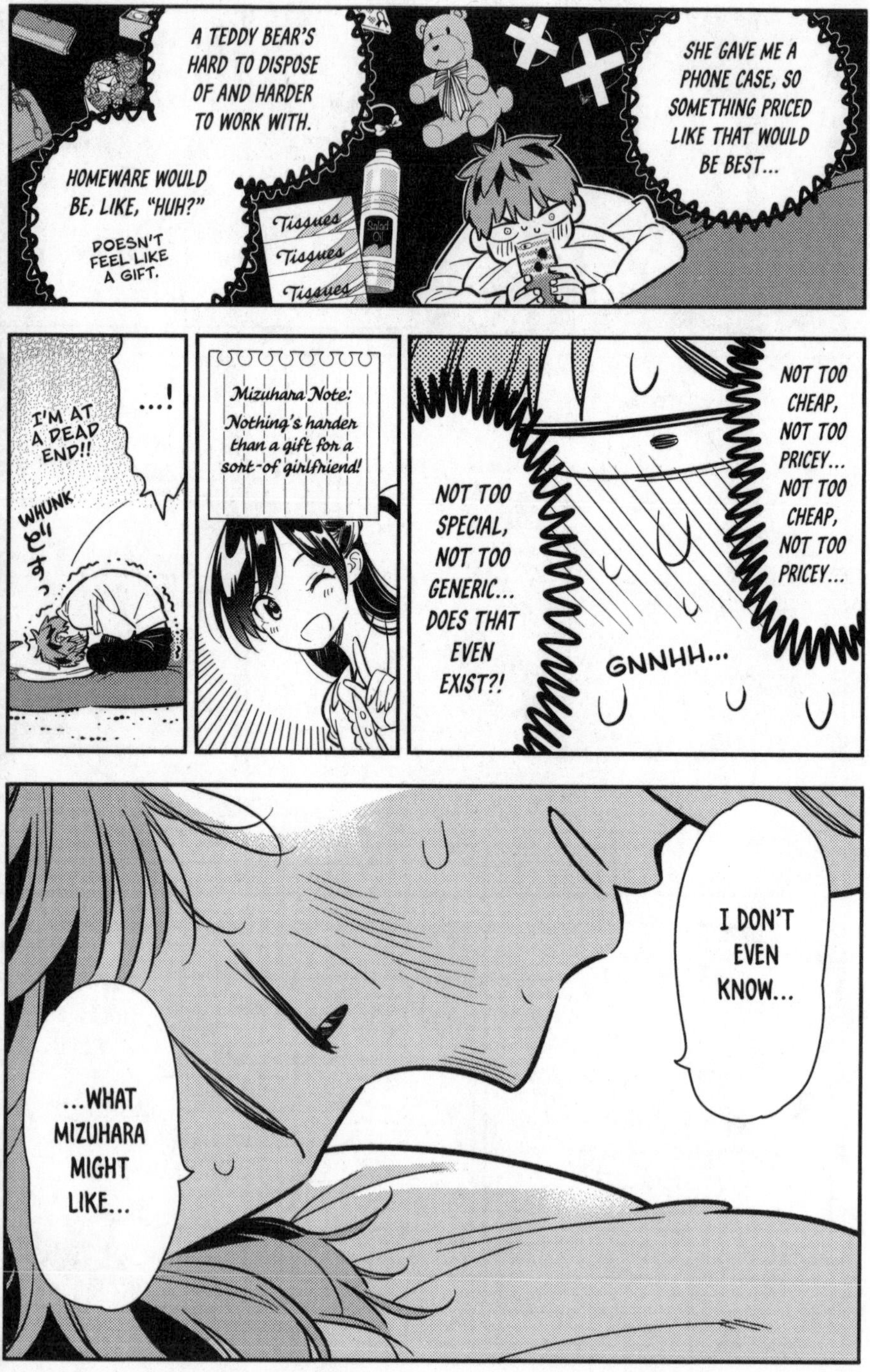
SHE GAVE ME A PHONE CASE, SO SOMETHING PRICED LIKE THAT WOULD BE BEST...
A TEDDY BEAR'S HARD TO DISPOSE OF AND HARDER TO WORK WITH.
Salad Oil
Tissues
Tissues
Tissues
HOMEWARE WOULD BE, LIKE, "HUH?"
DOESN'T FEEL LIKE A GIFT.
NOT TOO CHEAP, NOT TOO PRICEY... NOT TOO CHEAP, NOT TOO PRICEY...
NOT TOO SPECIAL, NOT TOO GENERIC... DOES THAT EVEN EXIST?!
GNNHH...
Mizuhara Note: Nothing's harder than a gift for a sort-of girlfriend!
...!
I'M AT A DEAD END!!
WHUNK
どすっ
I DON'T EVEN KNOW...
...WHAT MIZUHARA MIGHT LIKE...

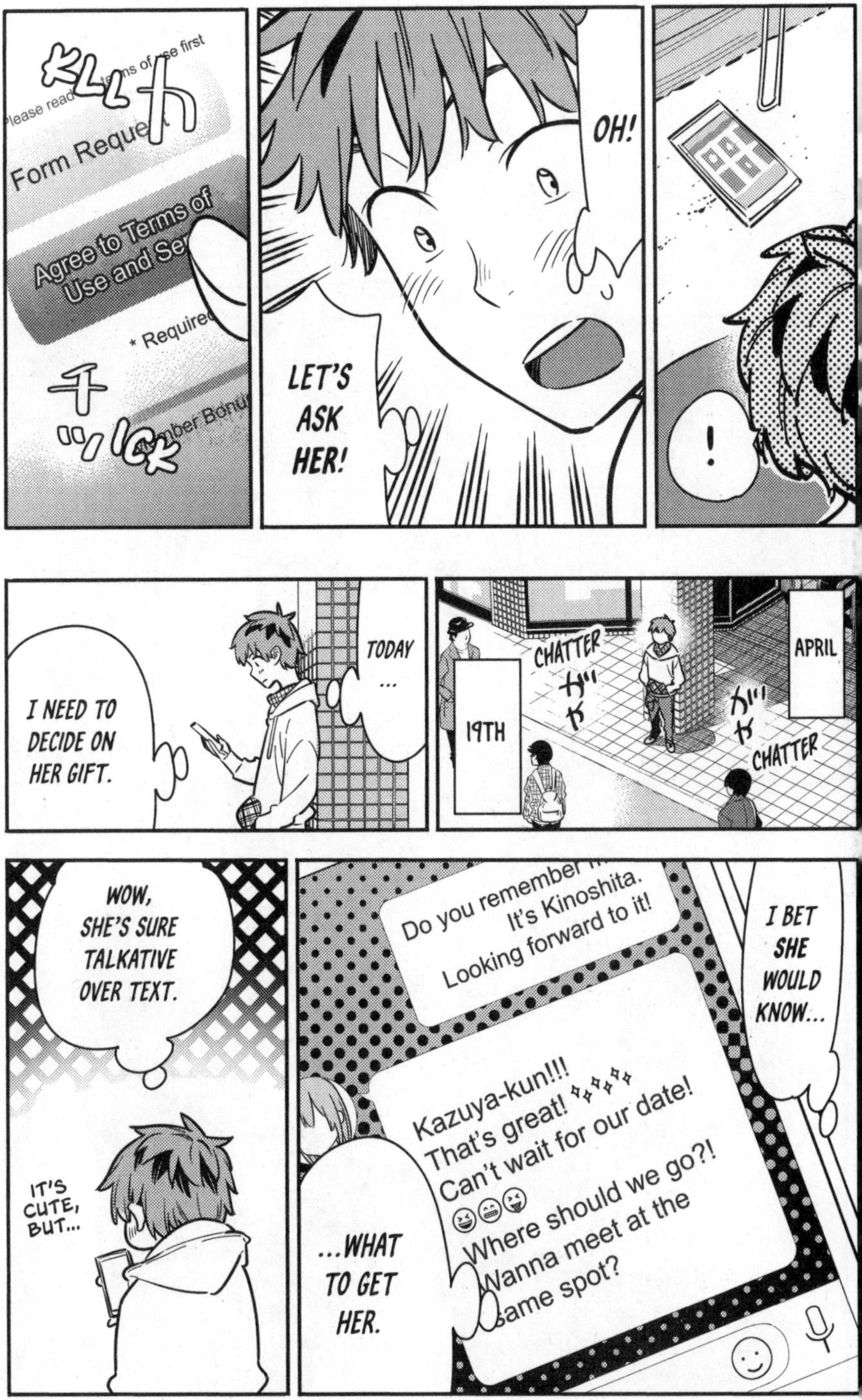
!
OH!
LET'S ASK HER!
Agree to Terms of
* Required
APRIL
19TH
CHATTER
CHATTER
TODAY...
I NEED TO DECIDE ON HER GIFT.
I BET SHE WOULD KNOW...
It's Kinoshita.
Looking forward to it!
Kazuya-kun!!!
That's great!
Can't wait for our date!
Where should we go?!
Wanna meet at the same spot?
...WHAT TO GET HER.
WOW, SHE'S SURE TALKATIVE OVER TEXT.
IT'S CUTE, BUT...

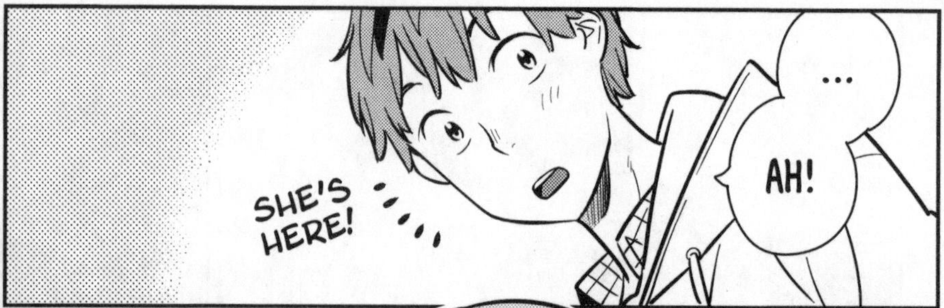
...
AH!
SHE'S HERE!
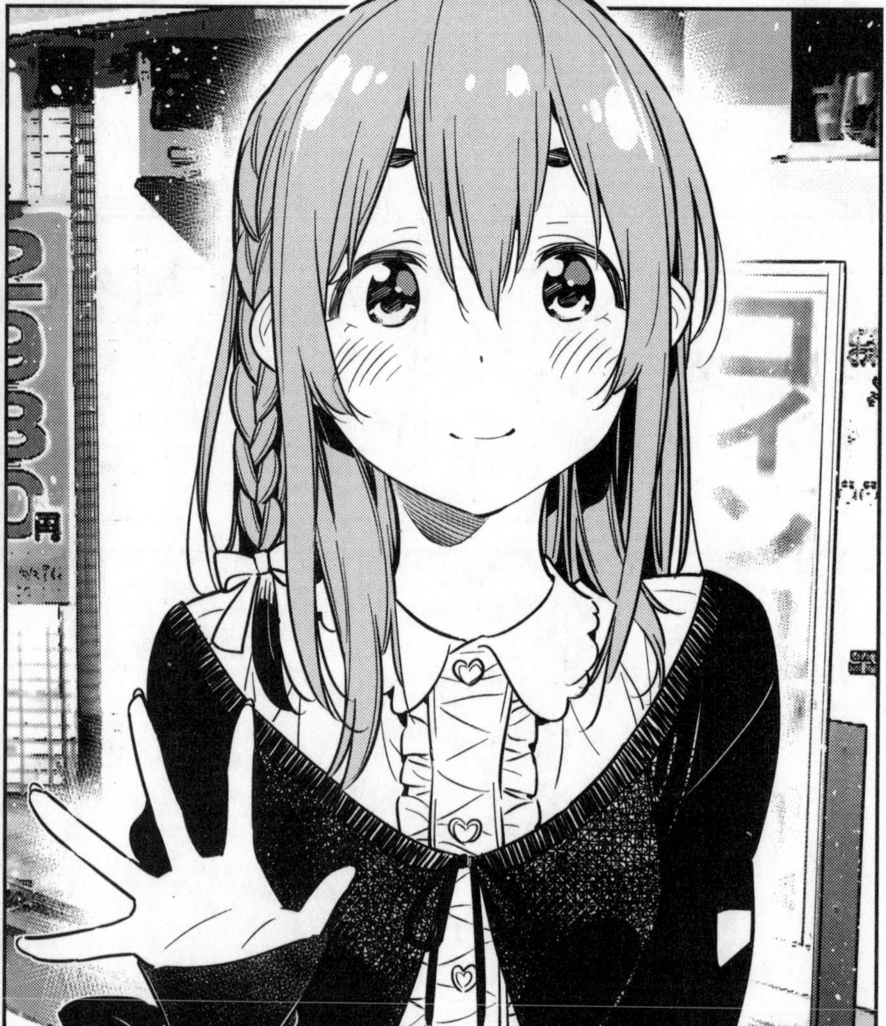
コイン

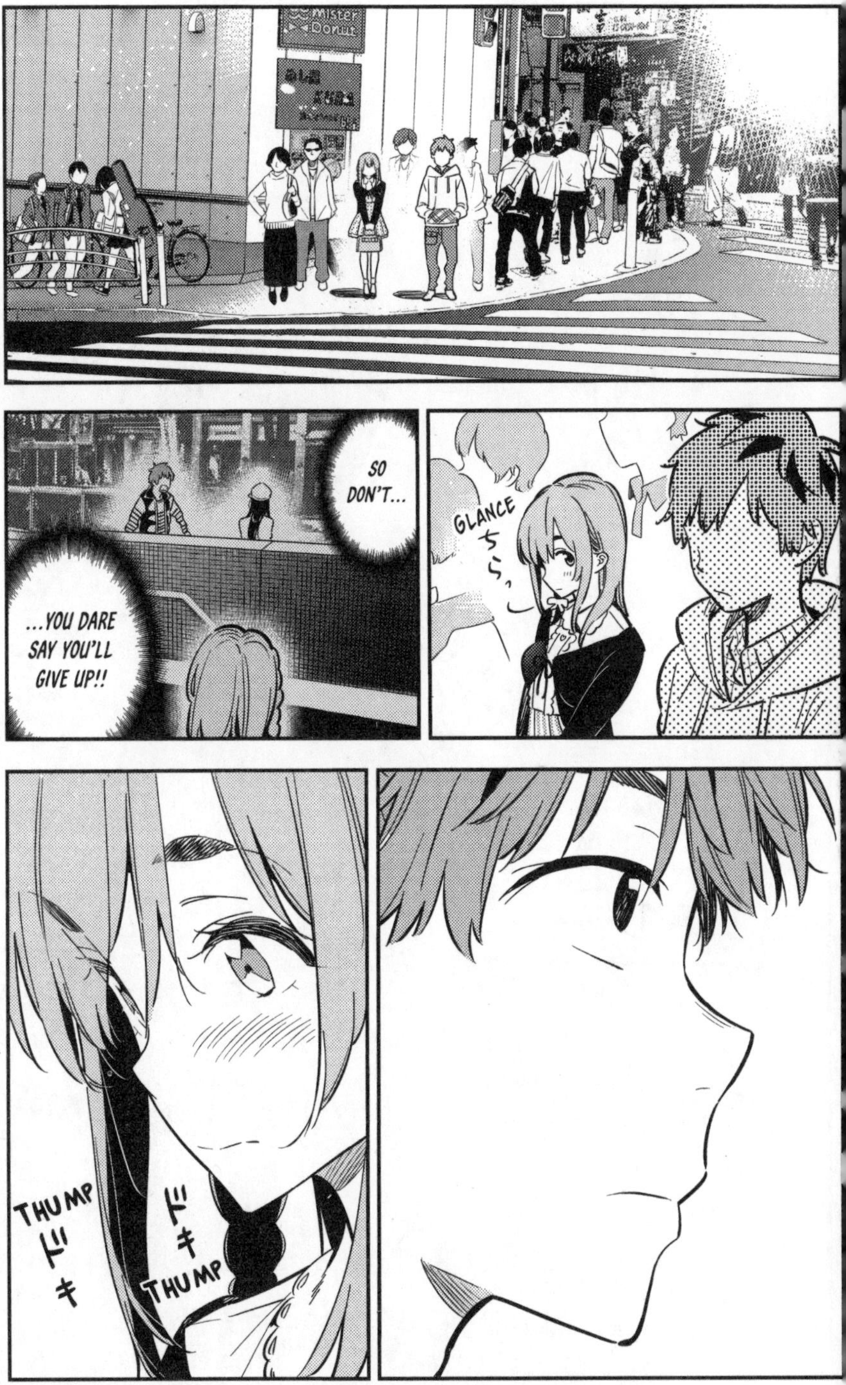
GLANCE
ちらっ
SO DON'T...
...YOU DARE SAY YOU'LL GIVE UP!!
ドキ
THUMP
THUMP
ドキ

RATING 67 THE BIRTHDAY AND MY GIRLFRIEND 2

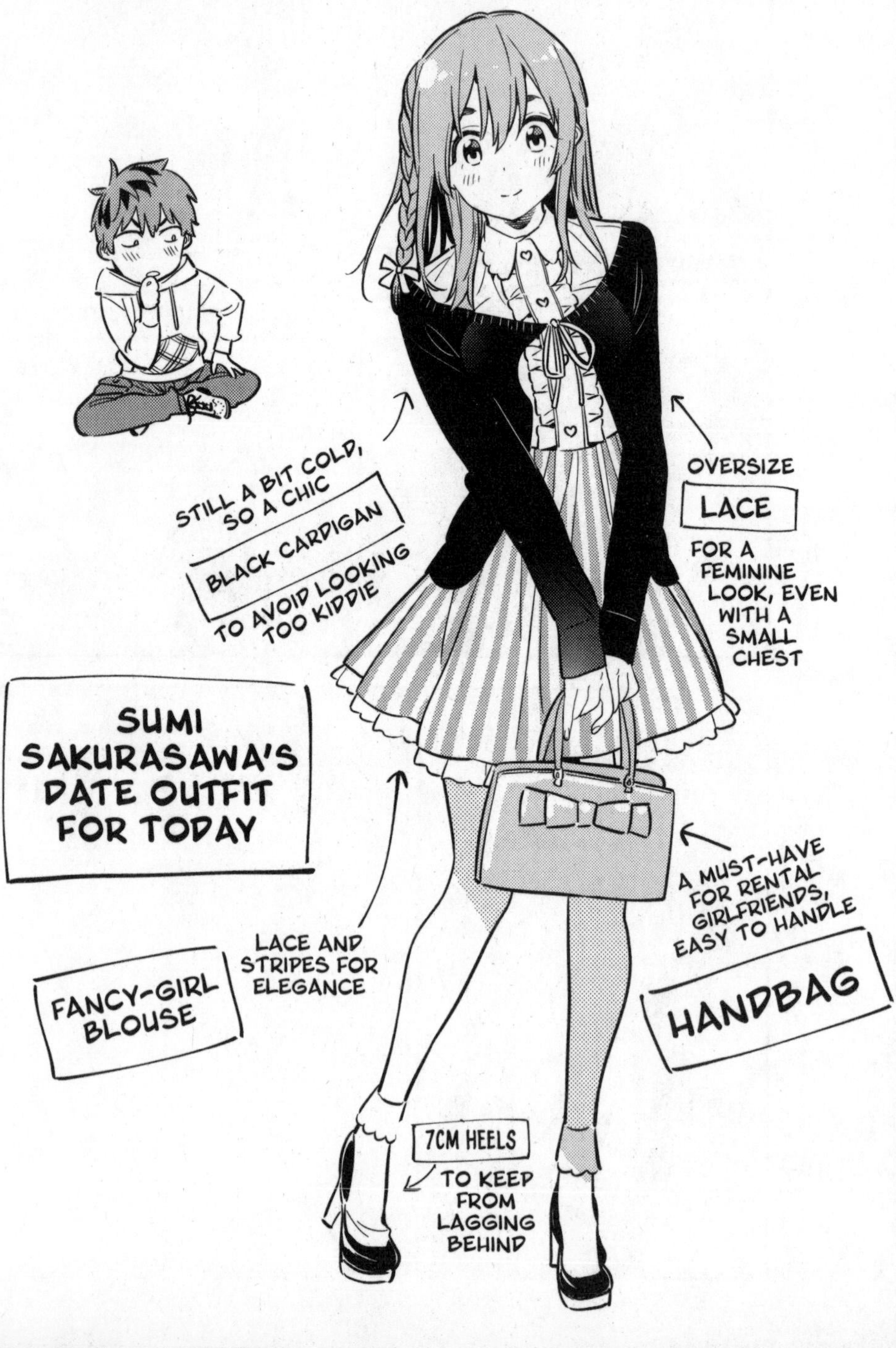
OVERSIZE
LACE
FOR A FEMININE LOOK, EVEN WITH A SMALL CHEST
STILL A BIT COLD, SO A CHIC
BLACK CARDIGAN
TO AVOID LOOKING TOO KIDDIE
SUMI SAKURASAWA'S DATE OUTFIT FOR TODAY
A MUST-HAVE FOR RENTAL GIRLFRIENDS, EASY TO HANDLE
HANDBAG
LACE AND STRIPES FOR ELEGANCE
FANCY-GIRL BLOUSE
7CM HEELS
TO KEEP FROM LAGGING BEHIND

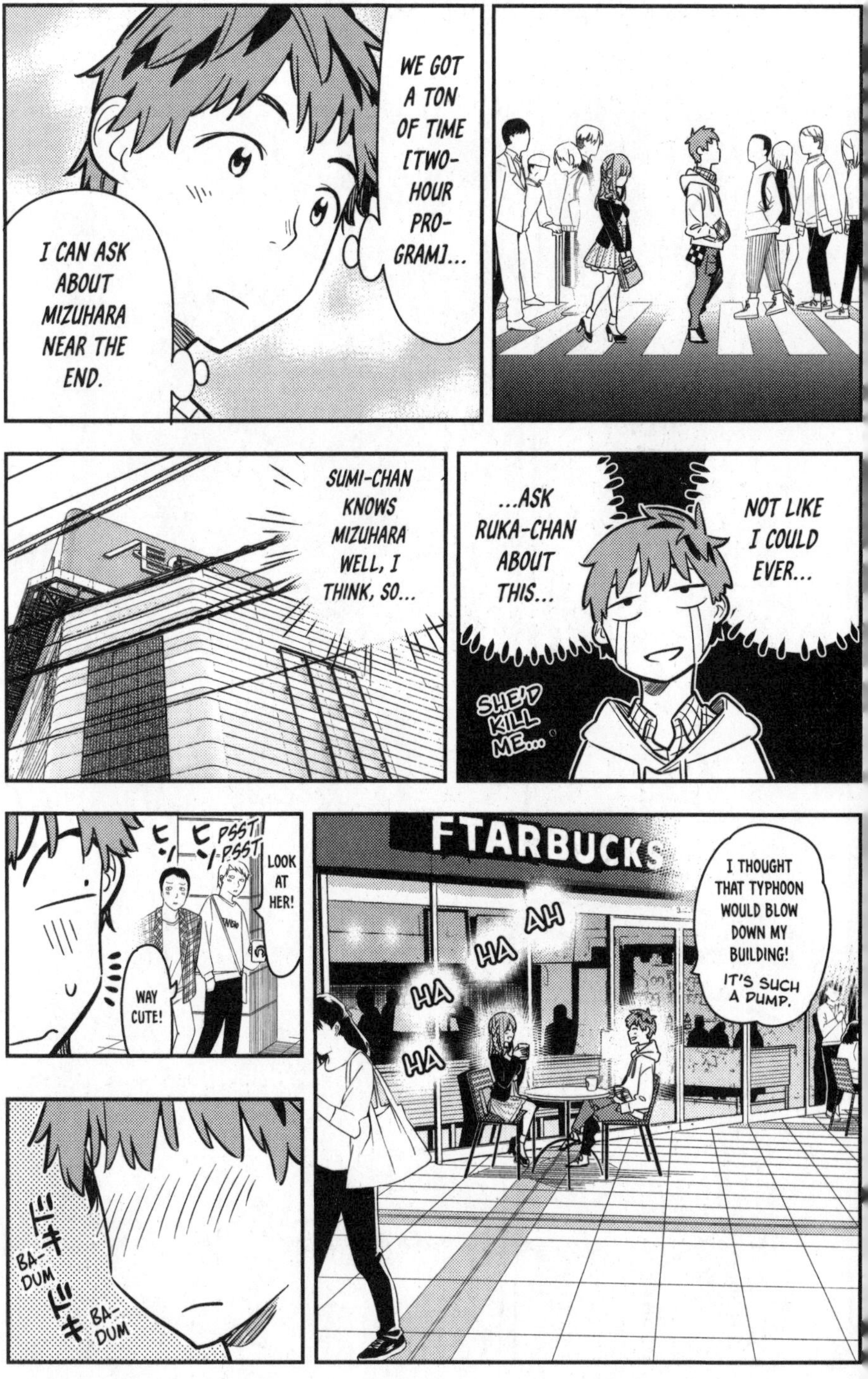
WE GOT A TON OF TIME [TWO-HOUR PROGRAM]...
I CAN ASK ABOUT MIZUHARA NEAR THE END.
NOT LIKE I COULD EVER...
...ASK RUKA-CHAN ABOUT THIS...
SHE'D KILL ME...
SUMI-CHAN KNOWS MIZUHARA WELL, I THINK, SO...
FTARBUCKS
I THOUGHT THAT TYPHOON WOULD BLOW DOWN MY BUILDING!
IT'S SUCH A DUMP.
AH
HA
HA
HA
ヒソ
ヒソ
PSST PSST
LOOK AT HER!
WAY CUTE!
ドキ
BA-DUM
ドキ
BA-DUM

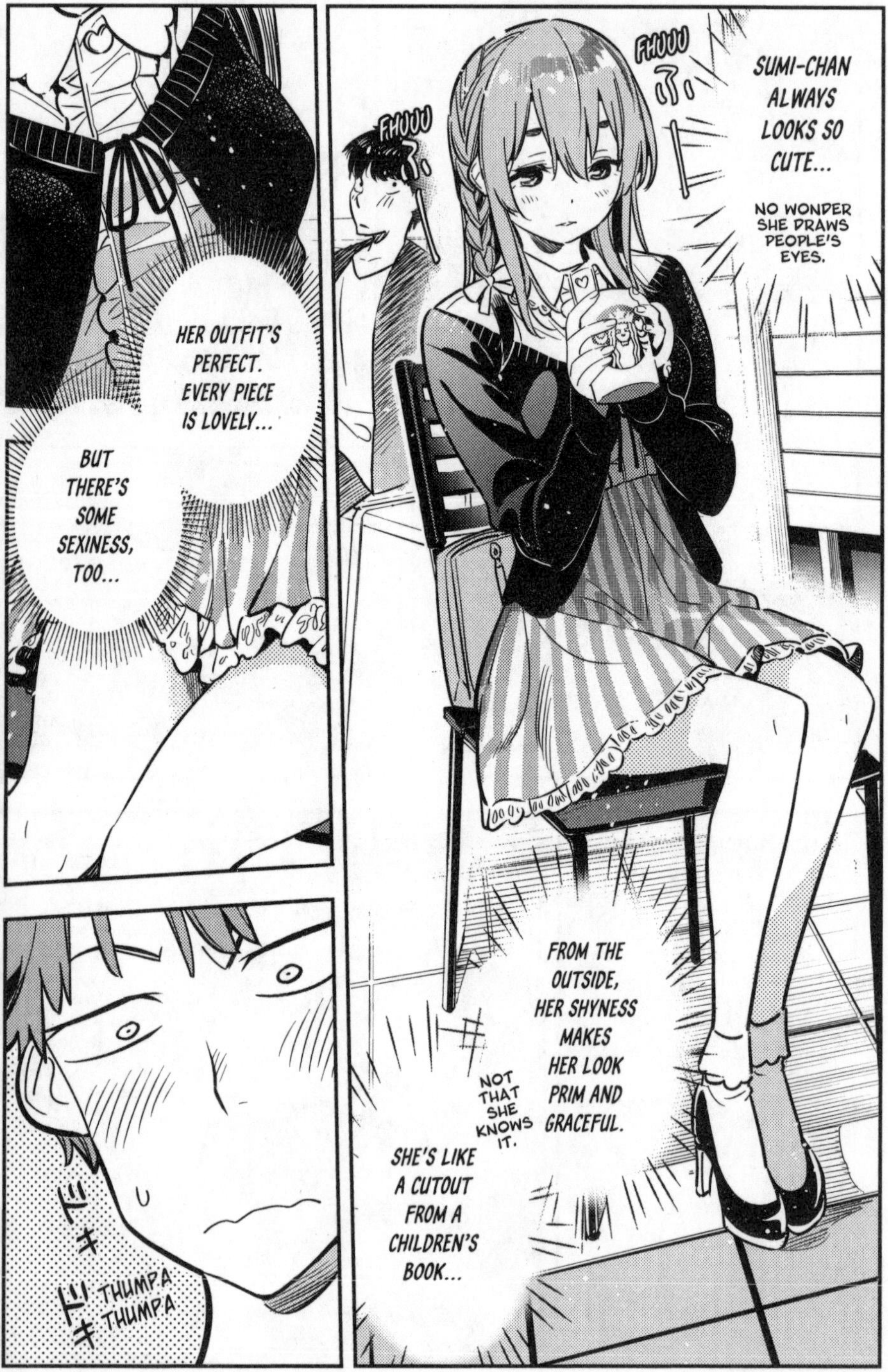
FHUUU
SUMI-CHAN ALWAYS LOOKS SO CUTE...
NO WONDER SHE DRAWS PEOPLE'S EYES.
FHUUU
FROM THE OUTSIDE, HER SHYNESS MAKES HER LOOK PRIM AND GRACEFUL.
NOT THAT SHE KNOWS IT.
SHE'S LIKE A CUTOUT FROM A CHILDREN'S BOOK...
HER OUTFIT'S PERFECT. EVERY PIECE IS LOVELY...
BUT THERE'S SOME SEXINESS, TOO...
ドキ ドキ
THUMPA THUMPA

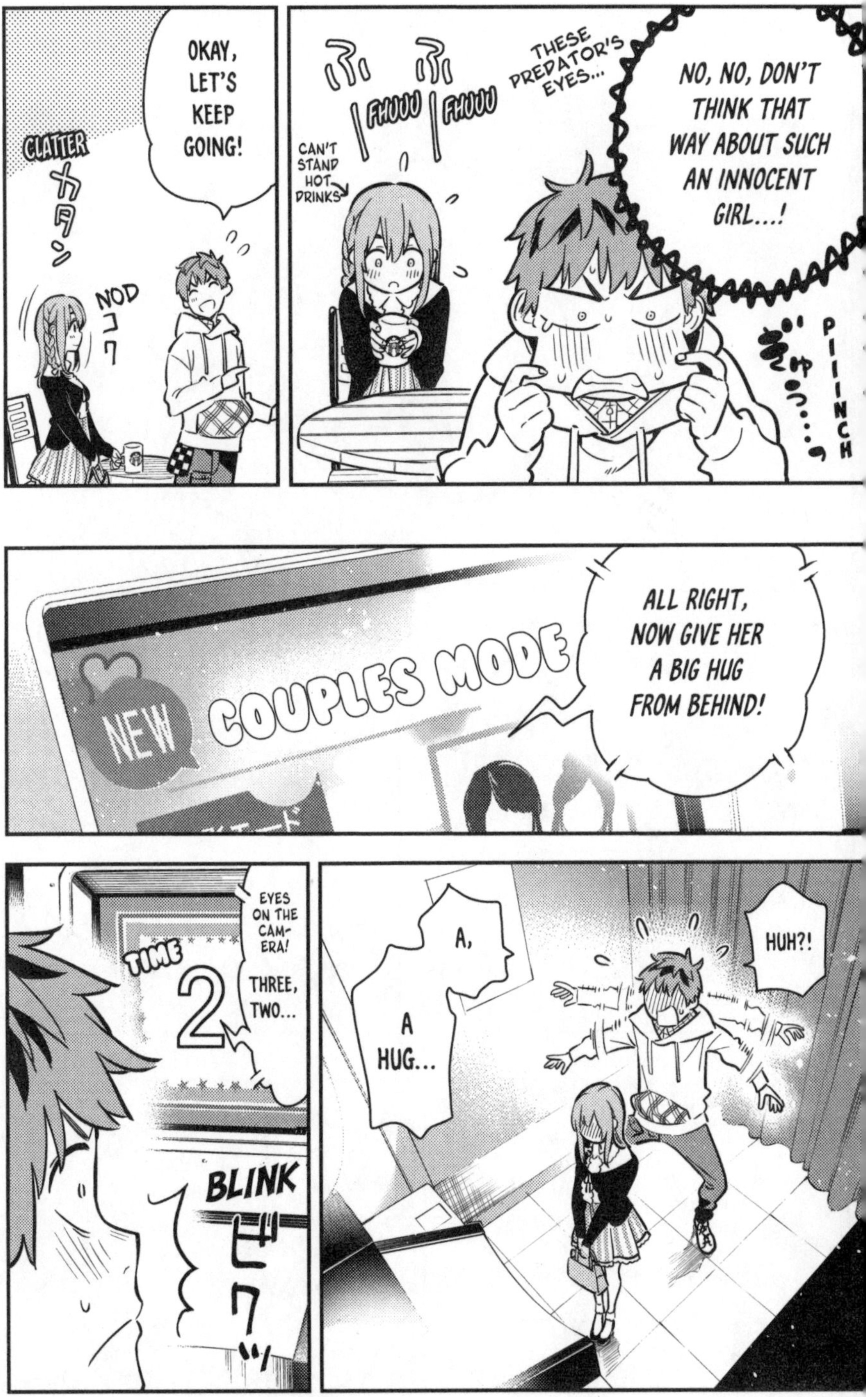
THESE PREDATOR'S EYES...
NO, NO, DON'T THINK THAT WAY ABOUT SUCH AN INNOCENT GIRL...!
FHUUU
FHUUU
CAN'T STAND HOT DRINKS
PIIINCH
OKAY, LET'S KEEP GOING!
CLATTER
カタン
NOD
コク
ALL RIGHT, NOW GIVE HER A BIG HUG FROM BEHIND!
COUPLES MODE
NEW
HUH?!
A,
A HUG...
EYES ON THE CAM-ERA!
THREE, TWO...
TIME
2
BLINK
ビクッ

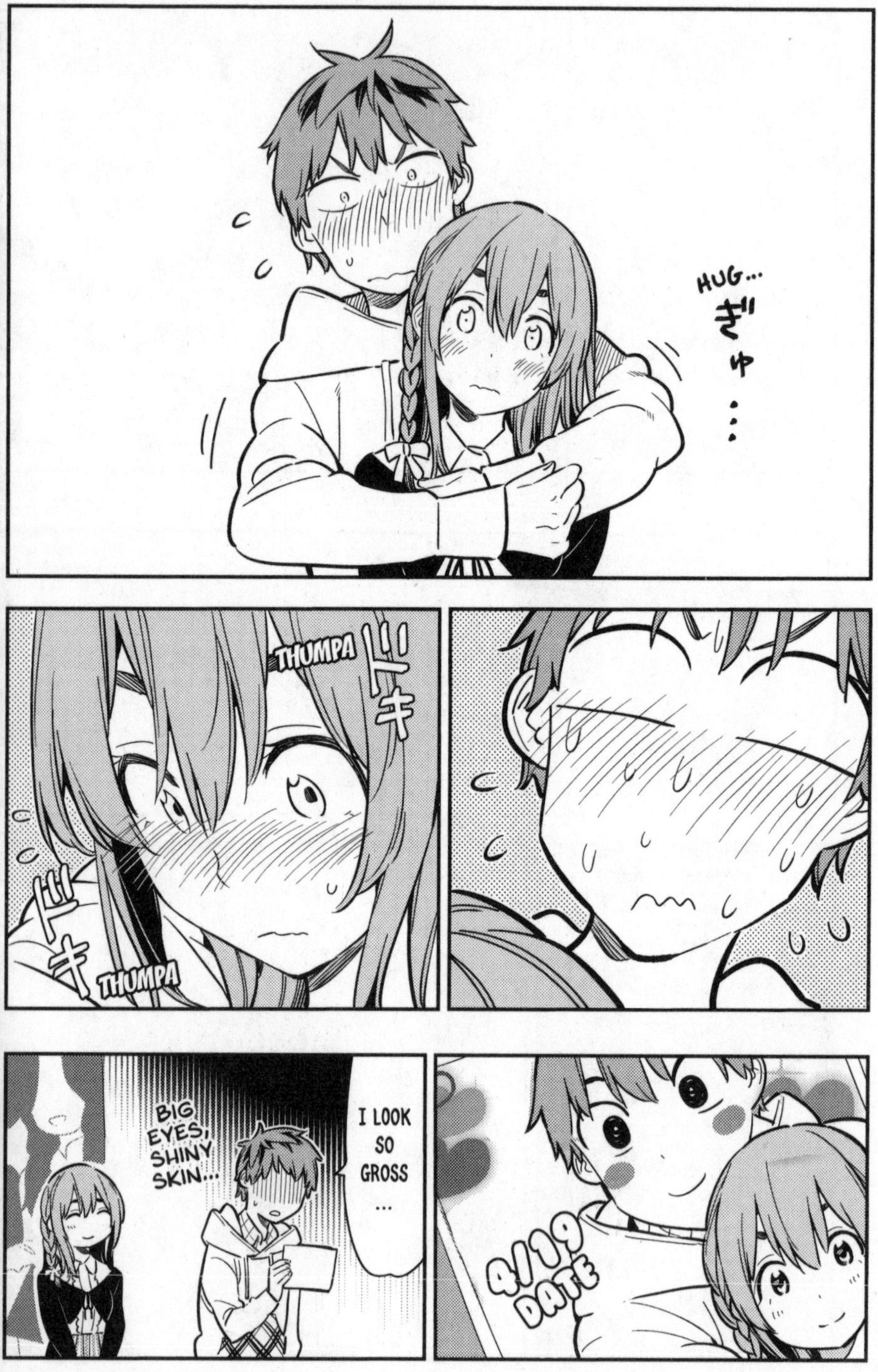
HUG...
ぎゅ...
THUMPA
ドキ
ドキ
THUMPA
4/19
DATE
I LOOK SO GROSS...
BIG EYES, SHINY SKIN...

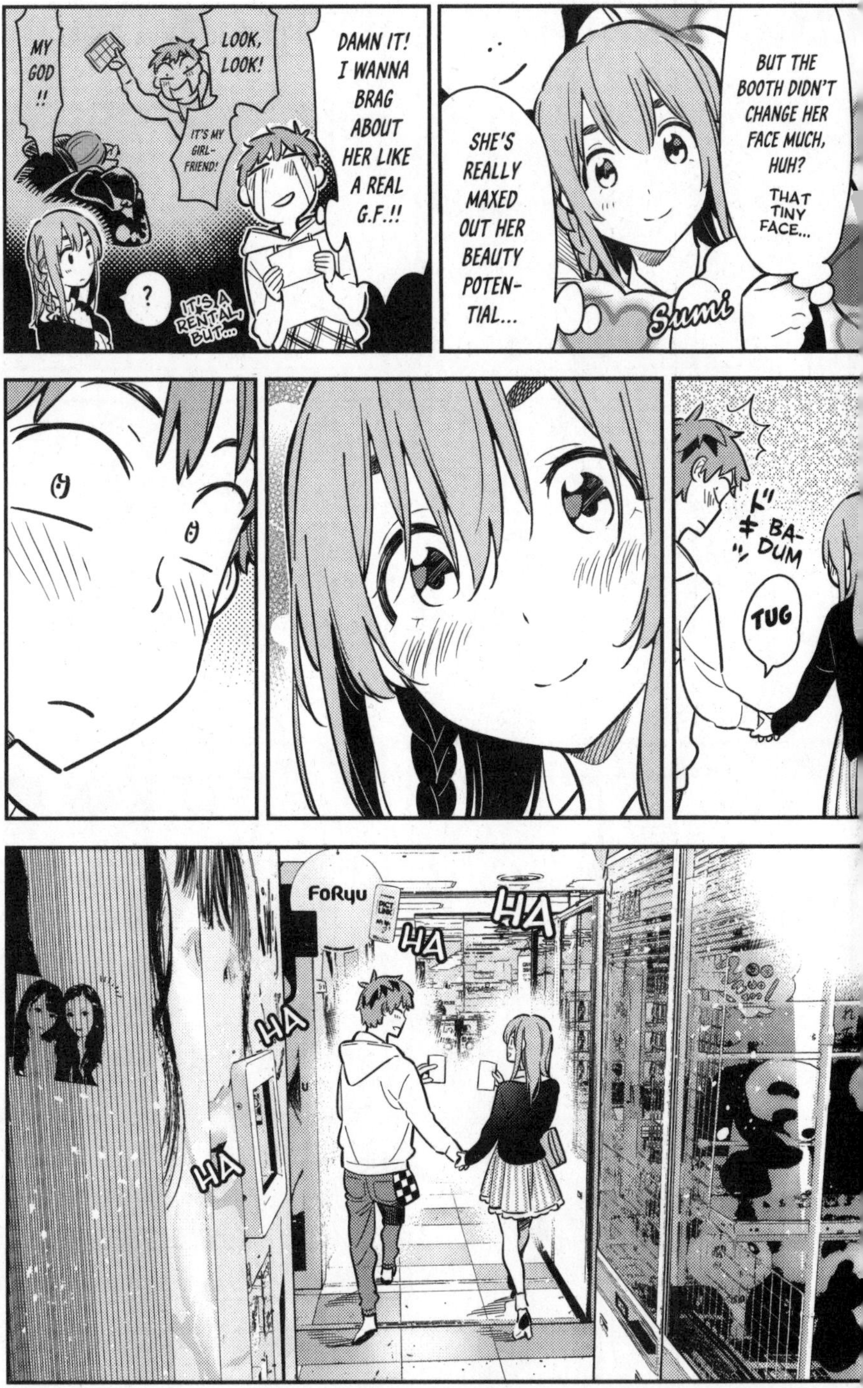
BUT THE BOOTH DIDN'T CHANGE HER FACE MUCH, HUH?
THAT TINY FACE...
SHE'S REALLY MAXED OUT HER BEAUTY POTEN-TIAL...
Sumi
DAMN IT! I WANNA BRAG ABOUT HER LIKE A REAL G.F.!!
LOOK, LOOK!
MY GOD!!
IT'S MY GIRL-FRIEND!
?
IT'S A RENTAL, BUT...
ドキッ
BA-DUM
TUG
FoRyu
HA
HA
HA
HA

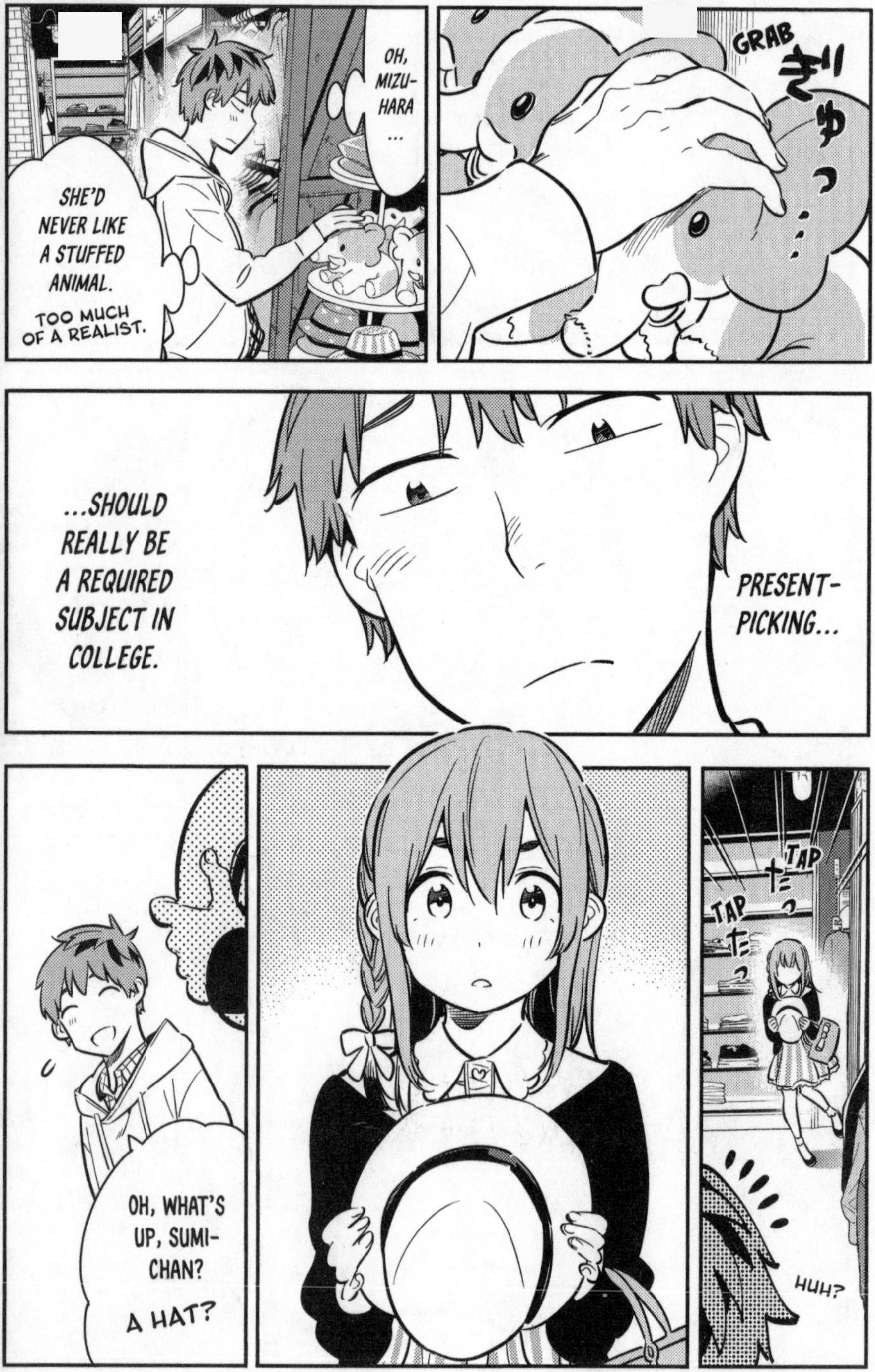
GRAB
ぎゅっ…
OH, MIZUHARA…
SHE'D NEVER LIKE A STUFFED ANIMAL.
TOO MUCH OF A REALIST.
PRESENT-PICKING…
…SHOULD REALLY BE A REQUIRED SUBJECT IN COLLEGE.
TAP たっ
TAP たっ
HUH?
OH, WHAT'S UP, SUMI-CHAN?
A HAT?

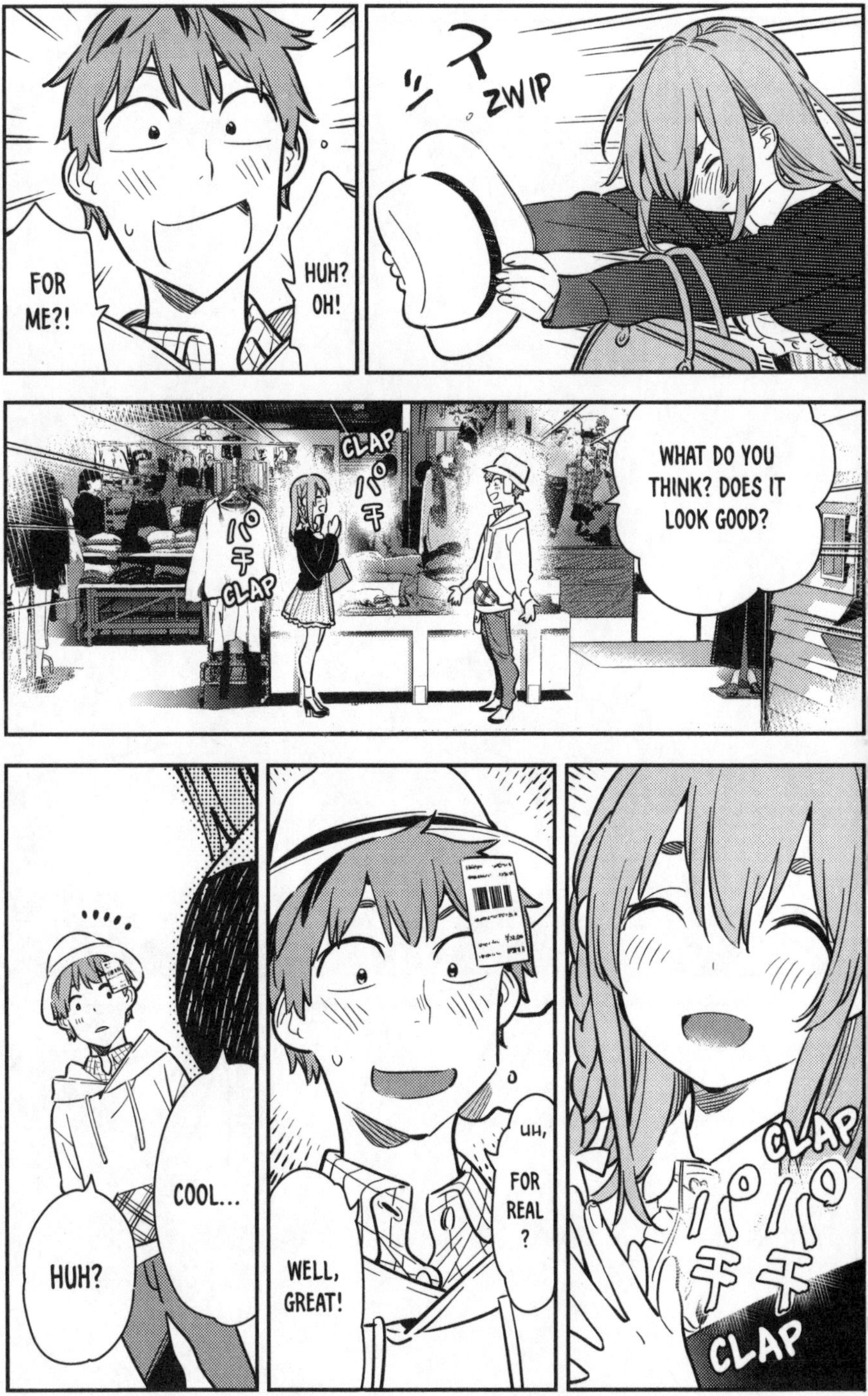
ZWIP
HUH? OH!
FOR ME?!
WHAT DO YOU THINK? DOES IT LOOK GOOD?
CLAP
パチ
パチ
CLAP
CLAP
パチパチ
CLAP
UH, FOR REAL?
WELL, GREAT!
.....
COOL...
HUH?

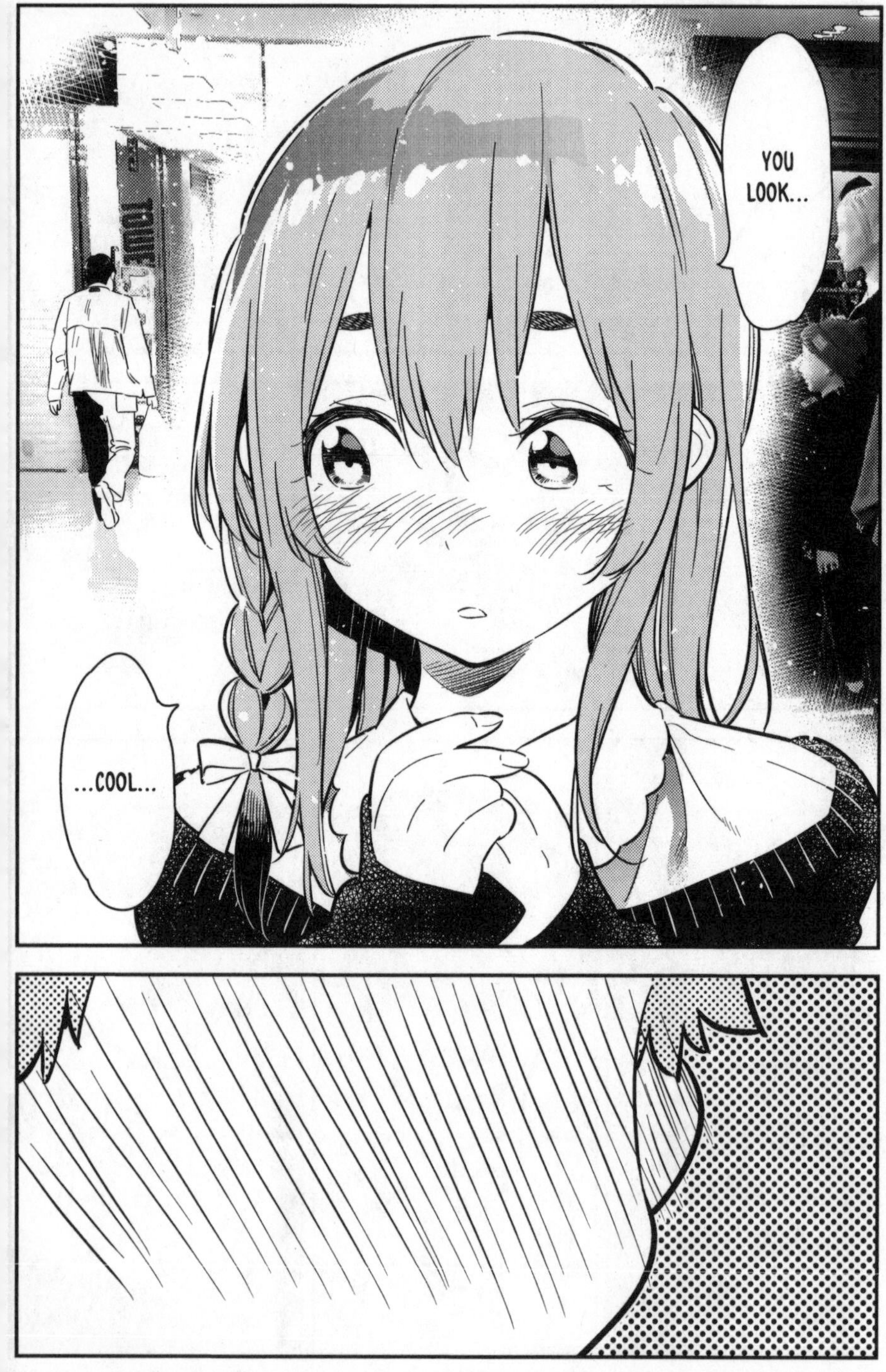
YOU LOOK...
...COOL...

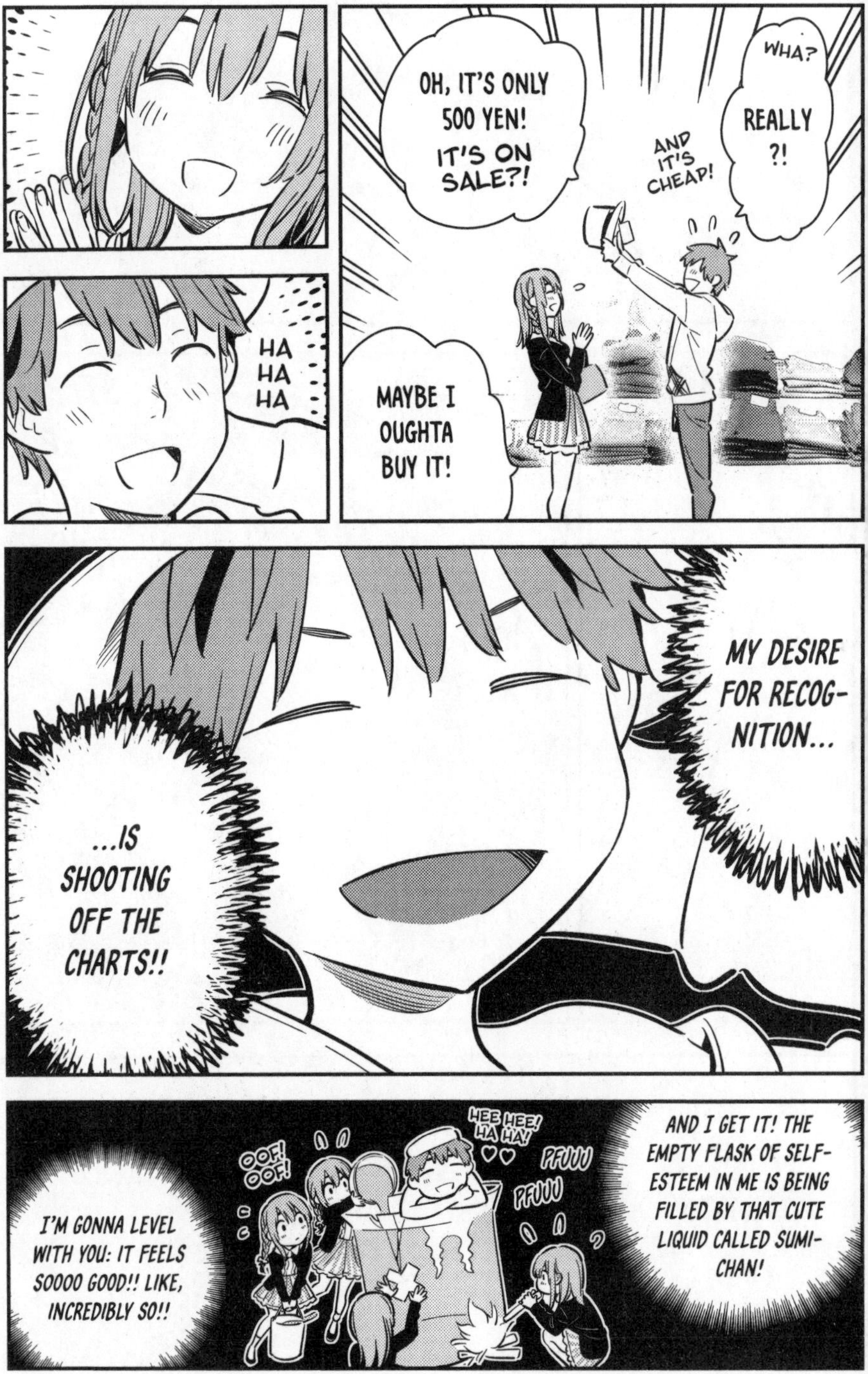
WHA?
REALLY?!
AND IT'S CHEAP!
OH, IT'S ONLY 500 YEN! IT'S ON SALE?!
MAYBE I OUGHTA BUY IT!
HA HA HA
MY DESIRE FOR RECOG- NITION...
...IS SHOOTING OFF THE CHARTS!!
AND I GET IT! THE EMPTY FLASK OF SELF- ESTEEM IN ME IS BEING FILLED BY THAT CUTE LIQUID CALLED SUMI- CHAN!
HEE HEE! HA HA!
PFUUU
PFUUU
OOF! OOF!
I'M GONNA LEVEL WITH YOU: IT FEELS SOOOO GOOD!! LIKE, INCREDIBLY SO!!

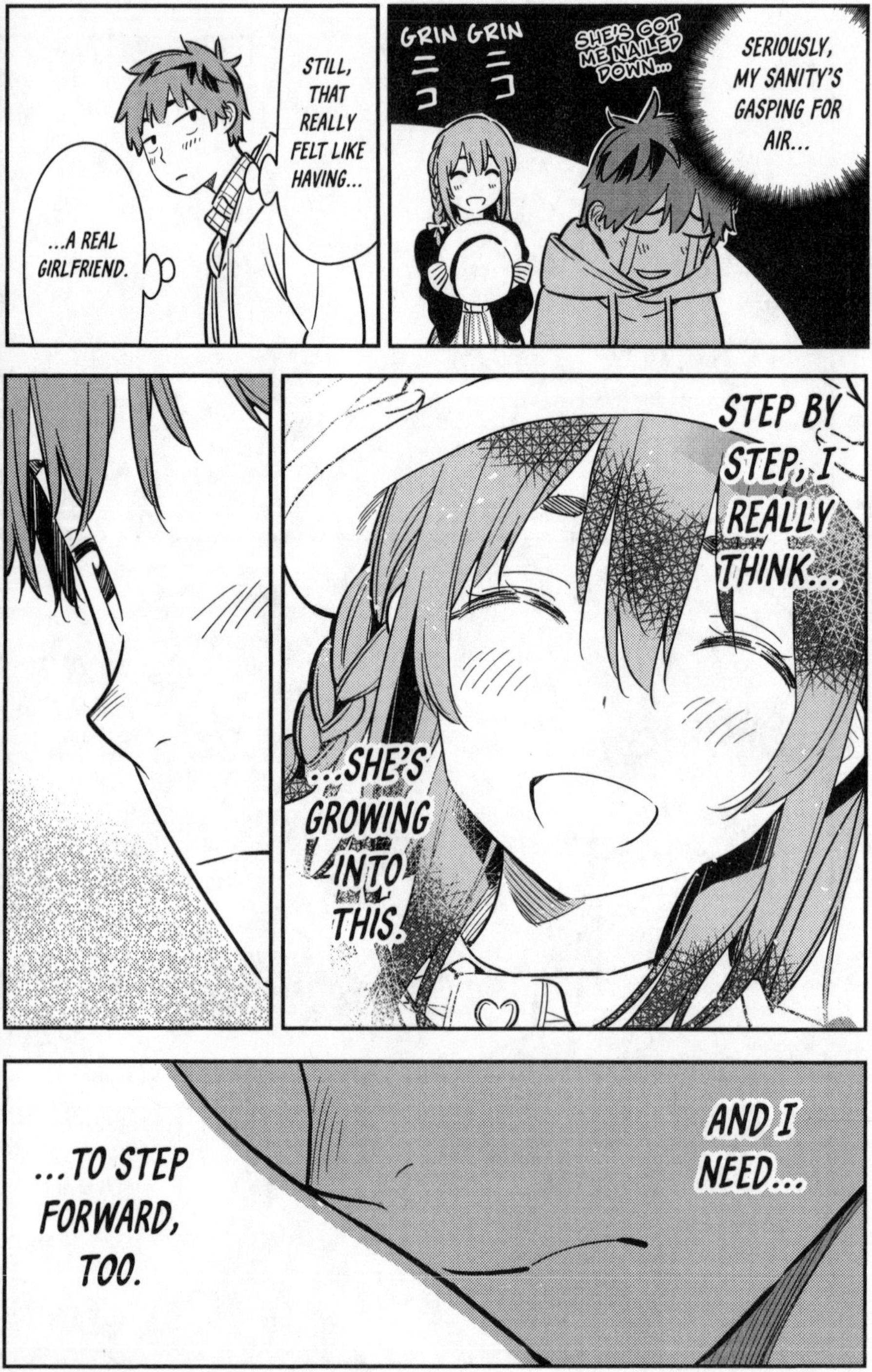
SERIOUSLY, MY SANITY'S GASPING FOR AIR...
SHE'S GOT ME NAILED DOWN...
GRIN GRIN
ニコ ニコ
STILL, THAT REALLY FELT LIKE HAVING...
...A REAL GIRLFRIEND.
STEP BY STEP, I REALLY THINK...
...SHE'S GROWING INTO THIS.
AND I NEED...
...TO STEP FORWARD, TOO.

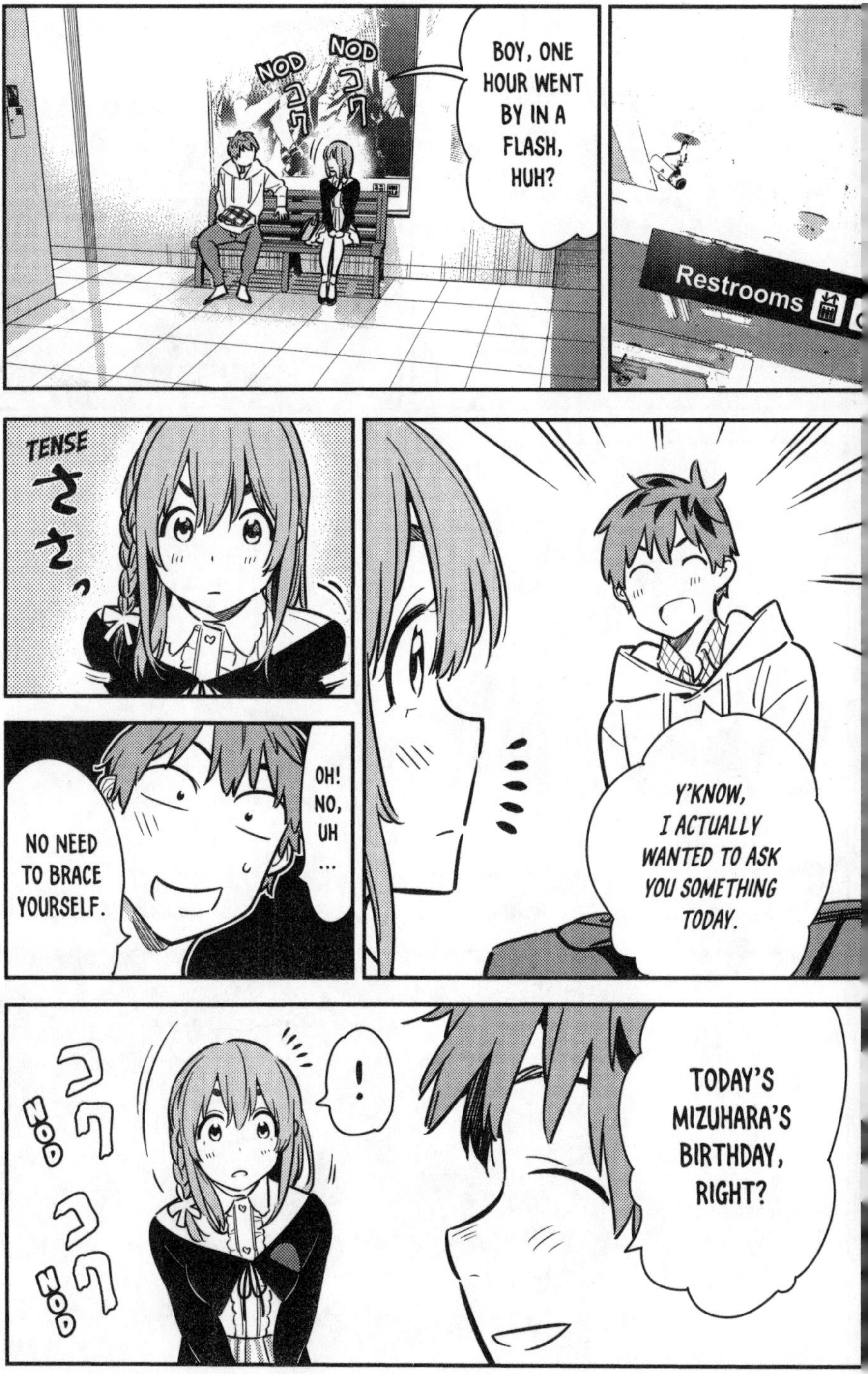
Restrooms
NOD
コク
NOD
コク
BOY, ONE HOUR WENT BY IN A FLASH, HUH?
Y'KNOW, I ACTUALLY WANTED TO ASK YOU SOMETHING TODAY.
TENSE
ささっ
OH! NO, UH ...
NO NEED TO BRACE YOURSELF.
TODAY'S MIZUHARA'S BIRTHDAY, RIGHT?
!
コク
NOD
コク
NOD

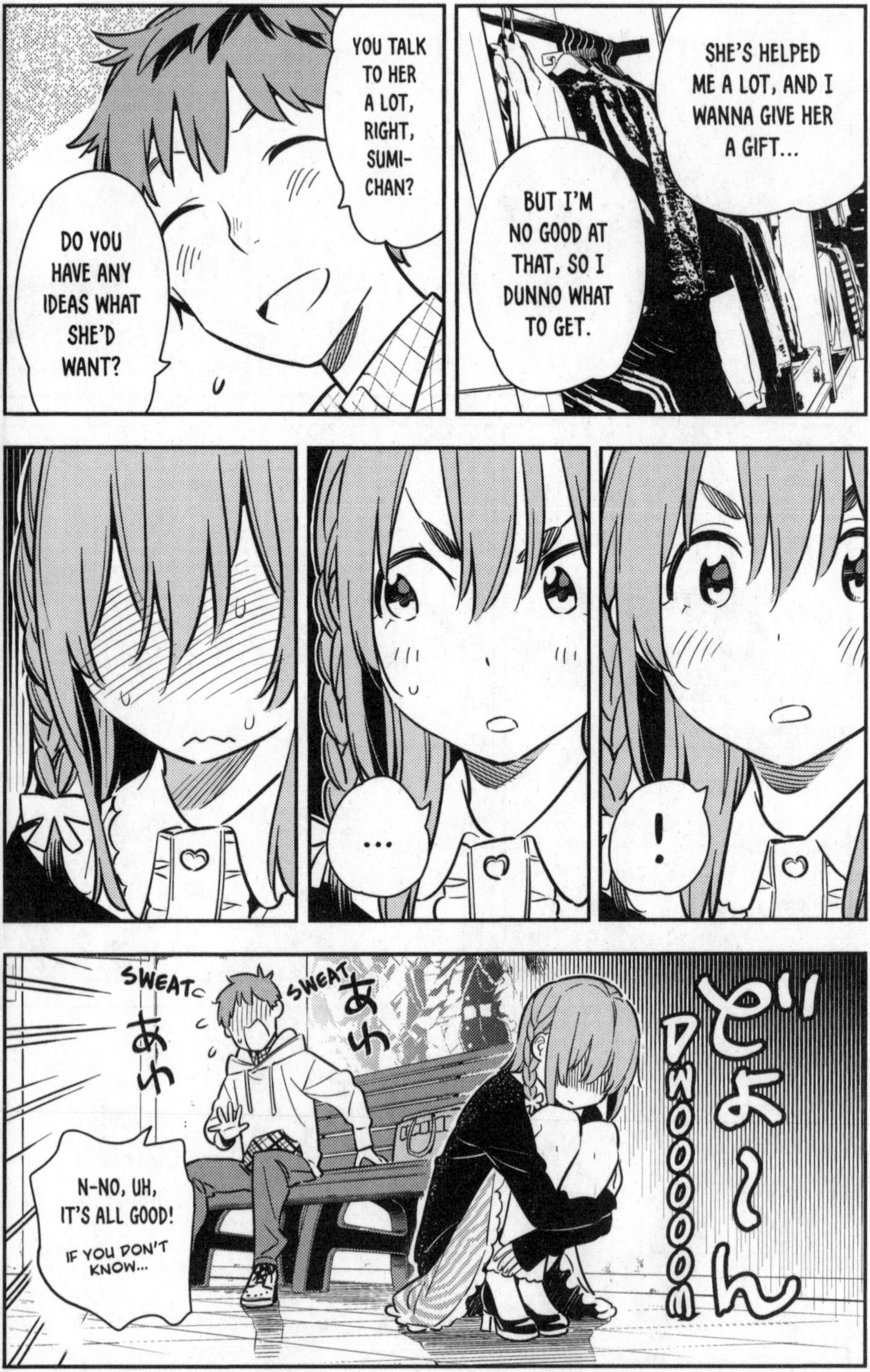
SHE'S HELPED ME A LOT, AND I WANNA GIVE HER A GIFT...
BUT I'M NO GOOD AT THAT, SO I DUNNO WHAT TO GET.
YOU TALK TO HER A LOT, RIGHT, SUMI-CHAN?
DO YOU HAVE ANY IDEAS WHAT SHE'D WANT?
!
...
どよ～ん
DWOOOOOOOM
あわ
SWEAT
あわ
SWEAT
N-NO, UH, IT'S ALL GOOD!
IF YOU DON'T KNOW...

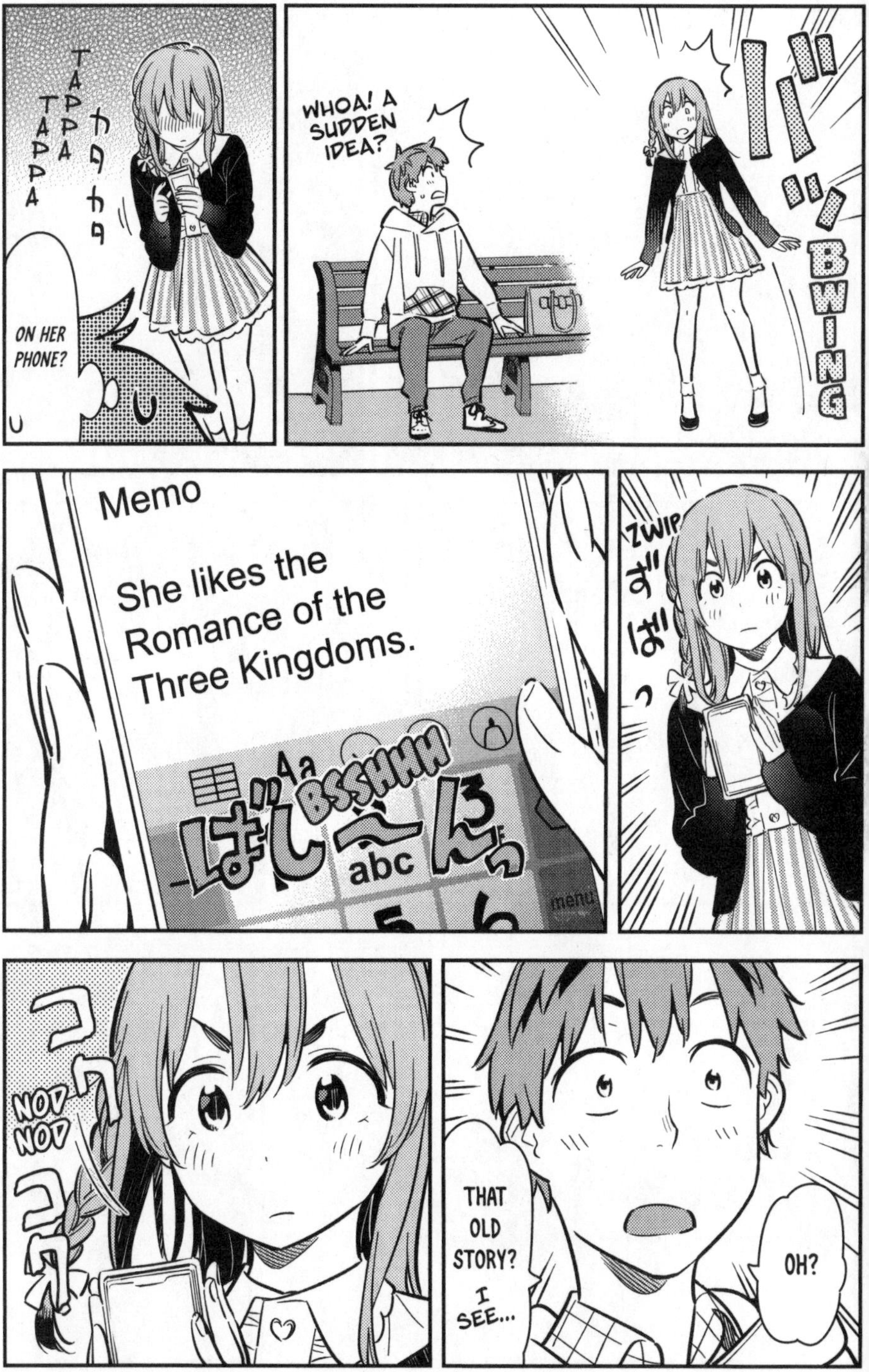
BWING
WHOA! A SUDDEN IDEA?
TAPPA TAPPA TAPPA
カタカタ
ON HER PHONE?
ZWIP
ずばっ
Memo
She likes the Romance of the Three Kingdoms.
BSSHHH
OH?
THAT OLD STORY? I SEE...
NOD NOD

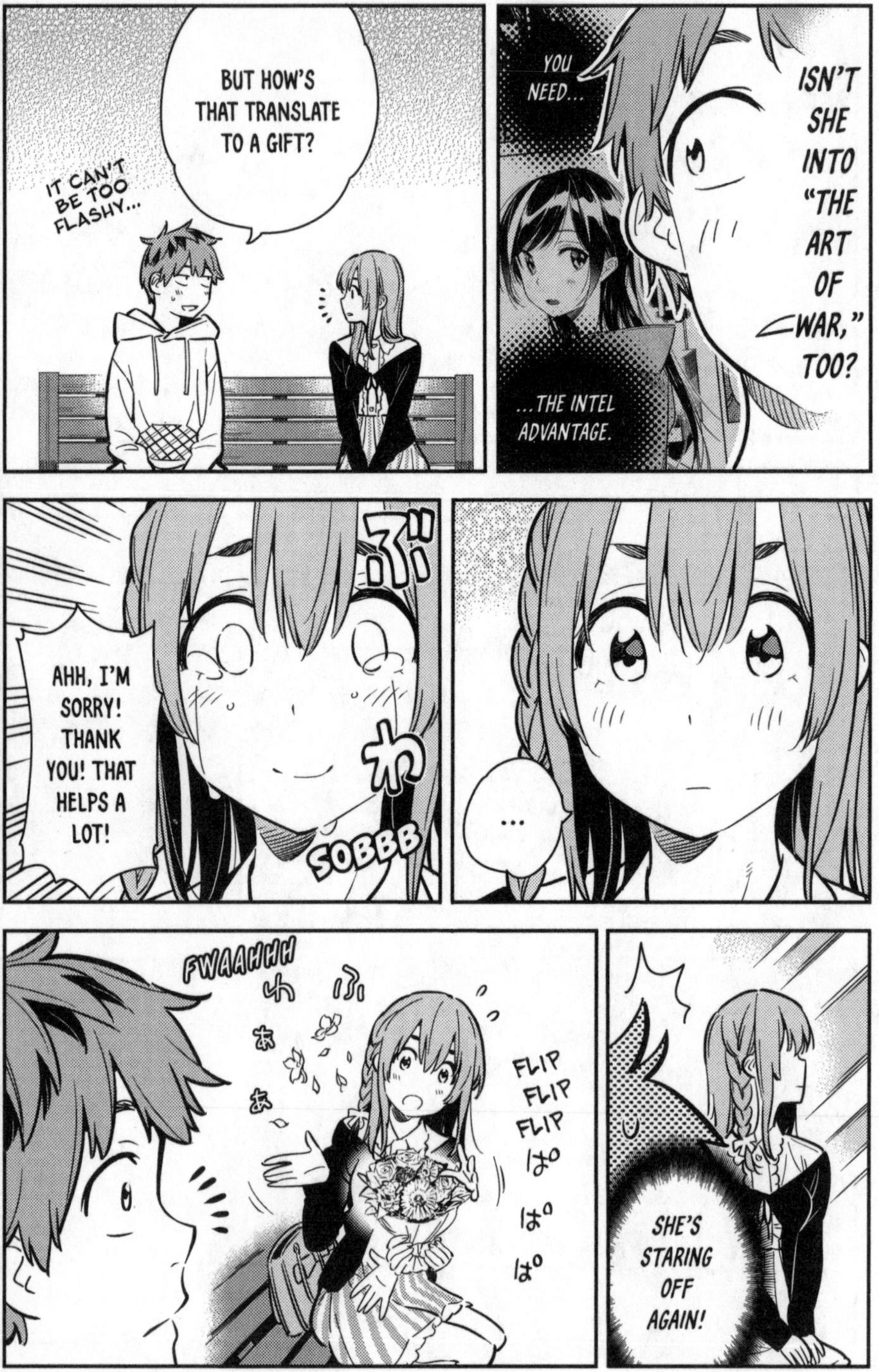
YOU NEED...
...THE INTEL ADVANTAGE.
ISN'T SHE INTO "THE ART OF WAR," TOO?
BUT HOW'S THAT TRANSLATE TO A GIFT?
IT CAN'T BE TOO FLASHY...
...
ぶわ
SOBBB
AHH, I'M SORRY! THANK YOU! THAT HELPS A LOT!
SHE'S STARING OFF AGAIN!
FWAAHHH
ふわああ
FLIP FLIP FLIP
ぱぱぱ

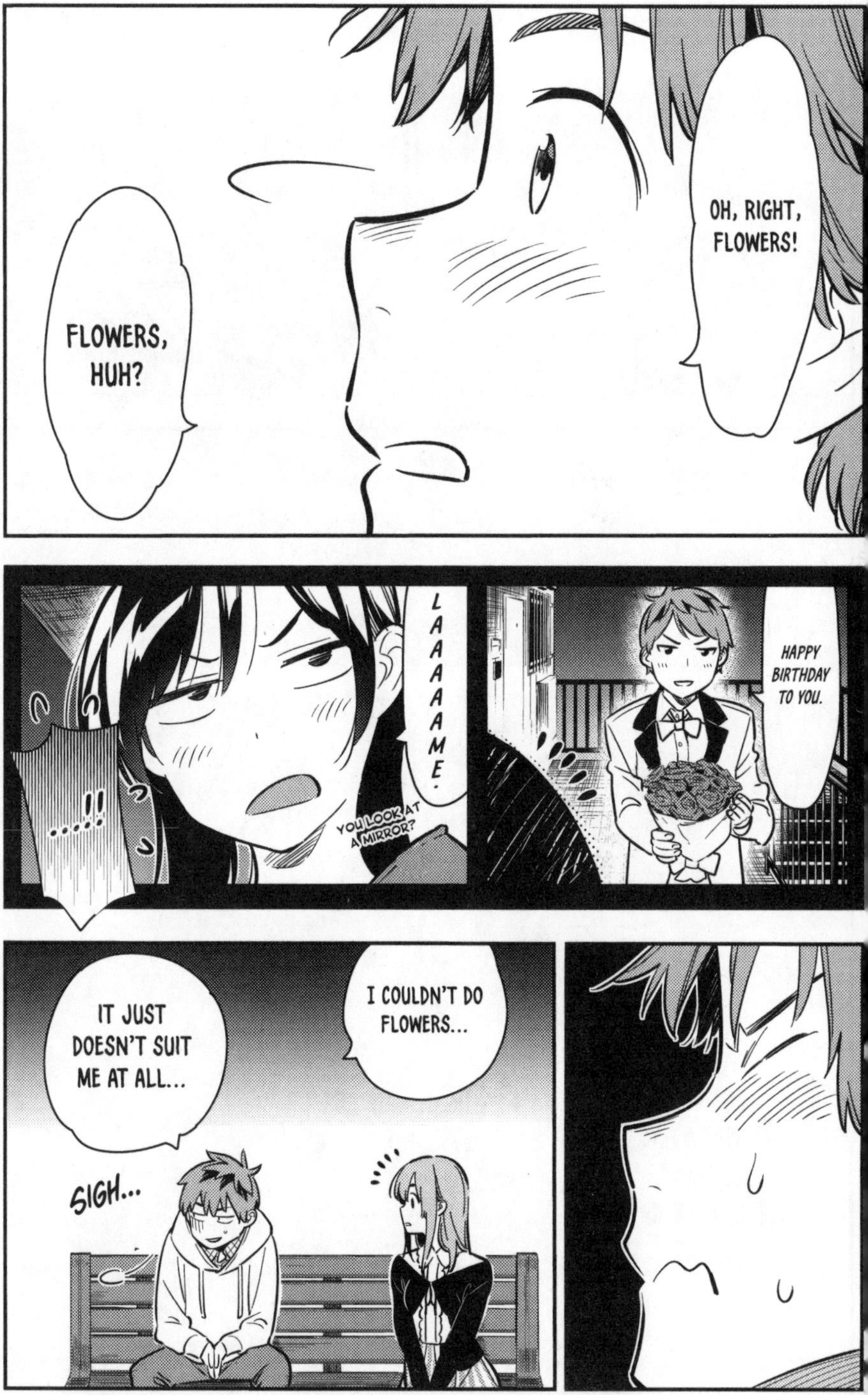
OH, RIGHT, FLOWERS!
FLOWERS, HUH?
HAPPY BIRTHDAY TO YOU.
LAAAAAAME.
YOU LOOK AT A MIRROR?
...!!
I COULDN'T DO FLOWERS...
IT JUST DOESN'T SUIT ME AT ALL...
SIGH...

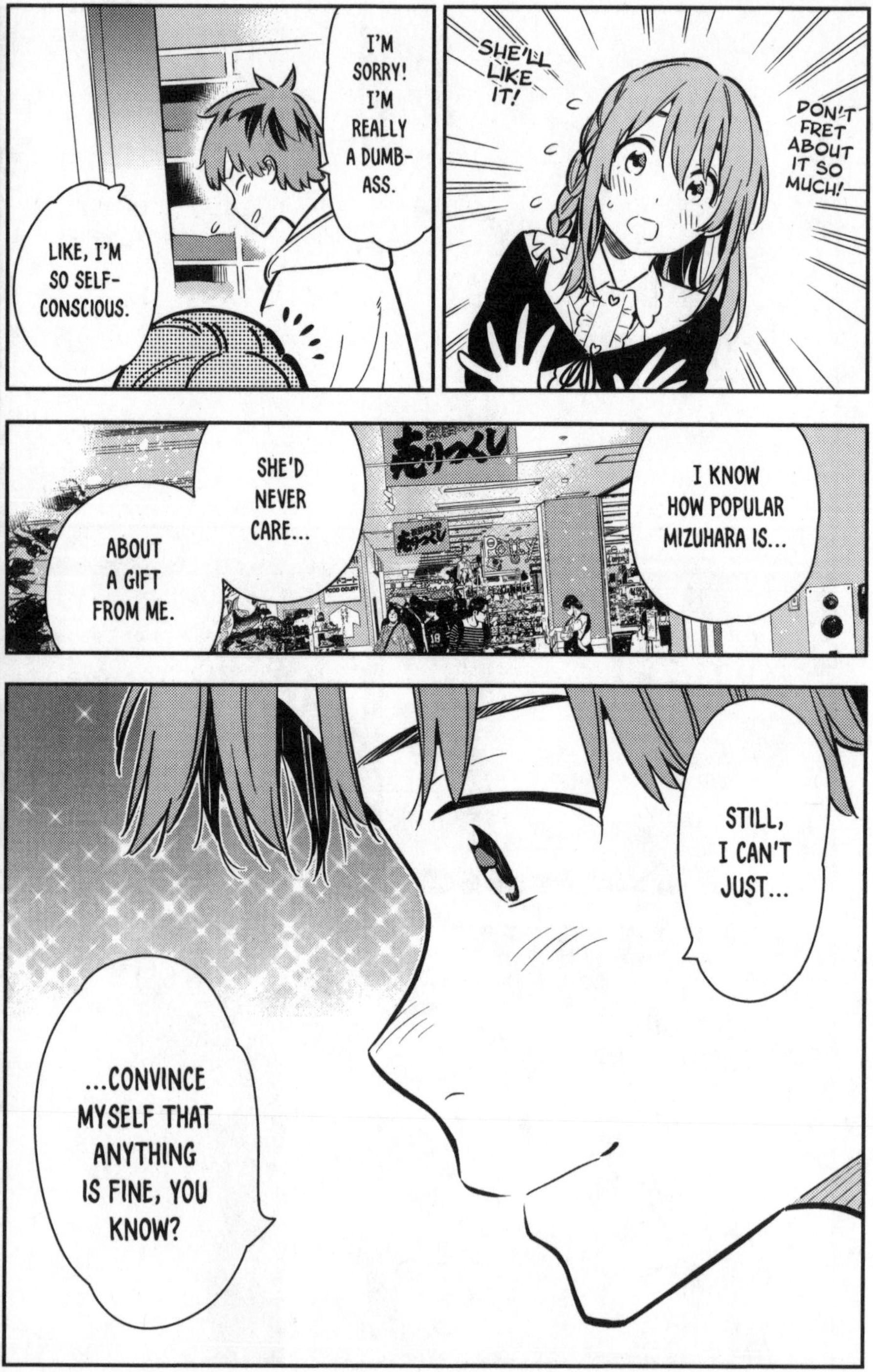
DON'T FRET ABOUT IT SO MUCH!
SHE'LL LIKE IT!
I'M SORRY! I'M REALLY A DUMB-ASS.
LIKE, I'M SO SELF-CONSCIOUS.
I KNOW HOW POPULAR MIZUHARA IS...
SHE'D NEVER CARE...
ABOUT A GIFT FROM ME.
STILL, I CAN'T JUST...
...CONVINCE MYSELF THAT ANYTHING IS FINE, YOU KNOW?

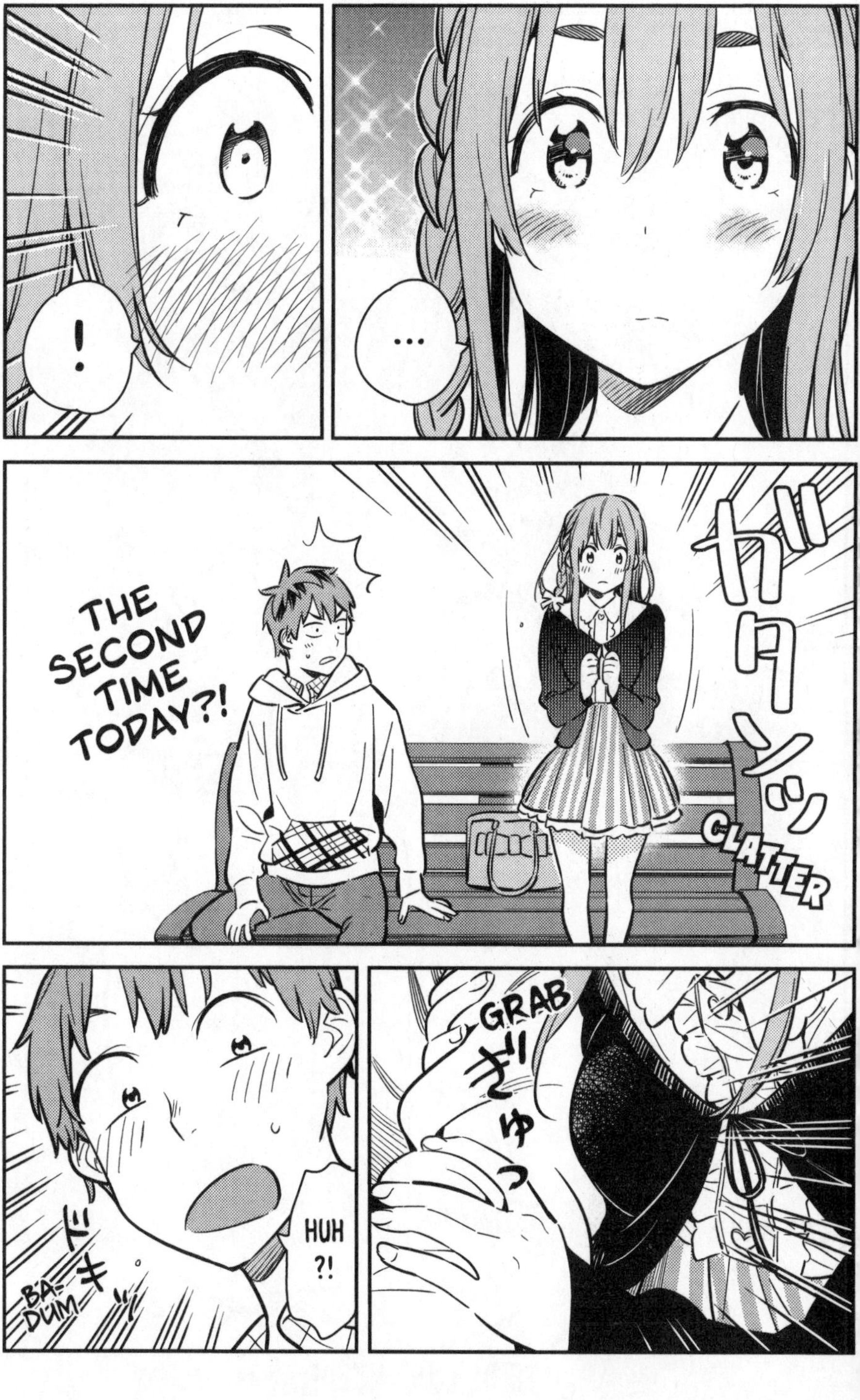
...
!
ガタンッ
CLATTER
THE SECOND TIME TODAY?!
GRAB
ぎゅっ
HUH?!
ドキッ
BA-DUM

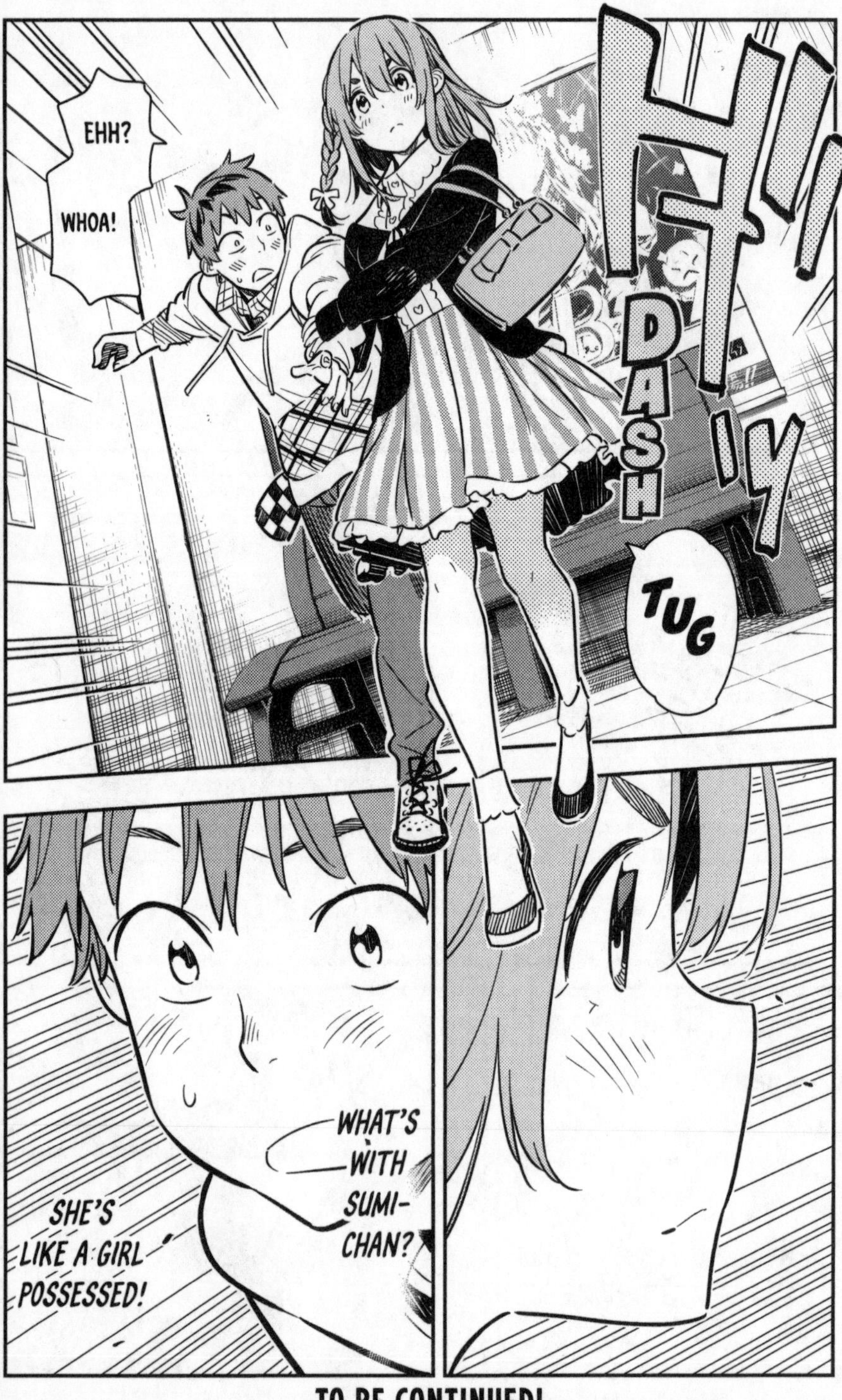
DASH
TUG
EHH?
WHOA!
WHAT'S WITH SUMI-CHAN?
SHE'S LIKE A GIRL POSSESSED!

TO BE CONTINUED!

SOMEONE COMMENTED THAT "THE END-OF-BOOK PAGE IS FUN," SO I WENT WITH IT AND AM SHAMELESSLY AT IT AGAIN.

THANK YOU VERY MUCH FOR BUYING RENT-A-GIRLFRIEND VOL. 8!

LET ME JUST SAY THIS FIRST. UNLIKE THE LAST VOLUME, I HAVE NOTHING TO APOLOGIZE ABOUT THIS TIME! THAT'S BECAUSE THERE'S SO MUCH I ***COULD*** APOLOGIZE FOR THAT NOT EVEN THREE PAGES (COUNTING THE "NEXT VOLUME" SPREAD) IS ENOUGH TO COVER ALL OF IT. IF I HAD TO PUT SOMETHING HERE, THOUGH, IT'D BE THE APARTMENT FENCE! (ALSO, IN MY MIND, I FIGURED WE REALLY NEEDED A "NEXT VOLUME" SPREAD IN THIS BOOK.)
THAT'S ALL! NOW, MOVING ON. SHOCKINGLY, I RECEIVED FEEDBACK THAT THIS PAGE ENTERTAINS PEOPLE, SO IT'S BACK YET AGAIN. WHAT SHOULD I TALK ABOUT? I JUST GOT BACK FROM THE COMITIA COMICS CONVENTION, AND EVERYONE'S SO CRAZILY GOOD AT DRAWING THERE, IT DRIVES ME INSANE. WHAT? YOU DON'T CARE? OKAY, THEN. HOW ABOUT I TALK ABOUT MIZUHARA? (OF COURSE, I COULD SPEND ALL NIGHT TALKING ABOUT PRETTY MUCH ALL OF MY CHARACTERS, BUT...) MIZUHARA IS, WELL, YOU KNOW... ***CUTE***, ISN'T SHE? WHAT'S CUTE, YOU ASK? THE WAY SHE'S LIVING IN THE APARTMENT NEXT DOOR. YOU'D NORMALLY ONLY SEE A GIRL THIS CUTE IN PLACES LIKE SETAGAYA. ALSO, THAT HAIR BRAID OUT FROM THE TEMPLE. WHEN KAZUYA FIRST RENTED HER, HIS REACTION WAS CLEARLY PRETTY TEPID, SO MIZUHARA MUST'VE COME UP WITH THAT AFTER EXTENSIVE CONSIDERATION. SHE GENERALLY ONLY GOES WITH THAT STYLE AROUND KAZUYA. (AS A 20-YEAR-OLD VIRGIN FRESH OUT OF HIGH SCHOOL, KAZUYA'S STILL THE SORT WHO LIKES THE KIND OF (TIDY) HAIR BRAID ONLY PEOPLE HIS AGE LOVE, SO I CAN'T BLAME MIZUHARA FOR HER DECISION. I'M NOT SURE HOW SELF-AWARE SHE IS OF IT, THOUGH, HAHAHA...)
BACK WHEN THIS SERIES WAS GETTING STARTED, I HAD JUST WRAPPED UP MY PREVIOUS ONE AND WAS DEALING WITH SOME TOUGH QUESTIONS, LIKE, "DO I REALLY HAVE ANY TALENT" OR, "IF I'M WORKING FOR A COMMERCIAL MAG, DO I HAVE TO CRAFT SOMETHING THAT SELLS, OR IS THAT INSINCERE" AND SO ON. BUT YOU KNOW, THAT APPROACH DOESN'T WORK—TALKING ABOUT SELLING, ATTRACTING HUGE AUDIENCES, OR WORRYING IF YOU DON'T HAVE ANY TALENT. THE MORE YOU THINK ABOUT IT, THE MORE IMPOSSIBLE IT BECOMES. SO ALL THAT REMAINS IS THE JOY OF DRAWING MANGA AND THE IDEALISTIC GREEDINESS OF DRAWING GIRLS THAT I THINK ARE SUPER-CUTE AND HAVING PEOPLE AGREE WITH ME. IT'S REALLY A LOT LIKE THE RELATIONSHIP BETWEEN KAZUYA—WHO THINKS HE CAN USE A RENT-A-GIRLFRIEND IN PLACE OF ACTUAL LOVE—AND MIZUHARA. THUS MIZUHARA IS KIND OF THE IDEAL "GIRLFRIEND." OR, TO ME, THE IDEAL "WORLD" ITSELF.
I'VE NEARLY RUN OUT OF PAGE WHILE I WAS GROSSING PEOPLE OUT. I REALLY DON'T MATTER, SO KEEP ON SUPPORTING MIZUHARA FOR ME, PLEASE. SEE YOU...

...NEXT VOLUME?

REIJI MIYAJIMA

IF I PUSH MY LUCK WITH THIS PAGE AND PEOPLE SAY, "IT SUCKS," I'D BE DEVASTATED, SO HERE'S MIZUHARA TO KEEP PEOPLE MORE SATISFIED

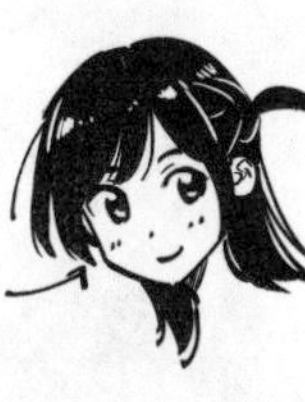

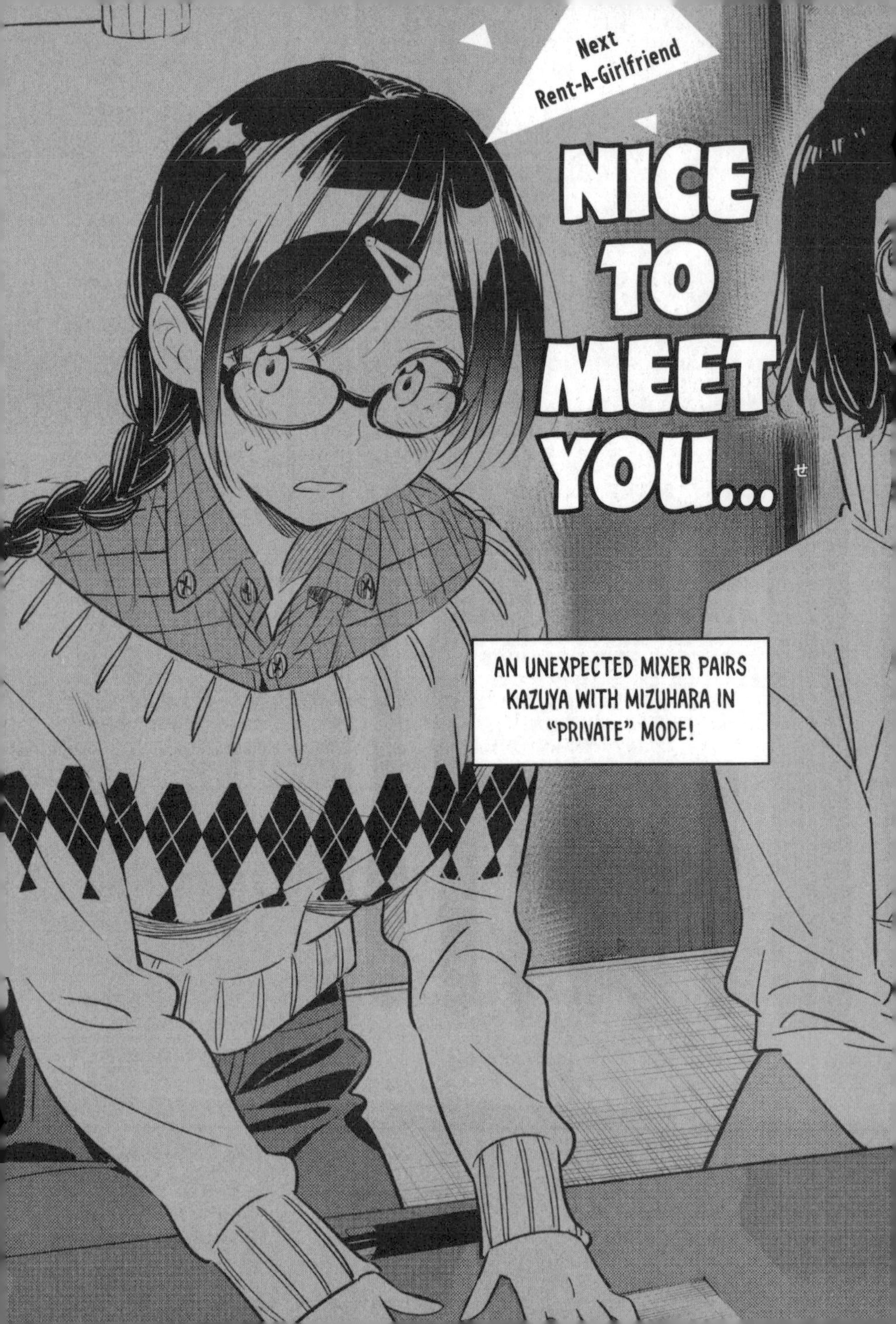
Next
Rent-A-Girlfriend
NICE TO MEET YOU...
AN UNEXPECTED MIXER PAIRS KAZUYA WITH MIZUHARA IN "PRIVATE" MODE!

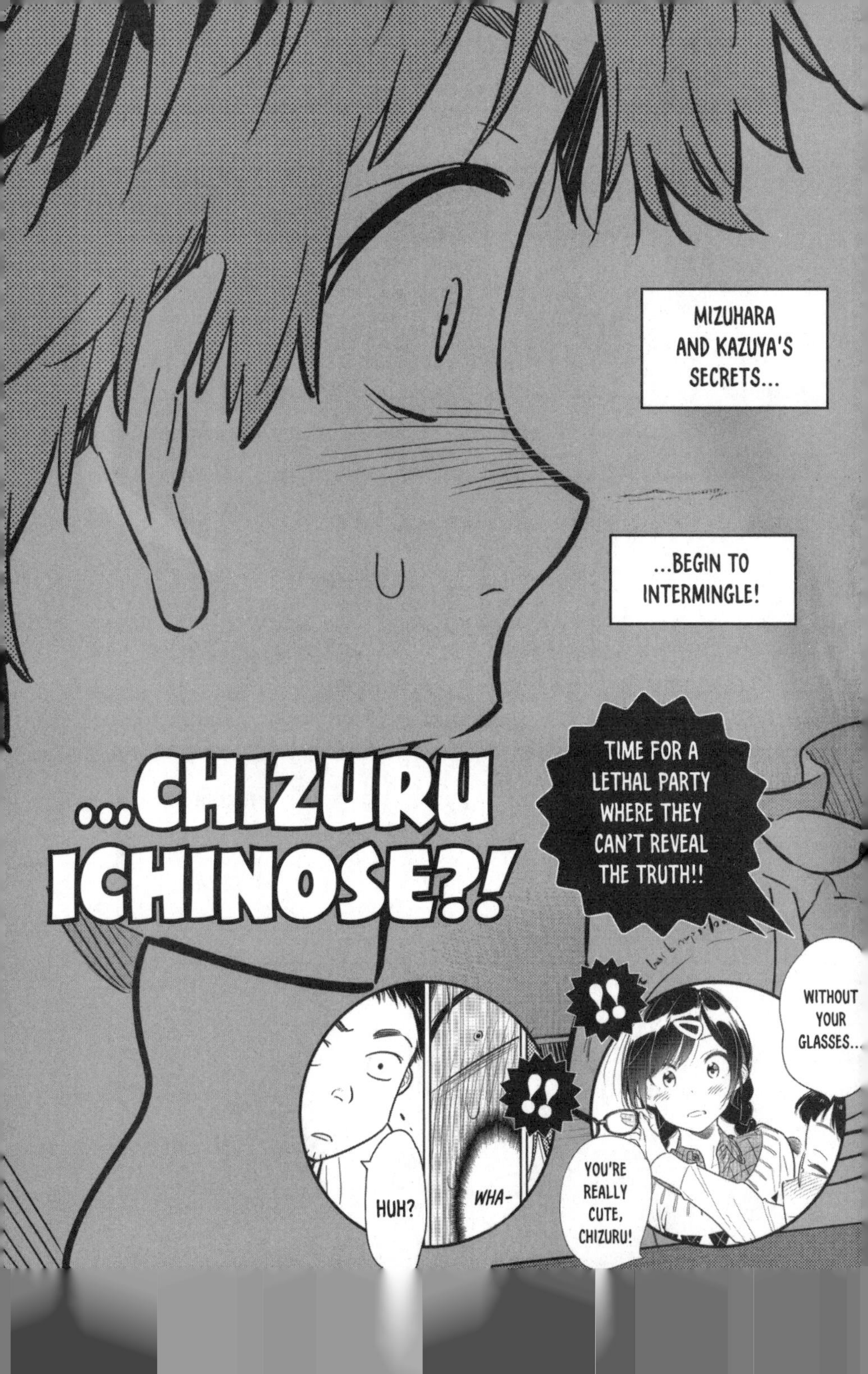
MIZUHARA AND KAZUYA'S SECRETS...
...BEGIN TO INTERMINGLE!
...CHIZURU ICHINOSE?!
TIME FOR A LETHAL PARTY WHERE THEY CAN'T REVEAL THE TRUTH!!
WITHOUT YOUR GLASSES...
YOU'RE REALLY CUTE, CHIZURU!
!!
!!
WHA-
HUH?

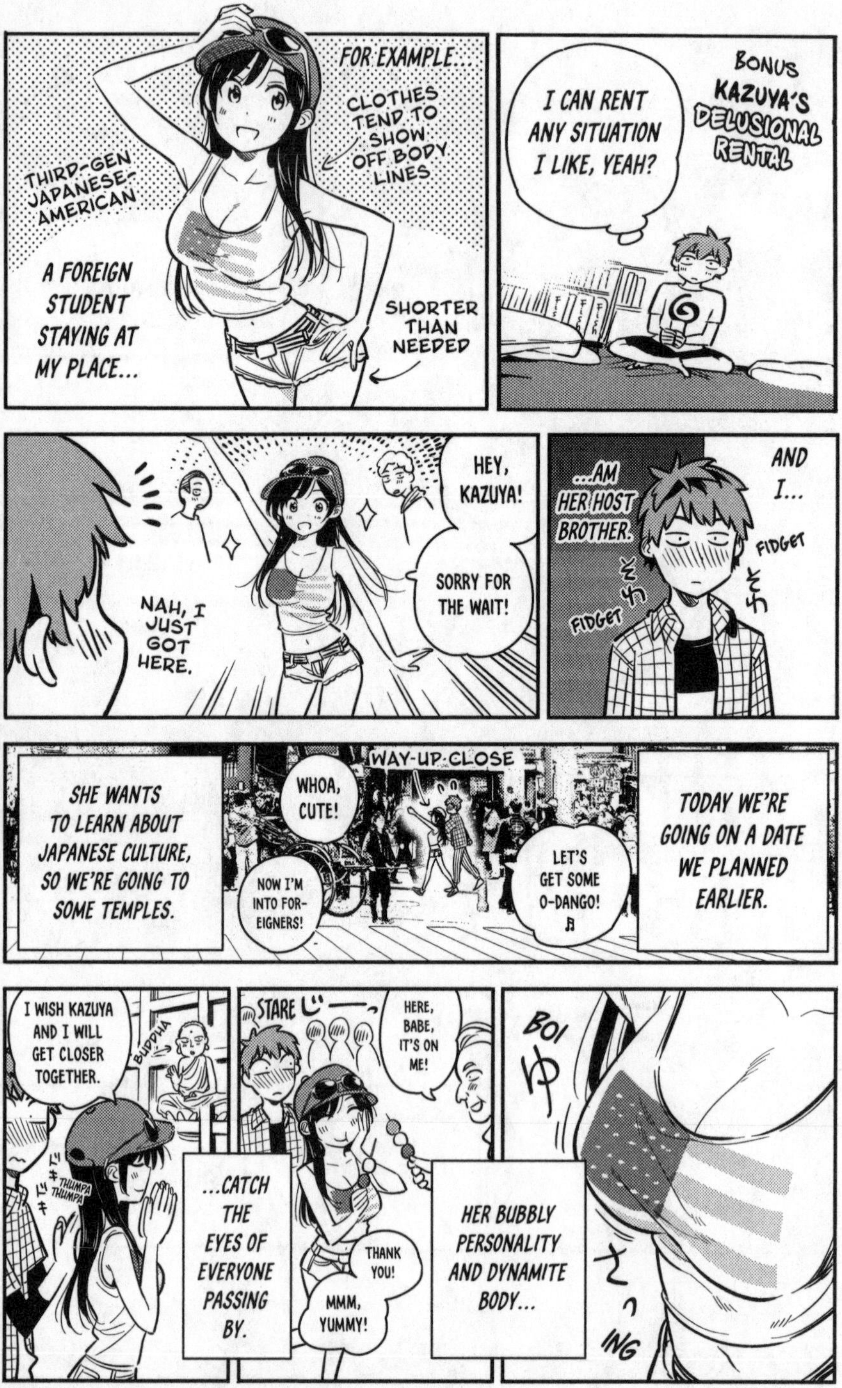
BONUS
KAZUYA'S DELUSIONAL RENTAL
I CAN RENT ANY SITUATION I LIKE, YEAH?
FOR EXAMPLE...
A FOREIGN STUDENT STAYING AT MY PLACE...
CLOTHES TEND TO SHOW OFF BODY LINES
THIRD-GEN JAPANESE-AMERICAN
SHORTER THAN NEEDED
AND I...
...AM HER HOST BROTHER.
FIDGET
FIDGET
HEY, KAZUYA!
SORRY FOR THE WAIT!
NAH, I JUST GOT HERE.
TODAY WE'RE GOING ON A DATE WE PLANNED EARLIER.
LET'S GET SOME O-DANGO! ♪
WAY-UP-CLOSE
WHOA, CUTE!
NOW I'M INTO FOR-EIGNERS!
SHE WANTS TO LEARN ABOUT JAPANESE CULTURE, SO WE'RE GOING TO SOME TEMPLES.
BOI
HER BUBBLY PERSONALITY AND DYNAMITE BODY...
ING
HERE, BABE, IT'S ON ME!
STARE
THANK YOU!
MMM, YUMMY!
...CATCH THE EYES OF EVERYONE PASSING BY.
I WISH KAZUYA AND I WILL GET CLOSER TOGETHER.
BUDDHA
THUMPA THUMPA

RENT-A-GIRLFRIEND STAFF: A, IROHKI, TEMAENO, KUSUMI, MITSUKI, MINATO

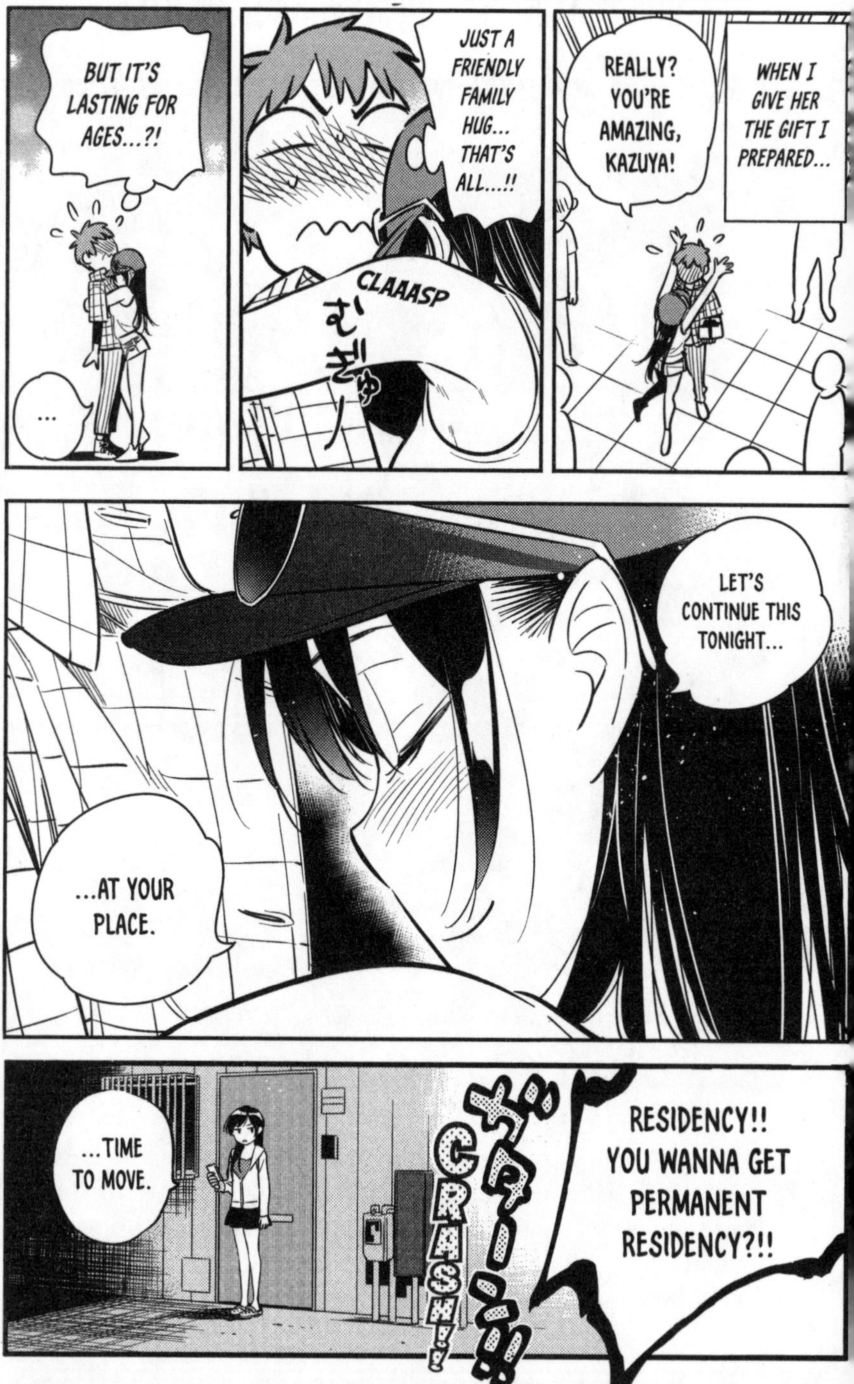
WHEN I GIVE HER THE GIFT I PREPARED...
REALLY? YOU'RE AMAZING, KAZUYA!
JUST A FRIENDLY FAMILY HUG... THAT'S ALL...!!
CLAAASP
むぎゅ
BUT IT'S LASTING FOR AGES...?!
...
LET'S CONTINUE THIS TONIGHT...
...AT YOUR PLACE.
RESIDENCY!! YOU WANNA GET PERMANENT RESIDENCY?!!
CRASH!!
...TIME TO MOVE.

EDITORS: HIRAOKA-SAN, HIRATSUKA-SAN, HARA-SAN, CHOKAI-SAN. ALSO THANKS TO EVERYBODY WHO PICKED UP THIS BOOK!! SEE YOU SOON! ♡

Young characters and steampunk setting, like *Howl's Moving Castle* and *Battle Angel Alita*

Beyond the Clouds © 2018 Nicke / Ki-oon

A boy with a talent for machines and a mysterious girl whose wings he's fixed will take you beyond the clouds! In the tradition of the high-flying, resonant adventure stories of Studio Ghibli comes a gorgeous tale about the longing of young hearts for adventure and friendship!

A SMART, NEW ROMANTIC COMEDY FOR FANS OF *SHORTCAKE CAKE* AND *TERRACE HOUSE*!

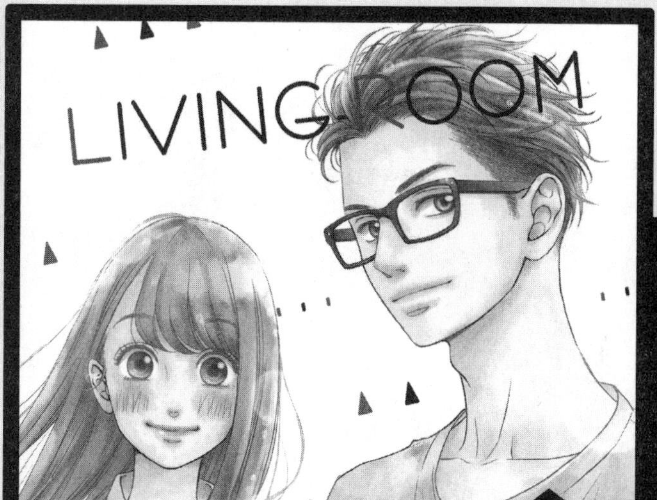
LIVING-ROOM
MATSUNAGA-SAN
1
Keiko Iwashita

KC KODANSHA COMICS

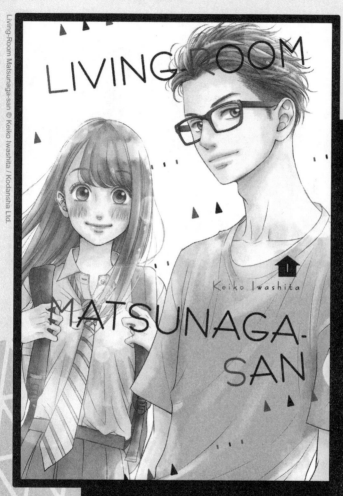

A romance manga starring high school girl Meeko, who learns to live on her own in a boarding house whose living room is home to the odd (but handsome) Matsunaga-san. She begins to adjust to her new life away from her parents, but Meeko soon learns that no matter how far away from home she is, she's still a young girl at heart — especially when she finds herself falling for Matsunaga-san.

PERFECT WORLD

Rie Aruga

A TOUCHING
NEW SERIES
ABOUT LOVE AND
COPING WITH
DISABILITY

An office party reunites Tsugumi with her high school crush Itsuki. He's realized his dream of becoming an architect, but along the way, he experienced a spinal injury that put him in a wheelchair. Now Tsugumi's rekindled feelings will butt up against prejudices she never considered — and Itsuki will have to decide if he's ready to let someone into his heart...

"Depicts with great delicacy and courage the difficulties some with disabilities experience getting involved in romantic relationships... Rie Aruga refuses to romanticize, pushing her heroine to face the reality of disability. She invites her readers to the same tasks of empathy, knowledge and recognition."
—Slate.fr

"An important entry [in manga romance]... The emotional core of both plot and characters indicates thoughtfulness... [Aruga's] research is readily apparent in the text and artwork, making this feel like a real story."
—Anime News Network

KC/
KODANSHA
COMICS

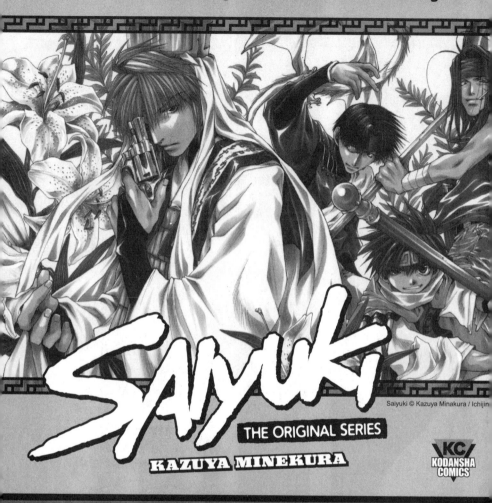

The art-deco cyberpunk classic from the creators of *xxxHOLiC* and *Cardcaptor Sakura*!

"Starred Review. This experimental sci-fi work from CLAMP reads like a romantic version of *AKIRA*."
—Publishers Weekly

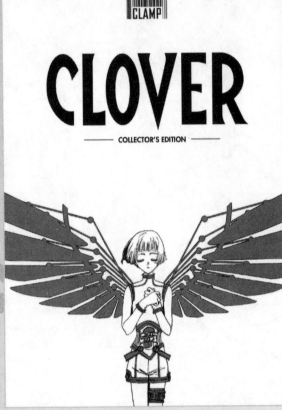

CLOVER © CLAMP-ShigatsuTsuitachi CO.,LTD./Kodansha Ltd.

Su was born into a bleak future, where the government keeps tight control over children with magical powers—codenamed "Clovers." With Su being the only "four-leaf" Clover in the world, she has been kept isolated nearly her whole life. Can ex-military agent Kazuhiko deliver her to the happiness she seeks? Experience the complete series in this hardcover edition, which also includes over twenty pages of ravishing color art!

KC
KODANSHA
COMICS

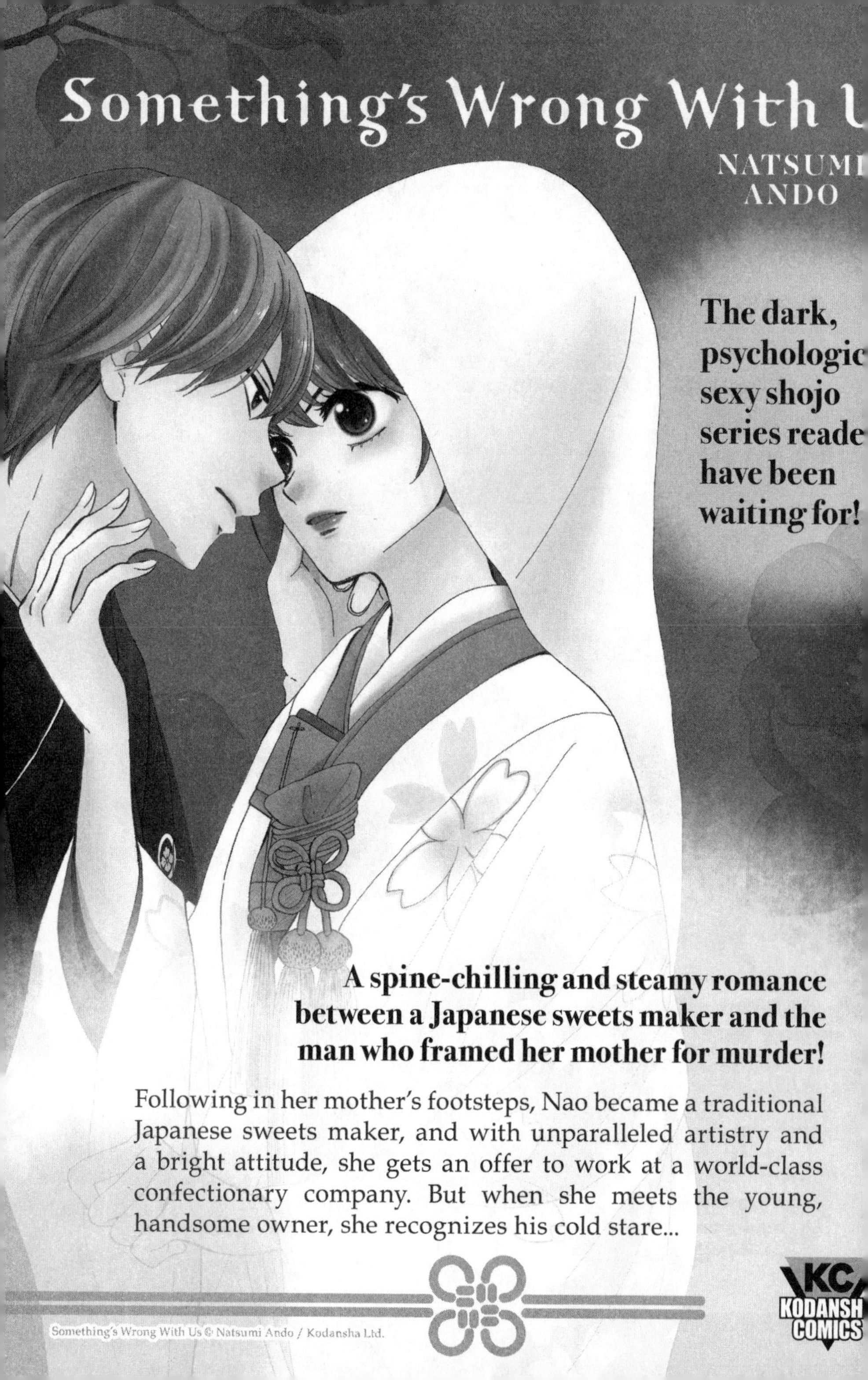
Something's Wrong With U
NATSUMI
ANDO
The dark,
psychologic
sexy shojo
series reade
have been
waiting for!
A spine-chilling and steamy romance
between a Japanese sweets maker and the
man who framed her mother for murder!
Following in her mother's footsteps, Nao became a traditional Japanese sweets maker, and with unparalleled artistry and a bright attitude, she gets an offer to work at a world-class confectionary company. But when she meets the young, handsome owner, she recognizes his cold stare...
KC
KODANSH
COMICS
Something's Wrong With Us © Natsumi Ando / Kodansha Ltd.

"Clever, sassy, and original....*xxxHOLiC* has the inherent hallmarks of a runaway hit."
—NewType magazine

autifully seductive twork and uniquely panese depictions of e supernatural will pnotize CLAMP fans!

xxxHOLiC OMNIBUS 1

CLAMP

xxxHOLiC © CLAMP-ShigatsuTsuitachi CO.,LTD./Kodansha Ltd.
xxxHOLiC Rei © CLAMP-ShigatsuTsuitachi CO.,LTD./Kodansha Ltd.

Kimihiro Watanuki is haunted by visions of ghosts and spirits. He seeks help from a mysterious woman named Yuko, who claims she can help. However, Watanuki must work for Yuko in order to pay for her aid. Soon Watanuki finds himself employed in Yuko's shop, where he sees things and meets customers that are stranger than anything he could have ever imagined.

KC KODANSHA COMICS

The adorable new odd-couple cat comedy manga from the creator of the beloved *Chi's Sweet Home*, in full color!

Praise for Chi's Sweet Home

"Nearly impossible to turn away... a true all-ages title that anyone, young or old, cat lover or not, will enjoy. The stories will bring a smile to your face and warm your heart."

–School Library Jo'

Sue & Tai-chan

Konami Kanata

Sue is an aging housecat who's looking forward to living out her life in peace... but her plans change when the mischievous black tomcat Tai-chan enters the picture! Hey! Sue never signed up to be a catsitter! *Sue & Tai-chan* is the latest from the reigning meow-narch of cute kitty comics, Konami Kanata.

KC KODANS COMIC

THE SWEET SCENT OF LOVE IS IN THE AIR! FOR FANS OF OFFBEAT ROMANCES LIKE *WOTAKOI*

Sweat and Soap © Kintetsu Yamada / Kodansha Ltd.

In an office romance, there's a fine line between sexy and awkward... and that line is where Asako — a woman who sweats copiously — meets Koutarou — a perfume developer who can't get enough of Asako's, er, scent. Don't miss a romcom manga like no other!

The beloved characters from *Cardcaptor Sakura* return in a brand new, reimagined fantasy adventure!

"[*Tsubasa*] takes readers on a fantastic ride that only gets more exhilarating with each successive chapter." —Anime News Network

In the Kingdom of Clow, an archaeological dig unleashes an incredible power, causing Princess Sakura to lose her memories. To save her, her childhood friend Syaoran must follow the orders of the Dimension Witch and travel alongside Kurogane, an unrivaled warrior; Fai, a powerful magician; and Mokona, a curiously strange creature, to retrieve Sakura's dispersed memories!

THE WORLD OF CLAMP!

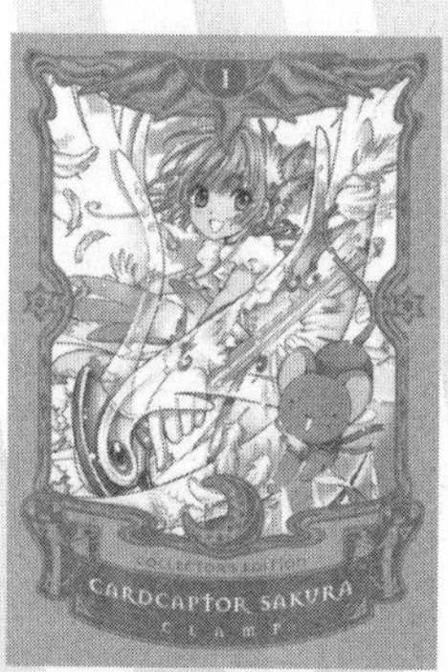
CARDCAPTOR SAKURA
CLAMP

Cardcaptor Sakura
Collector's Edition

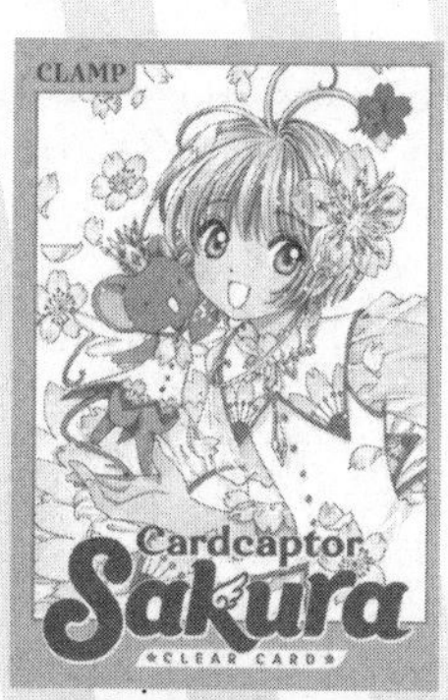
CLAMP
Cardcaptor
Sakura
CLEAR CARD

Cardcaptor Sakura:
Clear Card

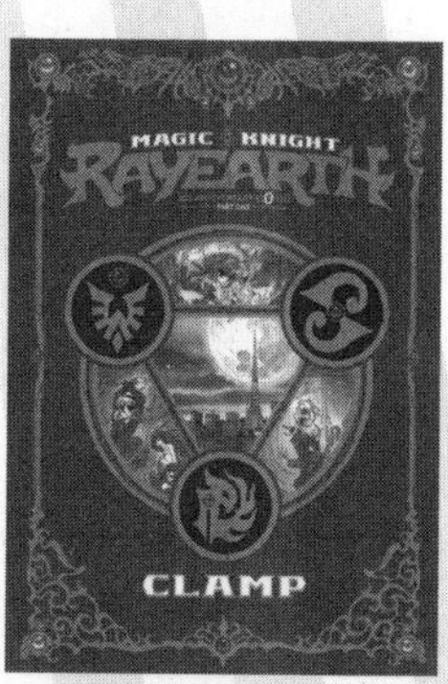
MAGIC KNIGHT
RAYEARTH
CLAMP

Magic Knight Rayearth
25th Anniversary Box Set

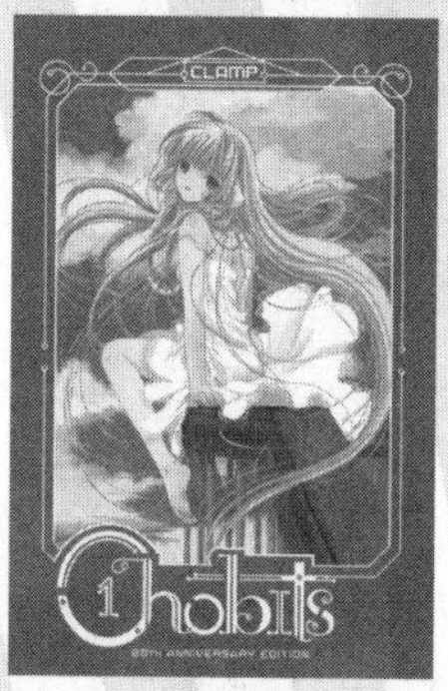
CLAMP
Chobits

Chobits

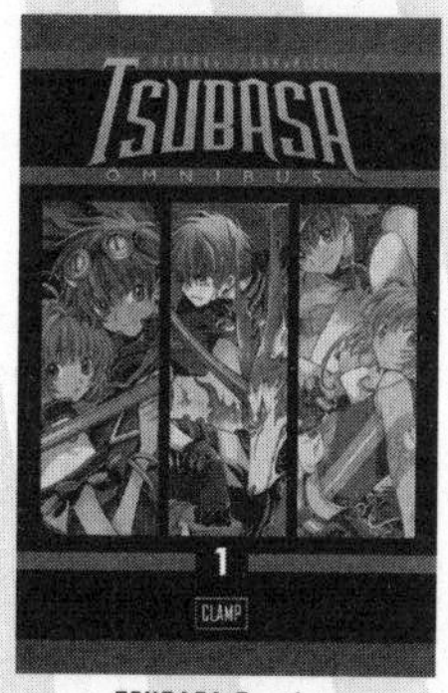
TSUBASA
OMNIBUS
1
CLAMP

TSUBASA Omnibus

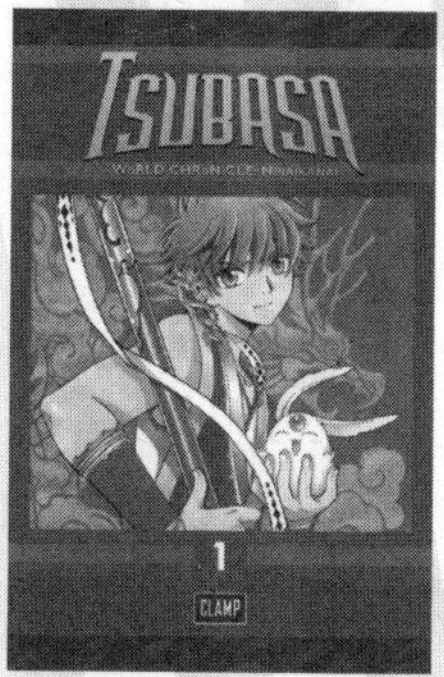
TSUBASA
1
CLAMP

TSUBASA WoRLD CHRoNiCLE

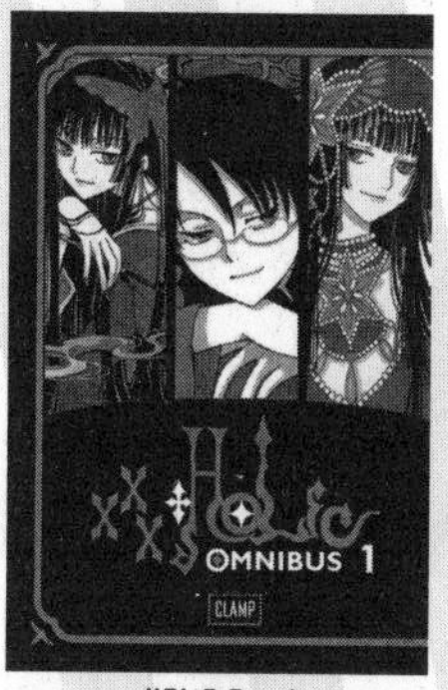
xxxHOLiC
OMNIBUS 1
CLAMP

xxxHOLiC Omnibus

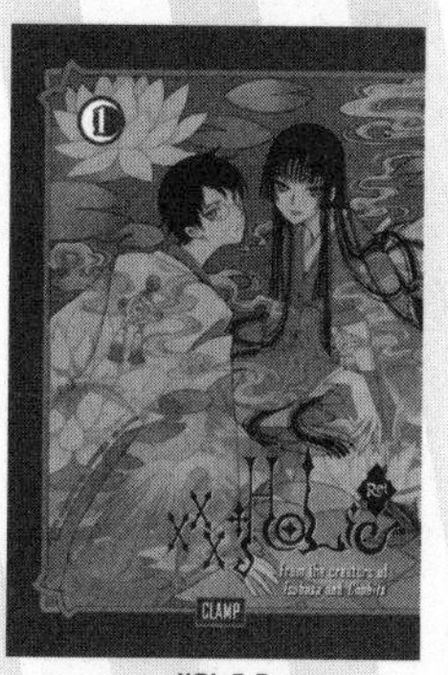
xxxHOLiC
CLAMP

xxxHOLiC Rei

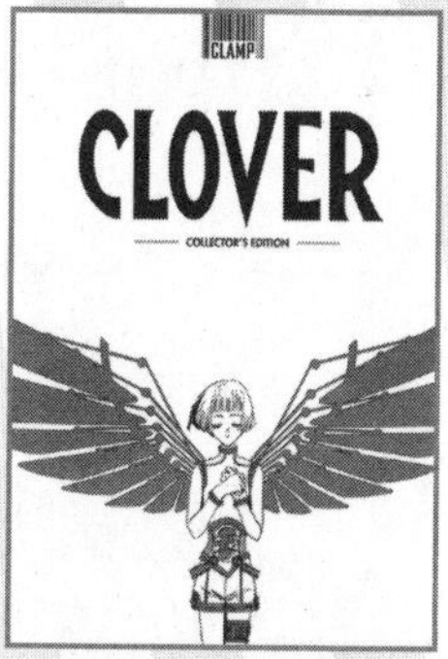
CLAMP
CLOVER
COLLECTOR'S EDITION

CLOVER Collector's Edition

KC KODANSHA COMICS

Kodansha Comics welcomes you to explore the expansive world of CLAMP, the all-female artist collective that has produced some of the most acclaimed manga of the century. Our growing catalog includes icons like *Cardcaptor Sakura* and *Magic Knight Rayearth*, each crafted with CLAMP's one-of-a-kind style and characters!

A Kodansha Comics Trade Paperback Original
Rent-A-Girlfriend 8 copyright © 2019 Reiji Miyajima
English translation copyright © 2021 Reiji Miyajima

All rights reserved.

Published in the United States by Kodansha Comics, an imprint of Kodansha USA Publishing, LLC, New York.

Publication rights for this English edition arranged through Kodansha Ltd., Tokyo.

First published in Japan in 2019 by Kodansha Ltd., Tokyo as *Kanojo, okarishimasu*, volume 8.

ISBN 978-1-64651-092-4

Original cover design by Kohei Nawata Design Office

Printed in the United States of America.

www.kodansha.us

1st Printing
Translation: Kevin Gifford
Lettering: Paige Pumphrey
Editing: Jordan Blanco
Kodansha Comics edition cover design by Phil Balsman

Publisher: Kiichiro Sugawara

Director of publishing services: Ben Applegate
Associate director of operations: Stephen Pakula
Publishing services managing editors: Madison Salters, Alanna Ruse
Production managers: Emi Lotto, Angela Zurlo
Logo and character art ©Kodansha USA Publishing, LLC